JOHN DRYDEN : SOME
BIOGRAPHICAL FACTS
AND PROBLEMS

JOHN DRYDEN 1631–1700
by an unknown artist, circa 1680
The Osborn Collection

JOHN DRYDEN : SOME BIOGRAPHICAL FACTS AND PROBLEMS

By

JAMES M. OSBORN

Revised Edition

UNIVERSITY OF FLORIDA PRESS

Gainesville

1965

To M-L

PREFACE

NEVER HAVE SCHOLARS BEEN so interested in British history of the later seventeenth century as they are today. Within the past two decades much of the history of the period has been rewritten; the economic and political history by scholars such as G. N. Clark, David Ogg, and E. S. de Beer, and the history of the theater by Allardyce Nicoll, Leslie Hotson, Alfred Harbage, and (*abusus non tollit usum*) Montague Summers. This trend of interest will undoubtedly continue—making allowance for the toll of war—because an invaluable tool will soon be available, Donald Wing's *Short Title Catalogue of English Books 1641–1700,* now in course of publication by the Index Society. Just as Pollard and Redgrave's *Short Title Catalogue 1475–1640* was followed by a burst of activity in Tudor and Jacobean research, so should Mr. Wing's volumes stimulate historians of the later seventeenth century.

A revival of interest in the greatest literary figure of this period, John Dryden, has been noticeable for some time. Led by T. S. Eliot and Mark Van Doren, present-day critics have found new significance in Dryden's poetry and critical writings. Louis I. Bredvold's examination of Dryden's intellectual milieu has gone far toward charting the mental patterns followed by Dryden and many of his contemporaries. The bibliographical information collected by Percy J. Dobell, George Thorn-Drury, and others has been augmented and recently published by Hugh Macdonald. An edition of Dryden's correspondence by Charles E. Ward is ready for the press, and plans for a complete edition of Dryden's works under the direction of Edward N. Hooker have been announced by the University of California. Mr. Dobell's collection of Dryden books has been acquired by the Folger Shakespeare Library and so made permanently available to American scholars.

Amid all this activity there is one noticeable lack—there is no adequate biography of Dryden. No other literary figure of his stature has been so neglected. The last attempt at a full-dress life was made in 1808

by Sir Walter Scott, and most of his materials came from Edmond
Malone's biography, published in 1800. In the century and a third since
Scott wrote, various items of information about Dryden have come to
light. They are scattered in half a hundred places, in calendars of official papers and catalogues of private libraries, in books on Dryden's
contemporaries, and in uncounted historical and antiquarian journals.
The need for a definitive life has occurred to more than one prospective biographer, but the task of gathering the evidence, of putting it in
order and thinking out its implications is not to be undertaken lightly.
The synthesizing of known facts is only half the work that will be necessary before pen can be put to paper. For dozens of years in Dryden's
life practically no information exists about what he was doing or even
where he was. These gaps are as numerous as they are broad, a situation
that is difficult to comprehend considering that for more than thirty
years Dryden was the most famous literary man in England. Dryden's
next biographer will have to be a handy man with the spade.

This volume is an attempt to do a little of the preliminary digging
for him. As a glance at the contents will show, it is divided into two
parts. The first half is devoted to an examination of the biographies of
the poet that have been published in the two and a third centuries since
his death. My purpose has been to sift out the facts about Dryden that
have good pedigrees and to set them off from the fictions that clutter
up much that has been written about him. Although the ups and
downs of Dryden's reputation do not come properly within the scope
of this inquiry, the subject has here received intermittent attention.
Students interested in the rise of literary scholarship will find a number
of pages that deserve their scrutiny, as, I believe, will historians of the
development of English biography. Since most of Dryden's biographers
—among them Dr. Johnson, Edmond Malone, Sir Walter Scott, and
George Saintsbury—were celebrated authors in their own right, I hope
my analyses of their work may have a double usefulness.

The second half of the book is made up of separate investigations.
Because these studies are largely unrelated, I have avoided trying to
link them together and have even repeated some statements several
times in order that each study may stand independent of the others.
These investigations are of various sorts—the presentation of new documents, the reëxamination of old ones, the synthesis of scattered evi-

dence, and the analysis of specific problems. In every case I have tried
to indicate the significance of the facts, new or old, except in a few instances where clearly drawn conclusions seemed unwarranted. But even
in such cases my object has been to print all the pertinent evidence, for,
as that self-appointed archivist of the Dryden family, Miss Honor
Pigott, wrote to Malone, "to an editor a trifle may lead to an event."

Because of the diverse subject matter treated in this book, my obligations to other scholars are very numerous. I am glad to have this
opportunity of thanking them again, even though it is not possible to
repeat all their names here. My initial obligation is to Charles E. Ward,
whose work is well known to Dryden scholars. While I was writing
this book he placed the results of his extensive Dryden researches at my
disposal and generously allowed me to make use of unpublished information. In addition he read the manuscript text and the proof sheets
—both much to my advantage. My colleague Benjamin C. Nangle also
read the proofs and saved me from many blunders. An intermediate
draft of the manuscript was read by my friends F. W. Bateson,
E. S. de Beer, and Hoxie N. Fairchild, all of whom made numerous
fruitful suggestions. Separate chapters have benefited from the criticism of Allardyce Nicoll, George Sherburn, and Homer E. Wood-
bridge. When an early draft of Part One was submitted for a research
degree at Oxford University, in 1937, the manuscript was read by
D. Nichol Smith, H. F. B. Brett-Smith, and Hugh Macdonald, from
each of whom I learned a good deal.

For permission to reproduce the letter from Dryden to Richard Salwey and the Salwey portrait of Dryden, I am grateful to the present
owner, Captain Roger Salwey, of Overton, Ludlow, England. I am
similarly indebted to Oliver R. Barrett, of Kenilworth, Illinois, for allowing me to make use of the document (now in the collection of
Roger W. Barrett) that is discussed in the chapter "Dryden and the
King's Company." Like all Dryden scholars, present and future, I am
under deep obligation to the generosity and learning of Percy J. Dobell.
Other acknowledgments for help on specific points will be found in the
text and notes, to which I should like to add my thanks to Strickland
Gibson, Giles E. Dawson, and Leonard Stevens. To Robert G. Sawyer,
who was my research assistant for several years before the war, I owe
much, as I do to his successor David R. Kerr, who is also responsible

for the index. But first and last my greatest obligation is to Edmond Malone, whose own researches into the life of Dryden have placed all later scholars in his debt and whose pen is responsible for so large a portion of the following pages.

JAMES M. OSBORN

Yale University
November 15, 1940

PREFACE TO THE SECOND EDITION

MOST AUTHORS, like parents, have a special affection for their first born. Hence, when after various publications in both Tudor and Hanoverian literature, I received the request from Aubrey Williams of the University of Florida to prepare a revised edition of this book, it was a pleasure to agree. As I hope is obvious, Dryden has always occupied a special place in my literary interests, and I have attempted to keep my "Dryden files" up to date.

Because of the economic realities of scholarly publishing, especially the gulf in costs between photographic reproduction and resetting of type, nearly all of the text in this new edition has been reproduced by modern photographic methods. But enough changes have been introduced to make advisable the rechecking of any quotations from the earlier edition. Additions and revisions will usually be apparent, of which Chapter VII and the Addenda and Corrigenda are the most obvious. Aside from discussing the new publications noted in Chapter VII, little amendment has been required. Besides the welcome suggestions made by reviewers of the first edition, I have benefited from the marginal jottings of two Dryden specialists whose annotated copies of the book stand side by side on my shelf, those of Charles E. Ward and the late Percy Dryden Mundy.

Two portraits reproduced in the first edition have been omitted. The Grolier Club portrait, despite the belief of its former owners in its authenticity, is now considered highly suspect by Dryden specialists. They have convinced me that it is not Dryden, though I am unprepared to join in the opinion that it represents Otway. So, too, the miniature of Dryden ascribed to Richardson has been deleted. Here again the experts have argued persuasively that it is a later copy based on one of the well-known engravings.

The revival of interest in Dryden, remarked in the preface to the first edition of this book, has continued to be one of the tides of literary taste, as the columns of any of the "Annual Bibliographies" of English studies will substantiate. Indeed, it is not without significance that the eulogy of T. S. Eliot in the *Times Literary Supplement* the week after his death stated:

Of the two great Tory and Christian poets and critics whom he loved, Mr. Eliot resembled Dryden in the apparently casual and informal movement of his thought rather than Dr. Johnson in his orderly argumentation and combative briskness. He perhaps also resembled Dryden more as a person. Dryden, according to Congreve, had to be drawn out, and hated to appear to intrude; nobody could be kinder and more patient than Mr. Eliot with young poets who wanted to consult him, but the courteous reserve of his manner had something faintly deterrent about it, and his close friendships were few. . . . Important though he was as a critic . . . and dramatist, it is as a poet that Mr. Eliot made his deepest mark on his age.

The eulogy continues the parallel further, but the point need not be labored: the intellectual climate of the "age of Eliot" has been closely sympathetic to the "age of Dryden," as devoted critics and scholars of the twentieth century have demonstrated.

JAMES M. OSBORN

Yale University
January 27, 1965

CONTENTS

Part One
THE EARLIER BIOGRAPHIES

Part Two
COLLATERAL INVESTIGATIONS

CONTENTS

ILLUSTRATIONS

JOHN DRYDEN *Frontispiece*

This portrait is reproduced from the original oil, now in the Osborn Collection. According to the evidence of Miss Honor Pigott's letter to Edmond Malone (see p. 266 below) it is the portrait owned by the poet's "Honour'd Kinsman, John Driden of Chesterton in the County of Huntingdon, Esquire." It was purchased in 1832 by Charles Beville Dryden and later inherited by the late Major Percy Dryden Mundy of Caldrees Manor, Ickleton, Cambs., an authority on the history of the Dryden family, from whose estate it was purchased in 1961. Although previous owners considered the portrait to be by Sir Godfrey Kneller, David Piper, Director of the National Portrait Gallery, says the painter was some imitator of Kneller's style. Judging from the wig, it probably dates from the 1680's.

THOMAS BIRCH 12

This portrait is reproduced from the oil painting by an unknown artist, perhaps J. Wills, in the National Portrait Gallery, London.

DR. SAMUEL JOHNSON 34

This wax medallion, now in my possession, was purchased as item 219a at the Baker Gallery, New York, on May 28, 1940. The catalogue described it as by George Wyon (d. 1796), the name being under the base and the words "Wyon Fecit" written on the back in a modern hand. The authorities at the Metropolitan Museum date it *ca.* 1780–1800. In detail it is very similar to the Wedgwood medallion, but the distinguished Wedgwood collector the late Mr. R. T. H. Halsey has pointed out that the slight difference in size eliminates the possibility that this wax medallion was Flaxman's model from which the Wedgwood was cast. Similar ones are now in the collection of Mr. H. W. Liebert of Yale and Mr. Isham.

EDMOND MALONE 60

The portrait of Malone is an engraving by Armytage. It is from a print by Bartolozzi after the painting by Sir Joshua Reynolds, now in the National Portrait Gallery, London. The engraving was reproduced in Sir James Prior's *Life of Malone,* 1860.

COMPLAINT OF THE SHAREHOLDERS OF THE KING'S COMPANY 202

This important document is now in the collection of Roger W. Barrett, of Kenilworth, Illinois. It is reproduced by the courtesy of Oliver W. Barrett.

DRAFT OF A LETTER TO DRYDEN FROM WILLIAM WALSH 232

This letter is folio 59 verso of Walsh's letterbook, now Additional Manuscript 10434 in the British Museum.

LETTER FROM DRYDEN TO MAJOR RICHARD SALWEY 272

This letter is reproduced by the generous permission of Captain Roger Salwey.

JOHN DRYDEN 273

This portrait is reproduced from the original painting which belongs to the descendants of Dryden's cousins, the Salwey family of Worcestershire. It is ascribed to Sir Godfrey Kneller and has not previously been reproduced. I am grateful to the present owner, Captain Roger Salwey, of Overton, Ludlow, Shropshire, for permission to include it in this book.

Part One

THE EARLIER BIOGRAPHIES

I

THOMAS BIRCH

WHEN DR. JOHNSON sat down to write the "little lives and little prefaces" which ultimately became *The Lives of the Poets,* he was faced with the problem of finding facts about more than fifty men of letters. The task was relatively simple in some cases, since many of the poets had already been the subjects of earlier biographies. For Cowley there was the life by Bishop Sprat, for Milton the lives by Edward Phillips and John Toland, for Pope the two volumes by William Ruffhead. But when Johnson began to look for materials about Dryden, he found no such biography available and confessed his disappointment in the opening paragraph: "His contemporaries, however they reverenced his genius, left his life unwritten; and nothing therefore can be known beyond what casual mention and uncertain tradition have supplied." The sources from which Johnson ultimately derived the various facts in the Life of Dryden were many: books, pamphlets, documents, and even anecdotes remembered from conversation. His main indebtedness, however, was to that sturdy ancestor of the *Dictionary of National Biography,* the great English edition of Bayle's *General Dictionary, Historical and Critical* (1734-41).

The fourth volume (1736) contains eleven and one-half folio pages devoted to Dryden and is the first account of him worthy of being called a biography. It was written, like the entries for other English poets, by the chief editor of the *General Dictionary,* the learned Doctor Thomas Birch. Since these pages remained for three decades the chief source of information about Dryden, it is useful to inquire where Birch found the "casual mentions and uncertain traditions," as well as the solid facts, which he inserted in this first biography of Dryden.

Various other volumes of collected biographies had been offered to the public before Birch's edition of the *General Dictionary,* some of them during Dryden's lifetime. Several were devoted entirely to poets and so contain references to Dryden. The earliest one which mentions him is *Theatrum poetarum,* by Edward Phillips, published in Trinity term, 1675. The subtitle, *with Some Observations and Reflections* indicates the nature of its contents, which are critical rather than biographical. Phillips was a nephew of Milton, and ever since the time of Thomas Warton the question has been raised whether the uncle was responsible for any of the "Reflections." According to John Aubrey, Milton counted Dryden among his "familiar acquaintance," and Dryden had visited him (to ask permission to make a stage version of *Paradise Lost*) only a year or so before the publication of *Theatrum poetarum.*[1] Though the volume contains frequent echoes from Milton's published opinions, there is nothing to indicate that Phillips derived other criticisms from him.[2] Nevertheless the book provides testimony to Dryden's position in the contemporary world of letters:

> . . . such hath been the approbation and acceptance his Poetry hath obtained, especially what he hath written of the Dramatic, with wonderful success to the Theatre Royal . . . if he have indulged a little too much to the French way of continual Rime and interlarding of History with ascititious Love and Honour, I am apt to impute it rather to his complying with the modyfied an[d] gallantish humour of the time, then to his own well examined judgment.[3]

These judgments are sound enough, but somewhat commonplace, coming as they did a few years after the *Rehearsal.*

Phillips's volume was followed twelve years later by another, with the promising title, *The Lives of the Most Famous English Poets . . . from the Time of K. William the Conqueror, to the Reign of His Present Majesty King James II.*[4] The compiler was William Winstanley,

---

[1] *Brief Lives,* ed. by Clark, 1898, II, 72. Dryden's name occurs about a dozen times in Aubrey's manuscripts, frequently as the source of anecdotes. Aubrey intended to get Dryden to write an autobiographical sketch for him, and left a blank page for it, with the notation "John Dryden, esq., Poet Laureate. He will write it for me himselfe" (I, 241). In passing it may be recorded that aside from Aubrey's endeavor the first attempt to collect materials for a biography of Dryden was made three years after his death by the booksellers Newborough and Rhodes. They wished to insert a sketch of the poet's life in the Supplement to Collier's *Dictionary.* Evidently no contributions were forthcoming. See *Term Catalogues,* III, 364.

[2] See Elbert N. S. Thompson's remarks on *Theatrum poetarum* in *Modern Language Notes,* XXXVI, 18–21.

[3] Part II, "The Modern Poets," pp. 107–8.

[4] *Term Catalogues,* Michaelmas, 1686; the title page is dated 1687.

who, under the pseudonym "Poor Robin," annually produced a series of almanacs and chapbooks. A paragraph on page 214 is given to "Mr. John Driden," but like most of the rest of the book this passage is merely diluted *Theatrum poetarum*. Neither Phillips nor Winstanley provided Birch with information about Dryden that was worth repeating.

In striking contrast to these little books is Anthony Wood's *Athenae Oxonienses* (1691). It will be recalled that Wood's plan for this work excluded accounts of living persons, but he could not refrain from inserting incidental remarks about many of his contemporaries. Under the entry for Sir William Davenant he slipped in the following passage:

> In the office of poet laureat succeeded Joh. Dryden, son of Erasmus Dryden of Tichmersh in Northamptonshire, third son of Erasm. Dryden of Canons Ashby in the same county, baronet: which John was born at Oldwincle (called by some Aldwincle) near to Oundle in the same county, (being the very same place that gave breath to Dr. Tho. Fuller the historian) educated in grammar learning in the college school in Westminster, elected thence a scholar of Trin. coll. in Cambridge, an. 1650, and is now highly celebrated among ingenious men for his poetry, and other polite learning.[5]

Scattered through the two folio volumes and among Wood's other writings are a number of other references to Dryden, the longest of which concerns the Rose Alley ambuscade. These passages proved highly useful to Birch, who quoted from most of them in the *General Dictionary*.

To one of Anthony Wood's Headington neighbors, young Gerard Langbaine, Birch was indebted for an extended treatment of Dryden's plays. In 1691, the same year as the *Athenae,* Langbaine had published *An Account of the English Dramatick Poets; or, Some Observations and Remarks on the Lives and Writings of All Those That Have Publish'd Either Comedies, Tragedies . . . in the English Tongue.* In this ambitious handbook of more than five hundred and fifty pages, the longest entry, forty-seven pages, was devoted to the recently deposed poet laureate. This number compares with twenty-six pages for Ben Jonson and sixteen for Shakespeare, who, measured by space, were the nearest rivals. The numerical proportion is also a fair indication of the attention Dryden received in other parts of the book, for many of the

---

[5] *Athenae Oxonienses,* ed. by Bliss, Vol. III (1817), col. 809. Much of Wood's information came from John Aubrey.

most interesting remarks about him are found in the entries other than his own. Langbaine's preoccupation with Dryden was not due entirely to Dryden's dramatic eminence, for Langbaine had a bone to pick with the old poet.

The relations between Langbaine and Dryden are discussed elsewhere in this book,[6] so that it will suffice to acknowledge here that for the next hundred years Langbaine's *Account* remained the basis for any criticism of Dryden's plays. Loaded as it was with abuse of Dryden, Langbaine's book has had, even until the present day, an unfortunate effect on the poet's reputation.

In 1698, seven years after Langbaine's *Account* and two years before Dryden's death, there was published *The Lives and Characters of the English Dramatick Poets . . . First Begun by Mr. Langbain; Improv'd and Continued Down to This Time, by a Careful Hand.*[7] The "careful hand" was that of Charles Gildon, but the Preface reveals that it did not always hold the pen.[8] Gildon's purpose was to condense Langbaine's material into a useful and saleable manual. The Preface frankly states ". . . I design'd . . . to bring my Book to an easier Price than Mr. Langbain's."

Gildon cut down the account of Dryden from forty-seven pages to seven, but here as elsewhere in the volume, he attempted to be fair to the grand old poet who had been so badly maligned by Langbaine. In the Preface he says,

Mr. Langbain seems every where to gratify some private Pique, and seldom to regard the Merit of the Person he reflects upon . . . He often commends Shirley, Heywood &c. and will scarce allow Mr. Dryden a Poet; whereas the former have left us no Piece that bears any Proportion to the latter; the All for Love of Mr. Dryden, were it not for the false Moral, wou'd be a Masterpiece that few of the Ancients or Moderns ever equal'd . . .

To Gildon's way of thinking, Dryden's general indebtedness to others for his plots does "by no means constitute the Character, (which is a

---

[6] See pp. 234–40.

[7] Entered in the *Term Catalogues*, Michaelmas, 1698 (Vol. III, col. 96). I have seen three title pages, two undated and one with the date 1699. The body of the page is identical, but one of the undated issues was printed for Daniel Midwinter and Thomas Leigh, and the other for Thomas Leigh and William Turner, while the dated issue was printed for William Turner.

[8] ". . . the following Piece is not writ all by one Hand . . ." Another line contains the phrase "one of my assistants," indicating that several hacks were employed by Gildon.

thing Mr. Langbain seems never to understand) . . ." [9] Buried in these remarks is Gildon's conclusion—a judgment in which posterity has concurred: "For I never found him in any Theft indeed, but what he gave a new Lustre to, when taken, ev'n from the best of the Ancients . . ." [10]

Considering that Gildon's primary purpose was to shorten Langbaine, it is a pleasant surprise to find a few additions and changes in the account of Dryden. Of *The Mistaken Husband* Gildon noted that Dryden "only added a Scene." And in the account of *The Indian Emperor* he observed that it was performed at the Theatre Royal, and he also appended Rycaut's *History of the Incas* to the list of sources.[11] The differences between the two versions, however, are rare, and condensation generally appears to have been Gildon's single aim.

The next publication (in point of time) that Birch used was Congreve's "character" of Dryden, which he found embedded in the Epistle Dedicatory before the 1717 edition of Dryden's *Dramatick Works* (6 vols., duodecimo). A close friendship had sprung up between Dryden and Congreve in 1691, at the time of Congreve's first literary efforts, and continued with unabated affection for the ten remaining years of Dryden's life. Apparently Dryden derived considerable stimulation from the company of the young poet. Conversely, it may be more than a coincidence that after Dryden's death Congreve practically ceased doing any creative writing. Although Congreve and Dryden were men with many friends, in the lives of both this relationship occupied a unique place. In 1694 Dryden had asked the young poet to "Be kind to my remains," [12] and this injunction apparently made a deep impression on Congreve, who undertook the edition of 1717 as a "Duty and Obligation to my departed Friend."

The biographical facts contained in Congreve's pages are very meager —only four in number: (*a*) Dryden gave not only literary assistance to his friends, but also practical help to those whose circumstances re-

---

[9] Charles Gildon, *Dramatick Poets*, p. 42.   [10] *Ibid.*, p. 41.

[11] Perhaps these additions were the result of perusing "Mr. Ash's admirable collection of English Plays," mentioned in the Preface. I have never seen other references to this collection. Could Ash have purchased some plays from Langbaine's library? Apart from the volumes in Worcester College, Oxford, few of Langbaine's "above Nine Hundred and Fourscore English Plays and Masques, besides Drolls and Interludes," are known to be preserved. According to Anthony Wood, most of Langbaine's plays passed through "the private shop of Nicholas Cox manciple of S. Edmund Hall, Oxon." (Bodleian MS Wood E. 4).

[12] Lines to Congreve "On His Comedy Call'd the Double Dealer," l. 72.

quired it; (*b*) "his Hereditary Income was little more than a bare Competency"; (*c*) Dryden considered that frequent reading of Archbishop Tillotson's writings had affected his prose style; and (*d*) "as his Reading had been very extensive, so was he very happy in a Memory tenacious of that he had read." [13] To Birch and his successors these pages possessed great value, because Congreve was the only one of Dryden's friends who left a deliberately composed account of Dryden's personality. Thus it is not surprising that nearly all Dryden's biographers reprinted Congreve's paragraphs as integral parts of their lives of the poet.

Two years later Congreve was indirectly responsible for a work of quite a different sort, which appeared under the title *The Poetical Register; or, The Lives and Characters of All the English Dramatic Poets, with an Account of Their Writings* (1719). The compiler was Giles Jacob, an ambitious young man, "bred to the Law, who between his more laborious studies has Diverted himself with Poetry." [14] That Congreve was the seminal force is apparent throughout the book and is clearly stated in the Preface: "I am in particular oblig'd to Mr. CONGREVE for his free and early Communication of what relates to himself, as well as his kind Directions for the Composing of this Work." [15]

Although Jacob's Preface states that "The Foundation of the Work is owing to Mr. *Langbain* . . ." [16] in point of fact the structure was taken over bodily and without acknowledgment from Gildon. Jacob was satisfied to bring Gildon's book up to date, but while rewriting the sentences of the 1698 text he introduced various details from the 1691 volume which Gildon had sacrificed in the interests of economy.

[13] Each of these statements is supported by independent evidence, some of which has become known long after Congreve's day. Taking them in order: (*a*) well-known examples are Dryden's literary assistance to Mulgrave and Walsh. Financial assistance may have been behind the "couzening" of which Dryden complained in his letter to Walsh in 1693 (Scott-Saintsbury edition of Dryden's works, XVIII, 184). Dryden also lent £500 to Charles II, as Professor Ward has shown in the *Review of English Studies* for July, 1937, p. 297. E. S. de Beer suggests that this may have been an impersonal investment. (*b*) For an account of his inheritance see Malone's Life of Dryden, pp. 440–42. (*c*) Apparent on examination, but of course Tillotson was not the only model. (*d*) Also obvious in nearly everything Dryden wrote, particularly the prose works. In fact, a few years earlier Langbaine had complained that Dryden's memory was *too* tenacious.

[14] Vol. II (1720), p. 299.

[15] Preface, p. [iii]. See also the letter printed by Curll in the Preface (pp. xv–xvi) of *Memoirs of Congreve* by "Charles Wilson" (1730), usually attributed to Oldmixon. It is dated July 7, 1719 and purports to be Congreve's reply to Jacob's request for information for the *Poetical Register*. The authenticity of this letter cannot be proved. Considering that Curll used it as evidence to support an argument, we are entitled to question its genuineness.

[16] Preface, p. [i].

But we remember Jacob for something more important than the improvement of a theatrical handbook, for the *Poetical Register* contains accounts of his contemporaries in which the details were often supplied by the individuals themselves:

As to the Accounts of the *Living* AUTHORS, most of them came from their own Hands, excepting such Parts as relate to the Fame of their Writings, where I thought my self at liberty to give such Characters of Praise or Dispraise, as the best Judges before me had pass'd upon their Performances.[17]

Thus it is apparent that Dennis, Savage, and others supplied information for the accounts of themselves. Perhaps this was Congreve's idea; at least it is tempting to conjecture that "his free and early Communication of what relates to himself" set an example which the lesser literary men were prevailed upon to follow.

The Dryden section of the *Poetical Register* occupies fourteen pages and contains ample evidence that some interested person had been gleaning biographical details from Dryden's writings. For example, the following points make their debut: "born, as he himself says, in a Village belonging to the late Earl of *Exeter* . . ."; "being King's Scholar [at Westminster] under the learned Dr. *Busby*"; "he pursu'd his studies [at Trinity College, Cambridge] with his worthy Friend Sir *William Bowyer* of *Denham Court*."[18] As we should expect, the author warmly defended Dryden against the hackneyed charges of plagiarism and irreligion, especially those made by Langbaine. Did Congreve have any part in this vindication? His connection with the book raises this question, for he knew as well as anyone that Langbaine suffered from delusions about Dryden and that this part of the book needed careful correction. Congreve may not have given active help in this revision, but the account of Dryden reads as he would have wished it to read.

The following year, 1720, Jacob published a companion volume[19] comprehending the nondramatic poets. Here he was breaking comparatively new ground, since no Langbaine had ploughed the field before him. In this volume four more pages were devoted to Dryden. They

---

[17] Preface, p. [iii].   [18] Page 72.

[19] *An Historical Account of the Lives and Writings of Our Most Considerable English Poets, Whether Epick, Lyrick, Elegiack, Epigrammatists,* . . . London, E. Curll, 1720. For his articles on the "ancient writers" he dipped into various sources, Phillips, Winstanley, the historians Fuller and Camden, and Sir Thomas Pope Blount's collection of eulogies (*De re poetica*, London, R. Bentley, 1694). The accounts of "modern writers," with few exceptions, are disappointing, but should not be neglected by any student of the period.

contain a list of his poems and conclude with Dennis's Ode to Dryden. Since this list adds a number of titles not found in Langbaine, it may be considered the first attempt to establish the Dryden canon.

Among the many references to Dryden sprinkled through the rest of the book, one requires particular attention. It is found under the entry for Tom Brown:

Towards the latter part of his Life, I am inform'd he was in favour with the Earl of *Dorset,* who invited him to Dinner on a *Christmas-Day,* with Mr. *Dryden* and some other Gentlemen famous for Learning and Ingenuity (according to his Lordship's usual Custom) when Mr *Brown,* to his agreeable surprize found a Bank Note of 50*l* under his Plate, and Mr. *Dryden* at the same time was presented with another of an 100*l.* Actions of this Nature, were very common and peculiar to this Great and Generous Spirited Nobleman.[20]

How authentic is this story? As Malone thought, the incongruity of the company invites caution, but he accepted the anecdote on the ground that Dryden "appears to have entertained no ill will towards Brown, speaking of him in one of his letters with perfect unconcern, as a mere pamphleteer who wrote against him solely for the purpose of getting a little money." [21] Although the financial figures may be inexact, the story does not conflict with the character of any of the persons named or with other known facts. Considering that it was printed within twenty-five or thirty years of the supposed event, there is no reason to be especially suspicious of this anecdote until contradictory evidence appears.

Each of these writers, from Wood to Jacob, enumerated some new facts about Dryden—facts that Birch synthesized, with others of his own finding, into the first biography. In doing so he followed the standard pattern of Pierre Bayle, the editor and author of the original version of the *General Dictionary.* Bayle had been the first to apply the inductive method to biography on a considerable scale. In compiling the English edition Birch and his colleagues followed the new method rigorously, and their careful authentication of information has made the 1734-41 edition permanently valuable.[22]

[20] *Ibid.,* II, 16.

[21] Malone, Life of Dryden, I, 453. Probably Malone had in mind the letter to Tonson dated Dec., 1697, in I (Part 2, Letters), 60.

[22] For an account of Birch's activities as editor of the *General Dictionary* see *Modern Philology,* XXXVI, 25–46.

The Dryden entry contains almost every fact about the poet that could be found in print. Because Birch's method required the careful labeling of all sources, later biographers have been able to check the authority behind his statements. An instance occurs in the very first sentence, where in his attempt to give a family background Birch stated that "Dryden . . . was descended of a worthy family in Huntingdonshire, often serving as Representatives in that County." The marginal note reveals the origin of the error:

A Letter to the Author of *Reflexions Historical and Political,* occasioned by a Treatise in Vindication of General *Monk* and Sir *Richard Glanville,* By the Right Honourable *George Granville,* Lord *Lansdowne,* page 6, edit. London 1732; in 4to.

Birch had good reason to accept the testimony of a man who had known Dryden. The mistake was due to a confusion in Lansdowne's memory between the Huntingdonshire and Northamptonshire branches of the Dryden family. Another example is Birch's error in ascribing Dryden's death to 1701. Here again he leads us to his source, in this case the inscription on Dryden's tombstone as reported by Alexander Pope.[23] These mistakes in Birch's Life of Dryden prove useful in tracing the derivation of some later biographies.

The most noticeable difference in procedure between Birch and his predecessors is that he went to the trouble to consult copies of Dryden's works. He made it a practice to specify the editions from which quotations were taken, for example, the 1716 octavo edition of the *Du Fresnoy* and the sixth edition (1735) of the translation of Juvenal. These, of course, are reprints, but Birch was not indifferent to early editions; on two occasions he dated books by means of their *imprimatur.*[24] And for three plays he found first editions, whereas Langbaine had been contented with later printings.[25]

In his quest for facts Birch also looked through some of Dryden's own writings for autobiographical passages. That he missed much goes without saying, but his range is indicated by the use of quotations, among others, from the prefaces of *Troilus and Cressida, Albion and*

[23] See *General Dictionary,* Vol. IV, p. 684, note 48.
[24] *General Dictionary,* IV, 681nn.
[25] The 1667 *Indian Emperor,* the 1670 *Tempest,* and the 1670 *Tyrannick Love.* Langbaine had in each case referred to a third edition, although as usual he was indifferent to the existence of other editions, either earlier or later.

Albanius, and *Cleomenes.* So, too, he paid careful attention to the *Miscellany Poems.* From these collections he extracted all of Dryden's verses that he could find and inserted the dates of their composition, whenever ascertainable, into the biographical narrative. His desire to establish the Dryden canon prompted him to list the titles of seventy-six of the poems in a long footnote (HH), a list which complemented the catalogue of plays begun by Langbaine.

Birch collected many other particulars about Dryden and discussed them at length in his notes, among others the following subjects: the controversy concerning the *Duke of Guise* (note Q); the quarrels with Stillingfleet and Burnet (notes S, T, and Z); the fabricated story of Dryden's funeral, repeated at length (note CC); and Congreve's "character" of Dryden (note EE). These instances demonstrate his use of Bayle's method: every shred of information Birch could uncover he handed on for the reader's use, and since all the information was documented, later Dryden scholars have been able to apply their own tests whenever reassessment has been required.

While giving Birch the credit that has been too long denied him, we must not overlook his shortcomings. The most noticeable of these is that he gathered, but did not sift. For example, he quoted at length the spurious story of Dryden's funeral, a tale that could easily have been confuted by the testimony of people yet living, as well as by the records and newspapers. In other instances he quoted information at second hand, without examining the evidence for himself. For instance, he reported Dryden's epitaph as given by Pope, whereas one look at the stone would have shown it to be erroneous. Lack of thoroughness mars Birch's work in other ways; though he examined a large portion of Dryden's writings, he passed by several not very rare books that would have been extremely useful to him. *King Arthur* is an excellent case in point; Birch supplied the title, size, and date, but no other details. If, however, he had taken the trouble to consult the actual quarto, he would have found there the list of Dryden's plays arranged in "the order in which they were writ."

Although in writing the other biographies for the *General Dictionary,* Birch had drawn on the knowledge of friends and relatives for information, his account of Dryden contains nothing that seems to have come from a verbal source. Indeed, except for the indirect quotation from one of Dryden's letters, "communicated by the very learned and in-

THOMAS BIRCH

genious Richard Graham Junior Esquire," [26] there is no indication that
he attempted to use manuscript material. Since Birch had already obtained information about Congreve from Thomas Southerne, he could
easily have applied to him or to other friends still alive for materials
about Dryden.

Yet when all these objections have been made, we must still remember
the debt we owe to Birch. The Dryden biography was just one of more
than six hundred that he produced within a few years, merely a few
pages from one of the greatest synthetic achievements of eighteenth-
century literature. If an equally brief account were necessary today, less
than a quarter of Birch's life of Dryden would need to be changed.
Through constant use by later scholars Birch's collection of Dryden facts
has become common property, while the man who did the work has
been all but forgotten.

[26] This letter was assiduously sought for by Malone, who acknowledged his failure in
his Life of Dryden, p. 286: "I had hoped to have found a copy of this letter among Dr.
Birch's papers in the Museum; but I have examined them for that purpose in vain." To
this passage he later added a MS note in his own copy of the book (Bodley Malone E. 61,
p. 286): "As Birch appears to have constantly copied every letter relative either to politicks or literature that came into his hands, I am inclined to believe that he never saw
this letter; and that Mr. Graham merely transmitted to him the paragraph above quoted."
That this conjecture was correct appears from a document printed in *Notes and Queries,*
May 19, 1877 (5th ser., VII, 386). Sent by one John Taylor of Northampton, who had
"lately obtained" it, the paper may well have been the very one Birch used.

"From a MS. of Mr Drydens in w^h he directs his Freind Mr Graham to settl' Acc^{ts}
w^h Mr J. Tonson his Bookseller, relating to his Virgil.

"He thinks Mr T. us'd him ill in ye Price of his Paper, considering some Additionel
Trouble he had been at in improving ye 2^d Edit, &c. Then adds:—'Upon ye third Edition, J. T. not be unwilling to give him in 3 Weeks more of Study to correct some
Parts of my Versification, tho^h ye Worst of them *are already more correct than any of
this Age can write.'*

Ditto.

Preface to Marq. of Normanby cost Mr D. above 2 months.
"He gave Mr T. his Ode on St Cecilias Day, w^h cost him almost a *fortnight in making & mending.*

"It appears further from y^s MS. that Mr D. had a Design to translate Homer—
"When you h' driven him (T.) as low as you can by ye Agreem't of future Dealing
w^h him f^r Homer, or some other Book, I see no Reason why I s^d not treat w^h him again.

"In Mr Graham's Hand. N. B. Mr Dryden own'd to me, that by ye money paid him
by Mr Tonson, by his Publicat' & by his Subscript^n he got 1400^l for his Translat^n of
Virgil.

"The MS. above contain'd ye rough Draught of Mr D^s Translat^n of Ovid de Art.
Amandi, and was com'unicated to me by my (late) Friend R. Graham, Esqr, F. R. S.
son to ye Gent. mention'd in it.

R. Nixon."

I am not able to identify Nixon.

One reason that the *General Dictionary* is often overlooked is that within a few years it was followed by the *Biographia Britannica* (7 vols., 1747–66), which, as its name implies, was composed entirely of the lives of British worthies. Imitating the *General Dictionary,* its pages are practically identical in appearance with the earlier work, as they also are in content. The Dryden entry, in Volume III (1750), was written by Thomas Broughton, who seven years earlier had published an edition of Dryden's poems in two volumes, duodecimo.[27] Like most of the other writers in the *Biographia,* Broughton went for most of his material to the *General Dictionary,* and his obligation to Birch is nowhere more noticeable than in the account of Dryden. True enough, most of the sentences were rephrased, and some shifting from text to footnote, or *vice versa,* has taken place; but these alterations are rarely improvements. Broughton's experience in editing Dryden's poems seems to have borne no fruit. His only additions were to call attention to Dryden's translations of the *History of the League* and the *Life of St. Francis Xavier,* to expand the explanation of the occasion of *The Medal,* and to quote once from the Preface to *Don Sebastian.* These small contributions were more than counterbalanced by Broughton's omissions. We look in vain for Birch's notes on *Annus mirabilis,* on Dryden's contemplated epic poem, on the *Duke of Guise,* and on Martin Clifford. Thus "Tom the second" merely imitated "Tom the first," and the reader who inquires after Dryden will find Broughton's original in the *General Dictionary.*

[27] *Original Poems and Translations by John Dryden, Esq. Now First Collected and Published Together, in Two Volumes.* London, 1743. Broughton's name is not given, but the Memoir in Vol. II of Kippis's edition of the *Biographica Britannica* (1780, Preface, p. x) establishes him as the editor.

II

SAMUEL DERRICK

FOLLOWING in the wake of the *General Dictionary* and the *Biographia Britannica* came a number of smaller biographical dictionaries, some of them devoted exclusively to poets or to dramatists, and all of them containing accounts of Dryden. These volumes are of considerable interest to the student of English biography and also to the historian of Dryden's reputation. They are not, however, of much value to anyone who seeks factual evidence about Dryden himself. All were derived from earlier compilations, particularly from the folio pages of Birch and Broughton. The time was now ripe for someone to write a life of Dryden, not an entry for another biographical dictionary, but a separate piece of work, independently executed. This development took place in 1760, in the form of a life prefixed to Dryden's *Miscellaneous Works* in four volumes octavo.

The honor of producing this handsome edition belongs to a young Irishman, Samuel Derrick. He is remembered today chiefly as Boswell's "first tutor in the ways of London . . . both literary and sportive," [1] but before Boswell met him Derrick had already achieved some success as a miscellaneous writer. A few years afterward he became the successor to Beau Nash as the "King" of Bath and Tunbridge Wells.

Derrick had begun work on his edition of Dryden's poems in 1757. Thanks to the help of his friend David Mallet, Derrick obtained an introduction to Birch, who gave the young man much kindly assistance. [2] The new edition was intended to include "the whole of his

---

[1] Boswell, *Life of Johnson*, ed. Powell, I, 456.

[2] I am indebted to Mr. William H. Miller for several details about Derrick. He has informed me that Mallet gave Derrick a letter of introduction to Birch on December 26, 1757. The choice of the Duke of Newcastle as dedicatee was also suggested by Mallet. Mr. Miller called to my attention a letter from Derrick among the Birch manuscripts in the British Museum, dated January 12, 1758, in which Derrick asked Birch's help in explaining a number of allusions in *Annus mirabilis*. The tone of the letter indicates that Derrick relied heavily on Birch's assistance.

original poems and translations (the plays and the Virgil excepted)," [3] and Derrick promised that if the poems should be well received, he would edit the remaining works also, "in the same size, which will make up a complete and uniform set of his works." [4] For one reason or another the undertaking was never carried to completion, perhaps because Derrick soon became absorbed in other projects, including a *Collection of Voyages,* published in 1762.

When writing the prefatory "Life of John Dryden, Esq.," Derrick was not content to depend on the *General Dictionary*. Instead he began by searching for documents. His most successful inquiry was at the house of Tonson, where he was rewarded by finding the Dryden-Tonson agreement covering the financial terms of the *Fables* and Dryden's receipt for a payment of two hundred and fifty guineas. Both of these Derrick printed in full. The helpful Tonson ("Jacob the Third") also lent him one of Dryden's letters, from which, for some reason, Derrick chose to print only an excerpt.[5] Why he failed to see the remainder of the Dryden-Tonson correspondence, I do not know, and it is useless to conjecture. Derrick's inquiries in other quarters were less successful, as the Advertisement tells in the third person:

He has with his utmost care been able only to recover two of Dryden's manuscript letters, one to Wilmot, Earl of Rochester; the other to Mrs. Thomas, otherwise known by the name of the Fair Corinna . . .

Other searches led to further disappointments,

though he applied to the present Sir John Dryden, through the means of a friend, who has considerable fortune in his neighbourhood. He also addressed himself on this head in person to a descendant of our poet's, near Berkeley-square; but cannot say he met with any information that gave him satisfaction.[6]

It happens that during these years Derrick and Dr. Johnson were moderately well acquainted, and the Doctor subsequently claimed that he was responsible for these applications: "I sent Derrick to Dryden's relations to gather materials for his life; and I believe he got all that I my-

---

[3] The Advertisement, p. vii.   [4] *Ibid.,* p. xii.

[5] Page xxix. According to Malone's numbering this is Letter XXIV.

[6] Page ix. From Oldys's notes to Langbaine, p. 131 (see p. 276, below) it is clear that Dryden's letter to Rochester was in the Harleian Collection, which had become the property of the British Museum by the time Derrick became interested in Dryden.

self should have got." "But," he told Boswell, "it was nothing." [7] Johnson's statement sounds reasonable enough, but we should like to know more about his relations with Derrick, and whether Johnson made the suggestions that led him to Tonson and to Montague House. Two of Johnson's friends also helped Derrick, the "Reverend Mr. Walter Harte, one of the canons of Windsor," [8] and David Garrick. He acknowledged in the Advertisement (p. xi) that he was "particularly obliged to Mr. Garrick, who with great civility gave [me] the use of his fine collection of old 4to plays." This was the most extensive dramatic library then in existence, and Garrick's copies of Dryden's plays enabled Derrick to make several corrections to the titles of prologues and epilogues and supplied him with a few new poems for the edition.[9] Although Derrick may have gained an introduction to Harte and Garrick through Mallet or some other acquaintance, it is not unlikely that Johnson "sent" him to these friends, as he had done to representatives of the Dryden family.

The biographical structure of Derrick's life of Dryden marks a notable advance over that of his predecessors. They had followed the dictionary formula and had divided discussion of his writings into dramatic, nondramatic, and other set categories. Derrick was not bound by these restrictions of space or style, and throwing the categories aside, he wove the life in a chronological pattern. As a result his narrative flows more smoothly than the earlier ones. The following passage is a good sample of Derrick's style:

He has been accused as a time-server and hypocrite in religion, because it was his fortune at a particular season to conform to one patronised at court; but this charge must fall to the ground on recollecting that he always continued therein firm and unshaken, though he might have gained considerably by recanting after the revolution, and his writings on that head carry with them the strongest marks of sincerity. Perhaps before he declared himself a Roman Catholic, he had no settled form of religion; and his Religio Laici is not a defence of any particular sect of Christianity, so much as of Christianity in general.[10]

---

[7] For the first reference see Boswell's *Life*, ed. Powell, I, 456. The second comes from the *Tour to the Hebrides*, ed. Powell, V, 240. See also my note on p. 24, below.

[8] Page viii. See pp. 283–84 for a discussion of a copy of Dryden's *Heads of an Answer to Rymer*, owned by Harte.

[9] The Prologue to the *Loyal General* is a case in point; Broughton had headed it simply "A Prologue" in his 1743 edition, as it had been titled in the *Miscellany Poems*, 1702. See Vol. II, p. xlvi, for Derrick's note telling how he found the play and so was able to give the Prologue the proper title.

[10] Pages xxxii–xxxiii.

Without exaggerating Derrick's abilities as critic, I wish to call attention to two passages from his summary of Dryden's literary powers. They contain echoes of Congreve, but go far beyond him in the development of critical judgment. When reading them, perhaps others besides myself will be tempted to see Derrick writing these words after sitting at the elbow of Samuel Johnson:

What a prodigious field for admiration opens upon us in contemplating our author as a poet! Here, in whatever light we view him, he is sure always to excel; and if universality of genius gives a title to pre-eminence, perhaps we shall be scarcely excused for admitting any to rank above him. In elegy he was plaintive and tender; in panegyric he had the art of throwing a lustre round a character that sunk all its imperfections. In satire he was strong, bold, penetrating, and severe; in didactic or controversial writing, concise, clear, and persuasive. His epistles are familiar, easy, and entertaining. His prologues and epilogues abound with wit, pleasantry, and often excellent traces of criticism. In his songs the thoughts appear new; the phraseology unconstrained; and the conclusions pointed. His odes are strong, forceful, soaring and sublime; the numbers are happily varied, the harmony is inimitable, and the whole seem to breathe the spirit of inspiration.[11]

In prose he was equally excellent, his words were always happily chosen, his periods round and flowing, his meaning clear, his arguments supported with masterly elocution, and his conclusions well deduced. In his prefaces, indeed, we find him sometimes a deserter, and opposing his own arguments in a manner to which Dryden only was equal; he has appeared unanswerable till he answered himself.[12]

Although in critical understanding Derrick went beyond his predecessors, in refashioning the incidents of Dryden's biography he perpetrated many of their mistakes and retained their apocryphal anecdotes. To these he contributed a few of his own, for example, the report that in return for the famous *Epistle,* the poet's cousin John Driden of Chesterton "made him a present of 500*l.*" So also with *Alexander's Feast:*

Mr. W. Moyle, who wrote the essays, used to say, "That it was composed for the Cicilian concert, and that our author for the use of it received 40*l.*" This volume [the *Fables*] was introduced into the world with a poetical address to the dutchess of Ormond, who rewarded the poet with a bill of 500*l.* as I have been credibly informed by one of his collateral descendants.[13]

---

[11] Page xxxiii.   [12] Page xxxiv.

[13] This and the previous quotation are from p. xxviii. For Malone's examination of these anecdotes see his Life of Dryden, pp. 278, 327–28, 437, and following.

Malone wisely questioned these figures and produced some evidence to qualify them. Two other statements may have been derived from the Dryden family: ". . . on his father's death [he] came into the possession of an estate of 200*l.* per ann. He is said to have been bred an anabaptist . . ." [14] But whatever Derrick's source, it was a poor one; Malone established that the former figure was grossly exaggerated, and no evidence has ever been discovered for the latter statement. On the same page Derrick made the curious suggestion that the Third Satire of Persius, which Dryden had "translated for a Thursday night's exercise" at Westminster School, was retained by Dryden and touched up for the complete translation of Persius more than forty years later.

It is interesting to note that Derrick came close to laying the ghost of a poem that had been ascribed to Dryden ever since the 1704 volume of *Poems on Affairs of State.* Printed there as "A Satyr on the Dutch," and included by Broughton in his edition, the poem was a composite of lines from the prologue and epilogue of *Amboyna.* Derrick recognized the connection, but thought that Dryden had written the "Satyr" first, and then adapted part of it for use in *Amboyna.*[15] Another of Derrick's innovations is found on page xxi, where he expanded the history of Rose Alley by quoting from a contemporary paper, *Domestic Intelligence,* the issues of December 23–26, 1679, and January 2, 1679/80.[16] By this evidence he gave the incident its true date, for Anthony Wood, on whom previous biographers had relied, not only had placed the attack in Will's Coffee-house, but also two days before it actually occurred.[17]

Our interest in Derrick's edition extends further than the life, however, for this is the first edition in which a serious attempt was made

[14] Page xiv. See Johnson's Life of Dryden, ed. G. B. Hill, I, 331–32. Also Malone's Life of Dryden, pp. 23, 37*n.*

[15] I, xiv. Derrick had searched for a pamphlet wrongly titled in *Biographia Britannica.* There are abundant indications that he went over other of the previous biographies and also Dryden's prose works with some care. Pp. xvii–xviii. Cf. his use of the Preface to the *Mock Astrologer,* p. xvi, and *All for Love,* p. xx, where he is the first to repeat Dryden's references to the three unities.

[16] Pages xxi–xxii. The second date is misprinted "September."

[17] *Life of Wood,* December 16, 1679, ed. Bliss, I, lxxxvii; Bliss did not explain how this entry happens to be dated two days before the occurrence of the event it describes, nor did Clark in the 1892 edition. Perhaps Wood was "maggotty headed" on this occasion. Robert Bell censured Wood severely for this discrepancy: "Such a mistake would be of little importance in a retrospective narrative, but occurring in a diary which professes to have been written from day to day, recording incidents as they happened, it is calculated to shake very materially the reader's confidence in the integrity of the writer." ("Memoir of Dryden" prefixed to his edition of Dryden, 1854, p. 46.)

at annotation. Notes to the poems take up 140 pages (88 in Vol. I, and 52 in Vol. III). Considering the date at which they were written and that they were the first attempt at this task, Derrick's notes constitute an important advance in Dryden studies. Nearly all the proper names that occur in the poems are glossed, and many are followed by expanded explanations. These notes contain material of more than passing interest to both the Dryden specialist and the historian of English studies.

A number of the annotations deserve comment. Derrick had done some reading in the pamphlet attacks on Dryden, as is shown by the note, "Dryden is said to have been the son of a committeeman." [18] Several pages further on he printed the Dedication of *Annus mirabilis,* remarking, "This dedication has been left out in all editions of the poem but the first." [19] To illustrate one passage in it he inserted a short essay on the changed meaning of "wit" in the century since Dryden had written on the subject.[20] That Derrick had the true zest of a literary historian is shown by his resourcefulness in documenting the narrative of the sea fight with a quotation from the *London Gazette* of June 4, 1666.[21] In similar fashion the notes to *Absalom and Achitophel* [22] supply a surprisingly full background to the poem, especially when we consider that this was the first attempt to explain a very complex situation that nowadays even university students find difficult to master. The passage on Settle, which is buried among these notes, exemplifies the patches of biographical information which are scattered through Derrick's pages.[23]

One of these notes provides another glimpse of Derrick's friendship with Dr. Johnson. Referring to "Randal" in line 251 of the translation of Boileau's *Art of Poetry,* Derrick stated: "Mr. Samuel Johnson thinks that this should be Randolph, Ben Jonson's adopted son, who wrote some pastorals." [24] This and previous echoes cause the reader to speculate as to what other notes he may have derived from Johnson. Yet Birch was probably consulted even more often.

Thus Derrick's edition, despite its deficiencies and errors, marks a definite advance in the history of Dryden scholarship. Derrick was the first of Dryden's biographers who made an effort to collect documents and family traditions, though in practice he proved inept at us-

---

[18] Notes (at end of Vol. I), p. iv.   [19] *Ibid.,* p. xix.   [20] *Ibid.,* p. xx.
[21] *Ibid.,* pp. xxx–xxxi.   [22] *Ibid.,* pp. xlv–lxxii.   [23] *Ibid.,* p. lxvii.
[24] *Ibid.,* p. lxxiv. Probably Johnson made this suggestion verbally.

ing the documents and credulous in repeating the traditions.[25] Similar criticism applies to the explanatory notes to the poems. Though they do not measure up to the work done by his contemporary Zachary Grey on *Hudibras,* they do represent the solid unpolished work of a pioneer. Considered as a unit, the edition has many virtues. Dryden had fared less well in the hands of eighteenth-century scholars than Butler and Milton, but progress was being made, and the work of Samuel Derrick stands as an important milestone in this advance.[26]

[25] Derrick confessed his inability to use two of the letters he had found, one addressed to Rochester and the other to Corinna, "for these there did not appear any proper place in these four volumes" (I, ix). Although letters had been included in biographies since antiquity, their use as a conscious literary device did not begin until William Mason's *Memoir* of Gray, in 1774.

[26] In 1767 Tonson reissued the four volumes of Dryden's *Miscellaneous Poems.* The handsome format was replaced by smaller, crowded pages, which necessitated cutting down the engravings and omitting some altogether. Likewise many of Derrick's notes were omitted, and most of the rest were emasculated. Derrick's name is nowhere mentioned, and in place of his Life of Dryden stood one that had been printed in Flloyd's *Bibliotheca biographica* (1760).

III

SAMUEL JOHNSON

IN THE MIDDLE YEARS of the eighteenth century Dryden was the subject of other biographical sketches, which appeared in the various handbooks and cyclopedias turned out by the book trade to satisfy the hunger of a rapidly expanding literary public. Cibber's *Lives of the Poets* (1753), Flloyd's *Bibliotheca biographica* (1760), Mortimer's *British Plutarch* (1762), Heathcote's *New and General Biographical Dictionary* (1761), Baker's *Companion to the Playhouse* (1764), Towers's *British Biography* (1766), and Granger's *Biographical History of England* (1769), are some of the best known of these compilations. Based either directly or indirectly on Birch or Derrick, most of these accounts of Dryden are smoothly written, but none of them can be called examples of biographical art. It was not until 1778 that a master craftsman took up the subject —and Samuel Johnson's life of Dryden is one of the most distinguished products of his pen.

The story of the *Prefaces, Biographical and Critical* is familiar to all students of literature, and it will suffice to say that the Dryden filled the whole third volume of the ten octavos in which the *Prefaces* were first printed. It was published in midsummer, 1779, if we may judge from the *Gentleman's Magazine,* where it is reviewed in the July issue (pages 362–64). Because of the success of these *Prefaces* and the many times they have been reprinted as the *Lives of the Poets,* it is often forgotten that the volumes were, like the other biographical collections we have mentioned, primarily a commercial venture of the book trade. The astute stationers had the good fortune to engage a really great biographer to write the prefaces, and both their purses and English literature benefited in consequence. Though Johnson's ambition pointed no higher than "to write trifles with dignity," [1] these "trifles" turned out to be the finest body of literary criticism of their century.

[1] Boswell, *Life,* ed. Powell, IV, 34n.

When, on the eve of his seventieth birthday, Johnson began to write on Dryden, he brought special qualifications to the task. Like the life of Pope, these pages were "written *con amore*." [2] There is ample testimony of Johnson's "partial fondness for the memory of Dryden," [3] of which the most interesting is his admission made in 1776, "When I was a young fellow I wanted to write the 'Life of Dryden.' " [4] It is tempting to speculate what the biography would have been like if Johnson had undertaken it at that time, but no fair judgment can be based on the biographies Johnson actually wrote in these early years. The lives of Drake, Burman, Sydenham, and even the life of Savage are more like "profiles" than full length biographies. Rather than another one of these, Johnson's ambition may have been to make the life of Dryden a work on the grand scale, similar to the biography of Sir Walter Raleigh (1736) by his friend William Oldys. But like the other *Lives of the Poets,* the Dryden was cast into a mold only slightly developed from that which Johnson used in the biography of Boerhaave (1739) and other lives which he contributed to the *Gentleman's Magazine.*[5]

As is indicated by the phrase "Biographical and Critical," the *Lives of the Poets* followed a set pattern, being divided into biographical and critical halves, of about equal length. At the conclusion of the biographical portion is an extended discussion of Dryden's character, and at the end of the volume Johnson added the contents of two manuscripts, which will be noticed in the proper place. Several topics are treated twice, once in each half, and the nature of the repetitions suggests that Johnson wrote the two sections at different times.

The information from which the biographical portion is built up was primarily derived from Birch's account in the *General Dictionary.* This can be said with certainty, for Birch betrayed Johnson into the mistake of naming Huntingdonshire as the early home of the Dryden family. Similarly he added a year to Dryden's life by accepting 1701

---

[2] Said by the reviewer in the *Gentleman's Magazine,* July, 1779, p. 364. Could Boswell have picked up his application of the phrase from here? Compare Boswell, IV, 46.

[3] *Life of Pope,* par. 311, in Birkbeck Hill's edition. All subsequent references to the *Lives of the Poets* are to that edition.

[4] Boswell, *Life,* III, 71.

[5] Mr. George Lam has made an extensive study, as yet unpublished, of the *Lives of the Poets.* He points out that structurally Johnson's biographies in the *Gentleman's Magazine* were generally divided into three parts, (*a*) the narrative of the life, (*b*) an essay on the habits, peculiarities and character, and (*c*) the list of writings. Mr. Lam suggests that Johnson may have been influenced by Fontenelle's *Du Bartas,* which follows the same form.

from Birch as the date of his death. And there is additional evidence in the long quotation about the "vexatious events" at Dryden's funeral, which Johnson took from Birch word for word.[6] In contrast to this evidence, there is nothing to indicate that Johnson utilized any part of Broughton's article on Dryden in the *Biographia Britannica;* probably he recognized the derivative quality of the latter, and preferred to use the original version in the *General Dictionary.*

In addition to Birch, Johnson leaned heavily on the principal edition of Dryden's poems and its prefatory life. This was the edition of Samuel Derrick, whom, as we have seen, Johnson had assisted twenty years earlier. Going directly to Derrick's additions, he at once put his finger on several mistakes:

[Dryden] is reported by his last biographer, Derrick, to have inherited from his father an estate of two hundred a year, and to have been bred, as was said, an Anabaptist. For either of these particulars no authority is given.[7]

And on a later page:

Mr. Derrick, who consulted some of his relations, was informed that his *Fables* obtained five hundred pounds from the dutchess of Ormond . . . and he quotes Moyle as relating that forty pounds were paid by a musical society for the use of *Alexander's Feast.*[8]

In these cases Johnson mentioned Derrick specifically, but apparently not from choice, for he named Derrick only when other authorities were lacking. Perhaps the best evidence of this attitude toward Derrick is found in the statement: "By discoursing with the late amiable Mr. Tonson I could not find that any memorials of the transactions between his predecessor and Dryden had been preserved, except for the following papers . . ."[9] The papers he reprinted are the agreement and receipt for the *Fables,* both of which had been previously printed by Derrick. Although Derrick is not mentioned, a comparison of the texts clearly shows that Johnson took his copy from the one Derrick had printed rather than from the original documents.[10] Of course, there is

---

[6] Pars. 153 and following. Birkbeck Hill's note on this passage is an example of that editor's too-frequent carelessness. Hill jumped to the conclusion that Johnson was quoting from the *Biographia Britannica,* and without looking into the matter closely he printed a detailed note directing the reader to the funeral passage in Broughton. This however is a paraphrase of Birch's account of the funeral, but much reworded. A single glance at the text would have shown Hill that Johnson was quoting, not from the *Biographia,* but from the original account in the *General Dictionary.*

[7] Par. 3.   [8] Par. 188. See p. 13.   [9] Par. 184. This Tonson, Jacob III, died in 1767.

[10] As printed by Malone, Life of Dryden, pp. 560–62.

a bare possibility that Johnson may have retained a copy during the intervening two decades, but such a supposition is not supported by what we know of his habits. Rather, I believe that Johnson himself had gone to Tonson twenty years earlier in order to help Derrick and that now in reprinting these papers he had merely reclaimed the fruit of earlier effort.

Johnson probably also inherited from Derrick the mistake about that "poem exquisitely satirical, called *Mac Flecknoe*," which he thought had been written on the occasion of Shadwell's "inauguration" to the laurel.[11] This error could have been derived from Cibber's *Lives*,[12] but whereas we know that Johnson consulted Derrick, there is no other evidence that he used Cibber for the life of Dryden.

Just as he had recourse to Derrick's edition of the poems, so Johnson depended on Congreve's edition of the plays. We know he was conscious of the deficiencies of such reprints from his half-apologetic statement:

In settling the order of [Dryden's] works there is some difficulty, for, even when they are important enough to be formally offered to a patron, he does not commonly date his dedication; the time of writing and publishing is not always the same; nor can the first editions be easily found, if even from them could be obtained the necessary information.[13]

If Johnson had cared to borrow the plays from Garrick's library, the first editions could have been found. But I doubt if he used any early editions, for nowhere else has he quoted or referred to a single line of Dryden that is not contained in the collected editions of Congreve or Derrick.[14] Yet access to Garrick's library was his for the asking, and it was from Garrick that he received the volume containing Dryden's manuscript "Heads of an Answer to Rymer."

In addition to using Congreve's edition, Johnson frequently consulted Langbaine's *Account* for information about Dryden's plays. References to it are found every few pages. In the process of unraveling the Dryden-Howard controversy, Johnson wrote, "Langbaine affords some help." [15] And in the course of reviewing Dryden's plays, the volume

---

[11] Par. 136.   [12] III, 76.   [13] Par. 11.

[14] This is true even in one instance where Johnson makes a negative remark: *"Sir Martin Marall* is a comedy, published without preface or dedication, and at first without the name of the author" (par. 29). In this case the lack of preliminaries could be ascertained from Congreve, and the fact of anonymity had been remarked by Langbaine (p. 170).

[15] Par. 25.

was again well-thumbed and is specifically mentioned in the accounts of *Sir Martin Mar-all, Marriage A-la-Mode, Troilus and Cressida*, and *Limberham*.[16] Indeed, in the *Preface* which was added to the third edition of the *Lives*, Johnson made the declaration: "I have followed Langbaine, as the best authority for [Dryden's] plays." [17] This statement was used by Malone and Birkbeck Hill to explain the fact that in Johnson's review of the plays, several were treated out of their proper order.[18] But Johnson was not referring to the order of the plays, only to their dates. The difficulty is solved by observing that the misplaced plays are precisely those contained in the fourth volume of Congreve's edition. Perhaps Johnson took up the fifth volume before the fourth, or possibly his manuscript was disarranged when it reached the printer. The mistake was a simple mechanical one, and Johnson's use of source books is not involved.

In a passage which does concern the dates of the plays Johnson was led astray, however, by a too close dependence on Langbaine. He wrote: "It is certain that in one year, 1678, he published *All for Love, Assignation*, two parts of *The Conquest of Granada, Sir Martin Marall*, and *The State of Innocence*, six complete plays . . ." [19] Here Johnson was merely repeating the dates given by Langbaine, as is indicated by the fact that he gave the plays in Langbaine's order. This evidence eliminates from consideration other books which might have caused the mistake.[20] Probably Johnson's close adherence to Langbaine is also responsible for his error in supposing that Dryden did not become historiographer until the reign of James II.[21] Johnson culled information about Dryden from many corners of his bookshelves other than those containing standard source books. A list of the books would include Farquhar's *Letters*, the *Key to the Rehearsal*, Lamotte's *Essay upon Poetry and Painting*, and the *Memoir of the Earl of Rochester*, which passed under the name St. Evremond. But the range of Johnson's reading is not a point to be labored, least of all with the *Lives of the Poets* open before us.

More important than Johnson's use of printed sources is the question of the new information he added to Dryden's biography. Like most

---

[16] Pars. 29, 62, 65, 80.   [17] Birkbeck Hill's edition, p. xxvi.
[18] Malone, Life of Dryden, p. 56, and Hill, I, 335, note 2.   [19] Par. 92.
[20] For example, Jacob, *Poetical Register*. Malone, p. 75, quotes the passage as "following Jacob," although there is no evidence that Jacob was used for any part of this life.
[21] Par. 183; Langbaine, p. 130.

critics, Johnson disparaged the exact inquiries which are usually meant by the term "research." He stated his attitude several times:

Of translated fragments or occasional poems to enumerate the titles or settle the dates would be tedious, with little use.[22]

To adjust the minute events of literary history is tedious and troublesome; it requires indeed no great force of understanding, but often depends upon enquiries which there is no opportunity of making, or is to be fetched from books and pamphlets not always at hand.[23]

That Johnson spoke twice in this vein in one biography may well indicate that the breaks and tangles in the thread of Dryden's life perplexed him more than he was pleased to admit. But in spite of these irritable disclaimers Johnson made several sallies in search of facts about Dryden. His application to the house of Tonson and the documents which it produced have already been mentioned. Indeed, the contract for the *Fables* whetted Johnson's interest so much that he took the trouble to count all the lines of poetry in that fat folio volume of almost seven hundred pages, finally computing that it "contains about twelve thousand verses." [24] Some years earlier he had also gone out of his way to look up any of Dryden's contemporaries who still lingered on:

Of the only two men whom I have found to whom he was personally known, one told me that at the house which he frequented, called Will's Coffee-house, the appeal upon any literary dispute was made to him, and the other related that his armed chair, which in the winter had a settled and prescriptive place by the fire, was in the summer placed in the balcony; and that he called the two places his winter and his summer seat. This is all the intelligence which his two survivors afforded me.[25]

Johnson's action in questioning these men is similar to the inquiries which he prompted Derrick to make among Dryden's relations.

Johnson also presented his readers with several new documents, of which perhaps the most important was a long letter from Dryden to his sons in Italy. It is the only one known to have survived from what must

---

[22] Par. 117.　　　　　　　　　　[23] Par. 95.

[24] Par. 185. If we accept Birkbeck Hill's figure of 11,924 lines, Johnson estimated correctly within 2/3 of 1 percent. No formula of calculation would have been satisfactory because of the many title pages and the different founts of type employed. And it was Johnson who once spoke sarcastically about "numbering the streaks of the tulip"!

[25] Par. 190. From Boswell (III, 72) we learn their identity: Colley Cibber and Owen MacSwinney.

have been a very newsy correspondence.[26] Among other particulars this letter contains information about the composition of *Alexander's Feast,* and Dryden's astrological prognostications. Johnson learned of it from his friend Dr. Vyse, the Rector of Lambeth, who had encountered it in the archiepiscopal library. Another Dryden letter is mentioned in passing: "I have been told of another letter yet remaining, in which he desires Tonson to bring him money, to pay for a watch which he had ordered for his son, and which the maker would not leave without the price."[27] This letter was first printed by Malone (Number XVII).

Had he wished to, Johnson could have used several other letters, namely, those Derrick mentioned or quoted from in part. Probably the best explanation of Johnson's neglect of them is that the technique of decorating a biography with personal documents had not yet become accepted. His predicament was similar to Derrick's: Johnson simply did not know how to use letters effectively. Though he had read Mason's *Life of Gray,* it seemed "mighty dull"[28] to him. He failed to recognize that the deliberate inclusion of letters was bringing about a great development in the art of biography. The change occurred most notably when Johnson's own biographer chose the new course and "resolved to adopt and enlarge upon the excellent plan of Mr. Mason, in his Memoirs of Gray."[29]

Still another documentary contribution can be credited to Johnson. To use his own explanation:

Mr. Dryden, having received from Rymer his *Remarks on the Tragedies of the last Age,* wrote observations on the blank leaves, which, having been in the possession of Mr. Garrick, are by his favour communicated to the publick that no particle of Dryden may be lost.[30]

Unknown to Johnson, these notes had been printed in the 1711 edition of Beaumont and Fletcher.[31] A number of differences exist between the 1711 text, Johnson's transcript, and a manuscript copy used by Professor Saintsbury. Probably it will never be known which version is the most faithful to the original, because the volume has disappeared. It is

---

[26] Did this letter ever reach Italy? In a subsequent letter (Scott-Saintsbury, number XXVI) Dryden complained to Tonson that two letters had miscarried, in both of which he had discussed dedicating the *Virgil* to the king. This letter fits the description and was probably one of the two not received by his sons. How it reached Lambeth is not known.

[27] Par. 186.   [28] Boswell, III, 31.

[29] *Ibid.,* I, 29.   [30] Par. 358.

[31] Preface, I, pp. xii *et sqq.* But Johnson soon learned of the existence of the 1711 text. See Hill's edition, I, xxvi–xxvii.

quite possible that we are obliged to Johnson for the proper text of these jottings.[32]

Other items of new information which were included for the first time in a biography of Dryden were the fruit of Johnson's omnivorous reading. For example, from the Dedication to Prior's collected poems he culled the suggestion that one of the characters in the *Essay of Dramatic Poesy* represents the Earl of Dorset.[33] He was the first to notice Marvell's lines describing the "less skilful hand" which had in 1674 turned *Paradise Lost* into a *State of Innocence*.[34] Previously biographers had missed the Lamotte story which described Dryden's habit of preparing for a period of writing by being "blooded and purged."[35] And for another instance, Johnson was the first to add to the poet's bibliography his participation in the 1698 *Tacitus*.[36]

As we should expect of a great conversationalist, Johnson derived still another Dryden anecdote from the lips of a friend, an anecdote that has never been disproved:

Lord Bolingbroke, who in his youth had cultivated poetry, related to Dr. King of Oxford, that one day, when he visited Dryden, they heard, as they were conversing, another person entering the house. "This," said Dryden, "is Tonson. You will take care not to depart before he goes away; for I have not completed the sheet which I promised him; and if you leave me unprotected, I must suffer all the rudeness to which his resentment can prompt his tongue."[37]

Indeed there is little reason to cast doubt on the story, for it is entirely consistent with what we know from other testimony of the relations between Dryden and his publisher.

As well as adding new information Johnson made numerous corrections to statements of his predecessors. For example, he challenged Anthony Wood's ascription of *Azarai and Hushai* to Settle, his grounds being that Dryden has already imputed *Absalom Senior* to Settle and that "it is somewhat unlikely that he should write twice on the same occasion."[38] Johnson's judgment was right, even though he may never have heard of Samuel Pordage, who has been asserted to be the author.[39]

---

[32] See pp. 283–85 for a fuller discussion of this subject.　　　[33] Par. 27.

[34] Par. 71. Johnson considered this to be "foreseen" by Marvell, but Masson in his *Life of Milton* (VI, 717) was convinced that Marvell was making a calculated hit at Dryden.

[35] Par. 99. This story is obviously based on the familiar passage in the *Rehearsal*: see p. 177.

[36] Par. 106.　　　[37] Par. 187.　　　[38] Par. 113.

[39] Mr. R. G. Ham, in a recent discussion, argues that Settle was the author (*Modern Philology*, XXV, 409).

Another correction concerned Derrick's naïve conjecture that Dryden polished up his schoolboy translation of Persius for use in the 1693 version of that poet. Johnson eradicated the error with these words: "Dryden says that he once translated it at school; but not that he preserved or published the juvenile performance." [40]

To turn from matters of fact to matters of interpretation, we may ask, how justly did Johnson judge Dryden the man, and how did he react to the incidents, both great and small, that tell us the little we know about Dryden's personality? In his characteristic way, Johnson focused his common sense on those particulars that had long been obscured by prejudice. To take one example, his judgment on Dryden's transition from the Cromwellian *Heroick Stanzas* to the panegyrics on Charles's restoration shines out strong as a beacon: "If he changed, he changed with the nation." [41] Small critics down to the present day have enjoyed harping on this insignificant incident in Dryden's life.

Similarly, in the matter of Dryden's other great "change," his religious conversion, Johnson uttered opinions distinguished for their common sense. In many ways this question is the core of any interpretation of Dryden's character, and so Johnson's treatment of it possesses special interest. He began by listing other distinguished converts, holding the attitude that:

If men of argument and study can find such difficulties or such motives, as may either unite them to the church of Rome, or detain them in uncertainty, there can be no wonder that a man, who perhaps never enquired why he was a protestant, should by an artful and experienced disputant be made

---

[40] Par. 302. Here one other point deserves mention, although it is not a definite correction. Baker's *Companion to the Playhouse* (1764) had stated, ". . . he appears, by his *Latin* Verses in the *Epithalamia Cantabrigiens. 4to. 1662*, to have been afterwards a Fellow [of Trinity College]." Without mentioning this account, Johnson took the opposite stand: "He obtained, whatever was the reason, no fellowship in the college. Why he was excluded cannot now be known, and it is in vain to guess; had he thought himself injured, he knew how to complain" (par. 6). Indirectly he helped to bring the discussion to a head. About two months later, Nichols's *Select Collection of Poems* was published, which contained several Latin poems signed "Jon. Dryden, Fellow." The reviewer in the *Gentleman's Magazine*, L [1780], 87, hailed this as a correction to Johnson's biography. But in the following November a correspondent signing himself "Eugenio" cleared up the confusion in names between the poet and his cousin Jonathan. Could "Eugenio" have been Malone? He was an occasional contributor to the periodical at this period: in fact the very next issue carried the first instalment of his Rowley criticism (p. 555). Malone made the point again in his Life of Dryden, p. 17, without reference to this *Gentleman's Magazine* letter. If it had been by someone else, he probably would have acknowledged the use of it.

[41] Par. 9.

a papist, overborne by the sudden violence of new and unexpected arguments, or deceived by a representation which shows only the doubts on one part and only the evidence on the other.[42]

Yet it may easily happen that information may come at a commodious time; and as truth and interest are not by any fatal necessity at variance, that one may by accident introduce the other. When opinions are struggling into popularity the arguments by which they are opposed or defended become more known; and he that changes his profession would perhaps have changed it before, with the like opportunities of instruction. This was then the state of popery; every artifice was used to shew it in its fairest form: and it must be owned to be a religion of external appearance sufficiently attractive.[43]

Yet in pronouncing these fresh opinions, Johnson did not omit a consideration of the traditional attitude toward this incident, and he qualified the case he had been making for Dryden by saying, "That conversion will always be suspected that apparently concurs with interest. He that never finds his error till it hinders his progress towards wealth or honour will not be thought to love Truth only for herself." [44] Ten years later, in the Life of Johnson, Boswell was justified in maintaining that Johnson had taken a courageous, open-minded, and unconventional attitude: "His defence of that great poet against the illiberal attacks upon him, as if his embracing the Roman Catholick communion had been a time-serving measure, is a piece of reasoning at once able and candid." [45] Despite the Gordon Riots, times had changed since the days when "no popery" was a cry still fresh in men's ears. The suffering of a generation upon the rack of religious controversy could not be healed in much less than a century. Earlier writers had been convinced that what was not conventional was heretical, but Johnson, definitely molded though his own convictions were, lived long enough after Dryden to judge him by a different standard, putting him on the scales, and balancing his weaknesses against his excellencies.[46]

[42] Par. 118.   [43] Par. 119.   [44] Par. 119.   [45] Boswell, IV, 44.

[46] These "scales" had previously been used by Johnson to judge the merits of different pieces of writing, a procedure he speaks of as follows:

"It is not by comparing line with line that the merit of great works is to be estimated, but by their general effects and ultimate result. It is easy to note a weak line, and write one more vigorous in its place; to find a happiness of expression in the original, and transplant it by force into the version: but what is given to the parts may be subducted from the whole, and the reader may be weary though the critick may commend" (par. 312). The same "scales" had been employed so judiciously by Johnson in his Preface to Shakespeare that it still stands as the greatest single piece of Shakespearean criticism ever written. Many other great pages in Johnson's criticism are due to this method, among them the famous passage on the Metaphysical poets in the Life of Cowley.

The second half of this life of Dryden is entirely taken up with criticism of Dryden's writings. In structure it roughly parallels the biographical portion. Following his usual practice, Johnson began with critical generalities, progressing from a discussion of Dryden's eminence as a prose stylist to his excellence as a poetical craftsman and as a translator. After these general remarks Johnson passed the major poems under critical scrutiny in chronological order. Many of these pages rank among Johnson's most brilliant criticism, and have provided succeeding generations with a foundation for understanding Dryden's poetry. It is to be regretted, however, that Johnson evaded a detailed examination of the dramas. In the biographical section he had protested at the necessity of enumerating them, but nevertheless had ploughed through Congreve's collected edition because he recognized that "the composition and fate of eight and twenty dramas include too much of a poetical life to be omitted." [47] Johnson shrugged off his responsibility for criticizing them with the frank admission that it was "labour too tedious and minute." [48] This remark is pathetically human, and brings before our eyes the tired old man at work on these "little lives and little prefaces." We can see him in his great chair, his weary eyes close to the paper, writing "in my usual way, dilatorily and hastily, unwilling to work, and working with vigour and haste." [49]

Just as the biography is capped with a "character," so the critical division concludes with a "critical character" or summary of Dryden's outstanding traits as a man of letters. Among these interesting passages, perhaps the best is Johnson's treatment of Dryden's mind. This keen characterization deserves generous quotation:

. . . [Dryden] appears to have had a mind very comprehensive by nature, and much enriched with acquired knowledge. His compositions are the effects of a vigorous genius operating upon large materials.

The power that predominated in his intellectual operations was rather strong reason than quick sensibility. Upon all occasions that were presented he studied rather than felt, and produced sentiments not such as Nature enforces, but meditation supplies. With the simple and elemental passions, as they spring separate in the mind, he seems not much acquainted, and seldom describes them but as they are complicated by the various relations of society and confused in the tumults and agitations of life.[50]

---

[47] Par. 15.   [48] Par. 266.   [49] Boswell, IV, 34.   [50] Pars. 321–22.

Johnson's concern with Dryden's mind led him to several passages in which he unconsciously described himself. He might have been writing a page of his autobiography in the following:

A mind like Dryden's, always curious, always active, to which every understanding was proud to be associated, and of which every one solicited the regard by an ambitious display of himself, had a more pleasant, perhaps a nearer, way to knowledge than by the silent progress of solitary reading. I do not suppose that he despised books or intentionally neglected them; but that he was carried out by the impetuosity of his genius to more vivid and speedy instructors, and that his studies were rather desultory and fortuitous than constant and systematical.[51]

Boswell was well aware of these parallels,[52] and among the many devices of biography that he picked up from Johnson, Boswell turned this idea of describing his subject's mind to very effective use. It may be fairly asserted that by focusing attention on intellectual characteristics, Johnson made one of his most important contributions to the development of English biography.

While dwelling on the brilliant pages of this biography, it must not be forgotten that, like the other *Lives of the Poets,* the Dryden is an uneven performance. Some examination of its weaknesses is necessary if we wish to appraise it properly. Of these weaknesses the most obvious is the disproportionate space Johnson allowed to the attacks on Dryden, of which the first and worst example is the pages on the controversy between Settle and Dryden over the *Empress of Morocco.* Johnson expended no less than eleven paragraphs on the *Notes and Observations.* Lengthy quotations were given from it, ostensibly to show "the criticism to which the genius of Dryden could be reduced, between rage and terrour." [53] Even though we realize that this was an unfamiliar story to Jŏhnson and his readers, nevertheless it is badly out of proportion. To the modern reader it is all the more obnoxious because we know that most of the violent words which Johnson put into Dryden's mouth do not belong there, but in Shadwell's and Crowne's.[54] Yet a few pages later Johnson repeated the performance with another insertion of about the same length from Settle's vitriolic reply, entitled *Notes and Observa-*

---

[51] Par. 211.
[52] Boswell, IV, 45. He also inserted in the *Life* (IV, 44–45) a quotation of sixteen lines from the *Hind and the Panther* (II, 64–79) that contain a picture of Dryden's mind.
[53] Par. 42.   [54] Cf. Birkbeck Hill's note 5 on p. 342.

tions Revised.[55] Taken together, these abusive quotations fill more pages than Johnson devoted to all of Dryden's twenty-eight plays.

Nor are these the only examples of offensive disproportion. Johnson regarded Martin Clifford's *Four Letters* seriously enough to allow it two full quotations,[56] Bishop Burnet's harsh words on Dryden are quoted *in extenso*,[57] and a little later he considered Tom Brown's abuse worthy to be perpetuated.[58] Apparently unsatisfied with these, Johnson drew on Luke Milbourne for several pages, though he had previously warned the reader of the worthlessness of Milbourne's captious criticism:

. . . his outrages seem to be the ebullition of a mind agitated by stronger resentment than bad poetry can excite, and previously resolved not to be pleased.[59]

The world has forgotten his book; but since his attempt has given him a place in literary history, I will preserve a specimen of his criticism . . .[60]

How can we excuse these faults of disproportion in the work of a master craftsman? I believe the explanation is found in the following quotations. Concerning the *Notes and Observations* he pointed out, "as the pamphlet . . . has never been thought worthy of republication and is not easily to be found, it may *gratify curiosity* to quote it more largely."[61] And in another case: "Clifford's remarks, by the favour of Dr. Percy, were at last obtained; and, *that no man may ever want them more,* I will extract enough to satisfy all reasonable desire."[62] The answer thus seems to be that Johnson had been forced to take considerable trouble to obtain these contemporary tracts, more trouble, incidentally, than he had gone to for any of Dryden's works themselves; the quest having cost him some effort, he easily fell into the error of imputing a proportionate value to their contents. Yet, if we may judge by the *Gentleman's Magazine,* even his contemporaries disapproved of the attention Johnson paid these pamphlets: '[Dryden's] illiberal abuse of Settle, now obsolete, and ever disgusting, we could well have spared. Dabbling in a puddle is never pleasing; and a puddle Dryden himself styles it."[63]

Another deficiency of Johnson as a biographer was caused by his

[55] Pars. 53–61.   [56] Pars. 50–53.   [57] Par. 124.   [58] Pars. 132–34.
[59] Par. 306.   [60] Par. 307.
[61] Par. 37. In this and the succeeding quotation the italics are mine.
[62] Par. 50.   [63] *Gentleman's Magazine,* XLIX (1779), 363.

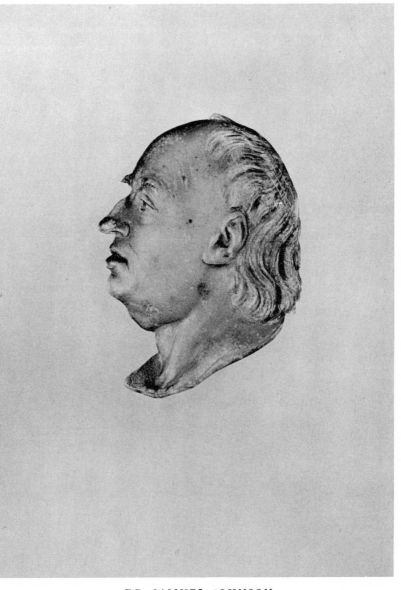

DR. SAMUEL JOHNSON
Wax Medallion

indifference to primary materials. His distaste for exact investigation has already been discussed, and we have remarked that in spite of this, on several occasions he did provide new information. Yet much of his carelessness is inexcusable, as, for example, his confused statements about *King Arthur*. Of it Johnson said at one place "it does not seem to have been ever brought upon the stage;" but he remarked on a later page, "When this was first brought upon the stage, news that the duke of Monmouth had landed was told in the theatre . . ." He evidently had confused *King Arthur* with *Albion and Albanius*.[64] Or again, one look at the epistle dedicatory of the *Life of Francis Xavier* would have cleared his doubts about Dryden's having "ever owned himself the translator," for the epistle "To the Queen" is signed "John Dryden." [65] No gain can be derived from chronicling his errors further, but we resent the fact that although Johnson took the trouble to read and quote generously from Settle, Clifford, and Hunt, he failed to do the same for Dryden, whose minor works he did not bother to consult. In general he was content with the results of inquiries made twenty years earlier by Samuel Derrick. Dryden had previously fared far worse in other hands, but the craft of scholarship was developing fast, and by 1780 the bud of a great age was bursting. The reviewer for the *Gentleman's Magazine* felt called upon to mention this deficiency: "He has the art of working up old materials so as to make them appear new; and, though he cannot give us much new information as an historian, that deficiency is compensated by his sagacity as a moralist and critic." [66]

Another weakness lay in Johnson's lack of perspective in many of his judgments. Johnson knew the need for an historical viewpoint, which he stated well: "To judge rightly of an author we must transport our-

---

[64] Par. 85.   [65] Par. 122.

[66] *Gentleman's Magazine,* XLIX (1779), 312. The contrast between the old and the new scholarship is piquantly illustrated in a report of a conversation between Johnson and Malone, who was at the time a precise young antiquary fresh from Dublin: "Having, however, as he himself [Johnson] told me [Malone], made no preparation for that difficult and extensive undertaking [Life of Dryden]; not being in the habit of extracting from books and committing to paper those facts on which the accuracy of literary history in a great measure depends; and being still less inclined to go through the tedious and often unsatisfactory process of examining ancient registers, offices of record, and those sepulchres of literature, publick repositories of manuscripts, he was under the necessity of trusting much to his own most retentive memory, which furnished him with many curious and interesting particulars concerning the most famous English Poets, collected during the course of a long life; but he was frequently, as in the present instance, obliged to rely for incidents and dates, on such information as had been transmitted by preceding biographers." (Malone, Life of Dryden, p. 2.)

selves to his time, and examine what were the wants of his contemporaries, and what were his means of supplying them." [67] But, being human, he sometimes failed to practice what he preached. Thus when Dryden's actions are considered from a broader view, he is freed from some of Johnson's censures. To quote a specific instance, Johnson took Dryden to task several times for complaints of penury after the Revolution, and when discussing the reputed benefactions of Dorset, he maligned Dryden on hearsay evidence.[68] Today we recognize that Dryden's pleas were merely part of the system of patronage as it was practiced in the time of the later Stuarts.[69] Moreover Johnson had the disadvantage of reading these calculated compliments and complaints in collected form, whereas Dryden had addressed them to a wide assortment of individuals over a period of forty years. A little historical dilution of Johnson's harsh words on the licentiousness of Dryden's plays [70] is also necessary. Dryden was guilty, as his age was guilty, and the connection is inseparable; Dryden should not be damned for his bawdy plays any more than Chaucer for his fabliaux. The mention of Chaucer suggests another parallel between him and Dryden: both of them frequently satirized the clergy, and did so quite independently of their attitudes toward religion in general. In Johnson's orthodox pages this distinction is nowhere indicated.[71]

It must also be recognized that in smaller matters Johnson was not always entirely fair to Dryden. Thus in some cases he freely imputed motives to Dryden when one guess is as good as another. To give specific instances, Johnson stated that Dryden, then newly converted, had translated Maimbourg's *History of the League* "with hopes of promoting popery," [72] whereas in fact, the purpose was political rather than religious, as Malone pointed out later.[73] Similarly Johnson announced that Dryden and his brother-in-law "were naturally rivals," [74] and a few pages later he described Dryden writing against that pretentious newcomer Elkanah Settle, motivated solely by the success of the *Empress of Morocco,* which made Dryden "think his supremacy of reputation in

---

[67] Par. 197.   [68] Par. 137.

[69] ". . . exaggeration in all complimentary and ceremonial language was a universal habit of the age."—G. N. Clark, *The Later Stuarts,* Oxford, 1934, p. 32.

[70] Par. 171.

[71] For another example of the discrepancy between Johnson's precept and practice in the matter of historical perspective see *Life of Cowley,* pars. 14–15.

[72] Par. 122.   [73] Malone, Life of Dryden, p. 186.   [74] Par. 25.

some danger." [75] Today we feel that statements such as these require careful modification.

Considered from the historical viewpoint, Johnson's Life of Dryden contains one important development in technique, the attempt to describe Dryden's mental qualities, to draw his intellectual character. As the art of biography has progressed since Johnson's day, this device has become a fundamental part of the biographer's craft. But in spite of this advance the biographical section interests the average reader much less than the critical section. The reason is that Johnson's treatment of the facts and fictions of Dryden's life is too general, as if these incidents were common knowledge. No doubt they were familiar enough to some of Johnson's circle, but few other readers come to Johnson's "Preface" with enough previous knowledge to appreciate the wisdom behind his generalities. As a result, the reader is overwhelmed by Johnson's personality, and Dryden seems little more than a name. The effect is most noticeable when the reader reaches the final leaves of the volume and comes upon the letter from Dryden to his sons in Rome.

Dear Sons,

Being now at Sir William Bowyer's in the country I cannot write at large, because I find myself somewhat indisposed with a cold, and am thick of hearing, rather worse than I was in town. . . . My *Virgil* succeeds in the world beyond its desert or my expectation. You know the profits might have been more; but neither my conscience nor my honour would suffer me to take them . . . [Tonson] has missed his of design in the Dedication, though he had prepared the book for it; for in every figure of Eneas he has caused him to be drawn like King William, with a hooked nose , . . I am writing a song for St. Cecilia's Feast, who, you know, is the patroness of musick. This is troublesome, and no way beneficial; but I could not deny the Stewards of the Feast, who came in a body to me to desire that kindness, one of them being Mr. Bridgman, whose parents are your mother's friends. I hope to send you thirty guineas between Michaelmas and Christmas, of which I will give you an account when I come to town . . . I am called to dinner, and cannot go on with this letter, which I desire you to excuse; and am

Your most affectionate father,
John Dryden. [76]

---

[75] Par. 32.

[76] Hill's edition, I, 479–81. In the interest of coherence the position of two sentences has been altered.

There is more of Dryden's personality in this letter than in all the rest of Johnson's pages.

But though the generalities are a cause of weakness in the biographical half, they are a source of strength in the critical section. Dryden's poems and prefaces are as familiar to the average reader as the biographical episodes are unknown. Johnson, it must be remembered, wrote as a pioneer, for Dryden "never had any critical examination before." [77] As with work of other pioneers, some flaws are easily discovered, but despite them, Johnson's criticism is the foundation of nearly all later interpretations of Dryden's genius. Though the success of the criticism compensates for the inadequacies of the biography proper, it is necessary to wait till after the turn of the century for a life of Dryden in which criticism and biography are properly balanced.

[77] Said of Cowley and Waller in a letter from Johnson to John Nichols. (Number 581 in Hill's edition).

IV

EDMOND MALONE

A HUNDRED YEARS almost to the day after Dryden's death his chief biographical monument was given to the public, Edmond Malone's "Account of the Life and Writings of the Author" prefixed to his edition of *The Critical and Miscellaneous Prose Works of John Dryden, Now First Collected,* and published late in April, 1800.[1] Including the Appendices and the "Collection of His Letters," Malone offered his readers more than seven hundred octavo pages of biographical gleanings about Dryden. He did this, moreover, without entering the field of criticism, which he considered belonged undisputedly to his late friend and mentor, Dr. Johnson.[2]

Malone's Life of Dryden occupies a special position in the history of English studies. Except for Oldys's exhaustive life of Raleigh (1736), no attempt had ever been made to collect every possible fact about one man into a single biography, and since Oldys approached Raleigh as a historical rather than as a literary figure, we can credit Malone with the first great literary biography. He attempted to discover every document, to assay every anecdote, to present every ounce of evidence that he could find about Dryden.[3]

To this undertaking Malone brought a rare combination of personal

[1] At the time when I was first introduced to Malone's edition of Dryden, Professor Samuel Lee Wolf, of Columbia University, raised the interesting question whether the exact interval of a century was not more than a coincidence. I have never found any evidence that Malone was conscious of the coincidence in dates, and there was certainly nothing deliberate about it.

[2] See pages 548–49.

[3] Shakespearean editors continued to reprint Rowe's life of Shakespeare with additions and appendices, and, except for the *General Dictionary* and later biographical compendia, no other life appeared in the eighteenth century. Tyrwhitt's *Chaucer* contains an "Appendix to the Preface" called "An Abstract of the Historical Passages of the Life of Chaucer," but this is more concerned with weeding out errors than with constructing a biography. Boswell's *Johnson* is the nearest exception to my generalization, but Boswell's aim was to write a personal biography, whereas Malone's was primarily scholarly.

and scholarly qualifications. Born the younger son in a distinguished family of Irish Protestants, he had passed a rather conventional youth in Dublin before entering the legal profession, which, because of family connections, offered every prospect of success. From the law he received the most exacting mental discipline that his century could afford.[4] During these years of legal training Malone engaged in several literary ventures, and while visiting London in his twenty-fourth year, he met the great Samuel Johnson, whose edition of Shakespeare had then just reached the restive public. It is not surprising, therefore, that Malone, after several years on the Munster Circuit, was ready to abandon both Ireland and the law when an estate received on the death of his father enabled him to move to London and embark, at the age of thirty-six, on a literary career.

At that time literary London was ablaze with enthusiasm for scholarship. The glow having lured Malone from a distance, it fired his interest at once, and he soon began to make a name for himself. This is not the place to review his part in Shakespearean studies, except to say that in 1783 George Steevens, the successor to Johnson as the editor of Shakespeare, designated Malone as his own heir. After much delay Malone's edition of Shakespeare appeared, in 1790. One reason that it had been held back so long was the heavy dependence Boswell placed on Malone in the task of putting together the *Life of Dr. Samuel Johnson.*

The result of these crowded years was that when Malone announced in the *Gentleman's Magazine* for June, 1793, that he was preparing an edition of Dryden's prose, he brought a remarkable amount of experience and equipment to the undertaking. Shakespearean scholarship, then as now, was the most advanced in technique and the most exacting of the literary disciplines. It was as a veteran of this discipline and a master of its technique that Malone turned to Dryden.

Malone brought something to the task that neither Steevens nor Reed nor Ritson nor any of the other Shakespeareans possessed—a practical training in literary biography. His experience began with an "Account" of Goldsmith prefixed to an edition of his fellow Irishman's poems in 1777. Similarly in 1797 Malone, as literary executor of Sir Joshua Reynolds, published an "Account" of the great painter. But these were acts of homage to countryman and friend, rather than serious biogra-

---

[4] A number of other great scholars had also passed through this discipline—Isaac Reed and Joseph Ritson, for example.

phies. Malone's chief knowledge of biographical practice was acquired at Boswell's side, in the painful process of turning the latter's masses of detail into publishable form. Malone's part in this feat of construction has recently been recognized,[5] but besides assisting in molding the original, it should be remembered that Malone was also the first editor of the *Life of Johnson*. Indeed, just at the time when he was putting the biography of Dryden into shape, in 1799, he was also preparing a new edition of Boswell.[6] His Life of Dryden frequently reflects the pattern of this greatest of English biographies.

In addition to this training and literary experience Malone possessed personal advantages which again and again opened the doors necessary for his researches. His character commanded universal respect, especially his industry, which became a byword. His courtesy and graciousness made him liked by everyone except a handful of rivals, and he benefited from an established social position, for he was known to be the heir to the title and estates of his brother, Baron Sunderlin. These purely personal factors were reflected both in his friendship with members of the literary *haut monde* like Horace Walpole and also in direct advantages when he applied for information to the descendants of Dryden and of Dryden's friends and patrons.

Although Shakespeare was the center of Malone's literary labors from the time he arrived in England until 1790, when his edition of Shakespeare appeared, Dryden also received occasional attention. The first fruits of this secondary interest are found in Isaac Reed's edition of Baker's *Companion to the Playhouse,* which was published in a much expanded form in 1782 as *Biographia dramatica.* Reed himself had added several new facts to the account of Dryden,[7] but they are less notable than those later inserted among the "Additions and Corrections"

---

[5] Cf. *The Literary Career of James Boswell,* by F. A. Pottle, 1928, pp. 164–65. Of this Dr. L. F. Powell wrote, ". . . justice has at last been done to Edmond Malone, without whose aid, it is certain, as the late Geoffrey Scott showed, the [*Life of Johnson*] would never have been completed" *Modern Philology,* Vol. XXX (No. 1, Aug. 1932. Page 116).

[6] After this third edition, Malone also edited the fourth in 1804, the fifth in 1807, and the sixth in 1811. Professor Pottle says, "Malone's editing was done with supreme tact and modesty . . . it is impossible to imagine any other person who could have done it as well as Malone" (*Literary Career of James Boswell,* p. 170).

[7] On p. 133 of Vol. I are found some new details about Dryden's residence at Trinity College, Cambridge: "he was entered a pensioner, and matriculated the 6th of July, 1650. He took his degree of Bachelor of Arts in 1653." The next page carries the statement: ". . . he engaged himself by contract to write four Plays in each year, which, notwithstanding the assertions of some writers, he never executed."

at the end of Volume I. Three columns of new information about Dryden were placed here, some of it of first importance in straightening out the facts of the poet's life.[8] And moreover, Dryden is the only name thus treated. The explanation is found in Malone's annotated copy of the volumes, among his books in the Bodleian.[9] On the margin of page 493 he wrote: ". . . all the other anecdotes here mentioned relative to Dryden except the last I communicated to Mr. Reed, the editor of this book. E. M." So here, almost twenty years before he published anything else on Dryden, Malone made valuable additions to the materials for Dryden's biography.

Thus when Malone finally concentrated all his attention on the biography of Dryden, he well knew where to turn for information. The first objects of his attention were, of course, the earlier biographies of Dryden. The derivative nature of their contents was readily apparent to his practiced eye, and he took occasion, while explaining the sources of Dr. Johnson's factual errors, to say:

[Johnson] was . . . obliged to rely for incidents and dates, on such information as had been transmitted by preceding biographers. Unfortunately, all the accounts of Dryden and his works were one continued tissue of inaccuracy, errour and falsehood. Very little had been handed down, and of that little the greater part was untrue.[10]

To this he added a more detailed footnote:

It is observable, that when once an errour has found a place in any original biographical work, it is generally transmitted from age to age by succeeding biographers . . .[11]

---

[8] These new facts may be enumerated as follows: (a) Reed's statement about Dryden's undertaking to write four plays a year is corrected to three. This is followed by other remarks about the complaint of the shareholders of the King's Playhouse against Dryden (cf. p. 203, below). (b) Attention is directed to "the satirical poem intitled *Description of Mr. Dryden's Funeral,* 1700, which Malone considered important because it "makes no mention of the outrages said to have been committed by the son of Lord Jefferies." (c) A footnote refers to Oldys's statement that Garth's epitaph had been in his possession. (d) The epigram on Dryden's "sleepy eye" is quoted. (e) Attention is drawn for the first time to the old man who "eat tarts with madam Reeve and plain John Dryden," as reported in the *Gentleman's Magazine* for 1745. (f) Dryden's reputed statement that *Alexander's Feast* was not only the best ode ever written, but also "the best Ode that ever will be written," is introduced. (g) the story is given that old Jacob Tonson had to borrow twenty pounds to publish the first play he printed for Dryden.

[9] Malone 154.   [10] Life of Dryden, p. 2.   [11] *Ibid.*

Malone's approach to these earlier biographies was highly characteristic, and he stated his principle in words that every scholar would do well to repeat before a new undertaking:

On reviewing the received accounts of his Life and Writings, I found so much inaccuracy and uncertainty, that I soon resolved to take nothing upon trust, but to consider the subject as wholly new . . .[12]

The contrast between this resolution and the inertia of Dryden's earlier biographers need not be labored, for Malone was applying the new scientific method of his age, the age of Erasmus Darwin and Bentham. A hundred years earlier scientific method had, in practice, consisted too often in the mere gathering of facts, irrespective of their genealogy. At the end of the eighteenth century researchers were still collecting facts, but they were learning to discriminate against those with faulty pedigrees. They were "resolved to take nothing upon trust."

Nevertheless, while "taking the subject as wholly new," Malone went carefully over the early biographies of Dryden and noted those facts and hints that seemed worth retaining. He ranged over any book touching on Dryden, always on the alert for traces of information that might serve to piece out incomplete deductions, culling and noting every reference or anecdote that threw light, no matter how glimmering and oblique, on any subject connected with Dryden. A full list of these books would be tedious, but Wood, Collins, Kennet, Spelman, Birch, and Lysons are a few of the names found frequently in Malone's pages.

Malone also made good use of Dryden's own writings as a field for investigation and systematically combed through them for biographical hints. Quite properly, he inserted this information wherever pertinent, but especially to illustrate Dryden's character:

To the various notices concerning himself, which Dryden, like Montagne, has very liberally scattered in his writings, we are indebted for many traits of his character; which are fully confirmed by the testimony of those with whom he lived.[13]

Malone was not the first to employ this practice, but, as with other good ideas, he adapted it very successfully to his own use.

There is no better example of Malone's application of a technique than his use of the historical method, which had been established long before

[12] Page vi of the *Advertisement*.   [13] Page 471.

Malone came on the scene, as Dr. Johnson's writings testify.[14] So extensive were Malone's researches into Elizabethan manners and verbal parallels that his *Life of Shakspeare,* half completed in 1794, never reached publication in his lifetime.[15] Of course Malone's era was still comparatively near to Dryden's, and the amount of illustration necessary to make Charles's reign understandable was very much less than for Elizabeth's. Yet Malone made contributions to an understanding of Restoration literature that have placed later historians deep in his debt.

He was assisted by a fortunate circumstance, his friendship with the learned owner of one of the most remarkable libraries ever assembled, James Bindley. Malone paid Bindley this tribute in his *Advertisement:*

My warmest acknowledgments are also due to my friend James Bindley, Esq. First Commissioner in the Stamp-Office, whose urbanity, classical taste, and various knowledge, are only exceeded by his great liberality in the communication of the very curious materials for literary history, and the illustration of temporary allusions, which his valuable library contains. By the aid of some very rare tracts and poems in his possession, several of which are wanting in my own Collection, I have been enabled to throw some new light on our author's history, as well as on many of his writings; as I have more particularly mentioned in the proper places.[16]

Apart from its extensive range, Bindley's library had a special advantage for the historian of Dryden's times, since it contained a portion of the annotated collections of Narcissus Luttrell. Malone was fully aware of the value of the Luttrell material, the accumulation of which he describes as being based on Luttrell's habit of

. . . purchasing the principal poetical productions that appeared in his own time, particularly those of a political kind; which he bound up in folio and

---

[14] Cf. the numerous references in Joseph Brown's *The Critical Opinions of Dr. Johnson* (1926), pp. 44–46. For literary critics the most important statement of this principle was made by Thomas Warton in his *Observations on the Faerie Queene of Spenser* (1754): ". . . in criticising upon . . . our elder poets, not only a competent knowledge of all antient classical learning is requisite, but also an acquaintance with those books, which, though now forgotten and lost, were yet in repute about the time in which each author respectively wrote, and which it is most likely he had red" [p. 243].

[15] "While the long days continued, I could amuse myself perfectly well, and worked very hard on the life of Shakspeare. After all, I have written but half of it, though the materials are collected for the whole. The scheme of giving an account of the manners of the time has delayed me much, and, after all, I have not fairly grappled with it, having done nothing in it yet but collect and make abstracts from various quarters." Letter from Malone to Charlemont, November 7, 1794. Historical Manuscripts Commission, *Report* XIII, Appendix, Part 8, p. 252.

[16] *Advertisement,* p. v.

quarto volumes, according to their respective sizes. He did not neglect even the single half-sheets at that period almost daily issued from the press, but preserved them with the rest; and marked on every poem, and half-sheet, the price it cost, and the day on which he made the purchase; which he appears generally to have made immediately after its publication.[17]

After outlining the portions into which this great harvest was divided, Malone says more particularly of the books on Bindley's shelves:

To this Collection I am indebted for the knowledge of many pieces that have contributed to illustrate our author's life and writings; and by the manuscript notices which it furnishes, am enabled to ascertain not only the precise date of some of his political poems, but the authors of the various Answers which were made to them, as well as the time of their publication.[19]

It is to Malone's examination of these Luttrell copies that we owe dates for the appearance of *Mac Flecknoe, Absalom and Achitophel, The Medal, Threnodia Augustalis,* as well as many of the attacks on Dryden, not to mention the names of the authors to whom the latter are ascribed.

In the process of painting in the background around Dryden, Malone made extensive use of early periodical literature. As far as I have been able to determine, Malone was the first literary biographer to utilize periodicals for literary history.[20] He used the quotations for a wide range of purposes. Investigation of muddled incidents such as the Rose Alley affair and Dryden's funeral made special search worth while, but many of the quotations were simply to illustrate contemporary manners and customs. For this purpose the *London Gazette* was particularly handy. The same periodical and others, such as the *Gentleman's Journal,* supplied him with the dates of many plays and books. Perhaps the most impressive means of demonstrating Malone's use of these tools is simply to give a list of the principal periodicals used by him, with a reckoning of the number of references to each. The figures in parentheses represent later references found among Malone's MS annotations.

Domestick Intelligence, 1 (1)
The Flying Post, or The Post Master, 3
The Gentleman's Journal, 19 (1)
The Gentleman's Magazine, 10 (1)
The Guardian, 5
The London Daily Post, 1

---

[17] *Life,* p. 156.   [19] Page 157.
[20] On two occasions Derrick had quoted from early newspapers, but his references were incidental; Malone's were deliberate.

The London Gazette, 22 (13)
The Post Boy, 12
The Postman, 3
The Spectator, 8 (1)
The Tatler, 5 (1)
The London Spy, 12

Although several of these papers were published after Dryden's death, they all contained grist for Malone's mill. Modern scholars are so accustomed to turning the pages of early periodicals that we may find it difficult to remind ourselves of the time when this was not a fundamental technique.

After announcing in June, 1793, that he had undertaken an edition of Dryden, Malone allowed several major distractions—a love affair, editorial labor on Robert Jephson and Reynolds, and most of all his Shakespeare researches—to delay work on the edition. Possibly he had been preparing the prose works in the intervals between these demands, but he does not seem to have settled down seriously to work on the essays until after publishing the works of Reynolds, in 1797.[21] Finally, on January 4, 1799, he wrote to Nichols, "Dryden's Prose is all printed, and the publication only waits for some account of him." [22] Accordingly the spring months of 1799 saw Malone bending every effort to gather material for the biographical volume.

Enough of Malone's correspondence remains to enable us to watch him at work and to follow the progress of his applications for information. When the time came to approach the representatives of the Dryden family, Malone tried every available avenue. On May 8 his friend the Reverend J. B. Blakeway, of Shrewsbury, who had already furnished Malone with the earliest known Dryden letter,[23] wrote to Malone that

[21] Malone's rabidly anti-Jacobinical note on p. 6 of Vol. II of the *Dryden* is dated Dec., 1797. A letter to John Price, Bodley's librarian, dated January 11, 1798 (Bodley MS Malone 26, f. 126) shows that his work was then far from complete. Another letter, from John Nichols, February 13, 1798, is the first devoted primarily to answers to biographical queries (MS Malone 39, f. 144).

[22] Nichols, *Illustrations*, V, 465. He also wrote to Bishop Douglas on January 15, 1799, that "a Collection of the Prose Writings of Dryden in three volumes octavo . . . are now printed . . ." (B. M. Egerton MS 2186, f. 104). But Baldwin printed the date December 24, 1799 at the end of the last volume. This contradiction to Malone's statement I am unable to explain.

[23] The 1655 letter to Honor Dryden. Honor Pigott explained the process by which it reached Blakeway's hands, by saying that his family had been servants to her grandmother, and had "monopolised" the letter (MS Malone 27, f. 150; dated June 15, 1799, from Bath). The letter had been printed in the *Gentleman's Magazine* in 1785, p. 337. It was

he had sent an inquiry to Miss Honor Pigott,[24] who was reported to have papers relative to the poet. She responded immediately and entered into the hunt with gusto.

In the Numerous Biographers of Drydens I am surprised Our Family has never been apply'd to before, But Dear Doctor Johnson (who was certainly his Best Biographer) was allways Toiling with Indolence & often found the End but never *the Easy* Road to Knowledge.[25]

Her long letters of family talk, it is to be feared, were a little too much for Malone, for she complained that he had not answered one of them.[26] When the book was finally published, Malone did not mention her assistance among the other acknowledgments in his preface. Although she repeatedly volunteered aid and even "writ sever[al] Letters," [27] to the representative of the Duke of Ormonde among others, Miss Pigott added little to Malone's and our own knowledge of the poet.

Malone was out for bigger game than family anecdotes, and he had one special quarry in mind, namely, the letters from Dryden to his cousin Mrs. Steward. That distinguished lady had lived on until 1743, and her granddaughter Mrs. Gwillim was still alive and in possession of the letters. Sometime before May 13, 1799, Malone called on her kinswoman Mrs. Ord, who chanced also to be his neighbor, and had prevailed upon her to act as an intermediary. On that date she wrote him the good news that Mrs. Gwillim would search for the letters as soon as her health permitted and included the following particulars about them: "The family having removed from the Old Mansion soon after the death of Mrs. Stuart, her Letters were most of them destroy'd —One box of papers however still remains with Mrs. G— . . ." [28] Though occupied with the many inquiries necessary for the Life of Dryden, the delay until these letters reached him must have been

---

sent from Shrewsbury, undoubtedly by Blakeway, who had made a copy of it for Bishop Percy on December 30, 1768 (note in Percy's annotated Langbaine, end papers of Part 1, Edinburgh University Library).

[24] Malone describes her family connection by saying that her "father was great-nephew to our author's kinsman, John Driden, of Chesterton" (Life, p. 233, note 2). Miss Pigott had demonstrated her zest for family lore by writing a letter to the *Gentleman's Magazine,* which was printed in March, 1792 (p. 225), entitled "Dryden Family Illustrated." This she acknowledges in her letter of May 31, 1799, to Malone (MS Malone 27, f. 144).

[25] MS Malone 27, f. 150ᵛ, dated June 15, 1799, from Bath.

[26] MS Malone 27, f. 60ᵛ, dated July 3, 1799, from Bath.

[27] MS Malone 27, f. 29ᵛ; undated, but probably late August, 1799.

[28] MS Malone 27, f. 175ᵛ.

tedious. They were sent finally on October 10, under the description "being all the Letters from the Poet Dryden now to be found among her family papers." [29] There were sixteen in all, and they reveal a side of Dryden's personality to be observed nowhere else. If Malone had not run them to earth, it is quite possible that they would have been dispersed before ever reaching the hands of an editor.

Another lady approached by Malone was the widow of Sir John Turner Dryden, herself a collateral descendant of the poet.[30] Malone had written her on April 12 and she replied immediately. The account books of Dryden's brother Erasmus were soon forthcoming, and from them Malone dug out a number of facts about the poet's wife, Lady Elizabeth, and his youngest son Erasmus-Henry. Several traditional matters were also discussed by Lady Dryden, and among them she quite unequivocally condemned the poet's wife, thus further complicating the task of apologists for that "fairest creature of the spotted kind." The passage runs as follows: ". . . but having, to bad conduct before marriage, united bad conduct afterwards, & having used Mr. Dryden very indifferently, the family confined their attentions to formal tea visits, as I have heard." [31]

From this correspondent Malone received a promising lead that only Napoleon's armies prevented him from following to the end. It is best described in his own words:

On his [John Jr.'s] removal to Rome, along with other recommendations, our poet's son carried with him a genealogical history of his family, drawn up in Latin by his father; which, to do him the more credit, was lodged in the Vatican, and is said to have contained a more ample and accurate account of the families of Dryden and Howard, than is to be found elsewhere.[32]

In this connection I may add that research in the Vatican Library has not turned up this document, if it still is (or ever was) "lodged" there.

But in these investigations Malone did more than record conjectures

[29] MS Malone 27, f. 177v.

[30] According to Malone she was "a great grand-daughter of Erasmus Dryden, the poet's younger brother." For a full account of these letters see pp. 251–68.

[31] MS Malone 27, f. 74. In paraphrasing this passage (pp. 394–95) Malone took the life out of it. He of course knew nothing of the Chesterfield letters at this time, although he later received copies of some of them from Lady Ailesbury, who had obtained them through the assistance of her Highness, Princess Elizabeth. Malone's letter of thanks to Lady Ailesbury is preserved in the Clark Memorial Library at Los Angeles. I owe knowledge of it to Dr. Claude E. Jones.

[32] Page 401.

and traditions. The Steward letters in themselves were a major discovery, and even the lesser points brought out in his researches, such as the recollections of the tenants on Dryden's small property at Blakesley, total up to more new information than any other individual has added from unpublished sources. More important to future Dryden biographers, however, was the fact that a careful scholar had gone over the ground, using all the skill and knowledge at his command. Lady Dryden expressed the family's attitude toward Malone when she wrote to him after receiving the Life and *Prose Works:* ". . . every branch of the Drydens will feel gratitude to the Author equal to the degree of estimation in which they hold the justly admired subject of it." [33]

With the same thoroughness that he had devoted to tracking down the Dryden family, Malone pursued the descendants of Dryden's friends and patrons. His rare but brilliant successes in tracing valuable collections tend to make us forget the almost numberless applications made to Knole, to Great Fenborough Hall, to Denham Court, and to other great houses from which the disheartening negative replies punctuate his correspondence. In the case of Knole three letters were admittedly preserved, but access to them was denied to him.[34] For the benefit of future biographers Malone tacked on at the end of the volume an appendix of "Persons in whose Cabinets letters written by Dryden may probably be found." [35]

The outstanding collection that this systematic search uncovered was, needless to say, the Tonson papers, most of which were preserved at Bayfordbury by William Baker, M.P., the descendant of the great publishing family. Malone handsomely acknowledged his obligation to Baker, "who most obligingly has furnished me with all the correspondence, now extant, which passed between our author and his bookseller, Jacob Tonson . . . which, besides exhibiting a lively portrait of this great poet, contain some curious documents respecting the price of his works, and some other interesting particulars concerning them." [36] There were seventeen letters besides the other documents. The opportunity of using the non-Dryden papers was too much for a confirmed antiquary to resist, and accordingly when he had once begun to write

[33] MS Malone 27, f. 190; dated May 14, 1800. A short time later Lady Dryden reinforced this sentiment by the present of a haunch of Canons Ashby venison (MS Malone 27, f. 181).
[34] For an account of these letters see pp. 277–81.   [35] Appendix V, pp. 567–70.
[36] *Advertisement*, pp. iii–iv.

about Tonson, Malone did not return to Dryden again for almost
eighteen pages. For nearly a century these pages remained the most
complete account of "Old Jacob" in print.

Having perused the printed materials and rummaged among the
family papers, Malone followed divers other paths and trails in his
search for information about Dryden. Refusing to accept any fact or
anecdote that was recommended by tradition only, he examined each
one with his own eyes and measured it against any documents that might
exist. As a result of his Shakespearean training, nothing brought fire to
Malone's eye like a traditional anecdote. The unreliability of such tales
was one of his favorite observations, and the Life of Dryden contains
many variations on the theme:

. . . the result has confirmed and increased my distrust of traditional anecdotes, many of which, on a close examination, I have found, if not wholly
false, yet greatly distorted by the ignorance, or inattention, or wilful mis-
representation, of those by whom they have been transmitted from age to
age. We do not indeed always find pure and absolute falsehood; but many
a plausible and well-attested story, when thoroughly sifted, has too often
proved what Dryden has denominated *a sophisticated truth with an allay
of lie in it.*[37]

. . . what is hoped is readily believed, and what is believed is confidently
told.[38]

The marvellous is always so much more captivating than simple truth . . .[39]

This anecdote . . . [has] a very fair genealogy: but after it has been carefully
examined, we shall find, that, like many traditional tales, it is not to be implicitly relied upon . . .[40]

. . . in traditional anecdotes of this kind, transmitted by oral communication, minute accuracy is seldom found.[41]

All traditional sayings appear to disadvantage, and are liable to misconstruc-
tion, when unaccompanied by the little circumstances with which they were
originally attended.[42]

In time this subject became almost an obsession [43] with Malone, and
one of his correspondents wrote rather plaintively,

[37] Page 148.   [38] Page 198.   [39] Page 224.
[40] Page 286.   [41] Page 327.   [42] Page 477n.
[43] Of course, the *Gentleman's Magazine* made reminiscences and anecdotes one of its
chief articles of content.

The Duchess of York's Paper reminded me about a scandalous anecdote relative to her conversion to Popery. I dare say you have heard it, but you have
so compleately shewn the danger of trusting to Traditions & exposed their
blunders and inconsistentcies, I shall hardly ever believe a good thing again.[44]

In the matter of unreliability, Malone considered tombstones to rival
traditional anecdotes. ". . . I have had frequent occasion to observe that
the information furnished by tombstones is by no means implicitly to
be relied on . . . "[45] said he in tracing the error in the date of Dryden's
death. And that Congreve's monument was four years astray on his age
Malone quoted as another "striking instance of the inaccuracy of tombstones."[46]

The documents that Malone discovered and made use of are in
striking contrast to these traditional stories and tombstone legends.
These documents form a very miscellaneous heap, and little organiza-
tion is possible in dealing with them. The best procedure is to take them
up as they come to hand, beginning with the various kinds of registers.
Malone went after every register he could find, especially in search of
entries that concerned Dryden, but also to throw light on persons or
events that he had reason to describe. Before Malone's time meager use
had been made of the various registers, except parish registers, which
had been utilized by several generations of antiquaries from the time of
Rowe and Browne Willis onward. In turning parish registers to account
Malone was hindered by the disappearance of several that might have
provided him with the key to various secrets, including the date of
Dryden's birth.[47] But he made good use of those that did exist, even
for such relatively minor points as the burial of one of Dryden's numerous cousins.[48]

The registers of schools and colleges supplied other items of information. The "Register of Elections into Westminster School" was extant
only for the years following 1663,[49] but Malone dug several facts out
of it about Dryden's eldest son, as he did also from the "Register of
Westminster Scholars."[50] The various records of Trinity College, Cambridge, yielded additional Dryden items. In this case he received the

[44] Bodley MS Malone 38, f. 171; from Andrew Caldwell, dated April 4, 1801.
[45] Page 5n.   [46] Page 226n.
[47] Cf. p. 7n; also MS Malone 27, f. 68, and pp. 285–86, below.
[48] Page 429, note 5.   [49] Page 13, note 8.
[50] Page 421n. He was much assisted in this by Bindley: cf. MS Malone 38, ff. 97,
101, 110. He also used the Charterhouse register: cf. p. 149, note 4.

substantial aid of Bishop Mansel, then master of the college.[51] His examination of the Trinity records was so complete that to my knowledge not a single addition has been gleaned from them by the scholars who have followed him.

Malone is seen at his best in the exhaustive combing he gave the registers of the Stationers' Company. Today we thumb over the Arber and Roxburgh reprints of the Stationers' registers so frequently that we accept them unthinkingly, but consulting the massive originals was a very different matter. After Thomas Tanner had made use of them about the turn of the century they gradually became known to literary antiquaries, and they had become a standard tool in the hands of the Shakespeareans by the time Malone joined their ranks. Yet the labor of creeping through their yellowed pages, crowded with a hodgepodge of handwritings, in search of a few particular entries, is an experience that we can give thanks for having been spared. Malone took special pains to find the dates of Dryden's plays, and his new list immediately superseded Langbaine's. He constructed a two-page table [52] in which the plays were listed, with parallel columns containing the names of the companies that acted them, the dates of entry at Stationers' Hall, and the dates of the first editions. This summary is the counterpart of Malone's previous study of the order of Shakespeare's plays, and it is still useful for reference purposes.[53]

Dryden's nondramatic writings also received due attention. In several cases the information proved to be of more than bibliographical value, such as, for example, in the controversy between Dryden and Bishop Burnet. The Whig churchman had written,

I have been informed from England that a Gentleman who is famous both for Poetry and *several other things,* had spent three months in translating Mr. Varillas's *History* [*of Heresies*]; but that as soon as my *Reflections* appeared, he discontinued his labour, finding the credit of his author was gone.[54]

---

[51] Cf. MS Malone 27, ff. 161, 163, 167–68. In the last of these, dated Jan. 12, 1800, Mansel planted a most fecund seed when he asked Malone, "Is it not possible that Dryden may have had a *Lambeth* M.A. degree?" By following this lead Malone found the document which proved to be the proper explanation of the puzzle. He was able to print a transcription of the Dispensation as a footnote to his "Appendix on Dryden's patent to the Laureateship" (Appendix I).

[52] Pages 218–19.

[53] Several corrections are now possible: for example, no copy of *The State of Innocence* has ever been found with the date 1674.

[54] *Defence of the Reflections on the Ninth Book of the First Volume of Mr. Varillas's History of Heresies. Being a Reply to His Answer,* Amsterdam, 1687, p. 138.

Malone pointed out the following circumstances which substantiate this charge:

The Stationers' Register . . . shews that Burnet's information was correct; for on the 29th of April, 1686, Jacob Tonson made an entry relative to this work, which is there said to have been translated by our author, by the King's command: but the translation was never published.[55]

If Malone had done nothing more for Dryden than comb out these entries from the Stationers' Register, his name would still be mentioned with honor.[56]

Wills were another type of document which Malone had mastered during his Shakespearean studies. In his Dryden researches wills supplied him with much useful information, and among others he quoted from the testaments of Dryden's father,[57] his mother,[58] of John Driden of Chesterton,[59] of Dean Lockier,[60] of old Jacob Tonson,[61] of young Jacob,[62] of old Jacob's father,[63] and even of Lady Elizabeth Dryden's maternal grandmother.[64] Unfortunately for him and for us, the main prize was not to be found in Somerset House, for the poet had died intestate.

Other hoards of information from which Malone extracted Drydeniana were the collections of anecdote mongers like Aubrey, Oldys, and Spence. As is well known, Malone nourished an ambition to publish the *Brief Lives,* and he has left extensive notes and transcriptions from the Aubrey MSS.[65] However, the familiar tale about "tag my verses if you will" was all that Malone found concerning Dryden.[66] Apparently he missed the other references or did not consider them significant.

[55] Page 194.

[56] The dependence Malone placed on the Stationers' registers is indicated by the frequency of his references to them: pp. 42*n*, 43*n*, 45*n*, 56, 57, 58 and note, 63*n*, 69*n*, 92, 93, 94, 99*n*, 107, 108 and note, 109*n*, 114*n*, 115, 116*n*, 118, 119, 167*n*, 181*n*, 185*n*, 186*n*, 194, 197 and note, 218–19, 220*n*. His manuscript annotations also refer to them on pp. 56 and 523.

[57] Page 440*n*.   [58] Page 446 and note.

[59] Page 325*n*. This information was communicated to him by the Reverend J. B. Blakeway; cf. MS Malone 27, ff. 77–79.

[60] Page 480*n*.   [61] Page 537*n*.   [62] Page 534*n*.   [63] Page 523.   [64] Page 447*n*.

[65] Of the many references to this project in his papers, only one deserves notice here. It is found on page 1 of MS Malone 33 and is dated "Oxon. July 10, 1792."

"These lives having taken seven days in the *perusal* alone, I cannot now make extracts from them, but at some future time will transcribe and publish them, with a vindication of Aubrey from A. Wood's *Calumny.* They contain many very curious particulars. July 16.

"I will now only prepare an *Apparatus* & incidentally note such other matters as may turn to account."

[66] Page 109.

Malone's acquaintance with Oldys's manuscript notes dates back to his first enthusiasm for literary antiquarianism. In 1776 he had taken Steevens's annotated copy of Langbaine to Ireland with him, and he had transcribed the manuscript notes of Oldys, Percy, and Steevens during the winter.[67] Malone also owned Oldys's annotated copy of Winstanley's *Lives of the Poets* (1687) [68] and had transcribed a number of Oldys's other notes, notably those in Fuller's *Worthies*.[69] Though there are a number of references in Malone's Dryden to Oldys's notes, they all prove on investigation to have been taken from Oldys's Langbaine. They are of course duly accredited to Oldys: Malone would rather have been caught without his wig than not to have properly acknowledged his authorities.

From Spence's *Anecdotes,* on the other hand, he succeeded in obtaining a good deal of information about Dryden. The manuscript had reached him in 1794, and he had then made a copy, regrouping the subjects somewhat, as well as adding a number of his own notes.[70] Without going into unnecessary detail, it suffices to say that Malone was the first to incorporate this body of anecdotes into a biography of Dryden.[71]

While discussing Malone's penchant for documentation we should say something about his acquaintance with the treasures of the two great national repositories, the Bodleian and its lusty young rival, the British Museum. Montague House was only a short walk from Malone's home on Queen Anne Street East (renamed Foley Place in 1807), and he was a frequent visitor. There is no way to determine how much he drew on the museum's collection of printed books for his work on Dryden, but there are ample references to the museum's manuscript collec-

---

[67] On the last leaf of his copy he wrote, "Mem. I finished this transcript 30 March, 1777. Edmond Malone." This copy is now in the Bodleian, Malone 129–32.

[68] As far as I know it has never been realized that this valuable book is in the Bodleian. The shelf mark is "Mal. 562."

[69] Bodley, Mal. 3. Also cf. MS Malone 26, f. 46.

[70] The Folger Library now owns Malone's transcript. It was printed by Murray in 1820. The note on p. 27 proves that he made some of his own notes in 1794, after finishing the transcript. The Preface to this edition reflects their fame before publication. Yet Andrew Caldwell wrote after reading the Dryden, "You often quote the Anecdotes of Spence, is that a work publish'd or in M:S: I never heard of it before" (MS Malone 38, f. 171, dated April 4, 1801). The story of the publication of the *Anecdotes* has been told by Richard Garnett in his article on Spence in the D.N.B.

[71] Although Dr. Johnson had use of a manuscript copy of the *Anecdotes* when writing the *Lives of the Poets,* I have not recognized any of the Dryden anecdotes in his account of that poet.

tions. He found the Harleian Collection the most useful, turning up, among other subjects, information about the migrations of Dryden's ancestors,[72] the circumstances of his first meeting with Congreve,[73] and the personality of Julian, the hawker of lampoons.[74] Other collections used by Malone include the Royal and Sloane manuscripts and the papers of Rymer and Birch.

As might be inferred from his interest in the Aubrey manuscripts, Malone made a number of visits to Oxford. In fact the university had awarded him an honorary D.C.L. in 1793.[75] His knowledge of Bodley's treasures can be judged better from references in his letters than from those found in the Dryden, which, however, allude frequently to the Rawlinson and Ballard collections. Bodley's librarian, the Reverend John Price, was an obliging correspondent whenever Malone had queries about the treasures of the Bodleian.[76]

By this time we have had enough examples to make our conclusions obvious. Malone was not only inspired by a passion for documentary evidence, he was also very open eyed in his search for it. Considering the facilities of his day, we must marvel at how little he missed that has since come to light.

In his literary sleuthing, Malone's chief tool was a simple one, chronology. He applied it rigorously, not unlike the use of the measuring rod in the hands of the archaeologists of his time.[77] His dicta on the subject are numerous:

. . . a little attention to dates will solve this difficulty.[78]

The chronology of a story is often of great service in ascertaining its authenticity.[79]

An examination of dates is generally fatal to tales of this kind . . .[80]

And in a letter to Percy he put this principle as an axiom: "Give me but time, place, and names, and the genuineness or falsehood of any story may be easily ascertained." [81] Perhaps his legal training was responsible for this aptitude, but at any rate "a little attention to dates" demolished

---

[72] Page 10.   [73] Page 222.   [74] Page 491n.   [75] Foster, *Alumni Oxonienses*, III, 906.
[76] Cf. MS Malone 26, ff. 122–23, 124, 126–27, 129, 134–37.
[77] Such as Stuart and Revett in their *Antiquities of Athens, Measured and Delineated,* the first volume of which appeared in 1762.
[78] Page 122.   [79] Page 505.   [80] Page 188n.
[81] Nichols, *Illustrations*, VIII, 369; dated June 5, 1802.

among other absurdities the tradition that Dryden had been the indirect cause of Creech's suicide.[82]

But chronology was not the only tool in Malone's scholarly kit. He utilized parallel passages on occasion,[83] and in one instance he employed the publisher to indicate the possible author.[84] Similarly in another case he attempted to determine an author's identity by means of his patron.[85] Moreover, he tells us that he used a "microscope" to solve a difficult reading in one of Dryden's letters.[86] If by this term Malone meant a compound microscope, he was one of the first to adopt this instrument of the scientific laboratory for the problems of English bibliography. I suspect, however, that he used a single lens.

But in addition to training and knowledge of technique, Malone possessed several qualities of character that had a great effect on his achievements. Sad commentary on his contemporaries though it is, Malone was distinguished among earlier scholars by his honesty. Against the lax standards of his day—and after—his integrity shines like a new sixpence. Warton, Steevens, Ritson, and Collier were all learned men, but they keep us constantly on our guard. Malone needs no watching: when he erred his errors were honest ones, and by conscientiously citing his authorities he generally left a way for his mistakes to be discovered. Even when a statement cannot be authenticated, we incline to accept his word until proved otherwise, because we know his character: he was sometimes the fool, but never the knave.

We have not far to seek for examples of this unaffected candor; ". . . nor have I ever seen any verses by Marvell on Oliver's death," [87] he says ingenuously. And in searching for an allusion to Dryden by Swift which Dr. Johnson had mentioned, Malone confesses, "I have in vain sought for any such observation in his very miscellaneous volumes." [88] Other modest confessions are sprinkled about Malone's pages:

---

[82] Pages 505–11. Unknown to Malone, the same point had been made by Oldys in the *Catalogue of Pamphlets in the Harleian Library*, p. 16.

[83] Page 351*n.*   [84] Page 383*n.*   [85] Page 347*n.*   [86] Vol. I, Part ii (Letters), p. 3*n.*

[87] Page 42*n.* That Malone failed to find these verses is a commentary on the meager library facilities of his day. Marvell not only wrote on Cromwell's death, but they are among his finest verses. They were first published in his *Miscellaneous Poems*, 1681.

[88] Page 240*n.* Malone had tried to find this out from Nichols, for he wrote to him on January 4, 1799, "I have in vain tumbled over my twenty seven volumes of Swift to find this passage. Have you any recollection of it?" (Nichols, *Illustrations*, V, 465. This letter is now preserved in the Folger Shakespeare Library). Birkbeck Hill, a mere tyro compared with Malone, found the quotation in *A Tale of a Tub* (Johnson's *Lives of the Poets*, I, 366*n*).

I do not know how to reconcile these three discordant accounts.[89]

This elegy I have never seen.[90]

I once thought that Lord Roscommon was shadowed under this name [of 'Crites' in the *Essay of Dramatic Poesy*]; but I soon saw and have acknowledged my errour.[91]

Among his manuscript additions we stumble upon a note in which pathos mingles with humility when we find the old gentleman scrawling above an earlier note, "Q[uaere] what I meant by this." [92] Malone was completely honest with himself, and that is why we know we can trust him.

But to say this does not mean that Malone was unbiased. He sprouted as fine a crop of prejudices as one could hope to find even in that fecund age. His chosen role as the scourge of Jacobinism will serve as an example. Scattered among his pages are denunciations of "French robbers" [93] and hortatory footnotes on the "eternal truth, peculiarly applicable to our own times." [94] These sentiments are easily understood when we remember his intimacy with Burke, Windham, and other champions of the old order. Fortunately this phobia does not often disfigure his pages. Indeed, instead of being obnoxious to us, it contributes a pleasant historical flavor.[95] This excuse, however, does not justify Malone for intruding his political feelings on the literary public of 1800.

To return to the discussion of Malone's more positive qualities, one of the most notable was that rare commodity, common sense. Others who were so inclined might set themselves up for wits, but he was content with the less glamorous role of literary antiquary. Combined with his industry and honesty, this simple quality, common sense, has placed his name second to none in the ranks of literary historians. Many of his exercises in deduction are merely the working of common sense. Thus he quotes the following anecdote about Dryden, inserted by Steele in the *Guardian* (No. 45):

---

[89] Page 210n.   [90] Page 383n.

[91] Page 63n. Professor George R. Noyes, to whom Dryden scholars will ever be indebted, has published a challenging article in which he maintains that Malone's first conclusion was correct and that Roscommon was indeed intended by Dryden. (Cf. *Modern Language Notes*, Vol. 38 [1923], 333–37).

[92] Page 61.   [93] Page 401n.   [94] Page 140n.

[95] The chief personal prejudice of Malone that finds record in the Dryden is against Sir John Hawkins. The notes on St. Cecilia give abundant evidence of his glee at finding errors in the parsimonious knight's *History of Music*: see pp. 268n, 270n, 288n, and 289n.

. . . "when a young fellow just come from the play of CLEOMENES, told him in raillery against the continency of his principal character, 'If I had been left alone with a fair lady, I should not have passed my time like your Spartan;' 'That may be,' answered the bard, with a very grave face; 'but give me leave to tell you, Sir, you are no hero.' " [96]

Most biographers would have been content to point out that the story was founded on an almost identical passage in Dryden's preface to the play. But Malone was not willing to accept such an obvious explanation as final, and sensibly suggests, "our author, however, might have made the reply mentioned by Steele, at Will's Coffee-house, and have afterwards availed himself of the same observation, when he published his play." [97]

Yet Malone possessed analytical powers that went beyond a mere ability to check off facts and probabilities against each other. For example he was the first biographer to judge analytically Dryden's relations with the stage and "commodiously" to divide his dramatic career into the four periods [98] which, by the justice of the analysis, have become standard in every subsequent treatment of Dryden and the theater. To illustrate further his propensity for analysis, I shall quote from one of his manuscript additions:

In his private letters to his friends he speaks of himself and his works with that modesty which was natural to him and truly part of his character. "In the mean time, says he in a letter written in 1698–9, betwixt my intervals of physick and other remedies which I am using for my gravel, I am still drudging on:—*always a poet, and never a good one.*" ["] My Virgil (he tells his son) succeeds in the world *beyond its desert* or my expectations." And of his *Fables* (addressing himself to his kinswoman, Mrs. Steward,) he says, —"They are a debt to you I must confess; and I am glad, because they are so *unworthy to be made a present.*" It was only among the criticks in Coffeehouses, or in his Letters to his bookseller, or when he was decried and run down by his adversaries, that he considered it necessary to keep up a proper port, and not to abate a jot of his poetical pretensions. In those cases he seems to have thought it fair to follow the example and adopt the language of Horace;—*Sume superbiam quaesitam meritis.*[99]

Another notable characteristic of Malone's work is his highly developed sense of historical perspective, a quality that can be judged only by comparing selected incidents with their previous treatment in the hands of other biographers. Thus in the case of *Absalom and Achito-*

---

[96] Page 498.   [97] Page 498n. The incident is treated more fully in II, 229.
[98] Pages 55–56.   [99] Malone's annotated copy in the Bodleian, p. 477.

phel, Dr. Johnson's explanation, such as it is, was highly personal.[100]
Although Malone gave the personal element due attention, he began
by outlining the history of Dryden's position as the leading Tory pen:
". . . it may be proper to give some account of those pieces which he
wrote in support of the party then first distinguished by the name of
Tories." [101] Similarly Malone threw the squabbles with Shadwell and
Settle against the proper setting of party journalism,[102] the very conflicts
which Johnson had interpreted as personal rivalries for literary honors.
By taking this wider view Malone also counter-balanced Johnson's harsh
words about the "hyperbolical adulation" of Dryden's dedications. After
pointing out that ever since his clash with Chesterfield, Johnson had
held a particular prejudice against dedications, Malone went on to put
the whole subject in a seventeenth-century perspective:

But the matter has been stated far more unfavourably for Dryden, than the
history of the period during which he wrote will justify. The encomiastick
language which is sometimes found in his Dedications, was the vice of the
time, not of the man. The Dedication of almost every other author of the
last age was equally loaded with flattery, and sometimes far surpassed any
of Dryden's in extravagance of praise; nor was any kind of disgrace annexed
to this exercise of men's talents; the contest among the whole tribe of writers of
every description, however humble, or however eminent, being, who should
go furthest in panegyrick, in the most graceful way, and with the happiest
turns of expression. Butler, as the late Mr. Burke several years ago observed
to me, has well illustrated the principle on which they went, where he compares their endeavours to those of the archer, *who draws his arrow to the head,*
whether his object be a swan, or a goose. The addresses prefixed to the various pieces issued from the press from the Restoration to the end of the reign
of Queene Anne, fully support this remark. Though very few of them are
written with the spirit and elegance that are found in our author's Dedications, they by no means fall short of them in hyperbolical adulation.[103]

A number of instances could be cited to show the variety of subject
matter which Malone inserted to give perspective to Dryden's career.
For example, stage history fills many pages, beginning with the state of
the theater before Dryden began to write for it [104] and continuing on
till the time of Collier's *Short View.*[105] Sometimes he also gave pointed
treatment to manners and customs of Dryden's day, such as the hour of

[100] Johnson, Life of Dryden, pars. 108–13. [101] Page 136. [102] See especially p. 166.
[103] Pages 243–45. The same kind of light is shed on the conventions present in the
letter to Honor Dryden, p. 26.
[104] Page 51. [105] Page 309.

dinner in the time of William III [106] or the condition of the London streets on the day of Dryden's funeral.[107] And for purely literary instances we may again take *Absalom and Achitophel* and read Malone's account of Nathaniel Carpenter's *Achitophel or the Picture of a Wicked Politician* (1627).[108] So, too, with the *Essay of Dramatic Poesy,* in which Johnson, after attempting to supply critical background, had mentioned Webbe, Puttenham, Jonson, and Cowley, and then had expounded the principle that "we must transport ourselves to his time, and examine what were the wants of his contemporaries, and what were his means of supplying them." [109] When Malone's turn came he replaced this generalization with two full pages describing the state of criticism before the *Essay,* adding such names as Gascoigne, Sidney, Campion, Daniel, and Bolton, as well as Hédelin and Corneille. The day of silhouette drawing in biography was passing: on Malone's canvas Dryden's figure was depicted against the manners of his time.

These comparisons between Malone and Dr. Johnson should not be carried too far, for essentially the two men represented complementary phases of scholarship—the antiquarian and the critic. Malone recognized this: he avowed it unmistakably in the "Advertisement" before the Life, and also reminded the reader of it again in the very last paragraph of the text of the book:

A critical examination of the merits and defects of [Dryden's] various productions formed no part of the present undertaking; and indeed may well be dispensed with, after Dr. Johnson's elaborate and admirable disquisition on his writings; than which a more beautiful and judicious piece of criticism perhaps has not appeared since the days of Aristotle.[110]

There were, of course, innumerable instances where Johnson needed correction, some of them so flagrant that Malone was hard put to soften the violence required. This he usually effected by praising the Doctor's great critical gifts: "Such trivial errours can diminish little from the value of his incomparable Lives of the Poets, and . . . are merely specks on the finest body of criticism extant in any language." [111]

---

[106] Page 494*n.*   [107] Page 364*n.*

[108] Pages 139–41. Here as elsewhere many particulars are found in the notes to the *Prose Works* which Malone did not repeat in the biography: see II, 293.

[109] Johnson, Life of Dryden, par. 197.   [110] Pages 548–49.

[111] Page 139. This tactful handling of the errors of the friend whom Malone loved and respected did not pass unnoticed by his critics. George Hardinge made great sport of it in *The Essence of Malone* (1800): ". . . I give Malone ample credit as the most gentleman-

EDMOND MALONE

In other places Malone went to some length to correct Johnson, and sometimes, as in the case of Dryden's reading, without mentioning his predecessor's name. Johnson had said that Dryden ". . . scarcely ever appears to want book-learning but when he mentions books . . ."[112] and "the knowledge of Dryden was gleaned from accidental intelligence and various conversation."[113] Malone handled this subject in a way that restored it to proper proportion. Following the positive statement, ". . . there can be no doubt that he had read a great variety of books . . ."[114] Malone went on to quote Dryden's own words from the *Life of Plutarch*. He then proceeded to illustrate the extent of the poet's reading by allusions to Montaigne, Tasso, Shakespeare, Cervantes, and even romances and ballads, without forgetting the ever-present evidence of Dryden's familiarity with the literatures of Greece and Rome.

Being essentially a literary antiquary, Malone's primary service to Dryden consists, nevertheless, in the factual material he dug out. Some of it corrected the errors of his predecessors, but most of it went to enlarge the body of the biography. Because the facts and documents are so numerous, it is sufficient to indicate a few of the general headings, instead of listing them in detail, as was done in the case of Birch, Derrick, and Johnson.

To begin with the darkest period of Dryden's life, Malone supplied most of the details now known about the poet's early years. These include not only additions to the literary canon, like the verses to Hoddesdon,[115] but more important matters as well. Thus Dryden's family connection with the Pickerings, and also its relation to his early career,[116] were first pointed out by Malone.

On the whole, perhaps his greatest contributions were to the dramatic side of the biography. These range from *minutiae* like the number of times a piece was acted[117] to such important documents as the complaint by Killigrew and the other shareholders in the King's Playhouse

---

like executioner I ever knew. His conquest over his predecessor is a perfect specimen of urbanity . . ." (p. 79; cf. also pp. 48, 63–65, and 67).

[112] Par. 212.

[113] Par. 211. See also p. 33, *supra*.

[114] Pages 511–12.

[115] Page 14.

[116] Pages 28–33. That Malone was pleased with discovering the Pickering connection may be inferred from his phrase intended to be inserted in the second edition of his Life of Dryden (p. 28). After the reference to Sir Gilbert Pickering Malone added "of whom no mention has been made by any of Dryden's biographers,"

[117] Page 93.

against Dryden for not producing the stipulated number of new plays.[118] Similarly Malone was the first to call attention to Dryden's own list of his plays in the order in which they had been written.[119] All in all, Malone brought to the treatment of the Restoration theater the deep fund of knowledge we should expect from the first great historian of the English stage.

In fact scarcely any corner of the biography passed under his pen without receiving substantial augmentation. Trained in the Shakespearean chase, he discovered Dryden's corrections to a number of his texts and supplied lists of variants for the *Essay of Dramatic Poesy, Absalom and Achitophel,* and *Mac Flecknoe.*[120] The computation of Dryden's income [121] and, more specifically, the reconstruction of the *Virgil* agreement [122] illustrate his penchant for calculation. Even the iconography came under his surveillance, and a python-length footnote extends for more than six pages with his collections on the portraits and engravings of Dryden.[123] Upon examination almost every page of the whole book will be found to carry equally new and solid information.

Mention of this lengthy footnote brings us to a discussion of Malone's particular forte as a scholar, the writing of dissertations. The writer who first developed this device can be left as a matter for dispute, but Joseph Warton's *Essay on Pope* was then credited as the prototype.[124] The dissertation at any rate became the most characteristic scholarly vehicle of the age, as Thomas Warton's *History of English Poetry,* Tyrwhitt's papers on Chaucer, and the swelling prolegomena to the editions of Shakespeare abundantly testify. Malone had particularly distinguished himself in this line, with his *Essay on the Chronological Order of Shakespeare's Plays,* his *Historical Account of the English Stage,* and his *Dissertation on the Three Parts of King Henry VI.* Having used this form so successfully, Malone naturally employed the same mold again whenever special subjects connected with Dryden tempted him to extensive outpourings. Those on Dryden's portraits and on Jacob Tonson have already been mentioned.[125]

---

[118] Page 73n. See pages 200–207.   [119] Pages 56n and 218–19.
[120] Cf. I (Part ii), pp. 135–42, and I (Part i), 150 ff., 170 ff.   [121] Pages 436–61.
[122] Pages 235–37. On the whole his conclusions were sound, as comparison with the original document shows.
[123] Pages 432–37.
[124] Malone knew the *Essay on Pope* very well; cf. *Advertisement,* pp. vii, 162n, 286n, also MS notes on pp. 320, 322, and 477,
[125] Cf. pp. 49–50.

Among these informal dissertations the longest are on the history of the laureateship and on the St. Cecilia odes. The laureateship had already been discussed at length by Thomas Warton on the eve of his appointment to that office, and Malone took much from the *History of English Poetry*. But he corrected and enlarged the account from Skelton onward, though, unfortunately, he was not able to finish the subject in one piece, but picked it up again twice later.[126]

The account of St. Cecilia shows Malone at his most thorough, most prolix, and most irrelevant. In bulk this dissertation takes up a tenth of the whole volume.[127] Such length might have been excusable if it had been set off from the rest of the text in some way, as in a special chapter or best of all in an appendix. But pouring out as it does, in the very middle of the volume, the history of St. Cecilia leaves Dryden marooned in space as it swirls from detail to detail. Even when Dryden's odes come to the surface, the discovery of the composer of *Alexander's Feast* sent Malone off on a six-page pursuit of an obscure organist, Jeremiah Clarke. Perhaps Malone's friendship with Dr. Burney, from whom he quoted at length, or his rivalry with Sir John Hawkins, whom he excoriated with zeal, prompted this excursion into musicology. But at any rate we are left gasping (to paraphrase Dryden), "Here is God's plethora." This dissertation, however, is an exception, and is the only one that really drowns the narrative.

One of Malone's contemplated improvements in the second edition would have had some effect in correcting this difficulty: I mean the division of the text into sections.[128] This imposition of form would have given the reader something to cling to. Here we recognize the old conflict of content versus form. Malone's weakness lay, not in the writing, but in the construction of the biography as a whole. Having "procured more materials than my most sanguine expectations had promised" [129] he proceeded to insert them all; and if they did not go easily, he forced them in. Unfortunately for his reputation as a writer, the opening pages in the book are probably the most crowded. Doubtless Leslie Stephen and other critics of Malone were soured at the beginning. Malone's ram-

---

[126] Page 205*n*, and p. 209. [127] Pages 254–307.
[128] Thus Malone wrote to Percy on June 5, 1802 (MS Malone 26, f. 41): "I have cast the Life into a much better form, by dividing it into sections, as I mean to do Shakespeare's also, & have made several small corrections & additions to it." There are eighteen sections, not including the conclusion, in this revised form. See p. 134.
[129] *Advertisement*, p. vi.

bling genealogical expositions are in themselves a major contribution to the biography of the poet, but no one can be blamed for objecting to the form in which Malone inserted them.

A number of shorter subjects were also inserted, which should be described more properly as digressions than as dissertations. They were usually limited to a few pages and were frequently concerned with matter not very germane to the life of Dryden. Thus they were often put in the form of extended footnotes. That on Samuel Dyer is a flagrant example (pp. 181–85). Although Dyer wrote more than seventy years after Dryden, he was lugged in on the thin pretext that both of them had been concerned with translations of Plutarch. Other digressions are the long footnote on Prior [130] and another on Sir Henry Sheres.[131] Malone was conscious of the extraneousness of the latter, as is indicated by his pencil note: "Q: erase all the note about Sheres." [132]

A good case could be made that Malone inserted these disquisitions in a conscious attempt to ornament the main narrative. They are frequently reminiscent of those with which Boswell had decorated the *Life of Johnson*. That Malone should imitate this great model of biography, as I have previously indicated,[133] was a natural step, since he had assisted at its birth and had been occupied with the duties of foster-parent at the very same time that he was working on Dryden. At any rate, an influential portion of his readers considered these asides an attractive feature of the book. Much of this incidental information is extremely interesting and should be better known beyond the circle of Dryden specialists. In fact it can be said that very few subjects left Malone's hands without an added luster. A good illustration is the footnote dismissing the claim that Minsheu's *Guide to the Tongues* was the first book issued by subscription.[134] The succeeding note on the same page provides another example:

Wood disposed of about 415 copies by subscription; and it appears from an advertisement in the London Gazette, June 8, 1691, that eighty-five copies only remained for sale to non-subscribers.[135]

In these digressions we also find material on the genealogy of Swift,[136] on certain anecdotes of Milton,[137] and numerous particulars about

[130] Page 545.   [131] Page 253.   [132] *Ibid.*   [133] Page 41, *supra.*
[134] This error is deeply rooted in Lowndes's *Bibliographer's Manual* and so flowers perennially in booksellers' catalogues.
[135] Page 234n.   [136] Page 239n.   [137] Pages 111–15.

Dean Lockier,[138] Congreve,[139] Obadiah Walker,[140] Sedley,[141] and a host of others, names both well-known and obscure. Thus this life of Dryden is decorated with plums for diverse palates and holds a series of pleasures in store for the literary historian. In fact the variety is so great that many who have sampled it have been distracted from the merit of the solid stuff underneath. It is these digressions that have confused readers and gained this Life of Dryden the title of a dull book.

My defense of the book does not imply that I champion Malone as a stylist, for as a structure of prose the volume has a number of weaknesses. Yet in nearly every case the cause of his trouble is the attempt to include too much material in too little space.[142] Like many another collector, Malone was simply swamped with his own success.[143] We are reminded of Thomas Rawlinson, who packed his house so full of books and manuscripts that he had to sleep in a passageway. And as Malone's guests we object to being entertained in this fashion. A good example is found on pages 88 to 92; these four full pages are covered by only one paragraph, which encompasses the following topics: (*a*) the case for the Earl of Mulgrave as chief influence in gaining the laureateship for Dryden; (*b*) the case against awarding this credit to the Earl of Manchester; (*c*) the case for crediting this influence to Lord Clifford, followed by a summary of Dryden's relationships with the Clifford family; (*d*) the possible assistance of Dorset, Rochester, and the Duchess of Monmouth; (*e*) the reasons why Sir Robert Howard should not be included in the former group; (*f*) a summary of the literary differences between the two brothers-in-law. Perhaps an argument could be made out for the general unity of this paragraph, but the average reader will not discover it. Another instance of paragraph trouble is that on pages 182 to 186; here a paragraph begins with an account of the 1684 *Miscellany,* but continues without a break into a discussion of Dryden's translation of Maimbourg's *History of the League.* The result is that

---

[138] Pages 478–82. Some of the notes and the main quotation are repeated in the Murray edition of Spence's *Anecdotes* (1820), pp. 108–10.

[139] Pages 222–30.   [140] Pages 422–23*n*.   [141] Pages 65–66*n*.

[142] This also probably accounts for the frequent mistakes in the numbering of footnotes.

[143] "In this, as on several other subjects, I have always found the pursuit pleasanter than being 'in at the death.' In collecting materials to any particular point, one's ardour and researches are daily rewarded by some new discovery; but the arranging and putting them into proper form is, if not a dull, at least an anxious and laborious business." Letter from Malone to Charlemont, dated Nov. 7, 1794. Historical MSS Commission, XIII, Appendix, Part 8, p. 252.

instead of pointing out the significance of the *Miscellany,* Malone distracts the reader with an anticlimax.

These paragraphs, of course, are exceptions. But time and time again we see Malone in difficulty for an allied cause: he could not draw a firm line between what belonged to the text and what to the footnote. His troubles in this direction crop out both in the conspicuous disproportion between notes and text and also in occasional manuscript notes. In a jotting on page 464 he can be seen struggling with this weakness, for there he scribbled, "Perhaps this note 5 sh^d be made text." The note in question is entirely personal and is actually a hit at Malone's literary enemies. In fact I have observed only one instance in the whole volume where a note could well have been merged into the text.[144] On the other hand, there are many examples of details clogging the narrative which would have been just as convenient to the reader if relegated to the bottom of the page.[145] To resolve the problem further Malone could have divorced many of these dissertations and digressions entirely from the body of the book and placed them at the end in appendix form, similar to the practice of his twentieth-century heirs. This would have remedied disproportions such as pages 213 to 219, where a veneer of text totaling only seventy-seven words is spread out to cover seven pages.

The answer to Sir Leslie Stephen's epithet "badly written"[146] is the challenge, "Compared with whom?" Unfortunately two of the greatest masters of English prose, Johnson and Scott, are his rivals, and Malone's pages are certainly at a disadvantage when placed next to theirs. But if we compare Malone with fellow laborers in general historical studies, the case is altered to his advantage. Considering all the facts and ideas that it carries in its stream, Malone's text flows both rapidly and smoothly. But if the reader stops to inspect many of the footnotes, he may soon lose his place in the narrative.

Malone was surprised and hurt at a pamphlet attack which charged him with pedantry and which killed the sale of his book. To the modern reader George Hardinge's *Essence of Malone* yields a number of good hits and slapstick blows that amuse until they become tiresome. Yet our sympathy is entirely with Malone, who is abused simply for giving too good measure, and we share with Dryden's ghost an increased debt of gratitude for this surplus of material.

---

[144] Page 70, note 8.   [145] Pages 28, 154, 175, 223, *et passim.*
[146] End of article "Dryden" in the D.N.B.

There are, however, vulnerable spots in Malone's scholarship. Reasonable as we may try to be in criticizing his clumsy literary form, little excuse can be made for some of the book's defects when judged as a serious piece of literary history. Of these deficiencies the most obvious are those in auxiliary apparatus, especially the lack of an index. Even his friend Percy upbraided him on this score, and Malone's only defense was to plead lack of time, a doubly weak excuse in the case of a "gentleman of the old school" who prided himself on his independence.[147] His intention to add an index to the new edition provides negative consolation for the reader who has occasion to search for a half-forgotten reference through five hundred and seventy pages which are not even divided into chapters.

Another of Malone's conspicuous sins, which is specially hard to condone in a man who had spent a large portion of his life in textual criticism, is the abandon with which he treated the texts of the quotations. For instance, in quoting two stanzas of *Fair Armida* from the *Covent Garden Drollery,* he made over thirty alterations.[148] This figure, I should think, constitutes some kind of record for sixteen lines. Malone's laxness is especially noticeable when one looks through his own copy of the book which he prepared for a second edition, for he seemed to have no hesitancy about raising words to italics or otherwise modifying them whenever it suited any emphasis he wished to infuse.[149] The text of the essays themselves is also handled very loosely. Not only are the spelling and punctuation altered, but in some cases even extra words have been inserted. Malone knew better than this, but evidently he had a double standard, one to practice in the temple of Shakespeare and the other for the lesser deities.[150]

Another weakness might have been noticed when we were discussing Malone's reliance on letters for the purpose of gathering information. As the title page asserts, this biography is truly "Grounded on Original and Authentick Documents." Yet in many cases Malone never saw the documents himself, but gained his knowledge at second-hand. Travel

---

[147] MS Malone 27, f. 157, letter from Percy to Malone, dated September 8, 1800: "your book (which I lament has not an index to the Life & Notes, &c.)" Malone's reply, MS Malone 26, ff. 33–34, dated September 13, 1800: "I was aware that an *Index* would be of great use to it, but I had not time for it: however, I hope to add one hereafter" (f. 34).

[148] Page 104. Other cases will be found on pp. 62, 101, 136–37.

[149] Among others see pp. 169, 195, 205, 207, 411.

[150] On this subject see "Dr. Johnson on the Sanctity of an Author's Text," *PMLA,* L, 928–29.

was not easy in those days, Cambridge being as far from London in terms of time and money as Wales is today, to say nothing of the physical demands placed on the passenger by a day's bumping in the coach. Nevertheless we are a trifle disappointed that Malone accepted the findings of Mansel and his other correspondents without inspecting them himself. Whether in this instance he would have located more documents is questionable, but in other cases he undoubtedly would have uncovered additional evidence. To the specialist a few lines of script may sparkle with significance, whereas the ordinary reader might pass them by unnoticed.

As we should expect from anyone who attempts to marshal a myriad of details, Malone did not escape without making a number of factual errors. Many of them might have passed unseen had it not been for the evidence of his own corrected pages, where they stand out like patches on a jacket. Some of them are mere slips of the pen,[151] but others occur because he failed to verify his references,[152] and there are occasions when he introduced conjecture in the guise of a fact.[153] His excuse is found in a passage on some inaccuracies in Southerne's account of Congreve:

> . . . how extremely difficult it is, at any considerable distance of time, to ascertain with precision the smaller incidents of biography; [which entitles biographers] to some degree of indulgence, who, however sedulous they may be in their researches, are still liable to minute errors.[154]

More important than an enumeration of these various faults is the judgment to be passed on the place Malone's Life of Dryden is entitled to occupy in the history of English biography. The verdict should be, I believe, that although it failed to command a wide public, it represents a definite development in the biographical formula. By this I mean that it is the first genuine scholarly biography of a man of letters. Malone's name should be mentioned with honor in every history of the development of English biography. In two other instances Malone appears to have contributed to the development of literary biography. The first we have already mentioned on an earlier page, his breaking of Dryden's dramatic career into "periods." [155] Since then

---

[151] As on p. 193, where *Religio laici* should be *The Hind and the Panther*.
[152] As on p. 392, where "Aristotle" should read "Plato."
[153] As on p. 17, "in 1657 was made Master of Arts."
[154] Page 227.   [155] Page 58.

biographers have drawn and quartered their subjects until such terms as "Horton Period" and "Experimental Period" have, by Gresham's law, gained universal circulation. In the second case Malone put his finger on a biographical sin that has continued to flourish in spite of the advance of scholarship. He was pointing directly at Hayley's *Life of Milton*:

To deduce an author's character from sentiments expressed in his writings, when they are at variance with the tenour and actions of his life, and to found an eulogy on such delusive ground, (a method which has lately been followed in the Life of a great English poet,) though it may please his zealous admirers, can afford no gratification to the lovers of truth. His works, however, may be safely appealed to, when they strongly enforce the practice of those virtues for which the writer, through life, was eminently distinguished.[156]

How often poor Chaucer, to name merely one example, has been accused of misogyny, and simply from the testimony of his own characters!

Malone's purpose, as we have already remarked, excluded critical appraisal of Dryden's various writings. He stated it specifically as follows:

To make Dryden better known to his countrymen than he hitherto has been; to delineate the *man* rather than the *poet,* by collecting from every quarter, and from sources hitherto unexplored, whatever might contribute to throw new light upon his character, and illustrate the history of his works, has been the principal object of the preceding pages.[157]

The idea of delineating "the *man* rather than the *Poet*" had received lip service long before, in the Advertisement for Cibber's *Lives of the Poets.*[158] But Malone appropriately reserved his claim to have done so until his concluding paragraph, when the reader could judge for himself how successful the attempt had been. The accomplishment had in effect been twofold, for not only did Malone record every factual particular he could discover, but—more important—he conceived of Dryden as an *individual* rather than as a mere bundle of human traits whose actions were to be criticized by abstract rules of conduct. This accounts for his attitude toward Dryden's conversion to Roman Catholicism. The Malones were Irish Protestants, and so doubly alert to fancied iniquities of the Roman Church, yet Edmond declined to be bound by the common

---

[156] Page 469, the text as modified for the second edition. Malone added and deleted a footnote, "See the late Life of Milton by William Haley Esqre."

[157] Page 548.

[158] Preserved in Isaac Reed's copy (British Museum shelfmark, 10854.a.1. Vol. 1).

Protestant syllogism that "we know popery to be false, therefore any conversion to it must be opportunism, therefore Dryden, since he was a convert, must have been an opportunist." Rather he looked at Dryden as a human being, who, among other human offices, was the father of a family. Accordingly Malone held as follows:

That his conversion was sincere, cannot be doubted; for he appears to have bred all his children papists, and was uniform in his adherence to his new faith from this time to that of his death . . .[159]

Moreover he bolstered his case with another very shrewd point:

I suspect, his wife, Lady Elizabeth, had long been a papist: her brother Charles, the second Earl of Berkshire, who . . . was probably godfather to our poet's eldest son, certainly was one.[160]

By treating Dryden as a human being rather than in "the character of an apostate" Malone made a step beyond Johnson's procedure, which, as we have seen, consisted essentially of "balancing probabilities." Here the subject remained until a few years ago, when Professor Bredvold's brilliant charting of the intellectual background of the age established this conversion as merely the final step in Dryden's intellectual path.[161]

Malone's attitude toward Dryden as a man among men took another form in his search for the poet's "petty habits." [162] In this particular he had learned a trick from Boswell, although the life of Dryden provided meager room for practice. But the few strokes it enabled him to add to Dryden's portrait go far in helping us to personalize the poet: "He was so great a taker of snuff, that . . . no box, however capacious, could serve him." [163] "He was fond of fishing; an amusement, which for

---

[159] Page 189. In the MS additions is the following, intended to be inserted in the text: "He even endeavoured to convert to his new faith those persons whom he esteemed. 'May God be pleased to open your eyes, (says he to a kinswoman in Nov. 1699) as he has opened mine. Truth is but one; and they who have once heard of it can plead no excuse if they do not embrace it.' "

[160] Ibid.

[161] The Intellectual Milieu of John Dryden, Louis I. Bredvold (1934). "As Dryden's sincerity may be discovered in his appropriation of exactly those ideas of his age which fitted him, so his consistency is to be understood from the historical development of those ideas" (p. 153). ". . . he was already in 1682 far along on the road to the Roman communion; he had already accepted the essential principles on which the Roman Catholics of the time based their apologetics. If the question of his sincerity is to be raised, it would therefore seem more discerning to raise it in connection with his Anglicanism [in Religio laici] rather than with his conversion a few years later" (p. 121).

[162] Malone, Life of Dryden, p. 518.

[163] Ibid., p. 518. A contemporary reference to Dryden's snuff taking, unnoticed by Malone, is found in Oldmixon, Country Wit (1696 Poems, p. 21).

those who, like Dryden, love quiet and retirement, has very strong attractions." [164] These homely details are a very welcome addition to the little we know about Dryden's personality and especially to the formal encomia of Congreve.

Considered as a whole, Malone's service to Dryden was very great. In our concentration on the biographical material we have failed to remark that Malone was the first person to call the attention of the literary public to the body of Dryden's prose. In order to gain a fairly comprehensive knowledge of these prose pieces, the reader before 1800 needed access to more than a dozen volumes; in their quite uncollected form the pieces numbered more than fifty, many of them of considerable rarity. The public voice could have spoken in the words of one of Malone's correspondents, who wrote him, "I was unacquainted with his prosaic works before." [165]

The most conspicuous weakness of this biography is, as we have noticed, in the construction. Though it sometimes seems choked by the very abundance of its information, we must never forget that it is a great piece of original scholarship. In that age the practice of distilling earlier compendia was still followed; but Malone dipped into the original sources. Malone was the first biographer to react consciously against the transmission of error and to emphasize his reaction by force of example. But our special interest in this examination has been to place Malone's Life against the whole range of Dryden studies. Here it looms large against the horizon and is the great plateau from which later peaks arise. In this perspective Malone's biography is undoubtedly the most important book on Dryden that has ever appeared.

"He went to *Wills* and borrow'd Snuff,
From *Dryden's* box with many more,
Who begg'd the liberty before;
For you must know amongst the Beaux
Wit always enters by the Nose,
And passing quickly to the Brain
Comes trickling down in verse again."

[164] Page 520.
[165] The Reverend John Chetwood. MS Malone 27, f. 110, dated December 23, 1800. His further comment (ff. 110ᵛ–111) illustrates the state of literature in Ireland at that time: "Our booksellers in Cork make their livelihood by selling Patent Medicines, of which there is a demand proportionate to the want of demand for literary productions."

V

SIR WALTER SCOTT

Thanks to Lockhart's great biography we have a fairly complete picture of Scott's reasons for undertaking a new edition of Dryden. It was primarily a publisher's venture, for Scott had secretly acquired a partnership in the printing business of his friend James Ballantyne. Thus he proposed to gain a double profit from the Dryden; [1] direct payments would be made to him for his work as author and editor, while at the same time he would be feeding the Ballantyne presses.

The project to reprint all of Dryden was a natural one for Scott to have chosen, since, as he tells us, "an edition of Dryden has been a hobby of mine for a long time." [2] At the beginning a complication arose, for a general edition of Dryden had been contemplated by the Reverend Edward Forster, of London. Forster was known to Scott through mutual friends, and so their rivalry was soon reconciled by a plan for joint editorship. Once embarked on the venture, Scott was immediately perturbed whether they could expect aid or opposition from Malone, who, as we know, was at this very time still contemplating a new edition of his own Life of Dryden. With this in mind Scott wrote to Forster, "I wish any means could be fallen upon to know what Malone proposes to [do;] if he can be brought to look with a propitious eye on our undertaking it would be very agreeable." [3] Another passage in the same

[1] J. G. Lockhart, *Life of Sir Walter Scott*, 1902, II, 205, letter to James Ballantyne, dated April 12, 1805: "There is a scheme for you! At least a hundred volumes, to be published at the rate of ten a-year . . . If the booksellers will give me a decent allowance per volume, say thirty guineas, I shall hold myself well paid on the writing hand. This is a dead secret." For a discussion of the relation of this scheme to the edition of Dryden see pp. 160–61.

[2] *Letters of Sir Walter Scott 1787–1807*, ed. Grierson, 1932, p. 246; letter to Forster dated March 29, 1805.

[3] *Letters 1787–1807*, p. 247. Malone refused to aid the rival publication; Scott considered he "behaved churlishly," but sent him a set of the edition just the same as an acknowledgment of assistance derived from Malone's Life of Dryden. See Scott's letter to William Miller in the *Yale University Library Gazette*, XIV (1940, No. 4), 68.

letter tells plainly that Scott felt the task was undertaken in Malone's shadow.

A very important part of this matter will devolve almost entirely upon you vizt the collecting materials both from the Museum and private hands. Malone in his Life of Dryden has pointed out some valuable sources & we must move heaven & earth to get at them.

A month later Scott again mentioned the great antiquary:

Malone's dates are very accurate & should be followed in arranging the plays —they differ considerably from those of Dr. Johnson & Congreve . . . If Malone be tractable it will be a pleasant circumstance: he is a very laborious editor though I think confused and tasteless.[4]

Scott's attitude was echoed a few months later in a letter from his friend George Ellis:

Quoad Malone,—I should think Ritson himself, could he rise from the dead, would be puzzled to sift out a single additional anecdote of the poet's life; but to abridge Malone,—and to render his narrative terse, elegant and intelligible,—would be a great obligation conferred on the purchasers (I will not say the readers, because I have doubts whether they exist in the plural number) of his very laborious compilation.[5]

The joint editorship was short-lived; a letter from Ballantyne to the London publisher Millar, discloses that the objection came from the latter:

If, as you have reason to think, his name would injure the work it would be absurd to pay for it; if it would ruin the work it would be madness to retain it. You only can feel the pulse of the London trade.[6]

Accordingly before many weeks had elapsed Forster was squeezed out by the pincer-like pressure between Scott's equivocal demand that Forster "make the best bargain you can" with Ballantyne on the financial side and his equally obdurate insistence on exercising the editorial dominance. Forster felt the impossible nature of the situation and withdrew from the undertaking. On October 27 Scott wrote to him,

I am extremely sorry to learn by your letter of the 21st that you are finally resolved to abandon Dryden . . . I hope you will give us a handsome & complete Ben Jonson which I have long thought a great desideratum . . .[7]

---

[4] *Letters 1787–1807*, p. 250; dated April 26, 1805.

[5] Lockhart, *Life of Sir Walter Scott*, II, 242. No date is given for this letter, but it answers Scott's of October 17, 1805.

[6] *Letters 1787–1807*, p. 245n.　　　　　[7] *Ibid.*, pp. 266–67.

From this time on Scott was able to travel alone. Forster would certainly have proved a Jonah to the venture, but Scott's part in the negotiations is not the most creditable page in his biography.

Having perused Malone's Life of Dryden with some care, we must feel that anyone who attempted to go over the ground again five years later would be heavily handicapped. Malone was a full-time antiquary, with only one diversion—dining well. But Scott's investigations, on the other hand, were confined to the hours not demanded by his legal duties. And these demands were considerable in the case of a young man just over thirty who was earning £1,000 per annum from the Scottish law. Scott had rival literary interests, too, for at the very time he was putting these eighteen volumes of Dryden into shape he was also deep in *Marmion*, a task which in itself would have been the keystone of a career for many poets. The poem was actually published two months before the Dryden. Scott's correspondence during this period contains many references to the twin projects,[8] and for a long time his letters indicate that he expected to finish the editorial task before the poetical. Of course the two undertakings were directed to different audiences, for then, as today, a hundred readers knew Scott's name as the author of *Marmion* for the one who had heard of his edition of Dryden.

Scott, however, was no ordinary man, and he brought remarkable ability to Dryden studies. Like Dr. Johnson he had been an insatiable reader since childhood, his favorite field having been British history. Consequently his knowledge of Restoration times was very extensive, in fact much more thorough than many of his admirers have recognized. History had become more than a body of knowledge to him, for by reading widely and deeply he had attained the goal of all education, a clear and steadfast perspective. To a writer on Restoration literature, no trait could have been more valuable.

The effect of Scott's unusual mind appears at once when we open the *Life of Dryden*. The first paragraph contains an attitude very different from that of his predecessors.

The Life of Dryden may be said to comprehend a history of the literature of England, and its changes, during nearly half a century . . . As he wrote

---

[8] Thus Scott wrote Anna Seward on August 11, 1807, ". . . my grand poem called Marmion has been entirely stopped even when half finished and Dryden has crept on very slowly." *Letters 1787–1807*, p. 374. Likewise, he wrote Southey on October 1, 1807, "I hope very soon to send you my Life of Dryden, and eke my *last* Lay" (*ibid.*, p. 386).

from necessity, he was obliged to pay a certain deference to the public opinion; for he, whose bread depends upon the success of his volume, is compelled to study popularity: but, on the other hand, his better judgment was often directed to improve that of his readers; so that he alternately influenced and stooped to the national taste of the day. If, therefore, we would know the gradual changes which took place in our poetry during the above period, we have only to consult the writings of an author, who produced yearly some new performance, allowed to be most excellent in the particular style which was fashionable for the time.[9]

This approach is quite new compared to that professed by any of the previous biographers. As we have seen, the early attempts to consider Dryden as a poet were brought to a climax by Dr. Johnson. Later Malone, who eschewed criticism, had far surpassed the efforts of his predecessors to delineate Dryden the *man*. On these twin pillars Scott designed a transcendent structure, comprehending no less than the whole of Restoration literature; the central figure, of course, was Dryden, but he was to be flanked by the lesser figures of the age.

It is the object of this memoir to connect, with the account of Dryden's life and publications, such a general view of the literature of the time, as may enable the reader to estimate how far the age was indebted to the poet, and how far the poet was influenced by the taste and manners of the age.[10]

Scott relied heavily on Johnson and Malone, and his introduction tells how much he depended on them:

In the Biographical Memoir, it would have been hard to exact, that the Editor should rival the criticism of Johnson, or produce facts which had escaped the accuracy of Malone. While, however, he has availed himself of the labours of both, particularly of the latter, whose industry has removed the cloud which so long hung over the events of Dryden's life, he has endeavoured to take a different and more enlarged view of the subject than that which his predecessors have presented. The general critical view of Dryden's works being sketched by Johnson with unequalled felicity, and the incidents of his life accurately discussed and ascertained by Malone, something seemed to remain for him who should consider these literary productions in their succession, as actuated by, and operating upon, the taste of the age, where they had so predominant influence; and who might, at the same time, connect the life of Dryden with the history of his publications, without losing sight of the fate and character of the individual. . . .[11]

What use did Scott actually make of Malone's collection of facts about Dryden? To anyone who is on the watch for it, Scott's pages seem dotted

---

[9] *Life of Dryden*, pp. 3–4.   [10] *Ibid.*, p. 4.   [11] Advertisement, pp. vi–vii.

with Malone's name, and in point of fact it is found about once in every three pages. Yet even so it is not repeated every time that Scott used Malone's material, or else it would occur in nearly every paragraph. But this circumstance is not to be wondered at, for the situation would be the same today if a biographer should conscientiously tag his facts with pedigrees. In the century and a third since Malone's edition, Dryden's biography has become the common property of literature, whereas to Scott, who began his task only five years afterward, the ethics of the republic of letters prescribed Malone's discoveries as still his property.

Of course a number of Malone's special contributions were borrowed and incorporated without being broken up, as for example, his table of Dryden's plays which Scott reprinted *in toto*.[12] But generally Scott's procedure was to take whatever details he wished and to weave them into his own pattern, as for instance, the description of Dryden's "petty habits," which was rewoven without a single addition.[13]

In a few instances Scott tried to pick up details which Malone had previously rejected, and it is not surprising that in doing so he came to grief. The 1662 *Satire on the Dutch* is a case in point: Malone had omitted any reference to this spurious poem, probably because one of Derrick's notes had challenged its authenticity, but Scott alluded to it in the *Life* and even printed the text of the poem.[14]

There are occasions, however, when Scott was able to take Malone's basic but rough material and mold it into its proper form. An excellent illustration is the anecdote of Milton's rejoinder to the proposal to dramatize *Paradise Lost,* "Ay, you may tag my verses if you will." Scott completed the incident with the words,

Perhaps few have read so far into the "State of Innocence" as to discover that Dryden did not use this licence to the uttermost, and that several of the scenes are not tagg'd with rhyme.[15]

So, too, Scott challenged Malone's contention that there is no allusion to *Marriage à la mode* in *The Rehearsal,* and made out a very convincing case for his side of the question.[16]

Perhaps the greatest contrast between the two biographers lay in their different attitudes toward details. Malone habitually examined each item of evidence until he was sure that no degree of its circumference was lacking, but Scott swept along without time for such *minutiae*. His nar-

---

[12] Pages 367–68.   [13] One anecdote was added in the 1821 edition. See page 163, below.
[14] Page 55.   [15] Page 170.   [16] Page 141*n.*

rative carries the reader along post haste, for having chosen his pace he knew that each superfluous detail would be a handicap. Accordingly many of Malone's choicest dates were left behind; for Scott usually would say merely that *"Aureng-zebe* was followed in 1678 by *All for Love"* [17] without offering the reader complete details. When quoting dates the months of the year were adequate for Scott, and even in his footnotes he sometimes omitted to give the location of the passages quoted. This practice implies that Scott knew that readers who sought for complete documentation could find it in Malone.

Scott's situation was indeed far from conducive to exact research; in his study competition for desk space was rife between piles of legal documents, papers of verses, and the volumes employed in his editorial labors. To sandwich scholarship between the demands of a law office and those of poetical composition was one thing; but geographical disadvantage was quite another. Certainly Scotland at that day was not the place to find new Dryden documents, or other source materials. Scott had no alternative but to go to London, and so February, 1806, saw him there, tasting the first fruits of literary celebrity. Some months before, he had written George Ellis, "Where dwelleth Heber the magnificent, whose library and cellar are so superior to all others in the world? I wish to write to him about Dryden." [18] In London Heber and Scott soon became cronies, much to the benefit of the Dryden.[19] Through Heber's offices Scott met James Bindley, and so the Luttrell collection was once again turned to good use.[20] At this time Scott also became well acquainted with the British Museum. He returned to Scotland for the summer, but a year later he was in London again,[21] and undoubtedly this time he had

---

[17] Page 218. [18] *Letters 1787–1807*, p. 264; dated Oct. 17, 1805.

[19] Scott's Preface makes special acknowledgment of Heber's assistance. He had known Heber before, as we learn from a passage in a letter to Forster, dated April 21, 1805: "Mr. Bindley of Somerset house has most of the rare controversial tracts relating to that period. I can get at him through my friend Heber to whom when the work is fairly set afloat I will intimate our intentions." *Ibid.,* p. 250.

[20] In two instances Scott got information from the Luttrell collection that Malone had overlooked. On p. 421 he tells us that Luttrell dated his copy of Blackmore's *Satire Against Wit* as purchased on November 23, 1699. This is of some importance, as Scott indicates in his note on the subject: "Mr Malone conceives, that the Fables were published before the 'Satire upon Wit'; but he had not this evidence of the contrary before him. It is therefore clear, that Dryden endured a second attack from Blackmore, before making any reply." The other instance is on p. 437, where Scott increased the ranks of Dryden's literary assailants by the anonymous author of *An Epistle to Sir Richard Blackmore, Occasioned by the New Session of the Poets,* "marked by Mr. Luttrell, 1st November 1700."

[21] "One of my principal reasons for visiting London this spring . . ." Letter from Scott to Lady Abercorn, dated February 11, 1807; *Letters 1787–1807,* p. 350.

fairly definite inquiries to engage his attention.[22] Much time was demanded by the text of Dryden, which he provided with the fullest annotations it has ever received. Indeed, when viewed from one angle the biography is just an introduction to the seventeen volumes of Dryden's works.

What, then, did Scott add to our actual knowledge of Dryden? Only one new document rewarded his inquiries, the letter printed with the conjectural date 1683,[23] which was written by Dryden as judge in a poetical argument. It came to Scott through his friend Constable, and was then owned by a "Mrs. White of Bownham Hall, Gloucestershire." The letter is more important from the literary than from the biographical point of view, since details of date and addressee are missing, but it provides a glimpse of Dryden's technical knowledge of language structure. Scott turned up other items of biographical importance in the research necessary in editing the poems. Most of them were not incorporated in the *Life,* but remain among the "illustratory" notes.[24] In reading the *Life* itself we are continually surprised by fresh information, additions ranging from the discovery of Dryden's great-great-grandfather to Dryden's supposed authorship of a number of Roman Catholic hymns.[25] These additions demonstrate that Scott's reading was both extensive and deep and, moreover, that the editor's chair provided him with the best discipline that a biographer can possibly obtain.

Just as in biographical matters Scott leaned heavily on Malone, so in the critical side of this biography he pored over his Johnson very thoroughly, and as we should expect, Johnson's name is printed most frequently in cases where some specific point is under discussion or where Scott made direct quotations. Yet Scott was far from a mere echo of Johnson and did not fear to contradict him on occasion. Thus for example Scott considered that the "Ode to Mrs. Anne Killigrew" "has been admired perhaps fully as much as it merits." [26] But in calling attention to these echoes of Johnson I am not speaking reproachfully. Far from it. Scott was merely doing his duty as it required to be done. Every

---

[22] See pages 163–64.

[23] This letter later belonged to Malone (Prior, *Life of Malone,* 1860, p. 264). It is now owned by the Marquess of Crewe.

[24] Henry Hallam also noticed this point: "The Life itself is, in many places, but an abstract of what is said more at length in the notes."—*Edinburgh Review,* XIII, 118.

[25] See pp. 161–62, below.

[26] Page 341. Joseph Warton (Dryden's *Poetical Works,* 1811, II, 259*n*) also felt that Johnson had been over-generous in calling it "undoubtedly the noblest ode that our language has ever produced" (Johnson's Life of Dryden, par. 278).

biographer who ever has written or ever will write on Dryden must take
the same course. In fact Scott's *Life of Dryden* has become in its turn
almost as much of a quarry for succeeding biographers as Johnson's had
been for him.

As a critic in his own right, Scott also deserves attention as his many
reviews in the *Edinburgh* and the *Quarterly* provide corroboration.
But the volume before us shows Scott's critical powers at their best,
especially his ability to judge a poem or a play in the light of its individual situation. He realized that knowledge of the occasion which
produced a literary piece was highly important in attempting to evaluate
it. This keenness is observable in his remarks on the *Verses to Lord
Chancellor Hyde:*

. . . in which Dryden has more closely imitated the metaphysical poetry
than in any poem, except the juvenile elegy on Lord Hastings. I cannot but
think, that the poet consulted the taste of his patron, rather than his own, in
adopting this peculiar style. Clarendon was educated in the court of Charles
I., and Dryden may have thought it necessary, in addressing him, to imitate
the "strong verses," which were then admired.[27]

Scott's historical imagination enabled him to explain the setting of *Absalom and Achitophel* better than it had ever been done before. By putting himself back into the maelstrom of the Popish Plot, Scott showed
the agitation that swept along Whig and Tory alike; Dryden, in writing *Absalom and Achitophel,* was throwing his strength into what he
and his party saw as an emergency.[28] To submit another instance, Scott
also perceived the political significance of *Cleomenes:*

The choice of the subject, the history of a Spartan prince exiled from his
kingdom, and waiting the assistance of a foreign monarch to regain it, cor-
responded too nearly with that of the unfortunate James.[29]

Malone had missed this entirely, for although he noted that the performance of the play had been delayed by "some obstructions on political
grounds," [30] he confessed, "What were the grounds of offence, does not
now appear." [31]

Scott also handled Dryden's critical writings very commendably.
When he chose to give the reader a summary of Dryden's argument, as
in the case of the *Essay of Dramatic Poesy,* the resulting passage is a

[27] Page 51.   [28] Pages 239 *et seq.*   [29] Pages 362–63.
[30] Malone, Life of Dryden, p. 213.
[31] *Ibid.,* p. 214*n.*

model of précis writing.[32] Other pages scattered throughout the book demonstrate that Scott was keenly interested in a variety of critical subjects, for instance, his remarks about the transition between Dryden's early ideas on the drama, as set forth in *Of Heroic Plays,* and his altered taste as evinced in the *Grounds of Criticism in Tragedy.*[33] Another example, on a later page, is Scott's discussion of Dryden's borrowings from the contemporary French critics in the *Discourse concerning the Original and Progress of Satire:*

> In that treatise, our author exhibits a good deal of that sort of learning which was in fashion among the French critics; and, I suspect, was contented rather to borrow something from them, than put himself to the trouble of compiling more valuable materials.[34]

For some reason Johnson had said nothing on this important subject, and it is doubtful whether Malone was much interested in it.

Numerous other passages could be singled out if Scott's critical ability really needed to be demonstrated. Among them his dramatic criticism should be mentioned, because Scott allowed himself something of a fling when he came to this part of the biography. The pages on the heroic plays make especially good reading,[35] although modern historians of the stage might qualify some of his points, particularly his emphasis on the personal influence of King Charles and the background of the seventeenth-century French drama. Yet all in all Scott gave remarkably good treatment to a subject that previously had received only jeers. Nowhere is his critical acumen better demonstrated than in recognizing the part that the elocution of trained actors had in the success of these entertainments:

> In representation, the beauty of the verse, assisted by the enunciation of such actors as Betterton and Mohun, gilded over the defects of the sense, and afforded a separate gratification.[36]

And this applied to Dryden's rich versification, which

> . . . abounded with such splendid and sonorous passages, as, in the mouth of a Betterton, awed into silence even those critics, who could distinguish

---

[32] Pages 92–96. Whether the expenditure of space for this summary can be justified is quite another matter.

[33] Pages 225 *et seq.*   [34] Page 376.

[35] Pages 69 *et seq.,* also 118 *et seq.* and 127 *et seq.* Observe the "critical scales" in his transition (p. 128): "But something may be said for the heroic drama."

[36] Page 129.

that the tumid and unnatural was sometimes substituted for the heroic and sublime.[37]

Equally commendable are Scott's summaries of other topics, such as Dryden's excellences in satire, elegy, and narrative. Because Scott had a strong mind and a vigorous pen he was an exceptionally well-equipped critic. Whenever he applied himself to a subject, he left his mark behind. Little did the writer in the *Monthly Review* realize how ridiculous he would appear to posterity when he said of Scott's performance in the *Dryden,* "if he anywhere fails, it is in that higher department which belongs to criticism and to taste." [38]

From the viewpoint of an historian of biography Scott's *Life of Dryden* represents a great advance over the work of Johnson and of Malone, an advance based on Scott's power to paint the historical background. If Johnson presented Dryden in silhouette and Malone drew a portrait of Dryden the man, Scott now achieved a canvas showing Dryden surrounded by his contemporaries, a skillful portrait of the individual placed among the figures of his age. To all who know Scott's novels this would seem a foregone conclusion, yet we must remember that at this early period even *Waverley* was only a fragmentary manuscript. Nevertheless the conception of historical portraiture was already in Scott's mind, and this biography contains the promise of what was to come.

This matter of historical background is a very important one in the history of biography. In talking of Boswell's *Johnson,* Lockhart's *Scott,* and other great masterpieces, we often forget that those writers faced no such problem as did Masson in his *Milton* or Scott in the *Dryden* now before us. Until almost our own day the great majority of biographies were really memoirs of deceased friends written by contemporaries, who often ignored the relation between a man and his time. This fact goes far to explain why Victorian biography so often degenerated into hagiography. Scott's background owed its excellence to his early reading; he had lived with these characters in his youthful imagination, even though his mastery of detail came from more recent and mature researches. The word "researches" is not used lightly, either. Though Scott's name ranks

[37] Page 131.

[38] New series, LVIII, 137. In the marked file of the *Monthly Review* in the Bodleian, this review is signed "Sym—s," which indicates without a doubt that the author was Charles Symmons (1749–1826). The twenty-three pages of this review are full of captious criticism upon trifling points. For example, being a Welshman, Symmons felt entitled to complain strongly of the young Scotchman's corruption of the English language.

high in the annals of ballad collecting, he was never a "literary anti-quary" in the specific sense of the term. Yet in his editorial work he de-voted considerable effort to acquiring detailed knowledge, and the an-notating of Dryden led him into many forgotten by-ways of inquiry.

During these long years Scott must have made voluminous notes about Dryden, as he did for the edition of Swift, but all of them are gone except for a few leaves. Only one of these papers is of any significance. It consists of passages copied or summarized from the *London Gazette*,[39] and is evidence that Scott selected not only items directly concerned with Dryden, such as the report of the Rose Alley indignity, but other items quite unconnected with Dryden. He gathered them in order to recreate the atmosphere of England under the Stuarts.

Scott's letters often testify to the energy that went into his researches. He wrote to his friend Lady Abercorn on September 20, 1806:

Your Ladyship is very good to enquire after Dryden. I have I assure you been labouring very hard through the old libels and pamphlets of the time to complete the historical notices upon his political poems; and I am at least willing to hope that I have been in some degree successful.[40]

The next spring he wrote on the same subject to another of his fem-inine correspondents, Anna Seward:

. . . the illustration of the poetical & historical passages have cost me much labour
> From my research the boldest spiders fled
> And moths retreating trembled as I read.[41]

The result of Scott's researches was that he successfully turned himself into a contemporary of Dryden. Almost every page is vitalized by his historical imagination, the power that later found its proper medium in the novel. The biography of Dryden is the first fruit of one of the most productive geniuses in the history of all literature.

Yet the author's genius is not the only explanation of the highly devel-oped background. Scott saw that one of the most important points about Dryden was his remarkable adaptability, that as a professional man of letters Dryden had learned to set his sails to suit the winds of fashion. This idea, now a familiar one in Dryden studies, has too often received only lip service, but in Scott's mind it was the key to an understanding of

Dryden. In itself it controverts the oft-repeated accusation that Dryden was "inconsistent," for why not say a ship tacking before the breeze is inconsistent? Like a ship Dryden was progressing steadily toward the harbor; in both politics and religion his course was toward belief in authority.

In describing these fashions in literature Scott did his best work toward reconstructing the seventeenth-century background. In fact many of his pages read like a history of English literature. The description of the "Metaphysicals" goes far beyond anything hitherto written on the subject, and as an elementary introduction it can be read with profit by students even today. He continued with the civil-war period, "the most unfavourable to literature which had occurred for at least two centuries," and then gave an excellent analysis of the great change that took place when the court of Charles had once more become re-established. And so throughout the rest of the book the same practice was followed. We have already mentioned the generous account of the theater and especially Scott's excellent critical analysis of the heroic plays. In the same way the background to the political and personal satires was fully developed. Furthermore Scott was alert enough to observe the minor literary renaissance of the 1690's,[42] a decade which has yet to receive its due from literary historians. But throughout the whole book Dryden is always the center figure, like Zeus in the center of the frieze on the Parthenon, while the lesser deities fill the wings on both sides.[43]

Another distinctive feature of this life is Scott's consciousness of Dryden's changing reputation among his contemporaries. He brings the subject to the fore so regularly that we can be sure it had more than casual importance for him. Take, for instance, this remark from the discussion on heroic plays:

The reputation of the poet himself kept pace with that of his favourite style of composition; and though posterity has judged more correctly, it may be questioned, whether "Tyrannic Love" and the "Conquest of Granada" did not place Dryden higher in public esteem, in 1670, than his "Virgil" and "Fables" in 1700.[44]

---

[42] Pages 385–86.

[43] See the sketch of Sir Robert Howard on p. 54 and of Villiers on p. 134. These are very different and more effective than Malone's footnotes, crammed with biographical dates. Observe also Scott's indication of certain *dramatis personae* that are concealed portraits of prominent contemporaries (p. 280*n*). As Scott points out (p. 284) Dryden did this in the *Duke of Guise*.

[44] Page 133.

Other passages illustrating this important line of inquiry are found under the remarks on *All for Love* [45] and also in "The State of Dryden's Reputation at his Death, and Afterwards," [46] which is especially well done. By calling attention to contemporary opinion Scott was once again exercising historical imagination.

Another device of biographical technique that Scott used was to parallel the periods of Dryden's literary career with brief surveys of his private life during the same years. Accordingly after we have read that the fire of London enforced a pause in Dryden's theatrical career, Scott used the lull to say, "We may take this opportunity to review the effect which the rise of Dryden's reputation had upon his private fortune and habits of life." [47] A similar parallel is made at the end of each of the remaining sections,[48] except the sixth, where it is carried over to begin the next division under the heading, "The State of Dryden's Connections in Society after the Revolution." [49] This device was handled very dexterously by Scott and it proved an effective, though simple, way to "show us Dryden the man."

The last point I should like to examine is Scott's interpretation of facts and situations. At the outset it should be observed that he very frequently did not wait on facts, but interpreted on the basis of "seems," [50] "it would appear," [51] and "we may suppose." [52] To a biographer faced with gaps in the factual record this procedure is certainly attractive enough. And Scott would have justified himself by saying that "facts make fine servants but are poor masters." Yet in our own day we have seen fictional biography developed into such a chimera that we react instinctively against supposition where proof is lacking.

Even in some cases where Scott appears to be safe enough, we cannot pass his statements unquestioned. He contends, for example, that Dryden "arranged for publication" the 1684 *Miscellany Poems* and did it as a direct result of being "coolly left to increase his pittance by writing occasional pieces." [53] Now this business should be weighed carefully. Why, if the pinch in Dryden's pocketbook was so great, did this *Miscellany* appear without a dedication? At this period even the most perfunctory string of phrases would have produced enough guineas to clink in his pocket. Scott's second assumption is qualified by a glance at

[45] Page 220.   [46] Pages 470 *et seq.*   [47] Page 86.
[48] Pages 112, 178, 292.   [49] Page 369.   [50] Pages 56, 58.
[51] Page 65.   [52] Page 360.   [53] Page 294.

the volume under discussion. Dryden, it is true, was the largest contributor to the volume, but only five of his poems made their appearance for the first time in print, and four of these were translations. Next there is the assumption that Dryden "arranged the publication." First of all, looking at Tonson's part in the transaction, we notice that he was still at the beginning of his career and that this was his first venture with a poetical miscellany.[54] Thus the most likely supposition is that Dryden was helping Tonson to embark on a publishing venture by allowing Tonson to reprint a number of his satires, prologues, and epilogues, to which, perhaps for a fee, he added several odd pieces that may have been lying about at the time. Two circumstances support this case: first, that *Absalom and Achitophel, The Medal,* and other pieces here reprinted were Tonson's property to republish as he pleased. The other is that Dryden's name is nowhere in the volume distinguished from those of the other contributors. In other words, this is a case where Scott was caught by the weakness of playing with "probablies."

But such instances are not frequent enough to be characteristic, and they are usually minor matters, about which Scott accepted Malone's conclusions without troubling to think himself. When he did concentrate, as he did on the important problems, his interpretations are magnificent. Such, for example, is his treatment of Dryden's conversion. Scott was the first Dryden scholar to search for clues in the two great religious poems, *Religio laici* and *The Hind and the Panther,* and he fastened at once on the autobiographical passage in the latter, which has since become so well known.[55] From this he proceeded to an examination of the theological arguments and to what is so evident in *Religio laici,* "Dryden's strong wish to believe." [56] Scott's mind then penetrated to the heart of the matter:

Dryden did not . . . except in outward profession, abandon the Church of England for that of Rome, but was converted to the Catholic faith from a state of infidelity, or rather of Pyrrhonism.[57]

As soon as he had comprehended this point, the whole knot of the conversion became loosened and untied in Scott's hands. He said in conclusion:

[54] The 1680 translation of Ovid was "By Several Hands," but the purchasers were paying for the Roman poet, not an anthology.
[55] Lines 72–77. "My thoughtless youth . . . false lights . . . new sparkles . . ."
[56] Page 308.   [57] Page 314.

... the change was adopted in consequence of [an] unbroken train of reasoning . . . Dryden, when he wrote the "Religio Laici," was under the impulse of the same conviction, which, further prosecuted, led him to acquiesce in the faith of Rome.[58]

Other brilliant interpretations flash from various pages in the book. Considering the modicum of evidence, his treatment of the marriage with Lady Elizabeth is excellent.[59] Yet it is not merely these major problems where his intellect shines through; it often glistens in out-of-the-way places as well. We thus have such admirable passages as the following, from the discussion of the Preface to *Tyrannick Love:*

And he concludes by exulting, that though he might have written nonsense, none of his critics had been so happy as to discover it. These indications of superiority, being thought to savour of vanity, had their share in exciting the storm of malevolent criticism, of which Dryden afterwards so heavily complained.[60]

The following from another page is good evidence that after three years of thinking about Dryden, Scott saw him steadily and saw him whole:

It was a singular trait in the character of our author, that by whatever motive he was directed in his choice of a subject, and his manner of treating it, he was, upon all occasions, alike anxious to persuade the public, that both the one and the other were the object of his free choice, founded upon the most rational grounds of preference.[61]

Scott's *Life of Dryden* marked as great an advance in the biography of the poet as the accompanying edition of his collected works did in the wider field of Dryden studies. In one place Scott used the phrase, "a biographer's duty." He did not proceed to define in words what this meant to him, but I have in this chapter tried to show how he defined it in practice. Scott placed Dryden the poet in perspective by making a critical comparison between him and his contemporaries. And Dryden the man lives in Scott's pages as he had never done in any other biography. The matter was summed up about as well as it can be when Scott wrote, "this essay [is] intended to contain the life, not the apology of the poet." [62]

The double aim expressed in Scott's opening pages was high: "to esti-

[58] Page 333.
[59] Pages 88–89. He wrote before evidence "dishonourable to the lady" was known. Cf. *Letters of Chesterfield* (Philip Stanhope, 2d earl), 1829, p. 95.
[60] Page 111.   [61] Page 91.   [62] Page 303.

mate how far the age was indebted to the poet, and how far the poet was influenced by the taste and manners of the age." [63] In the end Scott was not able to achieve both objectives, for he did not succeed in the former. His contention was quite correct; Dryden *did* influence the age; but Scott's demonstration became lost in the mass of other subjects crowded between these two covers. Yet viewed from any standard but his own, Scott's biography is a distinguished success. Not only does "Glorious John" walk and talk before us as he does later in *The Pirate*,[64] but so also do Dryden's friends and enemies. In fact this book is well on the way toward the "life and times," which has since dominated the field of scholarly biography. But to anyone who is conscious of literary form the chief impression Scott's book leaves is of the art with which his conceptions have been molded. Here is the work not only of a superior pen but also of a superior mind.

[63] Page 4.   [64] Ch. xiv.

VI

THE LAST HUNDRED YEARS

In the early decades of the nineteenth century two factors brought about a great change in publishing conditions—the extension of literacy and the development of the steam printing press. Among the many books that issued to supply the new demand were frequent reprints of the great poets, and among them Dryden. According to the custom of that day and of our own, most of these editions were preceded by memoirs. The volumes of Dryden were sometimes introduced by the old favorites like Dr. Johnson's *Life,* or other times by new biographical sketches representing more or less original work.

THE ALDINE EDITION

The first of these original sketches appeared in 1832, the year of Scott's death, in the form of a "compendious memoir" before the Aldine edition of Dryden's poems. The author was that prolific writer whom Lamb once described as "a pleasant layman spoiled," the Reverend John Mitford, friend of the publisher Pickering and of Samuel Rogers. Mitford's memoir was frankly founded upon Scott, Johnson, and Malone, especially the last, of whom he said, ". . . indeed, deprived of the result of his patient and praiseworthy labours, a life of Dryden would be little better than a romance." [1] Accordingly we are not surprised to find frequent excerpts from the work of these predecessors, sometimes with quotation marks and often without. This criticism applies especially to the footnotes, many of which are copied verbatim from Johnson, Malone, or Scott, with no indication that they are not the result of Mitford's own researches. The main body of the life, however, was rewritten. But in spite of Mitford's dependence on his great predecessors, his memoir cannot be wholly disregarded by present-day Dryden scholars.

[1] Page lxxxvi.

Although not a trained researcher, Mitford was a man of wide reading, and from one source or another he incorporated several new facts into the body of biographical material. Since this memoir was the first new account of Dryden after the publication of the Chesterfield letters, he was able to include the two which Dryden had sent to Lord Chesterfield on dedicating to him the translation of Virgil's *Georgics*.[2] Mitford also printed the letter of Lady Elizabeth Howard to Chesterfield, dated 1658, five years before her marriage to Dryden.[3] But the most important of Mitford's addenda is found tacked on at the conclusion of the memoir under the unobtrusive heading "Additional Notes." [4] In about a dozen lines of type he summarized the agreement, drawn up between Dryden and Tonson on June 15, 1694, to cover the translation of Virgil. Here was a rare find, indeed, but Mitford treated it in a rather off-hand way, not even telling where the document was located. As a result of this indifference later biographers could only refer to Mitford's incomplete note without being able to consult the agreement itself.[5]

Another of Mitford's additions was a development of the Ann Reeves affair. It had remained in the "tart-eating" stage until he took it in hand, but in his pages Mrs. Reeves's career was traced until her final retreat into a nunnery. And to mention two other small points, Mitford questioned the attribution to Villiers, Duke of Buckingham, of *Poetical Reflections on a Late Poem Entitled Absalom and Achitophel* (1682),[6] and he was also the first biographer to incorporate the account from Evelyn's *Diary* (published in 1818) about the dinner party at Ned Sheldon's in January, 1694, just at the time when Dryden was giving up playwriting and commencing his great period of translation. Scott had inserted some details from Evelyn into the second edition of his Dryden (1821), but had missed this incident.

These slight additions are paralleled by some interesting suggestions which Mitford raised about various small points. Concerning the *Rehearsal* he said, "Dryden's Play of Marriage a-la-Mode was alluded to,

---

[2] Page cxxxviii*n*.   [3] Page xxv*n*.   [4] Page clii.

[5] Christie had this experience (*Dryden*, Clarendon Press Series, 1873, p. xliii, note d). Professor Ward has recently rediscovered it in the British Museum (Add. MS 36933 and Add. Charter 8429), and has discussed it in RES, XIII (July, 1937), 301–3, and PMLA, LIII (Sept., 1938), 807–12. Professor J. M. Bottkol has pointed out that Charles MacPherson in his 1910 dissertation, *Über die Vergil-übersetzung des John Dryden* (University of Berlin) had also called attention to this document.

[6] Page lxxxvi. This he did simply by referring the reader to William Godwin's diatribe on the subject in the *Lives of John and Edward Phillips*.

though not acted nor printed till the subsequent year, but it probably had been shown about, as was the custom, in manuscript."[7] Recent investigation proves that the play was known in manuscript, although it had probably been acted before the *Rehearsal*.[8] Another of Mitford's suggestions concerned *Love Triumphant*:

This unsuccessful play is so inferior to some of his later productions, that I have often, while reading it, considered, whether in the hard necessities of his later days, he might not have produced a piece written in earlier life and which had been deservedly neglected by him, while the unimpaired vigour and luxuriance of his genius supplied him without difficulty.[9]

This consideration is not without merit, and no one, as far as I know, has ever studied the matter seriously. An interesting parallel exists in the case of the *Duke of Guise*, which Dryden began in 1660 and kept by him for twenty-three years.[10] Several circumstances, however, make the speculation questionable, of which the most important is that two of the poet's letters to Walsh mention this play, but say nothing to imply that it is not entirely new.[11]

Once these contributions have been noticed, Mitford's memoir can be allowed to rest in the limbo of literature with the remainder of his voluminous writings. For considered as a whole, the memoir is a negligible piece of work. Written in a style tumid with rhetoric, his pages are also marred by prejudiced judgments, as for example in his bitter and unfounded attack on the character of Lady Elizabeth Dryden. These problems, which Scott had labored to make matters of open inquiry, became more confused than ever in Mitford's treatment of them. Mitford's additions were due to the accidents of time, but his prejudices more than counterbalance any value they might have given to his pages.[12]

ROBERT BELL

A score of years elapsed before Dryden's life was taken up by another writer, once again to supply a prefatory memoir to an edition of Dry-

[7] Page xlv.
[8] Charles E. Ward, "The Dates of Two Dryden Plays," PMLA, LI (Sept., 1936), 786 ff.
[9] Page cxv.
[10] As Dryden acknowledged at the beginning of the *Vindication of the Duke of Guise*.
[11] Letters dated May 9, 1693 (Scott-Saintsbury, No. LI) and Dec. 12, 1693 (Scott-Saintsbury, No. LIII).
[12] In 1866 the Aldine edition of Dryden's poems was reissued with a new biography by the Reverend Richard Hooper. Although extending to 130 pages, the Life of Dryden contains very little of interest, for Hooper contributed nothing but a patchwork of passages snipped from the volumes of his predecessors.

den's poems. Like Malone, Robert Bell had come to London from Dublin to seek success in a literary career. After various editorial and journalistic occupations, he embarked on the task for which he is chiefly remembered today, an edition of the English poets. The plan, which unfortunately was never completed, called for "a revised and carefully annotated" text of the body of English poetry from Chaucer to Cowper, including not only the standard authors, but also "specimens, with connecting notes and commentaries . . . of those Poets whose works are not of sufficient interest to be reproduced entire." [13] The three volumes of Dryden (1854) were among the first of the projected edition to appear.

Rather than rely entirely on the earlier biographies, Bell threw his energies into extensive research, and as a result he was able to present some extremely important new evidence about Dryden. By great good fortune Bell discovered that one of the representatives of the Dryden family had lately taken a keen interest in the illustrious poet whose name he bore. This man, Charles Beville Dryden, had brought to light a remarkable series of new facts. The earliest of his discoveries, in the chronological order of Dryden's life, was simply a curiosity, being the name "I DRYDEN" carved on "an old form" at Westminster School.[14] His next find was more important, the entry in the marriage register giving the particulars and the date of the Dryden-Howard marriage.[15] Thirdly, he turned up an Exchequer warrant, dated May 6, 1684, showing that the Laureate's annuity was at that time four years in arrears, and that an additional £100 had been granted, beginning in 1680.[16] In addition to these items, he also supplied Bell with an extensive note on Dryden's portraits.[17] At Canons Ashby Bell was also able to recover two new letters. The first was "in the possession of Sir Henry Dryden . . . presented to his father, the later Sir Henry Dryden, by Dr. Samuel Butler, Bishop of Lichfield and Coventry." [18] It is without date, but written to Walsh. The other belongs to the series addressed to Mrs. Steward and was written in October, 1699. It is a "bread and butter" note from Charles Dryden, to which the poet had appended his own acknowledgment.[19]

A further discovery rewarded Bell's searches among Sir Thomas

---

[13] Advertisement prefixed to Vol. I of Bell's edition of Dryden.
[14] Page 25.   [15] Page 24.   [16] Page 56.   [17] Pages 97–98.
[18] Page 68. This letter is Saintsbury's No. XLIX.   [19] Page 80.

Phillipps's extensive collection of manuscripts. Since Malone's death the Walsh letters had come on the market, and Phillipps had acquired five of them.[20] Being very intimate in tone, these letters are a doubly valuable addition, for they illumine a side of Dryden's personality not to be seen in the Tonson or the Steward correspondence.

But Bell did not accept his good fortune passively, for in each case he deliberated on the significance of the evidence before him. The carved name, if indeed cut by the poet, indicated to Bell that early in life Dryden employed the "y" in spelling his name. The marriage register not only supplies an important date but also, as Bell emphasized, it proves that the marriage received the approval of the bride's father, the Earl of Berkshire. The Exchequer warrant delighted Bell immensely, and he hailed it with this conclusion: "the existence of this warrant indisputably establishes the fact, that, in the last year of the reign of Charles II, before Dryden had embraced the Roman catholic religion, this additional annuity was conferred on him." [21] And in printing the Walsh letters Bell annotated them carefully, though indeed, they largely explained themselves.

These, then, were the biggest nuggets that rewarded Bell's explorations, but there were also many smaller ones. At Canons Ashby he accumulated a new series of family anecdotes, but concerning other members of the family rather than the poet, and some of them modern in origin. Several of them involved Honor Driden. On the basis of her letters (which, however, had nothing to do with the case) Bell built up a five-page account of an apocryphal romance between the young Dryden and his cousin, who "according to tradition . . . haughtily rejected the poet's suit." [22] One letter, actually by Honor's sister Anne, enabled Bell to raise an interesting conjecture. In the postscript Anne had written to her father: "My sister Frances and myselfe humbly begs of you to let Mr. Conseat come down this sumer." [23] To this clue Bell responded: "Who was Mr. Conceit? Could he have been her cousin, the young poet? The conjecture is in some measure supported by the omission of the name of her sister Honor, who may, probably, have desired his company in reality more than either of them, but, for

---

[20] Scott-Saintsbury, Letters L–LIV.   [21] Pages 56–57.

[22] Page 15. This incident so fascinated Bell that he followed Honor to the grave, quoting the entry about her in the burial register of St. Chad's, Shrewsbury.

[23] Page 20.

obvious womanly reasons, did not choose to join them in the request." [24] This point is as alluring as it is unsubstantial, but it indicates that Bell possessed an active imagination, a trait too rare among his predecessors.

Two minor circumstances also found their way into a Dryden biography for the first time. The author tells us:

I have examined the Secret Service Expenses of Charles II. and James II. from 1678 to 1688 [printed by the Camden Society] and although I find the names of Killigrew and others, especially the King's mistresses, the name of Dryden occurs only once, and then . . . for the payment of an old arrear of salary.[25]

The second item concerned James II's action in eliminating the butt of sack from Dryden's official remuneration.

This fact, which escaped all Dryden's biographers, is stated from Mr. Macaulay, who discovered the authority for it in the Treasury Letter Book.[26]

It is sad to record that Bell's success in the chase after new facts was not accompanied by equal care in dealing with some old ones. Thus he blindly plunged after Mitford in stating that Dryden "was made Master of Arts in 1657 by dispensation of the Archbishop of Canterbury." [27] Since Malone had cleared up the matter by printing the 1668 document in full, Bell should have remembered it or at least have looked it up. Dependence on Mitford exposed him to yet another blunder: "in 1696 he published a Life of Lucian." [28] Moreover there are occasional instances of careless proofreading, such as "Du Fresnoy's Latin poem on the *Art of Pleasing*." [29]

Nor was Bell always careful to avoid the quicksands of inference; many times he fell into difficulty where he thought himself on solid ground. Take, for instance, this sentence: "From the grand and solemn chambers of Sir Gilbert Pickering's mansion to the obscure lodging in the house of Herringman, a bookseller in the New Exchange, was the transition that marked the new phase of the poet's career." [30] Whether Dryden was directly employed by Pickering is an open question, but to plunge beyond that to the supposition that he lived in Pickering's "grand and solemn chambers" is quite another. Bell also let his imagination run in describing the character of Lady Elizabeth Dryden: "Dis-

[24] Page 19. [25] Page 38. [26] Page 59n. [27] Page 17,
[28] Page 78. [29] *Ibid*. [30] Page 22.

similarity of tastes and tempers early clouded their domestic life . . . wayward and discontented disposition . . . repulsed his friends . . ."[31] From this and other abuse the poor lady became a caricature of uxorial vices—and all without a single fact to base it on.

What then is our estimate of Bell's services to Dryden? His good fortune in gaining the assistance of Charles Beville Dryden and his access to the Phillipps manuscripts enabled him to make such extensive contributions that we may tend to award him more credit than the short memoir deserves. But although available space and his interest in this one poet were limited, yet Bell brought active imagination and sane judgment to the study of Dryden the poet, as well as positive services to Dryden scholarship.

Although it has not been the purpose of this examination of Dryden's biographies to give a detailed record of the history of Dryden's reputation, it is interesting to observe Bell's treatment of the vexed question of Dryden's conversion. The mid-nineteenth-century attitude had been expressed by Macaulay in his *History* (II [1849], 199), that Dryden "knew little and cared little about religion . . . Finding that if he continued to call himself a Protestant his services would be overlooked, he declared himself a Papist." But Bell had printed evidence to show that Dryden gained no financial favors for joining the Roman communion, and so Bell was in a position to make an entirely new survey of the conversion. This he did with acumen and care, his vindication of the poet leading to the very logical conclusion, "The doubt is whether Dryden's conversion *did* concur with interest."[32]

And similarly Bell felt that the poet's personality had not been adequately appreciated by the readers of Dryden's poetry or by the writers of his life:

Looking back upon the life of the poet, we cannot fail to be struck by the affectionate regard with which he inspired all his contemporaries who were intimate with him, or who had opportunities for ascertaining how he was estimated by his friends. Investigating anew the materials for his biography, with the assistance of additional information, I have seen occasion to revise some opinions on other points; but the farther I have pursued the enquiry into his private character, the more it appears entitled to respect and admiration. He was devotedly attached to his family, and kind, forbearing, and gentle in all his personal relations. His nature was so noble, that he readily forgave

---

[31] Page 85.　　　　　　　　[32] Page 87.

offences, and even injuries; and his friendships were so sincere and earnest that he frequently strained his own limited resources in performing acts of generosity.[33]

But Bell was a voice crying in the wilderness, as we shall see in dealing with the next memoir to be published.

THE GLOBE EDITION

William Dougal Christie had been a member of Trinity, Dryden's old college. A few years after going down, he embarked upon a diplomatic career and served an apprenticeship in such posts as "consul-general in the Mosquito territory" before achieving the dignity and title of minister-plenipotentiary to Brazil. But, unfortunately, in several negotiations the Brazilians failed to act as this strong-minded envoy thought they should. Diplomatic relations went from bad to worse and were finally broken off entirely, with the result that Christie was recalled and retired on a pension. As a side interest he had for some years made a special study of the life and career of the first Earl of Shaftesbury, and when he returned to England, work on the Shaftesbury papers became his chief occupation. Besides editing many of these documents, he produced a two-volume biography of Shaftesbury in 1871.

Meanwhile Christie was also editing Dryden, and his edition of the poems was published in the Globe series in 1870. The success of this venture is indicated by what one of his successors has written of him:

The first, and down to the present century, the only serious attempt to present a correct text was made by William Dougal Christie . . . Christie had zeal and industry, and was a man of undoubted ability. He was at the pains to consult and in some cases to collate the original editions.[34]

But as heretofore our concern is centered on the memoir of Dryden which Christie prefixed to the volume. Extending to approximately forty thousand words, this Life interests us primarily because it comes from the hand of a trained historian. Christie's thorough familiarity with Restoration history is evident on nearly every page of this short biography, as, for example, on the subject of the delayed presentation of the *Duke of Guise*. The contemporary situation is unfolded in a few words:

[33] Pages 86–87.
[34] John Sargeaunt, Introduction to *Poems of John Dryden,* Oxford Standard Authors (1935 ed.), pp. x–xi.

It may be understood that the King's love for Monmouth would naturally make him view with displeasure a parallel which might suggest Monmouth's assassination; and the representation of this play was in fact delayed for some months by the interposition of the Court. At last, after the King had given orders for Monmouth's arrest, it was permitted to be brought out on the stage.[35]

An awareness of chronological relationships also enlightened Christie's page when he discussed the *Spanish Friar,* which, as he was the first to point out, was performed before the publication of *Absalom and Achitophel.*[36]

But such historical knowledge was not the only result of Christie's long devotion to Shaftesbury. For years his energies had been centered on one task, the vindication of Shaftesbury from the judgment which history had passed upon him. This loyalty colored Christie's attitude to other figures of the period, and in particular it stained the pages of this memoir of Dryden. Almost two centuries after the events, the author of *Absalom and Achitophel* and *The Medal* was thus delivered into the hands of an apologist for his opponents. The delayed retribution took the form of a continuous disparagement of Dryden's personal character. Quarter truths were expressed in abusive terms, a trick of which this ex-diplomat was a past master. The cumulative effect of these aspersions is to lead the unwary reader to the conclusion that Dryden had the character of a chameleon and the appetites of a viper.

One of Christie's principal charges was based on a strong disapproval of Restoration morals, for which Dryden was made the scapegoat. The subject was introduced with the dogmatic statement, "Dryden was a libertine." [37] Furthermore, we are admonished, his writings display "a prurient love of the indecent, which is a blot on his character and tarnishes his fame." [38] This contention Christie reinforced by a specific accusation of what, according to mid-nineteenth-century standards, was a cardinal sin:

Bitter sneers of married life abound in Dryden's plays to prove his own conjugal unhappiness: they cannot, under the circumstances, excite respect for him, and the discreditable licentiousness of much of his writing suggests blame for himself in connexion with his domestic discomfort.[39]

---

[35] Page liv.   [36] Page xlv.   [37] Page xxiv.   [38] Page xxvi.

[39] Page xlvi. But not one line from Dryden is included in the five columns devoted to this subject under the heading "Marriage: its Pains" in Stevenson's *Book of Quotations* (1934).

This was written of a man whose name during thirty years' activity in the Restoration theater was coupled with that of only one actress and whose private letters abound with evidence of affectionate home life.

So too with the question of Dryden's progression toward the "right" in politics and religion. Christie was in the position of many another man with set opinions, and he failed to understand an intellectual. growth that involved progress toward an ultimate goal. As a result of this blindness he condemned Dryden's participation in the nation-wide joy at the Restoration in these words: "A sudden change like this from one extreme to another, attendant on triumph of the newly-espoused cause over that which the poet abandons, cannot be complacently re-garded." [40] Christie's measure is taken by comparing these abusive lines with Dr. Johnson's words on the same subject.

This quotation sets the tone for Christie's unfair comments on Dry-den's religious conversion. Since Bell had exploded the old charge that Dryden had joined the King's church to gain a pension, a new motiva-tion for Dryden's act was found in the feeble explanation that Dryden's pension, although granted several years before, was now "placed on a better footing." [41] Next Christie reminds us of Dryden's disrespect for the clergy,[42] passing over the fact that anticlericalism had always been a stock item in the equipment of every generation of satirists. Then Christie stated his thesis:

. . . it is hard to believe that in this great change . . . visions of greater worldly advantage did not influence Dryden.[43]

His conclusion was reached after more discussion:

. . . I cannot but think that the brilliant and laborious historian [Macaulay] has taken a substantially just view of Dryden's conversion, and that impartial admirers of Dryden's poetry must confess that there is more truth than exag-geration in Lord Macaulay's stinging sentences.[44]

The latter's vituperations were then repeated at length. To Christie "impartial" had a special meaning, and it seems that the more he in-vestigated Dryden's life the more it corroborated the prejudices with which he had begun.

Under these circumstances special interest attaches to Christie's pages on Dryden's relations with Shaftesbury. He found *Absalom and Achit-*

<hr />

[40] Page xxiii.   [41] Page lvii.   [42] Page lviii.
[43] *Ibid.*   [44] Page lix.

ophel "marred by a low moral tone" [45] and he interpreted it primarily as a personal attack on Shaftesbury, which, as such, was unwarranted. By putting the relationship on this personal basis Shaftesbury became a much-abused individual, and by the same device Christie deprived Dryden of any credit for having thrown his strength into a national crisis. Here Christie exposed his elementary weakness as a historian, the weakness of seeing his characters like actors isolated on a stage and actuated by narrow personal motives. He apparently was unable to understand that Dryden and Shaftesbury were creatures of a tempestuous age, whose crosscurrents exerted pulls and pressures that made intellectual and emotional balance impossible.

After this unpleasant interlude, let us look into the more attractive qualities of this memoir. Since Christie was a trained historian, we should expect to encounter an abundant harvest of new information. Of course many of the additions were incorporated from the specialized researches of scholars in other fields. For example, from John Payne Collier he picked up the fact that Dryden's name appeared among the partners for the rebuilding of the new theater in 1672.[46] Similarly he gathered three new items from Peter Cunningham's edition of Johnson's Life of Dryden (1854). These included details about the poet's pension,[47] and the *Letter from a Gentleman to the Right Honourable Edward Howard,* which Cunningham attributed to Flecknoe.[48] He also introduced all the specific information about Dryden that could be found in the pages of Evelyn and Pepys, as well as the printed correspondence of the latter.[49]

Christie's own researches were equally productive and enabled him to print many other new facts. The most important of these was derived from the *Calendar of State Papers, Domestic,* namely, the record of the £3,000 granted to Lady Elizabeth Dryden by the Crown in consideration of her father's services.[50] Another item of more-than-passing interest is Dryden's project for "an English Dictionary, on the plan of the French Dictionary of the Academy, in which he was to work with Lord Roscommon . . ."[51] Christie does not say whence he derived this information. Presumably it was from the manuscript life of Roscommon

[45] Page lii.
[46] Page xxix. The information had appeared in the Shakespeare Society *Papers,* IV, 147.
[47] Page xliii.   [48] Page li. The third is on p. liii.
[49] Page lxxxi.   [50] Page xxv.
[51] Page xlvi. For other information Christie incorporated for the first time see pp. 166–67.

written by Knightly Chetwood, which is among the Baker manuscripts in the University Library, Cambridge.

Here it is proper to speak of a second biography of Dryden written by Christie a year after that for the Globe edition. He was engaged to edit a volume of *Select Poems by Dryden* for the Clarendon Press, and prefaced the poems by a "Biographical Introduction" of fifty pages, boiled down from the longer one. Of course it contained most of the same material, characterized by the same prejudices, but in a more concentrated form.[52] To the second edition of these selections (1873) he added two important pieces of information bearing on Dryden's departure from Cambridge. The first concerns his successor in the scholarship:

> He ceased to be a scholar of Trinity in April 1655, before the natural expiry by time of his scholarship, on account of his having ceased to reside at Cambridge. This appears from the following entry in the college Conclusion Book of April 23, 1655, 'That scholars be elected into the places of Sr. Hooker, Sr. Sawies, Sr. Driden, Sr. Quincey, Sr. Burton; with this proviso, that if the said Bachelors shall return to the College at or before Midsummer next, to continue constantly according to statute, then the scholars chosen into their places respectively shall recede and give place to them, otherwise to stand as proper scholars.' It further appears that a young man named Wilford was elected into Dryden's place on the above-mentioned condition. The Senior Bursar's book shows that neither Dryden nor any of the others for whom as scholars successors were elected at the same time, re-entered into their scholarships. They all received the scholars' stipends up to Michaelmas 1655, and no further payment is credited to any of them.[52a]

Aldis Wright, then librarian of Trinity College, had communicated to him a letter containing the testimony of a college contemporary of Dryden's, one Crichton, incorporated in a letter written in 1727 by a certain Mr. Pain:

> The Doctor [Crichton] also mentioned something of Dryden the poet, which I tell you because you may have occasion to say something of him. Dryden, he said, was two years above him, and was reckoned a man of good parts and learning while in College: he had to his knowledge read over and very well understood all the Greek and Latin poets: he stayed to take his Bachelor's degree, but his head was too roving and active, or what else you'll call it, to confine himself to a college life, and so he left it and went to London into

---

[52] For example: "His sudden change at the Restoration from flattery of the Protectorate to adulation of the Stuarts cannot possibly be explained by honest conviction . . ." p. liii (quoted from the 3d edition, 1883).

[52a] *Ibid.*, pp. xv–xvi. Malone learned of this Conclusion Book sometime after the printing of his Life of Dryden. He made a note about it in his Additions and Emendations, p. 134 (see p. 138, below).

gayer company, and set up for a poet, which he was as well qualified for as any man.[53]

There is little else that needs to be said about Christie. Although the memoir is a workmanlike performance, it has no literary value as biography or even as a piece of writing. To Dryden the poet, Christie performed great service, both in being the first editor to attempt seriously to establish the text and also by his excellent explanatory notes, which are the fruit of much historical research. But Dryden the man fared less fortunately in his hands. Between his disapproval of Restoration morals and his personal fealty to the Earl of Shaftesbury, Christie was heavily biased against the poet whom he chose to edit. In fact Christie probably has done more harm to Dryden's reputation than any other biographer. Not only did he blacken Dryden's portrait but also the resulting calumny has been read by every generation since. This is due to the fact that his memoir appeared in standard editions much used in schools; the Globe edition has been reprinted fifteen times.

SAINTSBURY

In 1881 appeared the first life of Dryden that was published independently and not as an entry in a biographical dictionary or as a memoir prefixed to his works. It was, however, a grown-up cousin of the former, being one of the *English Men of Letters* series. The author was a rising young critic who the year before had published his first volume, a *Primer of French Literature*. George Saintsbury had already made a name for himself by his articles in the periodicals and his contributions to the *Encyclopedia Britannica*. In the spring of 1880 he had delivered a series of lectures on "Dryden and His Period" at the Royal Institution, which may have attracted the editor's eye to him as a promising candidate for this volume of the series.

At any rate Saintsbury was bursting with ideas, and he swept through the biographical catacombs like a fresh wind. The vitality that fills his pages can, I believe, be easily explained. Saintsbury, a young man of extensive reading, was more than a mere reader. He *thought* about what he read and revalued it from the beginning.[54] Just as Malone in anti-

---

[53] 1883 ed., p. xvi*n.*

[54] Saintsbury had been senior classical master of Elizabeth College, Guernsey, as well as Headmaster of the Elgin Institution, and it was reputed that his "knowledge of French literature is certainly unparalleled among English men of letters" (*Saturday Review,* LIV, 507).

quarian matters had "taken nothing upon trust," so Saintsbury approached criticism. Although this procedure had its weaknesses, yet it is the only method by which literature can be seen with fresh eyes. This little volume thus became the most invigorating addition to Dryden criticism since Dr. Johnson's "Preface."

Saintsbury brushed aside the cant appraisals of Dryden that had accumulated in the seventy years since Scott's time. He accepted none of the verdicts without a revaluation, and in many cases his critical estimates were very different from the conventional ones. Thus, after the abuse that had been heaped on the *State of Innocence* by the worshipers of Milton, it is almost startling to see "considerable merits" ascribed to it.[55] And similarly with *Œdipus,* of which Saintsbury said, "both the friends are to be seen almost at their best. On Dryden's part, the lyric incantation scenes are perhaps the most noticeable, and Lee mingles throughout his usual bombast with his usual splendid poetry." [56] The *Spanish Friar,* he said, is "possessed of a good deal of merit, from the technical point of view of the play-wright, but which I think has been somewhat over-rated, as far as literary excellence is concerned." [57] These pointed judgments are refreshing challenges to the stereotyped utterances of Mitford, Hooper, and others.

But Saintsbury's critical powers are more clearly demonstrated by the new ideas that he introduced, than by these revaluations. For example, from his knowledge of early literature he recognized that *The Hind and the Panther* was related to the "beast-fable." [58] Dr. Johnson lacked this knowledge of early literary conventions and passed the myopic comment, "A fable that exhibits two beasts talking Theology appears at once full of absurdity." [59] Following this up, Saintsbury challenged the myth that *The City Mouse and the Country Mouse* is a masterpiece of high wit. He found the "heavy joking" of the piece very dull and "in the highest degree unworthy of Prior." [60] These new opinions were due to the fact that Saintsbury judged Dryden's writings as literature which did, and still does, concern people other than the writer himself.

Especially refreshing are the new considerations Saintsbury devoted to subjects long neglected or forgotten. His evaluation of Dryden as a lyric poet is a case in point. The great odes had always been properly

[55] Page 55.   [56] Page 60.   [57] Page 61.   [58] Page 97.
[59] Johnson, Life of Dryden, par. 127.   [60] Page 98.

appreciated, but the songs, which Dryden sprinkled so liberally through the plays, had never been adequately examined. Saintsbury said of these songs,

They constitute Dryden's chief title to a high rank as a composer of strictly lyrical poetry; and there are indeed few things which better illustrate the range of his genius than these exquisite snatches. At first sight, it would not seem by any means likely that a poet whose greatest triumphs were won in the fields of satire and of argumentative verse should succeed in such things. Ordinary lyric, especially of the graver and more elaborate kind, might not surprise us from such a man. But the song-gift is something distinct from the faculty of ordinary lyrical composition; and there is certainly nothing which necessarily infers it in the pointed declamation and close-ranked argument with which the name of Dryden is oftenest associated But the later seventeenth century had a singular gift for such performance . . . But Dryden excelled them all in the variety of his cadences and the ring of his lines. Nowhere do we feel more keenly the misfortune of his licence of language, which prevents too many of these charming songs from being now quoted or sung. Their abundance may be illustrated by the fact that a single play, *The Mock Astrologer,* contains no less than four songs of the very first lyrical merit . . . Nor are the other plays less rich in similar work.[61]

Other examples of Saintsbury's keen criticism abound in his book. Some of the best pages deal with large subjects, such as the state of English prose before Dryden and the French background of the heroic drama and Dryden's experiments and practices in versification. These were matters to which Saintsbury had given much careful thought. He was later to enlarge our knowledge of them beyond anything that had yet been written, and here in his first book on English literature we find many of them in the germ. When the time comes for some literary historian to assess Saintsbury's writings, he will find that the seeds of many of Saintsbury's critical ideas first sprouted in this small volume.

Apart from purely literary matters, Saintsbury filled his book with a number of fresh ideas, sometimes perceptions of relationships, causal or otherwise, and often merely new points of view. I shall select a number of them at random.

Nothing can be a greater mistake than to say or to think that the *Rehearsal* killed heroic plays. It did nothing of the kind, Dryden himself going on writing them for some years until his own fancy made him cease, and others continuing still longer.[62]

---

[61] Pages 61–62.   [62] Page 52.

. . . the farce [the *Rehearsal*] was what would now be called an advertisement, and a very good one.[63]

What a blow to the Dick Minims! The cant about the *Rehearsal* had been repeated so often that apparently no one thought it worth while to re-examine the facts of the case.

Another strictly unorthodox view is found on the same page:

Indeed, it may be said of Dryden that he was at no time touchy about personal attacks. It was only when, as Shadwell subsequently did, the assailants became outrageous in their abuse and outstepped the bounds of fair literary warfare, or when, as in Blackmore's case, there was some singular ineptitude in the fashion of the attack, that he condescended to reply.[64]

To Christie this would have seemed rank heresy.

Many of the passages are the result of brilliant interpretations of situations and character. Such is the generalization to which Saintsbury was led by his analysis of the prose style of the *Defence of an Essay of Dramatic Poesy:*

Its sentences are sharper, shorter, more briskly and flippantly moulded than those of the Essay. Indeed, about this time, the time of his greatest prosperity, Dryden seems to have passed, somewhat late in life, through a period of flippancy. He was, for a few years, decidedly prosperous, and his familiarity with men of rank and position seems a little to have turned his head. It was at this time, and at this time only, that he spoke disrespectfully of his great predecessors, and insinuated, in a manner which I fear must be called snobbish, that his own familiarity with such models of taste and deportment as Rochester, put him in a very superior position for the drawing of character, to such humble and home-keeping folks as the old dramatists.[65]

And in another place he speaks out boldly against the tendencies in the literary criticism of the day:

I am aware that this style of minute criticism has gone out of fashion, and that the variations of the position of a pronoun have terribly little to do with "criticism of life"; but as I am dealing with a great English author whose main distinction is to have reformed the whole formal part of English prose and English poetry, I must, once for all, take leave to follow the only road open to me to show what he actually did.[66]

As we should expect, he is at his best when firing at exposed targets like Macaulay, Christie, and J. R. Green.

[63] *Ibid.*   [64] Pages 52–53.   [65] Page 127.   [66] Page 31.

It was obviously Lord Macaulay's game to blacken the greatest literary champion of the cause he had set himself to attack.[67]

[Christie] unfortunately seems to have sworn allegiance to Shaftesbury before he swore allegiance to Dryden. He reconciled these jarring fealties by sacrificing the character of the latter, while admitting his intellectual greatness.[68]

But Mr. Green's twice-published history has followed in the old direction, and has indeed out-Macaulayed Macaulay in reckless abuse.[69]

Apart from Dryden's participation in the broad tastes of his age, the main evidence against Dryden's morality was his "tart-eating" with Anne Reeves and the prenuptial history of Lady Elizabeth. These hoary tales seemed to Saintsbury inadequately established:

As to the Chesterfield letter, the evidence it contains can only satisfy minds previously made up. It testifies certainly to something like a flirtation, and suggests an interview, but there is nothing in it at all compromising.[70]

Perhaps there is no more curious instance of the infinitesimal foundation on which scandal builds than this matter of Dryden's immorality.[71]

Modern scholars are in general agreement with this statement, although they differ from him about the Reeves affair. The number and nature of contemporary references indicates that the liaison, although conventional according to contemporary standards, did actually occur.[72]

The subject of Dryden's conversion has always provided a proving ground for his biographers, as we have seen in our review of the whole procession from Birch onward. Saintsbury came through the test very favorably, both for himself and for Dryden. He topped off the arguments of Scott and others with a crushing analogy:

Is Dryden's critic nowadays prepared to question the sincerity of Cardinal Newman? If he is I have no objection to his questioning the sincerity of Dryden. But what is sauce for the nineteenth-century goose is surely sauce for the seventeenth-century gander. The post-conversion writings of the Cardinal are not less superficially inconsistent with the *Tracts for the Times* and the *Oxford Sermons*, than the *Hind and the Panther* is with *Religio Laici*.[73]

Yet his argument does not rest on this hyperbole, but goes deeper, to the roots of the matter in Dryden's character: "If I judge his character

[67] Page 186.   [68] *Ibid.*   [69] *Ibid.*   [70] Pages 24–25.   [71] Page 26.
[72] See George Thorn-Drury, *Covent Garden Drollery*, London (1928), p. 136.
[73] Page 102.

aright, no English man of letters was ever more thoroughly susceptible to the spirit and influence of his time." [74] And this being true, he asks us to consider also the circumstances of Dryden's intellectual development:

It is probable that, until he was far advanced in middle life, Dryden had paid but little attention to political and religious controversies, though he was well enough versed in their terms, and had a logical and almost scholastic mind. I have already endeavoured to show the unlikeliness of his ever having been a very fervent Roundhead, and I do not think that there is much more probability of his having been a very fervent Royalist. His literary work, his few friendships, and the tavern-coffeehouse life which took up so much of the time of the men of that day, probably occupied him sufficiently in the days of his earlier manhood. He was loyal enough, no doubt, not merely in lip-loyalty, and was perfectly ready to furnish an *Amboyna* or anything else that was wanted; but for the first eighteen years of Charles the Second's reign, the nation at large felt little interest, of the active kind, in political questions. Dryden almost always reflected the sympathies of the nation at large. The Popish Plot, however, and the dangerous excitement which the misgovernment of Charles on the one hand and the machinations of Shaftesbury on the other produced, found him at an age when serious subjects are at any rate by courtesy supposed to possess greater attractions than they exert in youth.[75]

Here Saintsbury had unearthed the basic truth of the whole situation. To talk of "wandering fires" and "false lights" helps us to understand the direction of Dryden's religious development, but not the time sequence involved. His pace was like that of the hare in the well-known race—indifferent at the beginning, but a sprint at the end. Failure to recognize this time factor has led to the otherwise insoluble problem that only six years separated the *Spanish Friar* and *The Hind and the Panther*.[76] But Saintsbury was the first to put his finger on the essential

[74] Page 103.   [75] Pages 72–73.

[76] The question of how much Dryden's "interest" was involved is well answered in Saintsbury's verdict: "I believe Dryden to have been, in the transactions of the years 1685–7, thoroughly sincere as far as conscious sincerity went, but of a certain amount of unconscious insincerity I am by no means disposed to acquit him" (pp. 102–3). Writers on this subject have rather unaccountably overlooked Dryden's use of *The Hind and the Panther* as an apologia for his action. He anticipated the charge that he had been "bought" by James in the following references to the absence of financial inducement from the King to converts:

> Judge not by hearsay, but observe at least,
> If since their change their loaves have been increased . . .
> For not to ask is not to be denied.
> For what they have, their God and king they bless,
> And hope they should not murmur, had they less.
>   Part 3, ll. 1517–18 and 1536–38.

truth of the whole matter, that Dryden was shocked by the turmoil of 1678–80 into a serious consideration of his religious foundations. His immediate reaction, as the "Protestant play" shows, was strictly "No Popery."

His next step, it is important to observe, was to repeat exactly the method that he had followed fifteen years before, in the *Essay of Dramatic Poesy*. At that time he took pen and paper and carefully examined the controversy that touched him most, namely, which of the three kinds of drama—Elizabethan, classical, or French—he preferred to follow. Now he repeated the process with the three kinds of religion—the Roman, English, and dissenting churches. As in the case of the drama, he now attempted to think the matter out and make clear in his own mind what was the best course for him to follow. *Religio laici* was thus his "Essay of what I can believe."

This self-questioning was succeeded by the third stage of his religious experience. Having begun to seek an answer to this problem, Dryden progressed rapidly along what Professor Bredvold has shown to be a conventional pattern, and from Pyrrhonism took the path to Rome. Saintsbury, although he did not develop the sequence, deserves all credit for perceiving two points. The first step in this progression, he saw, was that Dryden had never before seriously considered his relationship with his God. Secondly, that once he had begun his pilgrimage, the distance was soon covered.

After praising Saintsbury as a critic, a word must be said about his deficiencies as searcher after new materials. Saintsbury was quite content to depend on the books of his predecessors, and it is doubtful how many of the documents or original sources he had actually seen. Even Dr. Johnson, aged and weary, made more of an effort to uncover new biographical materials than this young man with his career still to be made. There is no evidence that Saintsbury made a single move out of his library to search for unknown documents or even to check the known.[77]

There are indeed three items of new information in this book, but

[77] Like many scholars, Saintsbury was an enthusiastic walker, and appears to have made many excursions to Northamptonshire. Accordingly the "setting" for Dryden's boyhood is elaborately constructed, with many examples of sights and scenes that he may have known, such as "the grim and shapeless mound . . . which is all that remains of the castle of Fotheringhay . . . Dryden must have passed it constantly . . . he must have had it almost under his eyes . . . ." (pp. 5–6).

each of them was communicated by a friend. Edmund Gosse called his attention to a rare play in his collection entitled *The Mall, or the Modish Lovers*. It resembles in some particulars the *Ladies a la Mode* that Pepys had spoken of as Dryden's in 1668. This play, a very mediocre piece, was printed in 1674, but the Preface is signed "J. D." [78] J. Churton Collins pointed out a house in Fetter Lane which had anciently borne a slab stating that Dryden once lived there.[79] Saintsbury could find no supporting evidence that Dryden had ever dwelt in the house. And in the third instance W. Noel Sainsbury of the Record Office reported the discovery of a preliminary warrant, dated April 13, 1670, instructing the "Attorney or Solicitor Generall" to prepare a bill for the appointment of Dryden as Poet Laureate and Historiographer Royal.[80] The warrant itself had been discovered by Malone, and is dated August 18, of that year.

From this discussion the conclusion is obvious, that Saintsbury was not only the inheritor but also the pupil of Sir Walter Scott. His whole attitude toward Dryden and biography was the same as Scott's. Like Scott he took the facts where he found them, but fashioned them into a structure of strength and beauty. Both of them brought wide reading and vigorous intellects to the task; and to both of them the search for new facts was of less importance than the establishment of the true significance of the old ones.

The parallel between the two extends even to their announced objectives in surveying Dryden's works. Scott, it will be remembered, had set out "to estimate how far the age was indebted to the poet, and how far the poet was influenced by the taste and manners of the age." [81] When we discussed Scott's achievement we found that the first half of this aim was unattained. Saintsbury recognized, consciously or otherwise, that this important objective had still to be achieved and directed his study of Dryden's place in literature with this purpose in mind. Accordingly he announced early in the book:

It must be the task of the following chapters to show how and to what extent he effected a reform; what the nature of that reform was; what was the value of the work which in effecting it he contributed to the literature of his country.[82]

---

[78] Page 58. [79] Pages 66–67n. See pp. 210–11 for an examination of this subject.
[80] Page 67n. [81] Scott, *Life of Dryden*, p. 4. [82] Page 22.

How did Saintsbury follow out this program? In his conclusion he summed the matter up in a masterly fashion:

> . . . I can think of [no other] Englishman who, for a considerable period, was so far in advance of his contemporaries in almost every branch of literary work as Dryden was during the last twenty years of the seventeenth century . . . Not only did the immense majority of men of letters in his later days directly imitate him, but both then and earlier most literary Englishmen, even when they did not imitate him, worked on the same lines and pursued the same objects. The eighteen volumes of his works contain a faithful representation of the whole literary movement in England for the best part of half a century, and what is more, they contain the germs and indicate the direction of almost the whole literary movement for nearly a century more.[83]

I doubt if this statement of Dryden's place in literary history could be much improved upon. But it does require detailed treatment, which is what Saintsbury promised us. Yet, except for certain passages on Dryden's leadership in re-introducing blank verse to the stage [84] and another on teaching his opponents to write satire,[85] the book can be searched in vain for such details. And so once again we are offered generalities about literary influences instead of the demonstration we were led to expect. Excuses can be made for Saintsbury, particularly the space limits of the volume; but then why did he make promises? The volume which will examine Dryden's influence on the literature of his day and afterward has yet to be written.

Scott also taught his pupil how to respect Dryden the man. In this case Saintsbury did examine the evidence, and he sifted it very carefully. His conclusion is the best summary of Dryden's virtues written since Congreve's "character":

> I believe that I have put the facts at least so that any reader who takes the trouble may judge for himself of the private conduct of Dryden. His behaviour as a public man has also been dealt with pretty fully; and I think we may safely conclude that in neither case can the verdict be a really unfavourable one. Dryden, no doubt, was not austerely virtuous. He was not one of the men who lay down a comprehensive scheme of moral, political, and intellectual conduct, and follow out that scheme, come wind, come weather. It is probable that he was quite aware of the existence and alive to the merits of cakes and ale. He was not an economical man, and he had

---

[83] Pages 184–85.   [84] Pages 58 and 118.

[85] Page 83. Dryden had made the same point in the *Epistle to the Whigs* prefixed to the *Medal*: ". . . let your verses run upon my feet . . . turn my own lines upon me . . ."

no scruple in filling up gaps in his income with pensions and presents. But all these things were the way of his world, and he was not excessive in following it . . . On the whole, putting aside his licence of language, which is absolutely inexcusable, but for which it must be remembered he not only made an ample apology, but such amends as were possible by earnestly dissuading others from following his example, we shall be safe in saying that, though he was assuredly no saint, there were not so very many better men then living than John Dryden.[86]

Saintsbury's name is linked with Scott's for another reason. This short biography showed the publishers of Scott's *Dryden* that here was the man they were seeking to revise and re-edit that great work. Accordingly the first volume of "Scott-Saintsbury" was published in 1882, and other volumes followed at intervals until 1893. Much could be said about the deficiencies, textual and otherwise, of these volumes, but it remains to-day the only complete edition of the poems, plays, and prose. In this edition Scott's *Life of Dryden* was barely altered by Saintsbury, except to introduce whatever information had come to light in the intervening sixty years. He also supplemented a number of Scott's critical judgments by printing in footnotes his own opinions. Saintsbury's notes to the biographical sections contain little that is not found in his "English Men of Letters" life of the poet.

A word should be said about Saintsbury's style in this early book, for nothing could damn his later writing more than a comparison of the early and the late. Here is both neatness and charm, a definite contrast to the careless and "sticky" style of many of his later pages. The book is not free from idiosyncrasies, such as too heavy a sprinkling of foreign phrases and occasional gargantuan paragraphs; but they are the exception rather than the rule. Many attractive qualities abound all through it. A coruscating humor winks out from between the lines of type as Saintsbury discusses the topic before him. By introducing modern parallels he escapes the somber pall that too often chills historical writing, literary or otherwise. Take the following for example:

It should be observed, however, that a most unsubstantial romance has been built up on this letter [from Dryden to his cousin Honor] and that Miss Honor's father, Sir John Driden, has had all sorts of anathemas launched at him, in the Locksley Hall style, for damming the course of true love.[87]

---

[86] Pages 186–87.   [87] Page 9.

Perhaps the word that best describes Saintsbury's style is "jaunty." There is no question that his Life of Dryden is the most interesting of the many that have been written, and undoubtedly the chief factor in attaining this success has been its rollicking readability.

Of the keen perceptions which sparkle in Saintsbury's pages, one of the most interesting concerns Dryden's accomplishments before 1680: "Had he died in this year (and he had already reached an age at which many men's work is done) he would not at the present time rank very high even among the second class of English poets." [88] In reading this we may reflect that if Dryden had in fact died in 1680 his biography would not have been much less neglected than it was in spite of the great satires and translations. "Glorious John" had to wait exactly two hundred years after 1680 for a biography that stood within its own covers and was not prefixed to an edition of his works. The above quotation also illustrates the great virtue which characterized this independent biography when it did appear. Saintsbury, as we have seen, had the kind of mind which seized on significances. In general he did not inquire where biographical materials came from, but took them as he found them. But he did question the *significance* those facts had, and like his master, Scott, he excelled in the interpretation of Dryden's life and character in the steady light of common sense.

We are also frequently reminded of the man from whom Scott had learned so much, Dr. Johnson. Like Johnson, Saintsbury was a born critic, and the fact is apparent on every page of this book.[89] He was content to think and compare rather than to search for new materials. Although he seems to have enjoyed championing the character of Dryden and his ladies, yet we can see that his heart was with the literature of Dryden rather than with his life. After giving diligent attention for many pages to biographical incidents, when they were finished he plunged back into criticism with obvious relief. As a biographer, then, Saintsbury brought little that was new either in material or in form. But as a critic and interpreter of what Dryden did and wrote, Saintsbury has given us the most balanced, the most readable, and the most stimulating biography of the great poet that has appeared to this day.

[88] Page 71.
[89] On page 124, in a passage that has an autobiographical ring, Saintsbury describes St. Evremond as a "born critic."

LATER BIOGRAPHICAL STUDIES

In the fifty odd years since Saintsbury's volume in the "English Men of Letters" series, what have been the main events in the history of Dryden's biography? They are four in number, of which the first in time and importance is the entry in the *Dictionary of National Biography*. The· account of Dryden appeared in Volume XVI, in October, 1888, and bears the signature of the editor, Leslie Stephen. Extending to about ten thousand words, this biography possesses all the qualities that we expect from his distinguished and active pen. Every fact of importance is found in its proper position, accompanied by a reference either to the place where it first appeared in print or else to its most available location. Stephen had the ability to handle great quantities of material, and in the case of Dryden he showed a masterly grip of the whole subject.

Two qualities that distinguish all Stephen's work are present among the virtues of the Dryden article. These are the excellent sense of proportion with which the individual incidents are treated and the smooth, powerful flow of Stephen's narrative as a whole. The sense of proportion is shown to advantage in the treatment of such incidents as the letter to Honor Dryden, or Dryden's change of allegiance at the Restoration: "It proves only that Dryden was quite willing to do poetical homage to the power which seemed to be permanently established. The order which followed the Restoration was no doubt more congenial." [90] Of course there are many passages where Stephen was led astray by the earlier biographers, but the wonder is that he was able to make such a large number of improved interpretations, considering that the account of Dryden was only one of the many pieces of work on Stephen's crowded desk.

From his other biographical experience Stephen brought a number of new materials to the study of Dryden. For example, Alexandre Beljame's *Le Public et les hommes de lettres en Angleterre (1660–1744)* (Paris, 1881) contained much on Dryden, and he also found new information in Gillow's *English Catholics*.[91] This life of Dryden is an excellent example of the *Dictionary of National Biography* at its best.

The past fifty years have produced a continuous procession of prefa-

[90] 1908 reissue, VI, 65.
[91] Joseph Gillow, *A Literary and Biographical History or Bibliographical Dictionary of the English Catholics*, 3 vols., London, 1885–87.

tory memoirs, but very few of them require attention here. J. Churton Collins prefixed one to his edition of Dryden's *Satires* in 1893, which was largely derived from his sketch in the *Quarterly Review* for 1878. Another, prefixed to Professor Noyes's edition of Dryden's poetry (New York, 1909) deserves mention as typical of the workmanlike qualities to be found in these limited biographies. The most extensive of these prefatory lives is found in the elaborately printed Nonesuch Press edition of Dryden's *Dramatic Works,* 1931, edited by Montague Summers. The biographical introduction is an ill-digested and often inaccurate arrangement made from the editor's notes. Most of the material has been lifted from scattered sources, without acknowledgment, and the pages abound in statements for which proof is lacking. These prefatory sketches often contain original points of view and revaluation in points of emphasis, but they cannot be considered of importance in the history of Dryden biography.

The only independent biography of Dryden since Saintsbury's is the short volume issued in 1933 by Christopher Hollis. Unfortunately it is a product of the modern "biography mill" at its highest gear. Professor Bredvold has said the last word on this "comedy of errors":

The book is an hilarious performance . . .[92]
Its abundance of errors in even the most elementary matters can only be explained as due to a fertile combination of haste and ignorance.[93]

But although the years since Saintsbury's *Dryden* have been thin in the production of lives of the poet, yet they have been abundant in specialized studies. Professor Ker's edition of Dryden's *Essays* is pregnant with information for the Dryden student. And Professor Noyes's notes contain innumerable points of importance, as do his introductions to the individual poems. Mark Van Doren's study of Dryden's poetry will not be superseded for very many years. Special investigations such as Broadus's on Dryden as laureate,[94] Bredvold's on Dryden's *Intellectual Milieu,*[95] and Macdonald's on the "Attacks on Dryden" and his *Bibliography* [96] have contributed much to our knowledge of Dryden. And of course there have been innumerable shorter reports in the learned

[92] *Philological Quarterly,* XIII (Part 2, April, 1934), 118.
[93] *Ibid.,* p. 117.   [94] E. K. Broadus, *The Laureateship,* Oxford, 1921.
[95] Louis I. Bredvold, *The Intellectual Milieu of John Dryden,* Ann Arbor, 1934.
[96] "The Attacks on Dryden" in *Essays and Studies of the English Association,* Vol. XXI (1935); *John Dryden, a Bibliography,* Oxford, 1939.

journals, of which Thorn-Drury's *Notes on Dryden* [97] is perhaps the best example. All these studies are leading up to a comprehensive work that will cull from each specialized investigation whatever is important for a "definitive" biography. When a Masson or a Chambers does take up the task, he will be indebted to many of the "moderns" as well as to the "ancients."

[97] *Review of English Studies,* I (1925), 79, 187, 324.

VII
POSTSCRIPT:
ANOTHER QUARTER CENTURY

SINCE the first edition of this book, another quarter century has elapsed. These years have produced a veritable outburst of Dryden scholarship, books and articles that are interpretative, bibliographical, and biographical. As would be expected, the largest number are primarily concerned with literary and critical matters. This division is quite proper, for the products of Dryden's pen should always command the center of attention. Moreover, disappointingly little new biographical evidence has come to the surface, to the credit of Dryden scholars who worked the field in earlier generations. Because so little is known about Dryden's personal life, every shred of new evidence is to be valued the more.

The focus of this book is limited to biographical facts and problems, so no attempt will be made here to list or examine the many critical and interpretative essays, articles, and books that have led readers to a better understanding of Dryden's varied writings. The annual bibliography of *English Literature 1660-1800* published in *Philological Quarterly* [1] records these items, many accompanied by learned comments and criticisms. In 1950 Professor Samuel H. Monk produced a booklet titled *John Dryden, A List of Critical Studies Published from 1895 to 1948* which arranged in categories 768 items, [2] a volume highly useful to Dryden students. It may be hoped that new editions will appear from decade to decade, incorporating additions as they appear. [3]

The publication in 1939 of Hugh Macdonald's *Bibliography* was, of course, the most important event in Dryden studies of that decade. Because *Dryden Facts and Problems* was written before Macdonald's

---

[1] Those for the years 1926–60 have been published in book form by the Princeton University Press.

[2] The following year Professor W. R. Keast added about 125 others in *Modern Philology* XLVIII, 205–10.

[3] Besides the asterisks employed to designate noteworthy items, it would be helpful to have another symbol (perhaps a dagger †) to indicate those of minimum importance.

volume appeared there was no opportunity to include an analysis of it in the 1940 edition of this book. Although the merits and weaknesses of Macdonald's work are widely recognized, a brief summary of them is in order here.

The *Bibliography's* greatest value, obviously, is its usefulness as a reference book. Macdonald gathered information about Dryden and his writings from myriad sources, successfully synthesized it, and provided a full index to make it available. In doing so he stood on the shoulders of two forerunners, the learned bookseller, Percy J. Dobell, and the omnivorous collector of Restoration literary lore, George Thorn-Drury. Dobell spent the spare time of a long life gathering information about Dryden and his books. His catalogue of *The Literature of the Restoration . . . with particular Reference to the Writings of John Dryden,* published in 1918, was a valuable pioneer work, and still should not be neglected by any serious scholar. It contained 1,268 entries, among them 68 Dryden items with brief bibliographical descriptions, plus many informative annotations. In addition Dobell offered five documents bearing Tonson's accounts for Dryden's *Virgil,* and twenty engravings of Dryden portraits. During these early years and for two decades to follow Dobell continued to build up his own Dryden collection, the private catalogue of which covered forty-two typewritten pages. This collection ultimately came to America, the choicer section to the Folger Shakespeare Library and the remainder to Claremont College in California. Their sale occurred after Macdonald had had full use of them; indeed, many of the categories of Dobell's typescript catalogue were taken over by Macdonald.

Because his business as a bookseller did not permit Dobell to compile the full-scale bibliography that Dryden deserved, he persuaded George Thorn-Drury to carry on with his materials. Thorn-Drury, who combined a legal career with an avocation for Restoration studies, compiled a notebook of memoranda about Dryden's publications as the basis for the bibliography which he did not live to finish. After his death Mr. Dobell retrieved it, along with Thorn-Drury's other collections including notes of Luttrell's title-page annotations, and turned them over for Macdonald's use. Thus, the volume which emerged represented the cumulative work of three men, a harvest for which Restoration students were immediately grateful.

The weakest part of Macdonald's book is the technical bibliographical work which is untrustworthy in method, in transcription, and in the form and extent of the explanatory notes. Elsewhere I have discussed these shortcomings in some detail.[4] Suffice it to say that a check of Macdonald's descriptions against copies of books in American libraries revealed he had missed many canceled or inserted leaves. To cite one example, Northleigh's *Triumph of Monarchy*, 1685 (Macdonald 211, ii), examination of the Yale copy revealed twenty canceled leaves, and two more occur in the Harvard copy. The Bodleian copy (cited by Macdonald) has the same twenty cancels found in the Yale copy, but they were passed over unnoticed by Macdonald.

The present consideration is how much new information about Dryden Macdonald's volume offers. This, of course, was not his main purpose, which was to describe the poet's publications in various early editions. Yet nearly half of the volume is given over to Drydeniana, which Macdonald justified on the ground, "they give scraps of information about him or stray references to him or to his writings." The result is that Macdonald offered a Dryden allusion book, a useful compendium of contemporary references to him. But there is no single new piece of biographical information of significant importance.

The weakness of Macdonald's allusion-book approach is that he seemed to have an obsession to gather the attacks on Dryden, to repeat any satirical or dishonorable references to him, no matter how false or unimportant. In contrast, he often neglected passages that praise Dryden; for example on page 236 Macdonald printed a dozen lines from Otway's *The Poet's Complaint*, a poem containing some minor abuse, but omitted a portion that says Dryden's writing will in time come to rank with Jonson's and Shakespeare's. Similarly, he completely ignored Francis Atterbury's Preface to *The Second Part of Mr. Waller's Poems* (1690), which praises Dryden as "the living glory of our *English* poetry," especially for his blank verse.[5] Other examples could be cited, but these should suffice.

Every bibliography of such an important subject deserves to reach a second edition, and this is especially true of Macdonald's *Dryden*. Whoever undertakes the task must use modern techniques of bibliographical analysis to supplement the information here brought together. But whether or not a new edition of Macdonald's book is ever undertaken,

---

[4] *Modern Philology*, XXXIX, nos. 1, 2, and 3; see especially pp. 313–19.
[5] See Thorn-Drury's edition of Waller's *Poems*, 1893, p. xxvii.

the present one has been a boon to seventeenth-century scholarship in general, and a welcome stimulant to the revival of Dryden studies.

The next important volume in this survey is Charles E. Ward's edition of *The Letters of John Dryden with Letters Addressed to Him*, issued by the Duke University Press in 1942. Here Ward made the first attempt since Malone in 1800 to bring together all of Dryden's surviving correspondence with carefully transcribed texts and scholarly explanatory notes. The volume immediately became one of the essential books for Dryden students.

Malone had printed forty-five of Dryden's letters, plus two letters addressed to Dryden in his notes, omitting them from his numbered series. As we have seen, Scott reprinted these, and added one more that an acquaintance sent him. Saintsbury reprinted Scott's text, plus the six Dryden letters that Bell had given in his edition of the *Poems* (1854), and a seventh that had been published in the *Illustrated London News* in 1858. Neither Scott or Saintsbury felt called upon to compare their texts with the original documents.

Ward was able to print sixty-two letters of the poet himself, and fifteen letters to him. All of the new ones had been printed in scattered media. The thoroughness of Ward's searches is shown by the fact that no new Dryden letters have come to light in more than twenty years since he published, though two of the originals that he did not see have passed through the sale room. Ward's number 3, the 1666 letter to Sir Robert Long, formerly in the Alfred Morrison Collection, is now in the library of Robert Taylor of Princeton. And his number 17, Dryden's detailed criticism of Walsh's *Essay on Woman,* published by Bell, has found a home in the Osborn Collection at Yale. Of the forty-nine original letters in Dryden's hand known to be preserved, thirty-six are now in American collections. As far as Ward could determine, all fifteen letters addressed to Dryden survive in contemporary copies only.

Because the early decades of Dryden's career yield so few specimens, probably the most important new letter is that of July, 1677, to Edward Osborne, Lord Latimer, son of Lord Danby, which Ward turned up in the Historical Society of Pennsylvania. Although Dryden's purpose seems to have been to get the young man (then twenty-two) to jog his father, the Lord High Treasurer, to pay the delinquent £100 on Dryden's salary, the letter is unusually full of literary and biographical information, including references to *Limberham* and *All for Love.*

Yet, as heretofore, the bulk of the surviving letters are in three series beginning in 1684, when the poet was fifty-three. These three series are between Dryden and his publisher, Jacob Tonson (sixteen letters, plus one from Tonson), William Walsh (nine letters, plus two from Walsh), and his young cousin, Mrs. Elmes Steward of Cotterstock, Northamptonshire (sixteen letters, plus one to her sportsman husband). The most notable additions among these are to the Walsh correspondence. Ward printed the full text of the letters quoted in part in the chapter on "Dryden and William Walsh," pp. 226–33 below. As noted there, Professor Ward and I found that we had turned up these letters independently, and agreed that I should write the account of the Dryden-Walsh friendship, and he would print the full text of the letters.

Another significant new letter, Ward's number 6, is that addressed to Dorset written in 1677 (see p. 280 below). This letter was first known from a facsimile in the Catalogue of the *R. B. Adam Johnsonian Library* (1929, III, 87 verso). Along with other rarities from the Adam Library it is now in the collection of Mr. and Mrs. Donald Hyde, Somerville, New Jersey. In it Dryden reports his response to Rymer's *Tragedies of the Last Age,* a copy of which the author had sent him, a book which Dryden considered "the best piece of Criticism in the English tongue; perhaps in any other of the modern."

Of the new letters addressed to Dryden, perhaps the most interesting is number 21, from Walsh, dating from the early autumn of 1691 (pp. 231–32 below). Walsh's remarks on his reading of French and Italian followers of Cicero and other ancient prose stylists are highly revealing of the literary climate of the day.

Ward's transcriptions of the manuscript texts show commendable accuracy. A few minor slips could be cited, but in the wise words of the great Dryden scholar, George R. Noyes, "Each copiest of a manuscript is allowed a certain quota of errors." If a new edition is ever called for (unlikely until additional Dryden letters appear) the editor may wish to compare the texts of the Tonson letters, now based on Malone's revisions for a projected second edition, with the actual transcripts in Malone's hand from the manuscripts then owned by William Baker, M.P. for Hertford (p. 49 above). These transcripts are now in the C. B. Tinker Collection at Yale.

Ward's annotations throw much new light on various matters. He has been able to date a number of letters for the first time, most of them convincingly (e.g., numbers 1, 22, 24, 25, 26, 33, 35 [Malone's date bettered], 36, 40). In the case of letter 1, the flattering but conventional epistle to the poet's cousin, Honor Dryden, Ward disagreed with Malone's conclusion made after studying the date with what he termed "a microscope" that the figures read "1655," and argues that the events better fit 1653. The editors of the California *Works*, who reprint the letter (now in the Clarke Library) in facsimile, have used an ultraviolet light on the manuscript. While they report the faded number could be either a "3" or a "5," they follow Ward's reasoning. Despite this, it is possible that a century and a half ago the ink was still clear enough for Malone to be right, as he was about most factual matters. That Dryden wrote from Cambridge is no proof that he was still pursuing a degree there; he may have come over to visit friends at his old college. Similarly in letter 25 which Ward dated August 17, 1693, because the fleet had anchored in Torbay the day previously, I question whether it may not have been several days later. Torbay is about 200 miles from London, and it would take longer than one day for the news to reach the city and attain circulation.

One of the most valuable functions of this edition is the light the editor is able to throw on a number of names and references in the letters. For example, Ward identified, among other obscure people, Sir Matthew Dudley (letter 26), his brother (letter 27), and William Plowdin (letter 34). He gave contemporary references which Malone and other scholars have missed, such as the manuscript satire (pp. 158–59) which suggests that Dryden frequently held the pen in Walsh's *Dialogue concerning Women* (1691). This satire also calls Dryden "Mr Eat-finger," apparently a charge that he chewed his nails, a habit unmentioned by the swarm of other lampoonists. Also, Ward quoted from a letter by Cardinal Howard, a relative of Lady Elizabeth Dryden's, dated from Rome June 30, 1693, giving information about the poet's sons Charles and John, then in the Holy City (pp. 164–65).

Occasionally there are cases where the reader wishes for more annotation, or even a frank editorial aside, "I can't explain this." For example, in letter 11 Dryden wrote Tonson about the *History of the League* (1684), ". . . I hope the onely thing I feard in it, is not found out." Again in letter 45, to Chesterfield in 1697 where Dryden said, "I will not think, that, like Sylla, you rewarded a bad Poet and at the same time commanded him to write no more . . ."—the notes say, "Probably a reference to L. Cornelius Sulla, the dictator," but do not explain Dryden's allusion. Fortunately, such instances are rare.

In a few cases one may question or disagree with the explanatory notes. For example, in commenting upon letter 47 Ward said of the poet's son, Erasmus-Henry, who studied for the priesthood in Rome, "there is no definite evidence that he ever took orders." But Gillow's *Dictionary of English Catholics,* though often careless in slight matters, is so specific about his ordination in 1694 and subsequent career in the church that the statements should be strongly weighed and the Catholic records sought out, if they still exist. (See p. 288 below.) A few pages later on, in the notes on letter 53, Ward speaks of Sir Gilbert Pickering as Dryden's uncle. Actually, Sir Gilbert was a cousin-german, as Malone had noted in his "Additions" (p. 138 below). As an unimportant detail, it might be noted that two passages in letter 28 from Dryden to Walsh, December 12, 1690, were printed in William Seward's *Anecdotes of Some Distinguished Persons,* 1795, II, 102–5, a volume that somehow escaped the attention of Malone and Robert Bell who first gave the whole letter sixty years later.

Ward's volume also reproduced for the first time the portrait of Dryden that had come down through the collateral branch of the family to Major Percy Dryden Mundy, the family antiquary who contributed much genealogical information about Dryden to the scholarship on the subject. Now in the Osborn Collection, the portrait is reproduced again in this volume (see Frontispiece). Further details on its provenance will be found in the description of the illustrations.

Ward published only Dryden's personal letters, not the public ones such as the epistles and dedications to his works. Although this distinction has been questioned, the decision seems justified. The number of personal letters that survive seem meager until we compare them with those of other literary men of the age. Even such a prolific writer as Milton did not leave enough letters to make a collected volume possible. The age of letter writing as a literary form was yet to dawn. We can be grateful for every one of Dryden's letters that has come down to us for the information about his life and personality that it reveals, however barren some of the business letters may seem. In particular, the series to Tonson, even though largely on practical affairs, are invaluable records of Dryden's professional career. The letters to and from Walsh show Dryden's sweet willingness to encourage a literary aspirant, written in generous anticipation of the young man's achievements. Perhaps the most human side of Dryden is seen in his letters to his kinswoman, Mrs. Steward, about forty years younger than the poet (see pp. 224-25 below). Ward's edition of the *Letters* is a definitive volume in Dryden studies, in which he has performed a valued service to all students of the poet, especially those concerned with problems in Dryden's biography.

Brief mention should be made of two biographical accounts of Dryden in editions of his poetry which appeared after World War II. The first came from the pen of the distinguished French scholar of English Literature of the Restoration, Pierre Legouis, professor at the Université de Lyon. His *Dryden: Poèmes choisis* was issued late in 1946 in the Aubier "Littérature Anglaise" series, though a product of the occupation years, as testified by the Introduction which is dated two years earlier, and the brave statement, "Nous regrettons de n'avoir pu consulter l'édition Noyes (Cambridge, Mass.) 1909" (page 42). The latest scholarship available to the author was "un important article de E. S. de Beer dans la *Review of English Studies* (juillet 1941)," on *Absalom and Achitophel* ("Notes," p. 441).

Following the pattern of the series, Legouis gives sixteen of Dryden's best and most famous poems in parallel texts, his unrhymed translations appearing opposite Dryden's English lines. In a fifty-seven-page biographical and critical introduction Legouis does not, understandably, offer any new biographical information, such as he had produced in his earlier researches on Marvell when he had been free to work among documentary repositories in England. Nevertheless, a reading of Legouis's introduction will repay the serious Dryden student because of the Continental perspective he offers on Dryden's career in Restoration England, whether discussing a phenomenon such as the Popish Plot or "le châtiment dans la fameuse bâtonnade de la ruelle de la Rose en 1679." His sensitive translations of Dryden's poems also repay attention for his careful interpretations, though somewhat limited denotatively, as most verse translation must be.

A more important book, for obvious reasons, was the new edition in 1950 of George R. Noyes's one volume, *The Poetical Works of Dryden,* "Revised and Enlarged." Noyes was one of the outstanding philologists of modern times, who after taking his doctorate in English Literature at Harvard and producing the monumental edition (1909) of

Dryden's poems, shifted to Slavonic studies and ended his days as professor of that discipline at the Berkeley campus of the University of California. But during four decades after the original edition he cumulated the benefits of later Dryden scholarship, which resulted in the enlarged edition of the *Poetical Works* forty-one years later.

Of this new edition the only complaint that can be lodged is against the publisher. Motivated by the desire to offer almost 1,200 pages (containing more than 800,000 words) for a price that students could afford, the publisher reused the old plates from the 1909 edition for both the text and the notes. Few changes were necessary in the text, but many of the explanatory notes had been superseded by later scholarship. Noyes was allowed twenty-six pages of "Additional Notes" at the end, but in the same minion type, so small that most eyes require a glass to read it. Such a reading is highly worth while, for these pages incorporate the results of forty years of Dryden scholarship, as Noyes's scrupulous acknowledgments of his sources show, with frequent citations of the writings of Ham, Ward, Macdonald, Cyrus Day, and others, including even an unpublished dissertation.

The most notable accretion to the text consists of six "Additional Poems" (pp. 903–10): the "Epilogue to the *Rival Ladies*" (following Ham), the "Epilogue Spoken to the King in Oxford, 19 March 1681" (following Hiscock), the "Prologue and Epilogue to *Mithradates*" (following Wise), the translation of the "Epigram on Plutarch by Agathias" from Tonson's 1683 *Plutarch*, "On the Marriage of Lady Stafford" (from *Tixall Poetry, 1813*), and the "Prologue and Epilogue to the *Widow Ranter*" (following Ham). Among extensive revisions, mention should be made of the note on "Tarquin and Tullia" (p. 929) and that on "The Essay on Satire" (p. 1039). The long note on the "Epilogue to *Callisto*" (pp. 1052–53) is almost an article in itself.

The "Biographical Sketch" that prefaces the volume deserves special mention. Extending to fifty-five pages of closely packed type (about 35,000 words), it is greatly expanded from the twenty-six pages of the earlier edition. The footnotes show the wealth of subsequent scholarship that Noyes has incorporated into the biography. Although there are no discoveries of unpublished materials, the amalgamation of facts produced by others has been skillfully and judiciously woven into the narrative. Noyes's revisions reveal the maturity that came with half a century of thinking about Dryden the literary artist and the man. For its length, his "Biographical Sketch" has not been surpassed as a summary of Dryden's abilities, shortcomings, personality, and achievements.

The first book-length biography of Dryden since the "hilarious performance" of Christopher Hollis (p. 112 above) in 1933 appeared in 1954 from the pen of a rising young journalist, Kenneth Young. While a student at the University of Leeds Young had been inspired by his professor, Bonamy Dobrée, to whom he affectionately dedicated what he labels his "Critical Biography" of Dryden. Moreover, the Preface ends with special thanks for the professor's help, though Young earlier states that his attempt would have been impossible but for the work of recent scholars, however "academic." He added that these Dryden researches "have been carried out almost entirely by Americans, for reasons on which this is not the place to speculate." This self-denial is a pity, for it might have been the most original contribution in the book.

For, alas! here is another example of the impulse to write fictionalized biography, to show the "academics" the skill they lack. Thus the first chapter begins,

> In a quiet glade along the banks of the river Nene in Northamptonshire, a boy of about fourteen sits fishing. He is chubby, pink-cheeked and his auburn hair is close-cropped in the Puritan style; there is a slightly arrogant lift to his upper lip; his brow is creased with thought beyond his years.
> . . . That was the trouble: no one would talk to him about poetry. Indeed, his grown-up cousin, Sir Gilbert Pickering, took a positive pleasure in teasing him about reading poetry, telling him that it was a waste of time and a lot of lies, and anyhow people like Abraham Cowley were papist rogues.

And so the imaginative reconstruction continues for 220 pages until the final paragraph which begins, "Here the old lady rested her arm, and wiped a tear, and took up her labours another day."

Young's journalistic desire to avoid being academic manifested itself in remarkable ways. Ward's definitive edition of the *Letters,* though it had appeared twelve years earlier, is mentioned only in the "Select Bibliography," and citations are to the texts in the Scott-Saintsbury edition. Dryden's affair with Anne Reeves is apparently the basis for labeling him "the lover of actresses" (p. x). The gold watch Dryden ordered for his son becomes a "gold clock" (p. xiii). Such unsupported inferences and indifference to details can be passed over as the habits of Fleet Street, but it is difficult to excuse the reference to "one of Dryden's descendants [!], Percy Dryden Munday" (sic! p. 230). And even less forgivable is the reference in the very first page of the Preface to Edward (!!) Malone, repeated again on the very last page of the book in the "Select Bibliography." *Res digna in qua docti erubescant.*

It is a relief to turn to two examples of responsible scholarship, the first volumes of the California *Works of John Dryden* (1956, 1962) and the four-volume *Poems of John Dryden* (1958) edited by James Kinsley. The great California edition, under the general editorship of Edward Niles Hooker and H. T. Swedenberg, Jr., was long in gestation (p. vii above), appropriately considering its pachydermic proportions. But the edition has been well worth waiting for, and the first volume was greeted with the phrase Dryden applied to Chaucer, "Here is God's plenty." That its annotations will ever be superseded is inconceivable, though new evidence may be forthcoming, and new interpretations will be offered from generation to generation. To illustrate the scale of the undertaking, the first volume (poems to 1680) contains 200 pages of commentary to explain 165 pages of poetry. Volume VIII, which reprints Dryden's three earliest plays, offers 130 pages of notes, explanatory and textual.

Although no biographical memoir is offered, the editors demonstrate full familiarity with the background and events of Dryden's life, and occasionally make suggestions of biographical interest. For example, they suggest that during Dryden's long stay at Charlton in 1666, where he wrote the *Essay of Dramatic Poesie* and *Annus mirabilis,* he planned or wrote several plays (I, 260). There are frequent insights into Dryden's temperament and thinking habits (VIII, 297). Future biographers will find few new facts about Dryden in the California commentaries, but a wealth of background information and critical appreciation of Dryden as an artist.

Kinsley's edition is welcome for other reasons. His volumes, like others in the Oxford English Text series, provide a reliable text in readable type with the necessary notes. In these aims the editor has been highly successful. To save space, many of the notes have been cut to the bone, so that the scholar pursuing some particular point will be wise to consult Noyes's edition too. Reinterpretation, revaluation, and new light were not part of the editor's purpose, so that the student of Dryden's biography will not find these volumes essential. But they do provide Dryden's poems in attractive format, with a sound text and essential, concisely presented explanatory notes.

To the scholar interested in the man behind the printed page, the most important event of this quarter century was the publication in 1961 of Charles E. Ward's *Life of John Dryden*. For three decades, ever since the first "Biographical Note on John Dryden" appeared over his signature in 1932, Ward continued to accumulate materials for a full-scale biography. (His edition of the *Letters* in 1942 represented a halfway house.) The result of his endeavors is a book that takes its place on the shelf along with the work of Dr. Johnson, Edmond Malone, Sir Walter Scott, and George Saintsbury in the mainstream of Dryden biographies. It will be definitive for a generation, and probably more than one, an indispensable aid and valuable quarry for future students.

Because Dryden lived in an age of violent conflicts, during which he published poems, plays, and prose, both critical and polemical over a forty-year span, the chief problem faced by his biographer is how to keep his book down to moderate length. Ward faced it by choosing to limit his account to telling what contemporary evidence, especially that of Dryden's own pen, reveals about his varied activities, his purposes, and his attitudes towards men, literary problems, and political cruxes. In deciding to write this kind of biography Ward announced an impossible ambition, "to exclude critical pronouncement," for critical judgments are implicit in any attempt to explain literary events. Yet, he has kept such judgments at a minimum, quite properly considering his purpose. Accordingly, no scholar or librarian will wish to discard his copy of Van Doren's *The Poetry of John Dryden*, but rather wish to shelve Ward's *Life* next to this standard critical volume.

In making the decision to write a "straight" life of Dryden, Ward recognized the basic problem imposed by his subject, namely that even though Dryden was the most prolific and influential writer of his time, he has seemed to many students to be an elusive and faceless personality. The root of the problem lies in the fact that readers of literary biography have been spoiled by the abundant evidence available about Pepys, Swift, Pope, and Dr. Johnson, not to mention later personalities. Although Dryden's writings abound in subjective judgments and personal references he left no diaries or journals; nor were his conversations recorded by a Spence or a Boswell. Indeed, few writers before Pope (Drummond's conversations with Jonson excepted) have left much external testimony of their personalities.

Considering the lack of such evidence, which no biographer's private wishbone can summon up, Ward has succeeded beyond his predecessors in showing Dryden as a seventeenth-century Londoner. The reader gains a conception of Dryden the professional writer, living from day to day and year to year amid the tumultuous events of his time—the Restoration of Charles II, the revival of the theaters, the Dutch wars, the Popish Plot, the propaganda battles, the literary failures and triumphs. We get a sense of Dryden the experimenter in literature in the mainstream of political as well as literary events.

As a biographer Ward has shown marked skill in weaving together the diverse threads of his story: Dryden's family life, especially his relations with his wife's family (the Howards), the successive developments in politics, the evolution and dissolution in relations between the two theatrical companies, and the ever-shifting situation at court. Another important strand is Dryden's "Epic Dream," his unfulfilled plan to celebrate the Stuart dynasty; Ward's chapter on this subject constitutes one of his most signal contributions beyond earlier biographers. Similarly the chapter on "The Great Translation: *Virgil*" marks a notable advance, delineating in detail and perspective the travail and achievement of the crowning event in Dryden's literary career. The success with which these various aspects of Dryden's life have been woven together is a high achievement.

Among praiseworthy features of the biography the following may be noted briefly. Ward has shown an admirable awareness of the time factor, for example that the *Essay of Dramatic Poesy* was written before Dryden had made his reputation.

The *Essay* was a speculative adventure into the discovery of ways to write drama; and in 1665 he had not learned. For this reason, reticence and even a certain diffidence may be allowed him for not publishing a discourse on the writing of drama until he had sufficiently demonstrated a practical ability to succeed in the only proving ground known to the playwright—the theater. By the summer of 1668 he had progressed in his practice far enough to make his theories relevant and important. Earlier publication might have seemed presumptuous (p. 59).

The Rehearsal is described with a fine sense of proportion. Dryden, being a prominent shareholder in the Theatre Royal, undoubtedly followed the preparation of the farce for the stage as well as its performance: ". . . the box office returns could have mollified any injury he may have felt" (p. 84). Similarly, Ward has reduced to scale the parti-

san attacks on *Absalom and Achitophel,* a welcome corrective both to
Dr. Johnson (who gave more space to them than to Dryden's twenty-
eight plays) and to Macdonald's dual treatment of the subject, first in
"The Attacks on Dryden" (*Essays and Studies,* 1936) and then again
in the rambling "Drydeniana" section of his *Bibliography* (1939). These
attacks were as numerous as gnats, troublesome at the moment, but in-
capable of stinging deeply.

Indeed, one of the particular merits of the book lies in Ward's treatment of Dryden's political writings. His reading of *Annus mirabilis*
prompted some welcome qualifications to the lengthy interpretation in
the California edition (pp. 44, 342). Students of *Absalom and Achitophel* will benefit from the pathway he has cut through the tangled
political jungle. The *Vindication of the Duke of Guise* will be reread
with Ward's contention that it is ". . . more than a political tract; it is
also a personal defense of Dryden's own long established principles and
of his character" (p. 194). Similarly, in the dedication to the translation
of Maimbourg's *History of the League* Ward found significance that
earlier writers had overlooked (pp. 204–5).

For the first time all three parts of *A Defence of the Papers written by
the Late King* are attributed to Dryden, which led Ward to the following conclusion:

Had *A Defence* been recognized as Dryden's and studied as a document of
importance to an understanding of his conversion, much of the uncertainty
about his change of religion would have been settled long since. Suffice
it to say here that Dryden's quarto of 126 pages completely supports the conclusions of Professor Bredvold, who unaccountably makes no mention of
it (p. 219).

Whether Ward's attribution is accepted or not, his treatment of ideo-
logical issues marks a definite advance over his predecessors.

Another welcome characteristic of Ward's pages is his skepticism
when examining evidence. Beginning with the preface and continuing
through the thirty-eight pages of notes at the back of the book his statements of caution run like a leitmotif: "Assumptions . . . do not add to
our knowledge of Dryden; and speculation, though pleasant, may fal-
sify what little we can discover" (p. 20). He is particularly wary of as-
suming that references to "Mr Dryden" (however spelled) or even
"John Dryden" have any connection with the writer:

The temptation that besets literary scholars to identify the man best
known to them with men of the same name referred to in contemporary

documents is nowhere better illustrated than here . . . Whenever the name [Dryden] occurs, perhaps the safest procedure is to assume that it does not refer to the poet, unless it is accompanied by some distinguishing phrase (p. 324).

Despite this rule, Ward accepted the suggestion that the Dryden who purchased 146 books at the Digby sale, April 19, 1680, and at the Richard Smith sale, May 15, 1682, was the poet. Yet the christian name of the buyer does not occur in either catalogue to indicate whether he was one of the five contemporary John Drydens. Moreover, most of the books are tomes on obscure theological subjects, and only about a dozen of them can be shown to have been known to the writer.

Sometimes Ward's suspiciousness seems excessive. For instance, his treatment of Aubrey's story that Milton told Dryden "tag my verses if you will" receives only one sentence (p. 105); Dryden's connection with the actress, Anne Reeves, is dismissed in one-third of a sentence (p. 183). Spence's story that Charles II gave Dryden the idea of writing *The Medal* is not mentioned, even to be dismissed as hearsay too long after the event. Perhaps the extreme example of Ward's caution is his refusal to believe that the Dryden who had a minor post in the Cromwell government was the future poet. Yet, the "Heroique Stanzas, Consecrated to the Glorious Memory of his most Serene and Renowned Highnesse Oliver," Dryden's first ambitious literary endeavor, have every characteristic of being deeply motivated. Furthermore the earliest attack on Dryden, the *Letter from a Gentleman* (1668) possibly by Richard Flecknoe, speaks of his employment under his relative, "Sir Gilbert Pickering, a crafty councellor, in the late times." Though none of these items is conclusive evidence, the scale would appear to be tipped in favor of the traditional belief.

Considering the book as biography, the chief criticism is that Ward's overfamiliarity with his materials has led him to assume that an equal familiarity exists in his readers, especially that they will bring to his book a full knowledge of the literature of the Dryden era. Oddly, none of Dryden's letters is quoted in extenso, and usually passages from them are given in snippets or even paraphrased. Yet Dryden's personality is better crystalized in some of the letters than in the autobiographical passages in his published writings. Ward discussed Dryden's "fideism" (a word not in *OED*) without definition or explanation, apparently on the assumption that every·reader of his biography would be familiar with the theological concept. Dryden's relationships with his friends have been underplayed. John Oldham, on whose untimely death in 1683 Dryden felt moved to write an elegy, is not mentioned, at least in the index, and Ward names "his dear friend" Wycherley only in passing. The Shadwell-Dryden relationship receives only meager treatment; discussion of *Mac Flecknoe* occupies one paragraph, in contrast to seven pages devoted to quotations from *The Hind and the Panther*.

A second edition, when called for, should allow obvious corrections to be made, both of misprints and carelessness in the transcription of texts. The index is worse than inadequate; for example, no entry occurs for *The Medal of John Bayes*. Despite the author's devotion to factual accuracy, there are a number of minor slips, e.g., the verses "To my Honour'd Cousin, John Driden of Chesterton" could not date from 1694 (p. 14) because of the reference to the Treaty of Ryswick (1697); the prices paid for the items of silverware Dryden bought in 1668 differ from the printed record (p. 71); and Dryden's "first and best patroness the Duchess of Monmouth" did not marry Jack Churchill (later Duke of Marlborough) in 1688, but the third Baron Cornwallis (p. 251). Students will look forward to the new edition for these and other reasons.

Ward's biography was worth waiting for, and shows the advantage of a scholar's living with his subject for three decades. His *Life of Dryden* is successful both as biography and as a synthesis of his own and previous scholarship. The book brings Dryden alive as a man among men, a writer who lived by his pen while remaining loyal to his friends, consistent to his principles and his artistic conscience. The image that stands forth from Ward's pages should replace the picture of the inconsistent turncoat so cherished by Whiggish writers for two centuries after his death and ought to make unnecessary any future defense of Dryden's integrity, personal, political, or literary. The volume should serve as the standard biography for many years to come.

APPENDICES TO PART ONE

1

MALONE'S ADDITIONS TO HIS
LIFE OF DRYDEN

Preserved in the Bodleian, with the shelfmark Malone E. 61–63, is a very important set of books for the Dryden student, Malone's own copy of his edition of the prose works.[1] The most important volume is the first one, the biography of Dryden. Here, along the crowded margins and on innumerable inserted slips, Malone stored the additions and corrections that he discovered in the decade between the publication of the volumes and the twilight of his career.

These additions were inserted in preparation for a second edition, plans for which were made before the first issue was completely launched on the none-too-receptive public.[2] Although hope for the new impression haunted Malone's breast for the rest of his life, it was never financially justified, and so these patched pages remain to show the changes that additional researches and matured judgment would have introduced into the great compendium of Dryden biography.

In transcribing these notes I have aimed at making available all the additions and corrections that are likely to be of interest. Small changes such as those of spelling, punctuation, and diction have been omitted; and it has been considered unnecessary to repeat recurrent corrections of the same error (for example, "Andrew Bernard" is corrected to "Bernard André" only the first time it ap-

---

[1] Vol. I, Part 2, containing the letters, "Additions and Emendations" and the early prose, is missing from the Bodleian. When this volume is found it should provide the key to a number of interesting problems.

[2] The following note is in the Adam Library:

"April 5

"Mr. Malone requests that Messrs Cadell and Davies will advertise his book twice in the Sun and twice in the Star; for which purpose he sends a printed copy.

"He shd be glad to know their opinion about a second edition, as it will take three weeks to print at the least: and there ought not to be any stop in the sale."

pears). All the longer notes have been repeated, with the exception of those that stray too far from the Dryden path, such as the list of St. Cecilia odes. The volume is such a storehouse of literary history, however, that it has seemed advisable to preserve the majority of the notes just as they were poured from that overflowing crucible of literary and historical lore, Malone's graying head.

It remains to add that this is not a strictly literal transcription: the notes are here printed in the form they would have taken in Malone's second edition. Thus if he occasionally forgot to close a quotation with the proper marks, they have here been silently inserted. The text is taken from the transcript in my interleaved copy of the volume. I regret that it has not been possible to compare the text with the original, but the war has made such action impossible.

In order to make the reading of his *Life* easier, Malone divided it into "Sections"; and these begin at easily identifiable points on the following pages:

Page
iii   Advertisement, end of paragraph: delete "excepting" etc. Malone had apparently come across a copy of the *Defence of the Essay of Dramatic Poesy.*

Page

iv line 17: add "five letters addressed to William Walsh Esqre for which, with six written by Walsh, the reader is indebted to that gentleman's great nephew, William Bromley of Abberley in Worcestershire Esqre;" For an account of these letters see pp. 226–33.

vii line 11: a long footnote is inserted after the sentence about Burke. It begins with the sentence "Our author's description of Plutarch is extremely applicable to his own writings." and is followed by the passage from Dryden's *Life of Plutarch* beginning with the sentence "I have always been pleased to see him and his imitator Montagne" and continuing through "that he may instruct." (Malone, ii. 407–8).

xix line 7: Malone here added, as footnote to "imitated," "Accordingly, Pope, who in his early years made imitations of Chaucer, Spenser, Waller, Cowley, Rochester, Dorset, and Swift, did not attempt an imitation of DRYDEN. His own poetry indeed was only Dryden's versification, rendered by incessant care more smooth and musical, but less flowing and less varied."

3 To note 3 was transferred the note about the spelling of "Dryden" from "Additions and Emendations" (Vol. I, part ii, p. 133 [first pagination]). A sentence was added: "See the Dispensation granted by Archbishop Sheldon, in the Appendix.—"Joanni Dryden, . . . perantiqua Dreydenorum familia oriendo."

6 To the worthies of Northamptonshire Malone added: "Oundle was also the birthplace of Wm Hackets the fanatical presbyterian executed in Q Eliz time."
   line 4 from bottom: Malone altered the arrangement of the epitaph, from Add. & Em. p. 133.

7 line 4 from bottom: as additional evidence that Dryden was born in 1631, Malone inserted "So also in his Postscript to the translation of Virgil, he says he began it in his grand climacterick: and from other evidence we know that work was begun about the middle of the year 1694. This circumstance therefore, also, fixes his birth in 1631."

8 In an attempt to show that Dryden was born in Aldwincle All Saints, Malone supplemented note 6 with the fact that, "The Register of St Aldwincle St. Peters being perfect from its commencement in [*blank*] to the present time, and containing not a single baptismal entry of any one of Erasmus Drydens fourteen children, it is almost a certainty that our author was not born in that parish."

9 To note 1, about Dryden's birthplace, Malone added, "The house in which our author is said to have been born, fell down a few years ago." Where Malone got this information I do not know. The house mentioned by Bridges is still well preserved, and was put up for sale in 1937. For a description of it, see "Round Dryden's Birthplace" by J. Alfred Gotch, *Northamptonshire Notes and Queries*, Vol. II (1888), pp. 173–81.

Page

10 line 4: Malone deleted from "Were it not" to the end of the paragraph: evidently he had become convinced that Dryden was born at
Aldwincle.

On this page are the words "Q. Scotch origin—" Apparently this was
Malone's response to Scott's suggestion, based on the frequency with
which the name Dryden is found in the Lowlands. Lady Elizabeth
Dryden had raised the same point in her letter of May 18, 1799, but
Malone did not make use of it at the time.

In line 16 and note 3, Malone altered "Burnet" to "Oldmixon".

11 In the note about Dryden's grandfather, Malone deleted from "and
as at that time" (line 6) through "bred at Cambridge", and substituted, "but it appears from the most ancient Matriculation-Register of
that University that he was of Magdalene College in 1571, being
enumerated among the then existing members of that college: '1571.
Dec. Erasmus Dredon, Northamp. generosi fil. natus an. 18.'—It is
extraordinary that he should not have taken his first degree in arts
till he was of five years and a half standing in the university." At the
end of this note he added: "Wood relates that the first of the Dreyden
or Dryden family that migrated from Cumberland to Northamptonshire was a schoolmaster, that Erasmus stood godfather to one of his
children; (a tale derived I believe from Vincent the herald see his
Visitation for Northamptonshire in the Heralds Office) and that hence
this name continued in the family. But when we find that Sir Erasmus Dryden the first as far as appears who bore this name had a
maternal uncle whose Christian name was Erasmus, need we look
farther for his baptismal name?" This question was intended for
Scott, who had accepted the story about Erasmus standing as godfather to one of Dryden's ancestors.

12 As finally left by Malone, the passage about Dryden's brothers and
sisters reads: "Rose, another of the daughters, was the second wife of
John Laughton, D.D. of Catworth, in the county of Huntington, by
whom she had one son, whom our author honoured by a monumental
inscription; * Agnes was the wife of Sylvester Emelyn, of Stamford,
in the county of Lincoln, gentleman; Lucy of Stephen Umwell, of
London, merchant; and Martha according to Collins, was married to
—— Bletso, of Northampton.—Another of his sisters married ——
England, and became a methodist; and another as I learn from his
mothers will was the wife of —— Blunne. Of the other two, I have
not discovered any notices.

"Of the sons, Erasmus, who was in trade, and resided in King-
street, Westminster, succeeded at a late period of life to the title of
Baronet, and died at Canons-Ashby, Nov. 3, 1718, aged eighty-two,
(leaving two daughters; Elizabeth, the wife of Dr Richard Mar-
tyn, Prebendary of Westminster; and Mary, married to John Shaw,

Page

Esq. and five grandsons, the eldest of whom, John, succeeded to the title;) Henry went to Jamaica, where he died, leaving a son named Richard; and James, the youngest, died in the parish of St. Dunstan's in the East, in 1694, leaving two daughters."

*The following inscription on this lady in Catworth Church in Northamptonshire which was found, since the former edition, among the papers of the late Mrs. Gwillim of Whitchurch Court in Hereford- shire, grand-daughter of Mrs Elizabeth Stuart our author's kins- woman, was obligingly communicated to me by William Walcot, of Oundle, Esqre. From a circumstance mentioned, it appears to have been written between the years 1711 and 1718: [here follow the in- scription and verse as printed by Noyes in his edition of Dryden's *Poetical Works,* 1909, p. 268]."

13 Malone changed his mind about the age at which Dryden went to Westminster school. In place of "about the time . . . eleven years old" (lines 2–3) he inserted "when the Civil War was at its height, about the end of 1644, at which time he was above thirteen years old." Malone here quoted a letter from Dr. Simon Patrick to Dr. John Mapletoft, dated 8 February 1682/3, which I omit because it has no connection with Dryden.

15 note 5: of the translation of Persius, dated 1693, he inserted the phrase "(but published in Sept. 1692);"

16 line 12: the note to "tables" is inserted here from Add. & Em. p. 134.

17 This page is much marked up, for it was necessary to correct the false statement about Dryden's degree of Master of Arts. Malone learned about the Lambeth degree in plenty of time to have cancelled this page, and I am at a loss to understand why he failed to do so. The page was patched up as follows: for the date of Dryden's degree of Bachelor of Arts, read "Hillary term, 1653–4," then delete the rest of the paragraph substituting the note from Add. & Em. pp. 134–5, modified to read, "He did not indeed obtain the degree of Master of Arts at Cambridge, having probably left the University before he was of such standing as entitled him to it. At the regular time or at any subsequent period he might have taken that degree on performing the usual exercises, but for whatever cause (now perhaps undiscoverable) he was not indebted to Cambridge for this honour, being made a Master of Arts in June 1668 by the dispensation of Archbishop Shel- don in consequence of a recommendation of King Charles II." The long note about Lambeth degrees from pages 555–6 was also to have been inserted here.

Malone also inserted into note 7, line 6, the fact that the poet's cousin Jonathan Dryden "took the degree of B.A. in Hilary term, 1659–60,"

Page

and to the remarks about Jonathan's Latin letter to Busby Malone
added the detail "written at Cambridge."

18 Of course note 9 was now unnecessary.

20 In the note about the age of Dryden's father in 1632, Malone added
the observation, "In many of the ancient *inquisitiones post mortem*, I
have observed that when the heir was above thirty years old, his precise age was concealed under the indefinite words *and upwards.*"

23 Continuing about Dryden's father, the end of the top paragraph
should read, "He acted as a Justice of Peace and Committee-man, in
the county of Northampton, during the Usurpation, and was a zealous
presbyterian, as was his elder brother, Sir John Driden, who desecrated
the church of Canons Ashby, and was one of Cromwell's active parti-
zans in that eminently disloyal county during [*sic*] calamitous period."

26 line 8: here began Malone's Section Two, with the sentence modified
to, "After residing at least five years at Cambridge, Dryden probably
continued for some time at Tichmarsh with his mother, before he had
yet decided what course of life to pursue, and then removed to
London."

The last sentence of note 2 is also altered; with the help of a new fact
noted in Add. & Em., p. 134: "This passage induced me formerly to
suppose that our author continued at Cambridge for seven years; but
the following entry in one of the old books of Trinity College, obligingly communicated by the Reverend Doctor Mansel, Master of that
College, shews that the writer was mistaken; and warrants us in supposing that Dryden quitted the University at an earlier period:
    'April 23, 1655. At the election of Scholars, Wilford is chosen into
    Sir *Dreyden's* place.' "

28 Lines 9 and following were modified to read, "maternal grandfather
being cousin-german to Sir John Pickering, his mother was second
cousin to Sir Gilbert."

29 On a separate slip Malone drew up the genealogies of the Pickering
and Dryden families, showing their relationship.

33 At the end of note 2 Malone added, "His situation under his father
and his kinsman, Sir Gilbert Pickering, seems to have been particularly alluded to, in the following lines of the SATIRE TO HIS MUSE,
4to. 1682:
    My father wisely bade me be a *clerk*
    Thou whisper'dst,—boy, be thou a tearing spark."
The remainder of this footnote, on p. 34, was to have been omitted,
except for the allusion to Dryden's Verses on Cromwell.

34 The remark about Villiers in the text is replaced by, "It appears from
a poem ascribed to another of his opponents, Villiers, Duke of Buckingham, and from a controversial tract of that age, that his father,

Page

Erasmus Driden, (under whom also he acted as a clerk,) was likewise a committee-man."

37   In note 4, the paragraph about the Duke of Buckingham was replaced by the following: "The same fact is alluded to in another poem, (which seems to have originally appeared in 1687, and is reprinted in a miscellaneous collection by R. Cross, 8vo 1747,) entitled, THE PROTESTANT SATIRE, or some reason, not all rhyme, &c.

He honest kept as long as e'er he could,
But glitt'ring guineas cannot be withstood,
And BAYES was of Committee-men's flesh and blood.

These hitherto unknown circumstances of our author's early life are still more particularly mentioned in an extremely scarce tract, entitled 'A Letter from a gentleman to the Honble Edward Howard, Esqre occasioned by a civilized Epistle of Mr Dryden's before the second edition of the INDIAN EMPEROUR,' 4to 1668: 'His [Dryden's] fortune and that of the honourable gentleman [Sir Robert Howard] are different, for the Squire [Dryden] mistakingly charges him, that the corruption of a poet was the generation of a statesman; but on the contrary the Squire having been employed as a puny statesman under *his father, a zealous committee-man,* and Sir Gilbert Pickering, a crafty privy-counsellor, in the late times, it may be more properly applied to the Squire, that the corruption of a statesman is the generation of a poet-laureate.' "

39   To illustrate Walker's statement in his *Sufferings of the Clergy* that Sir Gilbert Pickering had "an uncle whose ears were cropt for a libel on Archbishop Whitgift," Malone added, "By an unkle, according to the usual licence of that time, Sr Gilbert Pickering's great uncle must have been meant: for his father could have had no brother so advanced in life previously to the death of Whitgift, to have incurred the censure of the Star Chamber by a libel. The person meant was unquestionably Mr. Lewis Pickering, (great uncle to Sir Gilbert) a zealous presbyterian, in the latter end of the reign of Elizabeth, mentioned by Fuller, Ch. Hist. of K. James, p. 56. His case forms the leading case de libellis famoris [?], in Sir Edward Coke's Fifth Report. It appears, from that case that the Attorney General proceeded against him in the Star Chamber *ore timus* [?] on his own confession for composing and publishing an infamous libel in verse by which Archbishop Whitgift, then dead, and his success^r Archbishop Bancroft, by description and circumstances, and not in express terms, were traduced and scandalized. The conduct of many of Charles's Judges may be traced to personal spleen and resentment. The punishment inflicted on this libeller was doubtless the cause of his kinsmans subsequent proceedings. In like manner the two Chaloners revenged themselves on their sovereign for the loss of the allum mine discovered in Yorkshire by

Page

their father many years before, and claimed by the Crown as a mine-royal."

45 The note on Herringman, the bookseller, was augmented by the addi-tion of these introductory sentences: "The New Exchange was situated in the Strand, opposite to Bedford Street (see the title-page of MIS-TAKEN BEAUTY OR THE LYAR, a comedy, 1685). Several book-sellers had shops in the lower walk of this Exchange."

45 To note 5, on Dryden's indebtedness to Howard, add: "In his Defence of the ESSAY ON DRAMATICK POESY, he says, that 'he had so many particular obligations to Sir R. H. that he should be very ungrate-ful if he did not acknowledge them to the world.' "

52 Malone wished to introduce here the two paragraphs from pages 55 and 56 which "consider our author as a dramatick writer."

55 At the end of the quotation from the *Session of the Poets* Malone added, "The Wild Gallant was revived in 1669, which probably was the occasion of its being noticed in these satirical verses, which, I be-lieve, were published either in that or the following year."

57 As a footnote to the discussion of the *Indian Emperor* Malone wrote: "Among the papers of Sir Henry Puckering in Trinity College, Cam-bridge, is a manuscript copy of this tragedy; but I know not whether it be in Dryden's hand-writing." This manuscript is not in Dryden's hand. For an account of it see Montague Summers's edition of Dry-den's *Dramatic Works,* 1931, Vol. I, p. 355.

58 After line 10 Malone inserted a new paragraph to conclude his re-marks about the *Indian Emperor:* "In this tragedy as originally ex-hibited, as we learn from a contemporary writer, there was a scene containing a disputation between a heathen and a Christian Priest, which does not appear in the printed copy.*
    * '—but if the Squire [Dryden] be, as he says he is, for distributive justice, we may justly presume that when his *Indian Emperor* was *first* acted he intended to instruct and reform all churches in polemical divinity by his admirable dispute between a Christian and a heathen priest, which also shows how great a loss the Church had of him when he was diverted from entering into holy orders.' A Letter from a Gen-tleman to the Hon. Edward Howard Esqre. &c. 4to 1668."

60 After the discussion of Ben Jonson's *Discoveries* (line 16) insert the sentence, "In Hobbes's Letter prefixed to Gondibert, published in 1650 and in Davenant's preface to the same poem, a few critical strictures are found."

61 At the end of the paragraph on the *Essay of Dramatic Poesy* and other dialogues, Malone appended the following note: "It is singular that Bishop Hurd should say in the Preface to his Dialogues, there are but three good dialogues in the English language, and that this of our author sh^d not be enumerated among them."

Page

64 The note on the spelling of "Sedley" was patched up by omitting the first three and a half lines, and inserting a sentence after that on the *Mulberry Garden*: "Such also was the orthography of several of his family at various times." This modification was undoubtedly caused by the passage on pp. 103–112 in Hardinge's *Essence of Malone*, (second edition).

66 Add to the note on Dryden's interchangeable use of "i" and "y": "He used them so indiscriminately that in a letter to Jacob Tonson, he even spells the Latin name, Euryalus, with an i instead of a y: Eurialus. Of the indiscriminate use of the letters y and i our author's own name also affords an instance." [Memorandum here: "another in Ded. of Æneid."]

68 lines 5–8 should read "and Sir Robert Howard had in 1665 collected into a folio volume four of his plays, two of which (THE COMMIT-TEE and the INDIAN QUEEN) had been acted with great success." Malone explained that Prior's *Heads of an Essay on Learning* (see the note) was "a MS. formerly in the possession of the Dowager Duchess of Portland." This manuscript was first printed in 1907, by A. R. Waller in his edition of the *Dialogues of the Dead*, etc. pp. 180–8.

74 In the account of the indenture of 31 December 1666, Malone corrected Thomas Killigrew's share to two shares only, rather than two and three-quarters.

82 In correcting the name "Andrew Bernard" to "Bernard André", Malone added the following note, which was clearly written with the projected second edition in mind: "In a former edition I had inadvertently followed Mr Warton in denominating this poet *Andrew Bernard,* into which slight errour I fell the more easily from Bernard being a French surname, and from his being frequently called by his contemporaries by the name of *Bernard,* without any addition. Thus in the record alluded to in the text. 'Item, to Master *Barnard,* the blind poet, c shilling.' So also Erasmus in one of his Epistles, speaking of this person, 'Si quid effeceris, velim cognoscere num meus Maecenas resolverit viginti nobiles illos *Bernardo,* quae res facit, &c.' Erasm. Epist. Edit. Bas. p. 321. His true name however certainly was, Bernard André."

[slip pasted in] "For Dryden On Henry VII entring London after the battle of Bosworth Barnard André saluted him with some Latin Sappicks [*sic*]. Speed."

83 To the note on the meaning of Poetae Laureati, Malone added the sentence, "Bale, however, says (Centuria Decima tertia, p. 139, article, Bernardus Andreas,) 'Hinc est ab Henrico Octavo illustrissimo Anglorum regi in aulam accitus, et *regii poetae* nomine statim insignitus.' " Malone deleted the last sentence of the note.

Page

84 After mentioning Skelton's claim to be regarded as poet laureate, Malone added, "The circumstance, however, of receiving a royal pension will not itself warrant our supposing every ordinary versifier who has participated of the royal bounty a poet laureat: for in particular cases his poverty rather than his poetry may have recommended him to the notice of the Crown."

To the account of Churchyard two new footnotes are appended: "Churchyard when he was extremely old, in the year 1593, obtained from Queen Elizabeth a grant of an annuity of eighteenpence a day for his life, in consideration of his services, age and infirmities." And, on his reputation, "This is so far from being the truth, that he was rated extremely low, as appears from one of Harrington's Epigrams, B. III. ep. [blank]."

87 The passage about Dryden's accession to the office of laureate was re-written to read: "It appears, however, from his Letters Patent, a copy of which will be found in the Appendix, that he was not legally invested with the laurel till August 18th, 1670. But a very scarce pamphlet of that time informs us that at least before the end of the year 1668 he was considered as possessed of the office [footnote: "see p. 37.n*", which refers to the 1668 *Letter to* Edward Howard, as quoted in these editions], probably in consequence of his having obtained a promise of it from the Crown; (about which time in consequence of an express recommendation from the King he was graced with an honorary degree of Master of Arts conferred on him by Archbishop Sheldon's diploma; and with respect to the emoluments" etc.

Of course, Malone was still far from correctly informed, although this manuscript note contained a germ of truth not realized before the researches of Professor Broadus, over a century after Malone wrote it.

88 The following footnote was added, to explain the relationship between the Earl of Manchester and Dryden: "Edward Earl of Manchester's third wife was Essex, a daughter of Sir Thomas Cheek, Knight, and widow of Sir Robert Bevil, Knight of the Bath, of Chesterton in the County of Huntingdon. By this lady he had five sons and six daughters. Our author's uncle, Sir John Driden, was married to her daughter by her first husband, Sir Robert Bevil; but this was but a slender claim to patronage, for not only the lady herself, but Sir John Driden was dead many years before the place of laureat became vacant."

92 On this page is pasted a slip of paper containing a note on the *Conquest of Granada;* except for the first line, it is in a hand other than Malone's: "This play was so popular that it was chosen for a private representation by a company of ladies and gentlemen in 1677. In Shipman's "CAROLINA, or Loyal Poems", 1683, are 'Lines in way of Pro-

Page

logue entit. 'THE HUFFER, 1677; spoken by *Ant. Eyre* Esq. and directed to the right Hon. the Lady Ross, when *he* acted Almanzor in DRYDEN'S GRANADA, at Belvoir.' These lines are followed by others entit. 'The Representation upon the Hon. Mrs. *Bridget Noel,* acting the part of Almahide in DRYDEN'S GRANADA, at Belvoir, 1677.'"

To note 9, on the subject of Dryden's relations with Sir Robert Howard, Malone added the information: "In the Notes on the fifth Æneid of Virgil (published in 1697) we find the following passage: 'Sir Robert Howard in his translation of this Æneid, which was printed with his poems in the year 1660, has given us the most learned and the most judicious observations on this book, which are extant in our language.' "

93   The footnote is deleted.

99   To the footnote on the actors who essayed the role of Bayes is added: "The elder Cibber was, I believe, the most celebrated performer of this part, and to him succeeded Garrick, who though he doubtless departed in some measure from the original idea, made the representation incomparably pleasant."

103 Footnote 5 is amended to read: "The 'fair Armida', who was *la belle Stuart* of the Comte de Grammont, was married to Charles Stuart, the third Duke of Richmond in 1667, and died October 15, 1702." The note is then continued with the passages from Add. & Em., pp. 135-6, slightly corrected.

111 To the criticisms which Dryden is reported as having been passed on Sathan's speech in Act I of the *State of Innocence,* Malone added the footnote: "I have some doubts whether the observations here alluded to ever appeared in print, except in this preface. They may have been remarks made in conversation by some of the Criticks who frequented Will's Coffeehouse."

113 Malone attempted to identify one "Sir W. L.", of whose conversations with Dryden, Richardson had preserved an anecdote, as "Perhaps Sir Wilfred Lawson, Baronet, of Isel in Cumberland."

115 To the statement that Charles II made certain suggestions about the writing of *Aurengzebe,* Malone contributed a footnote: "The subject of another play, MARRIAGE A LA MODE, was recommended to Dryden by Charles the second."

119 Concerning Kneller's portrait of Anthony Leigh in the role of the Spanish Friar, Malone added, "The picture is now at Knole."

121 In beginning his Section VI at line 19, Malone rewrote the introductory passage to read as follows: "We have now reached the close of that period which may be considered as the third portion of our author's dramatick life. Before we enter on the last period of his

Page

dramatick history, that chronological order, which contributes so much to perspicuity in narration of this kind, requires that we should take a slight survey of the various contests in which, during the most splendid aera of his scenic exertions, he was engaged with authors and others, the meanest of whom his admirable poetry has rendered immortal. To this survey may be properly subjoined an account of such of his literary productions as appeared between the time of his discontinuing to write for the stage and the Revolution."

126 Malone suggested in a new footnote that Lady Betty Howard was "Probably a daughter of Henry the sixth Duke of Norfolk, who was afterwards married to Alexander Duke of Gordon."

The discussion of the elaborately published *Empress of Morocco* led Malone to remark in a footnote: "It is remarkable that some of the worst plays in the English language have been ornamented with engravings. A few years after the appearance of Settle's tragedy, NOAH'S FLOOD, an opera, was embellished with similar decorations; and in the following century SCANDERBEG, a tragedy, was recommended to the public by the same ornamental appendage."

127 A footnote was given to the *Remarks on the Empress of Morocco:* "Crown in the preface to his [*Caligula,* 1698] says that above two thirds of these Remarks were written by him."

134 Malone had come across a good deal of new material on the Rose Alley ambuscade, and so he deleted his footnote on the subject and substituted the following one: "In a newspaper of the day is the following account of this transaction, with which I have been furnished by Dr Charles Burney, Junior.

" 'Dec.19.1679.

Last night Mr. Dryden, the famous poet, coming from a Coffeehouse in Covent Garden, was set upon by three persons unknown to him; and so rudely by them handled, that it is said, his life is in no small danger. It is thought to have been the effect of private grudge, rather than upon the too common design of unlawful gain: an unkind trespass, by which not only he himself, but the commonwealth of learning, may receive an injury.'

"In the London Gazette, No. 1472, Monday, December 29, 1679, I find an advertisement inserted by our author, with a view to discover the offenders; from which it appears that at this time he had adopted the ancient mode of spelling his family name:

" 'Whereas John *Dreyden,* Esqre was on Thursday the 18th instant, at night, barbarously assaulted and wounded in Rose-street, Covent Garden, by diverse men unknown: if any person shall make discovery of the said offenders to the said Mr Dryden or to any Justice

Page

of peace, he shall not only receive fifty pounds, which is deposited in the hands of Mr Blanchard, Goldsmith, next door to Temple-bar, for the said purpose, but if he be a principal or an accessary in the said fact, his Majesty is graciously pleased to promise his pardon for the same.'

"In a newspaper entitled 'Domestick Intelligence; or News both from City and Country,' Jany 2, 1679, the same reward (and pardon) is promised to the discoverer, though he should have himself committed the fact, provided he should make known the person who incited him to this unlawful act. But neither the persons who committed this outrage, nor their employers, were ever discovered: which affords a strong confirmation of what is stated in the text—that they were hired for the purpose by those whose circumstances enabled them to ensure secrecy by a larger sum than Dryden could afford to pay for the discovery.

"In a letter written Jany 2, 1679, by the pious Mr Nelson and addressed to one of Dryden's schoolfellows, already mentioned, Dr Mapletoft (see p. [13 in these additions]) are these words: 'Your friend and schoolfellow, Mr Dryden, has been severely beaten for being the supposed author of a late abusive lampoon. There has been a good sum of money offered, to find who set them on work: 'tis said they received their orders from the Duchess of Portsmouth, who is concerned in the lampoon.' The original letter is in the hands of Dr. Mapletoft's grandson, Mr Mapletoft, surgeon, of Chertsey, by whom it was communicated some years ago to the editor of *The European Magazine*."

135 To note 9, on the Duchess of Portsmouth, Malone added: "After the death of her royal paramour she returned to France, but in 1699 again paid a visit to England, when, according to Burnet, she told Mr Antony Henley of the Grange in Hampshire, that Charles the Second was poisoned. She died at Paris in 1728, near eighty years old."

141 Malone did not "remember right": he had to alter the reference to the "learned man" to "Hooker. See the first paragraph of his EC-CLESIASTICAL POLITY."

New information about the Absalom Allegory had come Malone's way, and he used it to introduce note 7: "Barten Holiday, during the Civil War, preached four Sermons against Disloyalty, one of which was on the subject 'of Absolon's Ambition', and was preached before the Prince Charles at Christ-Church in Oxford, Nov. 10. 1644. These four sermons were collected and published by Holiday in 1661. That on the subject of Absolon, I suspect, had been read by Dryden. Derrick asserts that 'the application of the story of Absalom *to this part of King Charles the Second's reign* was first made by a clergyman

Page

in the pulpit and his sermon was printed with the title of Absolom
and Achitophel;' but I have never met with it."

147   The note on Shaftesbury's memoirs was rewritten to read: "Biog.
Brit. lv.264* 2d. edit. Shaftesbury had written 'Memoirs of his own
time,' which, when he fled to Holland, he entrusted to Locke; who
after the execution of Algernon Sydney committed them to the flames.
Some of his pocket-books, however, containing a few short notes,
escaped the fire, and yet remain; and a curious character of Mr. Hastings, a Dorsetshire gentleman, (William third son of Francis, second
earl of Huntington) taken from those Memoirs, was published in
Howard's Collection of Letters, vol. i. p. 152. 4to 1756.—The *other
person'* mentioned by Dr Kippis as the *last* to whom the manuscripts of Mr. Stringer &c were consigned, was Dr. Kippis himself,
and he received £500 for his revision of them, as the late Sir W^m
Musgrave informed me."

150   To the lines on Shaftesbury there is added the following footnote:
"Had not the whole of Shaftesbury's political life made him so justly
odious, Dryden's connexions would naturally have led him to represent that nobleman in a favourable light; for Shaftesbury had married Margaret, a daughter of William the second Lord Spencer; and
Henry Howard, one of the brothers of Dryden's wife married Elizabeth, another of Lord Spencer's daughters."

156   A few details about the dispersal of Narcissus Luttrell's books were
given in a footnote: "The twenty four volumes of Ancient Poetry
were purchased by Dr Farmer for twenty four guineas; and being
cut up and sold piecemeal, produced at the sale of his books, I believe, near £200. They contained about three hundred articles."

157   The mention of Henry Care was illustrated by a footnote: "In a
ballad entitled 'The Treacherous Anabaptist,' published in April 1681,
are these lines:
'He writes twice a week news domestick and foreign,
    As seditious as Care, Ben Harris, or Curtis.' "
The note on *Absalom and Achitophel* was augmented into the following form: "Containing thirty-two pages, and the preface. Price one
shilling. The subsequent editions were in quarto. To the early editions
of this poem Jacob Tonson only put the initial letters of his name,
and the copies, though printed for him, were sold by another bookseller. He probably concealed his name from an apprehension that
Shaftesbury and his partisans might do him some prejudice in his
business."

166   To the note about Lord Somers Malone appended the following:
"How little he [Pope] knew of the terms on which that nobleman
and Dryden were, even to the latest period of the poet's life, appears
from Pope's verses in the Epistle to Arbuthnot, to which the note

Page

here referred to was appended. He there describes Lord Somers not only as the patron and admirer, but the *friend* of Dryden:

'The courtly Talbot, *Somers,* Sheffield, read,
Even mitred Rochester would nod the head:
And St John's self (great Dryden's *friends* before)
With open arms received one poet more.'

See also his note there.—Our author himself, however, in a letter to his kinswoman Mrs. Steward, written in Nov. 1699, expressly calls Lord Somers his *enemy."*

172 At the end of the list of textual variants in *Mac Flecknoe,* Malone aimed a shaft at Hardinge, who had ridiculed this page. The passage should read: "Two or three of these variations, however, are manifestly mere corrections of errours of the press; but many of them mark our author's care in revising this poem. The minute changes made in their compositions by eminent authors are always a matter of both curiosity & instruction to literary men, however trifling and unimportant they may appear to blockheads, one of whom in an impotent endeavour to ridicule all such notices, has had the impudence to assert that the *only* variations here noted were *papers* for *paper* & *poppeys* for *poppy* and *others of a similar kind."*

173 The paragraph on Shadwell's report that Dryden denied writing *Mac Flecknoe* was to end with the sentence: "However, in his Dedication of Juvenal to Lord Dorset in August 1692, the hero of the piece being laid in that grave where neither sarcasm nor wit 'could touch him further', he avowed himself the author of this admirable satire."

174 Malone had found a second edition of *Religio laici,* and amended the text to that effect.

181 Into the passage suggesting that Samuel Dyer was Junius, Malone inserted the qualifications that had appeared in Add. & Em. p. 137.

184 After the mention of Samuel Dyer's "pecuniary losses", Malone added the passage on the subject from Add. & Em., p. 137.

186 To the footnote (1) on the *History of the League* was added the detail, "It was published in the latter end of July, 1684. See London Gazette. No 1951."

187 Here is inserted the following unplaced note on *Albion and Albanius:* "Among the MSS of Richard Goodson Jun. Organist of Christ Church & St John Oxford—in the library of Ch. Ch. is

Albion and Albanus an Opera or representation in musick set by Lewis Grabu Esqʳ Master of his late Majesty's musick. large folio on wood. London 1687

The author tells us in his Dedication to King James II that his brother had honoured this opera with his presence at several rehearsals; that it had been *performed at his own theatre* when Duke of York; but complains much of the scarcity of good singers in Eng-

Page

land on which account he says the piece suffered very much. The overture airs and Recitative are all close imitations of Lully and the 1ˢᵗ violin part is put in the Tr. clif in the first line.

Burney MS."

[Here is pasted in a letter from Mr. W. G. Hiscock, 19 August 1932, Assistant Librarian of Christ Church, to Bodley's Librarian, making it clear that the above note refers to the ordinary printed folio, not a MS. copy].

188   Two slips are pasted in here, both containing quotations from the *London Gazette,* No. 2042, 15 June 1685, one about the landing of the Duke of Monmouth at Lyme, and the second about subscriptions for *Albion and Albanius.*

189   Into the paragraph on Dryden's constancy in his new faith, Malone inserted the following (line 11): "He even endeavoured to convert to his new faith those persons whom he esteemed. 'May God be pleased to open your eyes, (says he to a kinswoman in Nov. 1699) as he has opened mine. Truth is but one; and they who have once heard of it can plead no excuse if they do not embrace it.' "

190   The date of *Threnodia Augustalis* was inserted from that written on the title-page of Narcissus Luttrell's copy, 9 March 1684/5.

191   A note on the *Ode to Mrs. Anne Killigrew* points out that the poem was advertised in the *London Gazette* No. 2085, 9 November 1685.

193   Malone corrected his mistake in line 15 of saying *Religio laici* where he meant *The Hind and the Panther.*

196   Malone gave the source of the long quotation from Burnet: "A Defence of the REFLECTIONS on the ninth book of the first volume of Mr Varillas's HISTORY OF HERESIES. Being a *Reply* to his CENSURE. By G. Burnet, D. D. Amst. 1687. 24mo." This is the edition which Birch had quoted from, and probably Malone was merely quoting from Birch.

202   Among the events of 1688 Malone inserted the following reference to a fact that he had picked up from Scott's biography: "The Queen, during her pregnancy having recommended herself to St Francis Xavier as her patron saint, he had a few months before translated from the French * and published **Bouhours's Life** of that saint, doubtless in compliment to her Majesty.

* The Queen mother of France, we are told, having been long time childless, was persuaded to recommend herself to the protection of this saint; and to his intercession she owed Louis the Fourteenth; as all good Catholicks were then taught to believe. See 'The Reasons of Mr Bayes's changing his religion,' &c. by T. Brown, 4to 1690. Hence doubtless the English Queen's respect for St. Xavier."

202   Also to be inserted on this page was the note on Bossuet's *Doctrine of the Catholic Church,* from Add. & Em., pp. 137–8.

206   To the note on Dryden's successors in the office of Poet Laureate, the

Page

following particulars were added: [Shadwell] "to whom a salary of 300 £ p ann. was also granted." [Tate's succession was] "a promotion for which he is said in a poem of the last age to have been indebted to his translation of the *Psalms*". [Eusden] ("who had conciliated the new Lord Chamberlain Thomas Pelham Duke of Newcastle by an Epithalamium on his marriage with Lady Harriet Godolphin in 1716) was in the following year invested with this office; which he held till Sept. 27, 1730. About two months after his death, Dec. 3, 1730, Colley Cibber was appointed Poet Laureate."

To the last paragraph, concerning the practice of conferring the laureatship by a warrant, is added, the last nine words being deleted: "at least Mr. Warton, as he informed me was thus appointed: but the present laureat received no warrant but merely on his appointment took the oath of office before the Lord Chamberlain which is taken by all the King's household."

207 The account of Dryden's loss of the laureateship was augmented to read, ". . . Dryden's conversion to popery was an insurmountable objection to his holding his offices; and he was not divested of them by the strong hand of authority, as generally has been supposed, but as he himself has told us, 'conscientiously relinquished them' * on the 1st of August 1689, by refusing to take the oaths of supremacy and abjuration which were appointed by the first parliament of King William to be taken by every person holding an office under the crown.

* See his Letter to Mrs Stewart [blank] in which he says, 'I can neither take the oaths nor forsake his [sic] religion.'—In the Dedication of LOVE TRIUMPHANT to the Earl of Salisbury, in 1694, he mentions the lowness of his fortunes, to which he says, 'he had *voluntarily* reduced himself.' " [memorandum: "Q. where he says he conscientiously relinquished perhaps Ded to Juvenal"]

208 Malone later discovered that Shadwell's and Rymer's poems on the arrival of William and Mary were printed in *Poems on Affairs of State*.

210 Concerning Tate's official verses Malone added, "The Ode for New Year's Day by Tate 'as performed to musick before her Majesty Jany the first 1705', is printed at the end of a poem by the same author entitled THE TRIUMPH OR WARRIORS WELCOME. I have seen another official ode also by Tate."

211 The date of *Don Sebastian* was changed from 1690 to "the winter of 1689" and the reason given in a footnote: "The Reasons of Mr. Bays's changing his religion &c, which was licensed Jany 8 1689–90 contains some observations on DON SEBASTIAN."

212 Add to the account of Dryden's literary activities in 1690: "Between

Page

June and Sepr in that year while King William was in Ireland, he furnished Betterton with a prologue to the PROPHETESS, a musical drama, in which Cibber informs us * there were some sneers at the Revolution which occasioned its being stopped after the first night of its being spoken. As it now stands, nothing of this kind is found.

* APOL. for his Life; p. [blank] 8vo"

221   To the paragraph on *Eleanora*, Malone added the note: "It is a singular circumstance that Dryden should not have known that this lady died very suddenly at a ball in her own house in the midst of a gay assembly of both sexes; a fact, of which had he been apprized of it, he would not have neglected to avail himself. See Gould's Poems, 1708. Vol. [blank] p. [blank]."

228   Malone had come across an earlier publication by Congreve than the song in the *Maid's Last Prayer*, January 1693: "In the preceding year he prefixed some encomiastick lines to our author's translation of Persius."

230   Additional information about the 1694 *Annual Miscellany* was inserted in a footnote: "In the London Gazette No. 2929, Dec. 7, 1693 Tonson informed the publick that he was preparing for the press another volume of poems, to be published in the ensuing Hilary term; and such gentlemen as wished their verses to appear in that collection were requested to send them to him. This fourth volume of what has been usually called Dryden's Miscellanies was published under the title of the ANNUAL MISCELLANY in July 1693. [sic]. A similar advertisement *praying aid* for the THIRD MISCELLANY, appeared in the London Gazette, No 2856, March 27. 1693. That volume was published in July in that year."

Malone also hazarded the speculation that Dryden's version of the Third Georgic was "published, we may presume, as a specimen of his projected translation of that author's works."

233–4   The lines about early publication by subscription were changed to read as follows: . . . "Milton's great poem, as we have seen, had been printed by subscription some years before; in 1691, Wood's ATHENAE OXONIENSES and in 1694 Camden's BRITANNIA *, published by Gibson,§ were issued out in the same manner.

* The proposals for printing that work by subscription appeared in the London Gazette, No 2864, April 24, 1693.

§ Some works of less importance indeed had been pub^d by subscription at an earlier period: Dr Plotts History of Staffordshire in 1677 and [blank]."

235   The first sentence on the page, about the translation of Virgil, was modified to read: "It appears to have been begun in the summer of 1694, and was sent to the press when only eight books of the Æneid

Page

were translated; probably early in the year 1696. From a letter now before me" etc.

237 An entirely new paragraph was inserted here: "Though an author's sentiments with respect to his own works are not always decisive with his readers, it yet may be a matter of curiosity to many, to learn which part of this great work Dryden esteemed the most. He tells us, that of the original, the fourth and sixth Æneids were his greatest favourites; and he thought he had succeeded best in the translation of the fourth, sixth and eighth pastorals; the First and Fourth Georgicks; the fourth, fifth, seventh, ninth, tenth, eleventh and twelve [sic] Æneids. The first Georgick he thought more sublime than any part of Virgils Works; and he adds, if ever he copied that writing majestick style, it was in his version of that book; the 12th Æneid he informs us he translated with uncommon care by desire of Sir Wm Trumbull. It is remarkable that though he mentions the sixth Æneid as his particular favourite, he does not enumerate it among those in which he had succeeded best."
Lower on the page, among the authors who had made plural dedications, Malone added the names of Drayton and Sylvester.

238 One sentence about the relationship of the Swifts and the Drydens was emended to read: ". . . the Dean of St. Patrick's *father,* and our author, were only second cousins, and consequently the Dean himself who was born in 1669 [sic] and Charles Dryden our poet's son, who was born in 1666, were third cousins."

241 The footnote on the publication of Swift's odes contained several errors, as Bishop Percy pointed out to Malone (MS. Malone 27 f. 157^v). Accordingly it was emended to read: "An Ode to Sir William Temple, written in 1689; and an Ode to the Athenian Society, written in 1691. These Odes are inserted in the common editions of Swift's works. A Copy of Verses addressed by Swift to King William on his success in Ireland, written in alternate succession about the year 1690, was also probably submitted for Dryden's perusal. It long remained sheltered in Motteux's GENT. Journal and Dunton's ATHENIAN ORACLE (selected from a larger work, and published in three volumes, 8vo.) from which it has been reprinted in a supplemental volume to Swift's Works printed for C. Dilly in 8vo. in 1789."

252 The verses about "hook-nosed Æneas" were transferred here from the place where Malone had first printed them, Vol. I, part ii, pp. 55–6, note.

253 The first sentence of the note about Sir Henry Shere should begin "According to the ordinary corruption of the last age" and should end "this gentleman was generally called *Sheres* by his contemporaries."

256 The footnote on the death of St. Cecilia is augmented, but since this, as well as numerous emendations and alterations on pp. 260–83 about her and the musical performances in her honour, do not concern Dryden, I shall not reproduce them.

Page

259   Of the verses ascribed to Hughes, Malone wrote, "These very elegant lines are ascertained to be written by Hughes by a manuscript note in my copy."

286   Malone augmented his remarks on the letter to Dryden from Richard Graham, Junior, which I have already quoted on p. 13.

287   To the story printed by Joseph Warton that Dryden wrote *Alexander's Feast* at one sitting, Malone had replied with evidence that it was composed with more leisure. A new passage was to be inserted, as follows:

"This is the language of a barrister to whom some important cause had been comitted [sic] at a late hour in the evening, on which it was necessary for him to sit up the whole night to prepare himself to appear before the House of Lords on the following day. The original relater of this anecdote should seem to have supposed that Dryden had not much more time allowed him for the composition of this ode.

"It is observable also, that though Mr. Spence appears to have had frequent conversations with Pope concerning Dryden, and has left several anecdotes relative to that poet, Pope, who is said to have been one of the transmitters of this story, never mentioned it to him."

290   The note on Lady Elizabeth Howard was expanded by transferring to this page the first paragraph of the note on page 398. Other changes of less importance were made in the remainder of the note, on pp. 291–92.

302   The note on Jeremiah Clark received the addition of one sentence: "In 1697 he composed the musick of the prologue to THE WORLD IN THE MOON, an opera by Settle performed in that year."

318   Malone inserted a sentence into the paragraph about Dryden's modernization of Chaucer: "Some years indeed before 1697, as he has himself told us, he had thoughts of apparelling the old bard in a modern English dress, but did not then undertake the work, in deference to the Earl of Leicester, who greatly admired Chaucer's language, and thought it a kind of profanation to alter it.*
      * See vol. iii. p. 635."

321   A passage of note 6 has been rewritten into the following form: "In the Epistle to his kinsman our author alludes to his grandfather, (perhaps Sir Erasmus Driden, their common grandfather) who appears to have been imprisoned, for resisting some irregular levy of money; a circumstance which, it may be presumed, induced Sir John Driden to take so strong a part afterwards with Cromwell. See the Shrewsbury Papers, iii. 265: 'For Mr *Driden,* his Ma. greatly commendeth your grave and judicious proceedings, saying youe had sung the 101 psa. of mercy and justice.' These words are found in a letter written by Lord Shrewsbury to the Privy Council, Feb. 25, 1604–5."

322   Note 7, on the spelling of Dryden's name, was deleted, probably because

Page

Hardinge (*Essence of Malone,* p. 29) had made sport of its inconsistency with a previous note, on p. 3.

325 The beginning of the note on the will of John Driden of Chesterton was considerably rewritten: "The will of Mr. John Driden of Chesterton I have not been able to find in the Prerogative-office, though I examined the Calendar of Wills for several years subsequent to his death. It was 'sealed, delivered, and published the 2d of January, 1707,' three days only before the death of the testator, and probably was not proved till many years afterwards.*

* It is mentioned *as proved,* in a private act of parliament for the sale of the George Inn in Northampton, enacted in the 40th year of Geo. III. (1800)."

326 Note 2 was to be transferred to p. 434, because of the alteration of the text mentioned below:

The lines about the Kneller portrait of Dryden are deleted. The family tradition that Dryden received £500 in return for the famous address to his cousin of Chesterton was emended as follows: "That some valuable donation was made to Dryden in return for these animated verses, I had no doubt when I originally mentioned this circumstance in a former edition; and I afterwards found it fully confirmed by a letter of our author to Mrs Steward; in which he says, that on his sending the volume which contained these verses to his kinsman, he received from him in return to his great surprise *a most noble present.* But in traditional anecdotes of this kind, transmitted by oral communication, minute accuracy is seldom found. It seems much more probable, that the gift was one hundred pounds; for the receipt of so large a sum as five hundred pounds, in March 1700, at which time we know this donation was conferred, seems inconsistent with those distressed circumstances . . ."

The end of the footnote on the Fables is emended to read: ". . . 1699/1700; and we learn from one of Dryden's Letters to Mrs. Steward that the book (in folio) then first appeared; and it was sold for twelve shillings."

331 Footnote 5 was much altered by Malone, especially by the deletion of the quotation from Gildon's *Comparison Between the Two Stages.*

332 On the subject of celebrations to welcome in the new century, Malone pasted in a paper containing the following note: "The Jubilee was improperly celebrated in 1600, as well as 1700; if in either instance those years were considered as the commencement of a century. 'I do intend (says Puntarvolo in EVERY MAN OUT OF HIS HUMOUR acted in 1599,) this year of Jubilee coming on to travaile' &c.

"See also Farquhar's Trip to the Jubilee, which was performed in the spring of the year 1700."

333 The subject of whether the new century began with 1700 or 1701 drew

Page

several additions on this page, including the incorporation of the long note from Add. & Em., pp. 139. Dryden's own testimony was added: "In the Preface to the FABLES writing in Nov. or Dec. 1699, he says, 'if I may properly call it by that name which was the former part of *this concluding* century.' The year then began on *March 25.*"

335   The note on Mrs. Oldfield should begin with a new sentence: "Mrs. Oldfield had at this time been on the stage about a year, unnoticed."

350   Malone had discovered that Dr. Glisson died in 1677.

353   Corrections on this and the following page show that Malone had encountered a copy of "Corinna" 's 1722 volume of poems.

356   Note 5, on the subject of fees for interment in Westminster Abbey, should read as follows: "This was set down at random, the *whole* of the fees for the interment of any person excepting the nobility, amounting at that time only to *ten pounds.* In 1694 the treasurer of the Dean and Chapter of Westminster received from Mr. Nathaniel Povel *ten pounds* for a licence of interment in the Abbey for himself or *any person whom he should nominate.* In 1721 ten pounds were paid for the interment of Prior the poet. Larger sums, however, were then and before paid for the interment of the nobility; and since that period, the fees of interment both for nobility and gentry have increased."

368   Malone had collected the advertisements of William Russel, the coffin-maker, out of the *London Gazette,* Nos. 1957, 1963 and 2035.

371   To conclude the first paragraph of the note on Dryden's funeral, Malone inserted the following: "Tanner's letter as well as the order of the college of Physicians then that Lord Jefferies was not the sole or even the principal person concerned in the honourable interment of Dryden: but that his private was converted into a publick funeral by the interposition of several persons of quality."

377   To the list of those who "doubtless" were found in Dryden's funeral procession Malone added, "Dr. Radcliffe, Dr. Gibbons, Dr. Mapletoft."

381   After the quotation from the *London Spy* are added the details: "The author of this work, which though meanly written, is curious as a picture of the manners of the time, survived Dryden about thirty years. He died June 21, 1731, and was buried at Pancras. Lysons's Environs of London, iii. 371."

386   The mention of Catherine, Duchess of Buckinghamshire, is followed by the detail, "at whose request Pope in 1735 wrote an Epitaph for her son Edmund, the second Duke of Buckinghamshire."

392   Malone learned that he had confused Plato and Aristotle in saying that the latter had defined man as "an unfeathered two-legged thing."

398   The first paragraph of the note about Lady Elizabeth Howard was of course transferred to p. 290 (see above).

400   To the account in note 4 of Charles Dryden's Latin verses on Lord

Page

Arlington's Gardens is added, "A translation of them may be found in Boyse's Poems, 8vo, 1734, p. 32."

401   On this page is a note about the emoluments received by the Chamberlain of the Pope at the Vatican.

403   The note on Granville's generosity to Charles Dryden was modified as follows: "It is very probable that he had, in like manner, given Dryden the profits of his two plays, the SHE GALLANTS and HEROICK LOVE, the former of which was acted in 1696, and the latter in January 1697/8. Before HEROICK LOVE are some encomiastick verses by our author.

"In the Preface to the SHE GALLANTS, Granville says, that he gave the benefit of it to *a friend;* and that if his friend had a *third* day to his satisfaction, [he] had obtained his end. At that time this kind of treaty was not uncommon." etc.

419   To the note on the popularity of astrology Malone added: "No discredit was attached to this foolish study. There are several sermons in print, preached before the *learned society of Astrologers.*"

423   Malone had learned that Obadiah Walker had not died abroad: "He afterwards returned into England, where he remained concealed, not venturing to prefix to his books more than the initial letters of his names. He died in 1699, and was buried in Pancras Churchyard, with this inscription only. O. W. *per bonam famam et per infamiam.*"

432   At the end of the paragraph about Riley's portrait of Dryden, Malone added the further information, "Another portrait said to be painted by Riley was in the collection of the Earl of Besborough, and was sold at a sale of his pictures &c in 1801: whether a duplicate of Mr. Bromley's picture, I have not been able to ascertain. It is now in the collection of [blank]" (Malone identified the person as follows: "the same person who bought the high priced Guido or Coreggio for 1000 gs at Mr Furlings.")

434   The second half of the first paragraph about the Kneller portraits of Dryden was to be deleted (see note for p. 326 above).
A footnote was inserted to explain Dryden's nickname of "Poet Squab": "The precise meaning of *Squab* may be learned from Coles, who in his Dictionary renders it by—*pinguiculus.* I do not vouch for the goodness of his latinity." The *OED* gives the meaning with equal precision: "short and stout, squat and plump."

435   The paragraph on Kneller should conclude with this sentence: "Another portrait of Dryden by Kneller is in the possession of that painter's great nephew, John Kneller Esqr at D [onhead] Hall in Wiltshire."

439   After the long quotation from the letter written by Swift to Thomas Beach, Malone added a note about Beach's poem which Swift had corrected for him: "The poem here mentioned after it had received Swift's corrections was published in London in quarto under the title of

Page

'EUGENIO, or Virtuous and Life' [sic] and inscribed to Mr. Pope. A few days after its publication, May 17, 1737, the author, who was a winemerchant at Wrisam, killed himself in a very shocking manner."

444   Malone emended the note about Spence's report of Dryden's estate, to read, "probably from the information of Sir William Trumbull, Congreve or Garth."

454   Here are pasted three slips about the custom of giving an author the receipts for the third day's performance of his play: [i] "Lacy in his Epilogue to the Old Troop 1698 but written before—1682 & I believe then acted

My poet's day I mortgage to one act

At least six months before the play is writ

In Prologue to Alphoncorlys

And then I'll laugh at wits on *my third day.*

Prol to Duffets Devil of a Wife 1695

And since penance at this time's in fashion

Come *three days* for mortification.

[ii] Dryden mentions his *third* day in Dedn. of Amphitryon 1690 To author only *one* benefit thus

[iii] The 3rd and 6th night only talked of in Farquhars Twin Rivals 1702–3

The charges in 1730 ascertained in the 4° Life of Mrs. Oldfield."

458   In his estimate of Dryden's earnings Malone inserted the following note: "For Dryden's contribution to each of the four volumes of Miscellanies published in 1684, 1685, 1693, and 1694, he appears to have got either fifty pounds or fifty guineas. See Tonson's Letter to him. Lett. V."

464   Malone augmented the note on Dryden's relations with Pope so that it read: "We learn from Dr. Warburton, that when he was very young, he prevailed with a friend to carry him to Will's Coffee-house, that he might see Dryden. 'Who does not wish (says Dr. Johnson) that Dryden could have known the value of the homage that was paid him, and foreseen the greatness of his young admirer?' Dr. Warton mentions, that Mr. Walter Harte informed him, 'that Dryden gave Pope a shilling for translating, when he was a boy, the story of Pyramus and Thisbe.' Probably he carried this early specimen of his abilities in his pocket when he went to Will's Coffee[house] to see our author." etc.

467   At the end of the note on the Mulberry Garden, the passage from Add. & Em. p. 140, was inserted.

475   Further remarks were added to the note on Dryden's caricature of Burnet as the "Buzzard" in the *Hind and the Panther:* "It was an aggravating circumstance that this unfavourable character was dispersed in his native country by authority: for the Hind and the Panther was printed in quarto in 1687 at Holyroode House 'by James Watson, Printer to his Majesties royal family and houshold.' "

Page

477 To illustrate Dryden's modesty the following passage was appended to note 6: "In his private letters to his friends he speaks of himself and his works with that modesty which was natural to him and truly part of his character. 'In the mean time, says he in a letter written in 1698-9, betwixt my intervals of physick and other remedies which I am using for my gravel, I am still drudging on:—*Always a poet, and never a good one.*' 'My Virgil (he tells his sons) succeeds in the world *beyond its desert* or my expectations.' And of his FABLES (addressing himself to his kinswoman, Mrs. Steward,) he says,—'They are a debt to you I must confess; and I am glad because they are so *unworthy to be made a present.*' It was only among the criticks in Coffee-houses, or in his Letters to his bookseller, or when he was decried and run down by his adversaries, that he considered it necessary to keep up a proper port, and not to abate a jot of his poetical pretensions. In those cases he seems to have thought it fair to follow the example and adopt the language of Horace:—*Sume superbiam quaesitam meritis.*"

484 At the end of the note on negus, Malone recorded an item of social history, about Augustan drinking customs: "In the last age, it was a common practice to grate both ginger and nutmeg into ale and other similar beverages."

485 To the note on Will's coffee-house, add the following: "The situation of Will's is alluded to in the Epilogue to THE PERJURED HUSBAND, a tragedy, by Mrs Centlivre, acted in 1700.

'Let at yond *corner house* the *Wits* and *Bards*
Gain by religion what they lose at cards;
Let snarling peevish critics cease to bite
Or in a false sublime dull plays to write.' "

494 More social history appears in an addition to note 8, on the hour when theatrical performances began: "In 1699, however, they appear not to have begun till five o'clock. Thus in the DISPENSARY, C. iv, which first appeared in that year:

Not far from that frequented theatre
Where wandering punks each night *at five* repair &c."

496 As additional evidence that Dryden was an easy conversationalist Malone inserted the following note: " 'Here', says his kinswoman Mrs Creed, speaking of Tichmarsh and our author, 'he has often made us happy by his kind visits, and *most delightful conversation.*' See Appendix, No. IV."

498 Malone here deleted the anecdote about Lady Elizabeth Dryden, and inserted the remarks on the "Dryden Almanac Story" which I reported in the *Philological Quarterly*, XVI (1937), p. 412 ff.

499 To the note on the fondness for bowling of Sheffield, Duke of Buckinghamshire, is added the passage from Add. & Em., p. 140.

502 Dryden's remarks about Homer, from his letter to Montague in 1699,

Page

were here deleted, because they had already been printed on p. 313.

512 Inserted in the list of Dryden's favourite authors is "Cowley [who] he himself tells us was the darling of his youth". This carries the footnote "Dedication to Juvenal, Vol. [blank] p. [blank]. He lived however to think less highly of him. In the Preface to his FABLES, he observes" [unfinished].

515 Malone added Swift's name to the ranks of those poets who read badly, with the footnote: "This deficiency in this respect is ascertained by the testimony of George Faulkner, who in a note in the Irish edition of his works speaks of it as an acknowledged fact."

To note 6 on this page, Malone appended an additional example of Dryden's readings of his works before publication: "See also his Dedication of the THIRD MISCELLANY to Lord Radcliffe, in 1693: 'Your lady and you have done me the favour to *hear me read* my translations of Ovid; and you both seemed not to be displeased with them.' "

To note 7 Malone added a conjecture as to how Dr. Johnson knew the anecdote that Southerne used to relate about Congreve's wretched reading of his own plays: "probably [Johnson learned of it] from the information of John Earl of Corke and Orrery."

523 Pasted on this page are a number of citations from the books of the Stationers' Company, concerning Richard Tonson, Jacob Tonson I, and Abel Swalle:

4 July 1676 Richard Tonson Servt to Mr S. Walbanck, sworn & admitted into the freedom of the Company

iii^s iiij^d

20 Dec. 1677 Jacob Tonson Servt to Thos Bassett sworn and admitted into the freedom of the Company iiis. iiijd

5° Junii 1670

Jacob Tonson sonne of Jacob Tonson late of *Holborne* in the county of Midd. Barber Chyrurgeon deceased hath put himselfe an Apprentice to Thomas Bassett for eight years from this day.

iis. vid.   Free

5° December 1676

Abell Swalle sonne of Abraham Swalle late Citizen and Weaver of London deceased hath put himselfe an Apprentice to Robert Boulter for seaven years from this daye.

admitted & sworn into the freedom of the Company, iii.iiijd

1 Aprilis 1668

Richard Tonson sonne of Jacob Tonson Citizen and Barber Chirurgeon of London hath put himselfe an Apprentice to Elizabeth Walbanck widow for seaven yeeres from this day.

ii. vi.d   free

533 Here is another bit of social history, the definition of a "cold loaf", a dish enjoyed by Vanbrugh at "a very humble ale-house": "A *cold loaf,*

Page

is a loaf of bread from which all the crum has been taken, after which operation it is filled with the limbs of *cold* chickens, slices of ham or tongue, &c."

534 The occupant of Tonson's villa at Barn Elms about 1800, Malone tells us, was Sir Richard Hoare.

564 In the epitaph on Dryden's father, Malone found an error in the statement that the poet's mother was a granddaughter of Sir Gilbert Pickering: "This is a mistake. Mary was the granddaughter of Henry Pickering, a younger brother of that Sir Gilbert Pickering who died Feb. 28, 1612–13. Esc. 10 Jac. p.1. n. 94."

567 In the catalogue of "Persons in whose Cabinets letters written by Dryden may probably be found" are listed "The Representatives of Sir Robert Howard, Bart." To this a note was added: "Thomas Howard Esq. a son of Sir Robert Howard was married at Twickenham to Diana Newport Sep. 4. 1682. Perhaps some female descendants of this marriage may have carried some of the Howard papers into other families."

568 Here is found an unplaced memorandum: "Samuel Briscoe the bookseller soon after Dryden's death said in the preface to his Collection of Familiar Letters, that after he had finished his Collection, he had received several of Mr. Dryden's. Q where they now are."

569 To the list of those who informed Malone they had no Dryden letters, he added "John Kneller of [blank] Hall in Wiltshire, Esqre." Accordingly Kneller's name was deleted from the list on the opposite page.

This page also notes that a letter of Dryden addressed to William Oldys, Senior, was in the possession of the antiquary; this had already been noted on p. 376, note. The fact comes from Oldys's MS. notes in his well-known copy of Langbaine, p. 131.

At the bottom of the page Malone recorded the loss in Sir John Hawkins's fire of Dryden's annotated copy of the Rymer's *Tragedies of the Last Age Considered,* which I have discussed in some detail on pp. 283–85.

2

NOTES ON SCOTT'S *LIFE OF DRYDEN*

SCOTT'S *DRYDEN* AND THE "COMPLETE WORKS"

LOCKHART's account of Scott's early publishing ventures has led later biographers astray as to the relation between Scott's *Dryden* and his project for a "complete edition of the British Poets, ancient and modern." Stephen Gwynn, in his *Life of Scott* (1930), says, "The first of these proposed undertakings was no less than a complete edition of the British Poets . . . The scheme did not go through; and in the upshot Scott undertook only an edition of Dryden's Works . . ." (p. 127). Lord Tweedsmuir followed the same erroneous path in his *Sir Walter Scott* (1932, p. 78). The letters from Scott to the Reverend Edward Forster prove conclusively, however, that the edition of Dryden was projected earlier than the complete edition of the English poets. Scott discussed the Dryden with Forster in letters dated March 17 and 29, 1805; whereas he did not propose the complete edition until April 12.

The letter of March 17 contains an interesting exposition of Scott's plans for the edition of Dryden. Since it does not appear in Sir Herbert Grierson's edition of the letters, I quote it here:

On the subject of Dryden I have to trouble you with the following observations. I think what you propose as to pecuniary matters would be very fair vizt, from 30 to 40 gns. a volume. No doubt this will be greatly too much for some of them & too little for others for example neither you nor I could do the life & general critique under £100, & I would willingly undertake to do the Drama at 20 guineas a volume. The political poems and translations will take an equal degree of attention and should be on a level in point of emolument. But if you can drive a good bargain with the Booksellers I think there will be no difficulty in arranging the proportion of labour & recompense betwixt ourselves. The reason I am anxious to take the Drama, at least the one half of it, is that I can be ready to go to press immediately having a copy lying by me corrected and almost ready for printing, whereas the waiting for yours would lose us at least three or four months. What renders it indeed most essential for us to gain all the time that we can is that I do not think it possible for Ballantyne to push on at the rate which would otherwise be necessary to obtain our object of publishing early, unless he is immediately set a-going. Besides this is my own period of leisure so that I could dedicate much more time to setting the old Bard in motion than when our courts sit down. Upon the whole I wish very much to send three volumes at least of the Drama to press instantly & I hope the criticisms & notes though few will do them no discredit. As to the rest of the arrangement I agree with you perfectly, & think you will find a pleasing employment in making notes on the Translations &c. which I dare say you will mingle so judiciously as to interest both the learned & English Reader . . .

As to my name for the reasons already stated it must remain a subject for future consideration. You will be a better judge of how much or rather of how little importance this matter is when after some progress in the work you can speak to the Trade.

This letter was purchased at Hodgson's (lot 520) on January 19, 1939, by the National Library of Scotland. I am able to quote it through the kindness of Mr. W. Park.

NEW INFORMATION ADDED BY SCOTT

The following items are chosen as examples of the new information Scott added to the biographical materials he derived from Malone and other biographers of Dryden.

"David Driden, or Dryden, married the daughter of William Nicholson of Staff-hill, in the county of Cumberland, and was the great-great-grandfather of our poet" (p. 21).

Scott pointed out that "Sir Gilbert Pickering was not our author's only relation at the court of Cromwell. The chief of his family, Sir John Driden, the elder brother of the poet's father, was also a flàming and bigotted puritan, through whose gifts and merits his nephew might reasonably hope to attain preferment" (pp. 37–38).

For the first time another brother-in-law of Dryden, the Honourable Edward Howard, was introduced into the family party on the question of blank verse *versus* rhyme (pp. 97–99).

Sir Walter was the first to point out that the "H. D." to whom *Religio laici* was addressed waş Henry Dickenson (p. 275).

From Octavius Gilchrist Scott learned of "Dryden's Walk" at Rushton, Huntingdonshire (p. 325). See also page 220.

His knowledge of Scottish history enabled Scott to add an interesting fact about *The Hind and the Panther*. "It was printed about the same time at London and in Edinburgh, where a printing-press was maintained in Holy-rood-House, for the dispersion of tracts favouring the Catholic religion" (p. 333).

Dryden's hymns had previously passed unnoticed by his biographers (p. 343).

The poetical epistle to Etherege was also remarked for the first time (p. 346).

Sir Walter was the first to call attention to the *Poem on the Camp at Hounslow*, which indicates that Dryden made frequent visits to the camp of King James in the anxious days of his short reign (p. 348).

The suggestion is here introduced that Dryden privately circulated "light pieces in favour of the exiled family" in the years just after the Revolution (p. 356).

Oldmixon and Parker's defences of Dryden's *Virgil* were mentioned here for the first time (pp. 401–2).

Scott here showed that many suggestions were made to Dryden that he should write an elegy on the death of Queen Mary. And in this connection Scott discovered the story that "Dryden's only interference was, in character of the first judge of his time, to award the prize to the Duke of Devonshire, as author of the best poem composed on the occasion of the Queen's death" (p. 406).

scott's alterations and additions in the second edition (1821)

Most of the alterations in this second printing are unimportant, many of them being mere corrections of grammatical slips or Scotticisms. Occasionally a word or two is inserted in the text, usually to clarify or qualify earlier statements. These changes, numerically the largest group, need not be listed here.

The following differences, however, are worth mentioning, for they are changes in the matter of the text rather than of the manner only.

Asterisk note adds, "The Satire in Cinthia's Revels is directed by Ben Jonson against this false and pedantic taste" (p. 8).

On p. 84 and on p. 110 Scott inserted notes from Evelyn's *Diary*, which was first published in 1818, that is, ten years after the first edition of the *Dryden* (p. 84).

In the note on p. 107, Scott added the clause about Liston.

Since 1808 Sir Walter had presented Kemble with a copy of *The Empress of Morocco*, which fact he added to the footnote on this page (p. 186).

In the footnote to pp. 264–65 Scott made a rejoinder to Gifford, who in his edition of Ben Jonson had challenged the truth of one of Scott's points concerning Jonson.

The note in the first edition does not contain the sentence, "Sir Gideon's son had been married to the Duchess's eldest sister" (p. 285).

The hymns are transferred in the second edition from the *Life* to the *Works,* so that from this point on there is a difference in the pagination of the two editions (pp. 343–45, 1808 edition).

The following is inserted after "subject" in l. 4: "A contemporary authority, the reference to which I have mislaid, says that Dryden was shy and silent in society, till a moderate circulation of the bottle had removed his natural reserve, and that he frequently justified this degree of conviviality by saying, 'there was no deceit in a brimmer' " (p. 457, in the 1808 edition, pp. 454–55 in 1821 edition).

Where Scott encountered this anecdote, I know not. In fact I have never seen it in print elsewhere, except in biographies after Scott's.

After "chivalry," l. 4, Scott added, "The most pathetic verses which Dryden has composed, are unquestionably contained in the epistle to Congreve, where he recommends his laurels, in such moving terms, to the care of his surviving friend. The quarrel and reconciliation of Sebastian and Dorax, is also full of the noblest emotion. In both cases, however, the interest is excited by means of masculine and exalted passion, not of those which arise from the mere delicate sensibilities of our nature; and to use a Scottish phrase, 'bearded men' weep at them, rather than Horace's audience of youths and maidens" (p. 484).

SCOTT'S MANUSCRIPT NOTES ON DRYDEN

All the industry and intelligence that has been put into the Scott Collections at the National Library of Scotland by Dr. Meikle and his learned colleagues does not help us to reconstruct much of the editorship of the Dryden. Many papers have survived from the edition of Swift, but only one volume (MS 894) contains any traces of the earlier undertaking. Folios 31–33 contain *Verses to Dryden* in Scott's hand, beginning, "But thou, great Bard, whose hoary merits claim." Folio 34 contains a copy of *Verses to Dryden* further described as "Miscellaneous Poem, inscribed to the Earl of Oxford, 5. April 1712." Folio 88 contains "Part of a poem on Dryden in Scott's hand." It begins, "Thus bold, thus great & all in the extreme."

But on Folio 89 are the "Notes on Dryden in Scott's Handwriting," which have been already referred to on page 82. The first of these is the advertisement offering a reward for the discovery of the Rose Alley assailants, taken from the *London Gazette,* No. 1472, dated Dec. 24–29, 1679.[1] The next reads, "Bonfires prohibited on the 29th May being the Birthday & Restoration of Charles or at any other time w^{t}out Leave from the board of Council. By Order of Council 7 April 1680. Gaz. No. 1503." These other notes then follow:

Proclamation by the Lord Mayor & Alderman offering a reward of £500 for discovering of the person who committed the indignity against the Duke of Yorks picture at Whitehall. 27. Jany 1681. No. 1691.

The Hist^y of the League advertised in Gazette from July 28 to 31. No. 1951. Whitehall July 31. 1685. Earl of Feversham created a Knight of the Garter; probably in place of D. of Monmouth.

From these it would appear that Scott had obtained grist for his mill by painstakingly thumbing over the files of the *London Gazette.*

With the exception of certain original letters which I have referred to as printed in Sir Herbert Grierson's edition, the National Library yields nothing else that throws light on our present enquiry. But even this is more than can be found at Abbotsford. Through the courtesy of the honorary librarian, Mr. Paul Stevens, and the present representatives of the Scott family, I was allowed to examine the volumes which pertain to Dryden. They consist of a number of early editions which without doubt had been employed by Scott in creating his text of the poems and plays. None of them contained any notes or marginalia. They would be of interest only to a historian of Dryden's text.

My chief hopes had been to find additions and corrections in Scott's own copy of the *Life of Dryden* but the volume at Abbotsford is quite

---

[1] Malone later inserted a manuscript note of this advertisement in his copy of the Life of Dryden. From his tone I believe he came upon it quite independently. (See p. 144 above).

untouched. Considering the numerous alterations which Scott made to the 1821 edition of the biography, there is reason to believe that he sent a marked copy of the 1808 volume to the printer. Perhaps it may yet come to light.

3

NEW INFORMATION IN CHRISTIE'S
MEMOIR OF DRYDEN

CHRISTIE's work as editor helped him finally to eradicate the *Satire on the Dutch* (1662). He says,

The fact is that the alleged Satire was made up from the Prologue and Epilogue of [*Amboyna*] by the publisher of the "State Poems," and first published by him in 1704, with the invention of its having been written in 1662.[1]

The "State Poems," however, were usually taken from manuscript versions or broadsheets, and manuscript copy was probably the origin of this one rather than the iniquitous mind of the publisher.

Christie derived some helpful information from the Rector of Aldwincle, namely, the date of the marriage of Dryden's parents and the true epitaph for his grandfather, Henry Pickering.[2] From the former he was able to confirm the fact that the poet was the eldest son, and from the latter that Dryden was undoubtedly born in the parsonage at Aldwincle, which tradition had long argued to have been the case. The moot point of why Dryden did not take the degree of M.A. at Cambridge is well explained by Christie:

As to his not taking the degree of Master of Arts, this would probably be explained, as he was not a Fellow, by the expense, which would have been greater for Dryden, in consequence of his inheritance from his father. The ancient statutes of the University required anyone possessed of any estate, annuity, or certain income for life amounting to £26 13s. 4d. to pay £8 6s. 4d. in addition to the ordinary fees for any degree; and these for the M.A. degree for one not a Fellow of a College would be as much. It may be supposed that Dryden with his income of forty pounds might be unable, or might not care, to incur the expense of this degree.[3]

---

[1] Page xxxv.   [2] Pages xvi–xvii.   [3] Page xx.

Christie definitely assigned to Dryden the authorship of ". . . an unfortunate production, 'Ladies à la Mode' which did not survive the first night, and was never printed . . ." [4]

No earlier biographer had pointed out that Dryden and Charles Montagu were related by marriage: "The wife of Sir Gilbert Pickering, Dryden's first cousin, was first cousin of George Montagu, the father of Charles, Earl of Halifax." [5]

Tonson's reputation had suffered from Dryden's statement in the letter to his sons at Rome that "I am of your opinion that by Tonson's means almost all our letters have miscarried for this last year." Christie explains the charge by saying, "It is, however, clear from a subsequent letter to Tonson himself that the complaint as to loss of letters imputed nothing more than carelessness or choice of a bad agent." [6]

On page lxxiii Christie refers to the folio Spenser containing Dryden's marginalia which is in the library of Trinity College, Cambridge. I believe he was the first Dryden scholar to take notice of it. For a detailed account of the volume, see pages 241–44.

[4] Page xxx.   [5] Page lxiii*n*.   [6] Page lxx.

Part Two

COLLATERAL INVESTIGATIONS

THE MEDAL OF JOHN BAYES

Most of the attacks on Dryden are painfully dull reading. The majority of them contain nothing but the same stock charges against him, such as his early verses on Cromwell, the ignominy of Rose Alley, or more personal insults repeated from the *Rehearsal*. A contrast to these lampoons is *The Medal of John Bayes* (1682), which, though equally scurrilous and obscene, is deservedly the best known and most quoted poetical assault on Dryden.

This superiority in matter and manner is explained by the fact that Shadwell has been accepted as the author. Malone discovered the first evidence, the copy that belonged to Narcissus Luttrell,[1] which bears the autograph note, "6ᵈ. By Thomas Shadwell. Agt Mʳ Dryden. very severe 15 May." But recently this ascription has been challenged by a distinguished authority on Restoration literature, the late George Thorn-Drury.[2] He questioned Shadwell's authorship on four grounds: first, that the publisher of the libel, Richard Janeway, "had not been concerned in the issue of any single scrap of Shadwell's identified work": secondly, that

As Shadwell had been his most conspicuous victim among the literary men, his name was most readily associated with anything and everything in the nature of a retort, and that it is for this and for no other reason that he has been saddled with *The Medal of John Bayes* [and other anti-Dryden libels].

To substantiate this argument, Thorn-Drury gave the dates of several other lampoons which came after *The Medal of John Bayes*.[3] On this basis he contended that "it is to the last degree improbable that within [this] short period . . . any one man should have produced them all and should have returned three several times to the attack upon Dryden."

---

[1] Now in the Dyce Library at South Kensington.   [2] RES, I (1925), 190–92.

[3] *Satire to His Muse by the Author of Absalom and Achitophel*, advertized in *The True Protestant Mercury*, July 22–26, 1682; *The Tory Poets*, dated by Luttrell "Sept. 4" [1682]; *The Address of John Dryden Laureat, to His Highness the Prince of Orange*, 1689. Luttrell's copy is dated January 30, 1689/90.

In the third place, Thorn-Drury called in witness the dedication of Shadwell's translation of *The Tenth Satyr of Juvenal* (1687). In this he found neither "scurrilous violence or obscenity," nor any acknowledgment of Shadwell's authorship of *The Medal of John Bayes* (though it is not clear why he should have expected acknowledgment of either):

> There are, I suppose it must be admitted, no limits to hypocrisy and untruthfulness, but it is very difficult to believe that a man who had shortly before disgraced himself by the disgusting obscenity of his attack upon Dryden, should, while actually addressing him in public, put forward this unctuous claim to make excuse for himself, because he is neither base nor dishonest.

Finally, there is the core of the argument, Thorn-Drury's attempt to depreciate Luttrell's authority. He did this by labeling it "a single unsupported statement," in contrast to which "there is not to be found, as far as I am aware, a trace of a suggestion of his authorship of it throughout the full and free exchange of abuse which the religious and political differences of the time provoked; the above inscription is, in fact, the ground, and the only ground, for heaping upon Shadwell the disgrace of this scurrilous production." It must be admitted that Thorn-Drury has made a plausible case against Luttrell's ascription, but nonetheless I believe that Shadwell was indeed the author.

Answering the points in the order stated, I shall first examine the argument based on Janeway. That he published nothing else for Shadwell is suggestive rather than conclusive: Janeway's press was very active in the Whig interest and was useful for many writers who wished the maximum of anonymity. The poem before us is so obscene and vitriolic that the author may well have preferred to send it to a party printer rather than merely to take the chance of concealment behind title-page anonymity. Moreover, Thorn-Drury neglected to take into account Shadwell's publishing habits during this decade: after he ceased writing for Herringman, in 1678, and until he settled with Knapton, in 1689, Shadwell did not, so far as I can discover, use the same publisher twice consecutively.

Next, the matter of the many poetical libels fathered on Shadwell. It is true in literature as in life that nameless brats are usually laid at the doors of notorious rakes, but in the present instance this circumstance does not invalidate the authority of Luttrell's ascription. The fact that other libels were attributed to Shadwell *after* the appearance of *The*

Medal of John Bayes in no way detracts from the likelihood that Shadwell wrote the first and most powerful of them: indeed, this explanation strengthens the case for Shadwell's authorship, for it is entirely consistent with the qualifications propounded by Thorn-Drury. *The Medal of John Bayes* is ascribed to Shadwell on positive evidence, and there are no corresponding grounds for the attribution of succeeding libels to him.

The interpretation of the epistle to Sedley before *The Tenth Satyr of Juvenal* seems to me to have been oversimplified by Thorn-Drury. Written five long years after *The Medal of John Bayes* and the publication of *Mac Flecknoe* (regardless of its composition date, we must remember that a poem circulated in manuscript has a restricted audience compared to the same poem in print), this dedication was framed consciously as a "vindication," the very word Shadwell used. Although he could not foresee how many centuries he would live as monarch of Dullness, Shadwell realized that he had been caricatured unmercifully and was deeply hurt by what he regarded as the injustice of Dryden's exaggerations. Five years earlier his method had been to meet abuse with abuse; but now that the quarrel had died down to embers, his method changed into an attempt to prove that Tom Shadwell was not such a bad fellow after all.

I hope Sir [he wrote to Sedley] you will not think me guilty of Arrogance in my own Vindication, especially since there have been such strong endeavours to depress me, and by those who had least reason to do it.

But sure he goes a little too far in calling me the dullest, and has no more reason for that, than for giving me the *Irish* name of *Mack,* when he knows I never saw *Ireland* till I was three and twenty years old, and was there but four Months. . . . But he is not content with [pronouncing me dull], but has another fling at me for playing upon the *Lute*. I must confess that that and all other Gentlemen-like Exercises, which I was capable of Learning, my Father was at the charge of, and let the Libeller make his best of it.

I was provoked to this first [venture in translation] by the supposed *Author* of *Mack-Fleckno,* who saies in another Pamphlet; that to his knowledge, I understand neither Greek nor Latin, though in *Bury* School in *Suffolk,* and *Cajus* Colledge in *Cambridge*, the places of my Youthful Education, I had not that reputation, and let me tell him he knows the contrary.[4]

Having taken this tack, Shadwell naturally avoided saying anything at all about his earlier attempts to repay blow for blow. His whole

---

[4] *Works,* ed. Summers, V, 292. These quotations show how well acquainted the two poets were with incidents in each other's life.

purpose now was to show that Dryden's shafts were never deserved. Thus it was the very essence of Shadwell's remarks to omit references to his attack on Dryden, though he nowhere denies or even implies that he failed to retaliate to the best of his ability. In the absence of an implied denial this "vindication" is a slender thread upon which to hang the contention that Shadwell did not write *The Medal of John Bayes*.[5]

And now for the core of the argument, the authority that should be accorded to Luttrell's title-page inscription. Luttrell's habit of jotting on title pages clearly reveals that he was unusually well informed. I have approached the matter by collecting data from several thousand of Luttrell's books and have found no instance where Luttrell's ascriptions are mistaken in the case of such a well-known figure as Shadwell. Luttrell's note is positive evidence of established quality, which cannot be controverted except by evidence equally positive. So far none has been produced. Neither Thorn-Drury nor any other scholar has put forward as author any other candidate who is worth consideration. If during "the full and free exchange of abuse which the religious and political differences of the time provoked," the poem had been ascribed to another writer, Thorn-Drury would certainly have urged this candidate in Shadwell's place. The negative evidence *against* Shadwell is not a whit stronger than the negative evidence *for* him. Moreover, we should not lose sight of the fact that another writer with an equal knowledge of Dryden's affairs and an equal capacity for virulence in verse could not easily be found in 1682.[6]

In addition to the previous arguments, an important new piece of evidence has recently been brought forward by Dryden's bibliographer, Mr. Hugh Macdonald.[7] In the library of Trinity College, Cambridge, is a copy of *The Medal of John Bayes,* on the title page of which an unknown contemporary recorded his reaction to the abusive poem. It

[5] Even if Shadwell *had* categorically denied the authorship, Thorn-Drury's argument could be turned inside out: why should we be expected to accept Shadwell's denial of *The Medal of John Bayes* any more than he accepted Dryden's denial of *Mac Flecknoe?*

[6] D. M. McKeithan, in his study of "The Authorship of the *Medal of John Bayes*," (Texas Studies in English, pp. 92–97, 1932), has examined passages of this poem in comparison with Shadwell's acknowledged verse.

[7] *Essays and Studies by Members of the English Association*, XXI (1935), 59. In his *Dryden Bibliography* (1939) which appeared after this study was written, Mr. Macdonald points out (p. 233) the contemporary evidence of *A Journal from Parnassus* connecting Shadwell with *The Medal of John Bayes*.

reads, "Shadwell is run mad." With this statement corroborating that of Luttrell, I believe we must accept Shadwell as the author until there are new grounds for thinking otherwise.

Once Shadwell is accepted as the author, it is necessary to reëxamine with care the passages in *The Medal of John Bayes* that tell us anything about Dryden. Sprinkled in the poem or in the preliminary *Epistle to the Tories,* there are about a score of such passages, of which half a dozen or so are repetitions of old charges that had been bandied about by Dryden's opponents for more than ten years. Before going on to the dozen passages which contain new biographical information about Dryden, it is convenient to glance at Shadwell's restatement of these stock charges.[8]

The first of them, mentioned in the *Epistle to the Tories* and expanded in the poem, is that Dryden, ever prompt to discover dullness in others, was himself "lumpish and flegmatick" in conversation. Shadwell was especially sensitive to this contradiction, for he had won a name as a clever conversationalist, and so was doubly insulted that a whole poem should celebrate him as the monarch of Dullness. His vanity punctured and his wit impugned, Shadwell sought revenge with personal abuse. His task was comparatively easy, because fourteen years earlier Dryden had confessed in print that he was backward in company:

I know I am not so fitted by nature to write comedy: I want that gaiety of humour which is required to it. My conversation is slow and dull; my humour saturnine and reserved; in short, I am none of those who endeavour to break jests in company, or make reparties.[9]

To what degree Dryden described himself fairly it is now impossible to determine, but his admission was used for several decades by his opponents as a stick with which to beat him.

The next circumstance of which Shadwell reminded Dryden was his relations with the actress Ann Reeves.[10] From the many contemporary references to this affair, we may safely conclude that she was the poet's

---

[8] Shadwell's critical opinions, such as that Dryden "has an easiness in Rime, and a knack at Versifying," or that his dedications are full of "nauseous flattery," have been passed over as not coming within the scope of this present inquiry.

[9] "Defence of an Essay of Dramatic Poesy," in Ker, *Essays of Dryden,* I, 116. This trait is again mentioned many years later in a letter to the Earl of Chesterfield, dated February 17, 1696/7: "I have humoured my natural bashfulness by not addressing you sooner." *The Letters of Chesterfield,* (1829), pp. 376–79.

[10] See Thorn-Drury's discussion of the subject, *Covent Garden Drollery,* 1928, p. 135.

mistress, although to the credit of both it must be acknowledged that amidst the loose living of the age Dryden was apparently constant in his affections: for unlike his notorious contemporaries, Dryden's name is never linked by gossip with that of any other woman of the theater or the town.[11] Even Shadwell pays tribute to his "constancy in Love," although the venereal consequences cannot be substantiated.

Mention of the Reeves affair is followed by this paragraph:

> You who would know him better, go to the Coffee-house (where he may be said almost to inhabit) and you shall find him holding forth to half a score young fellows, (who clap him on the back, spit in his mouth, and loo him on upon the *Whiggs,* as they call 'em) puft up, and swelling with their praise: and the great Subject of his Discourse shall be of himself, and his *Poetry;* What Diet he uses for *Epick* what for *Comick;* what course he is in for *Libel,* and what for *Tragedy.*

That Dryden did "inhabit" Will's has become a commonplace in all accounts of him. We also know that he got on easily with younger men: Southerne, Congreve, Walsh, Lockier are a few that immediately come to mind. Dryden was past fifty at this time, so the contrast between him and the rising generation of wits was easily noticed. Yet there are passages in the 1668 *Letter to Edward Howard* by the unidentified "R. F." and also in the *Rehearsal* which provide earlier analogues for this reference to the flattering attentions of "half a score young fellows."

The joke about "What Diet he uses for *Epick* and what for *Comick*" is repeated in full anecdotal form lower down the page:

> 'Tis not two years since he consulted with an Eminent and Learned Physician of this Town; telling him, he was obliged to write a Play, and finding himself very dull, desired he would prescribe him a Diet, and course of Physick fit for his Malady: the Dr. merrily asked him Whether 'twas *Comedy* or *Tragedy* he designed? he answered, *Tragedy;* the Dr. replyed, The Steel Diet was most proper for *Tragedy;* whereupon the Poet desired to have it prescribed, and did undergo it for six weeks.

It would be tempting to believe this anecdote, for such pseudo-science and credulity were possible in an age when modern empirical medicine was just beginning. However, a likely source for the tale makes specula-

---

[11] There is a little-known story that Dryden and Henry Cromwell competed for a mistress and that Cromwell won. For a refutation of it see *Dryden, Pope and Curll's Corinna,* by W. M. Thoms, in *Notes and Queries,* First Series, XII, 277–79.

tion futile. I refer to the well-known passage in the *Rehearsal* where Bayes describes his preparations for literary composition:

If I am to write familiar things, as Sonnets to *Armida,* and the like, I make use of Stew'd Prunes only; but when I have a grand design in hand, I ever take Phisic, and let blood: for, when you would have pure swiftness of thought, and fiery flights of fancy, you must have a care of the pensive part. In fine, you must purge the Belly.[12]

Even so late as 1730, in Lamotte's *Essay on Poetry and Painting,* the anecdote was repeated that Dryden customarily was "blooded and purged" before sitting down to serious work. Both Shadwell and Lamotte follow their source too closely to warrant belief that their testimony is independent of the *Rehearsal.*

Another stock charge repeated from the *Rehearsal* was that Dryden depended on other men's work for his wit and his plots:

> All written Wit thou seizest on as prize;
> But that will not thy ravenous mind suffice;
> Though men from thee their inward thoughts conceal,
> *Yet thou the words out of their mouths wilt steal.*

There could be no better measure of the paucity of valid complaints against Dryden than the fuss made over his careful reworking of the *materia poetica.* Yet in the twenty years between the *Rehearsal* and Langbaine's 1691 *Account of the English Dramatick Poets* this was one of the chief accusations against him.[13]

So much, then, for the conventional items of abuse; and now to consider the original information to be found in this pamphlet. The second paragraph of the *Epistle to the Tories* contains two anecdotes that have an air of verisimilitude about them. The first is as follows:

You may know he is no concealer of himself, by a story which he tells of himself, *viz.* That (when he came first to Town) being a young raw fellow of seven and Twenty, as he call'd himself when he told the story, he frequenting but one Coffee-house, the Woman (it seems finding him out) put Coffee upon him for Chocolate, and made him pay three pence a dish for two years together: till at length, by what providence I know not, he discovered the Cheat.

---

[12] *Rehearsal,* ed. Summers, p. 18. From a letter to Tonson (Scott-Saintsbury, Letter IX) we learn that, whatever his affection for stewed prunes, Dryden was apparently very fond of damsons: "Pray, Sir, let [my wife] know that I am well; and for feare the few damsins shou'd be all gone, desire her to buy me a sieve-full, to preserve whole, and not in mash."

[13] For a somewhat fuller treatment of these charges of plagiarism, see pp. 237–39.

Surrounded as it is by violent abuse, this story is so feeble that no reason can be suggested for the prominence given to it except that it is true. Certainly the phrases "a story which he tells of himself," "as he called himself when he told the story," "it seems," "by what providence I know not," have the ring of authenticity about them. They may be mere devices of conscious art, but when taken in conjunction with the mild pointlessness of the anecdote itself, the combined factors make me believe that Shadwell was really repeating a story once told to him by Dryden.

This story is followed by what Shadwell considered a jesting explanation of Dryden's incredible stupidity:

> . . . there is somewhat to be said for it; for (as he said of himself at the same time) the opening in his head (which in Children usually closes about the age of three) did not close in him till he was seven and twenty; which may be the reason he has had such a devilish soft place there ever since.

The reasons already given for accepting the anecdote of the coffee hoax incline me to believe that Shadwell based his quip about the "devilish soft place" on what he considered to be a fact. The tardy closing of the fontanelle is a not uncommon occurrence, but only in very abnormal cases has the fontanelle been known to remain soft until manhood. If Dryden suffered from this trouble it was probably caused by rickets, usually the result of diet deficient in vitamin D and lack of sunlight.[14] Although the connection is not implicit, it is suggestive that Dryden was one of the slowest to mature of all the great poets.

Leaving the preliminary prose epistle and turning to the poem itself, we are arrested by a phrase in line 13, "this Cherry-cheeked Dunce of fifty-three." At this time Dryden was actually only fifty-one, an error devoid of importance. The adjective "cherry-cheeked" is, however, one to be remembered, as it is in many ways the happiest description of Dryden that has come down to us. The touch of color cannot be discerned in the dark portraits of Kneller and is lacking in most other references to "Poet Squab." [15]

---

[14] I am indebted for this medical opinion to Clarence W. Lieb, M.D., and Allan K. Poole, M.D.

[15] Malone (Life of Dryden, p. 430*n*) mentions Radcliffe's *News from Hell* (1682):
> "Laureate who was both learn'd and *florid*,
> Was damn'd long since for *silence horrid.*"

And in *The City Mouse and the Country Mouse* (Malone, p. 431*n*) is a reference to Bayes's "rosy-coloured" appearance.

Allied with a point already discussed—Dryden's lack of mirth in company—is the charge that his repartee consisted chiefly of bawdy talk:

> An old gelt Mastiff has more mirth than thou,
> When thou a kind of paltry Mirth would'st show.
> Good humour thou so awkwardly put'st on,
> It sits like Modish Clothes upon a Clown;
> While that of Gentlemen is brisk and high,
> When Wine and Wit about the room does flie.
> Thou never mak'st, but art a standing Jest;
> Thy Mirth by foolish Bawdry is exprest . . .

To substantiate the allegation Shadwell quotes an obscene remark supposedly made by Dryden "At *Windsor* in the company of several persons of Quality, Sir *G*[eorge] *E*[therege] being present." [16] Considering the standards of the time, especially those of Sedley, Etherege, and others, I see no reason to doubt this story. The general charge of bawdy talk, it will be recalled, had previously been made in the *Rehearsal.* Dryden was always thoroughly responsive to his audience, and in this instance as elsewhere we can be sure that he gave the company what it wanted to hear.

Shadwell next developed still another theme from the *Rehearsal,* that Dryden "boasts of Vice which he did ne'er commit." The contemporary readers of the poem probably did not notice that this allegation directly contradicts the claims previously made about his conduct with Anne Reeves. But consistency is not to be sought for in abuse, and Shadwell hurled at Dryden's head all the filth available.

Of course the Rose Alley beating was the delight of Dryden's foes, and throughout the following years it served as a cudgel with which to chastise the old poet in print. Shadwell alluded to it several times, but only once in a way that is of interest to posterity:

> After the drubs, thou didst of late compound,
> And sold for th'weight in Gold each bruise and wound . . .

The only other reference to monetary compensation for this disgraceful episode is dated thirty years after the event and is found in Defoe's *Review,* the issue of May 17, 1712: Here the story goes that Buckingham "can'd him very smartly; *there Sir,* said the Duke, *is for your ill Man-*

---

[16] Dryden apparently visited Windsor on several occasions. See the discussion of his absences from London, pp. 215–16.

ners; and *here, Sir,* says he, *is for your Wit,* and threw him a Purse with Thirty Guineas at the same Time." [17] But there is no reason to connect Buckingham with the event, and even Rochester's part in the beating is open to question. The most likely explanation of such reparation would be that the Duchess of Portsmouth, probably the chief protagonist in the ambuscade, may have discovered that, not Dryden, but Mulgrave was responsible for the satire and afterward may have attempted to salve the bruises of the poet in the manner reported by Shadwell. Conjecture on the subject is futile, yet Shadwell's statement must not be disregarded.

Leaving these small points, we shall now consider the main biographical passage—more than thirty lines which chronicle in detail the unfortunate incidents of Dryden's early years. This much-quoted passage begins with the lines:

> At *Cambridge* first your scurrilous Vein began,
> When sawcily you traduc'd a *Nobleman,*
> Who for that Crime rebuk'd you on the head,
> And you had been Expell'd had you not fled.

As with other incidents in Dryden's early life, details are lacking of this overflow of youthful impertinence, but Shadwell probably knew what he was talking about. Dryden was still at Cambridge in May, 1655, and Shadwell came there in December. The records do not tell when Dryden departed, and his movements in this year are entirely conjectural. Even if the incident occurred some time before Shadwell came into residence, he had ample opportunity to pick up the tale from contemporaries who knew both him and Dryden. Dryden was punished at least once during his college years, in July, 1652,[18] and this event may have provided the foundation for Shadwell's story.

The next lines describe Dryden's move to London:

> The next step of Advancement you began,
> Was being Clerk to *Nolls* Lord *Chamberlain,*
> A Sequestrator and Committee-man.

For years this triplet was the chief authority for the tradition that Dryden held a small position on Thurloe's staff. The public records

---

[17] This was first pointed out by E. G. Fletcher in MLN, L, 366.

[18] "His crime was, his disobedience to the Vice-master, and his contumacy in taking his punishment inflicted by him." Conclusion-book, Trinity College, Cambridge, quoted by Malone, Life of Dryden, p. 16,

have yielded confirmation, although little more than the bare fact
can be ascertained from them.[19]

After the Restoration Dryden was forced to seek new employment,
and his progress is continued in the already-quoted lines:

> He turn'd a Journey-man t'a * Bookseller;
> Writ Prefaces to Books for Meat and Drink,
> And as he paid, he would both write and think.
> * *Mr*. Herringman, *who kept him in his House for that purpose.*
> [Original note].

Shadwell's claims that Dryden worked for Herringman and lived in
his house are still unconfirmed and probably never can be proved posi-
tively. Yet here again the known facts are consistent with Shadwell's
statements.[20]

In similar fashion Shadwell alluded to Dryden's relations with Sir
Robert Howard:

> Then by th'assistance of a § Noble *Knight,*
> Th'hadst plenty, ease, and liberty to write.
> First like a *Gentleman* he made thee live;
> And on his Bounty thou didst amply thrive.
> But soon thy Native swelling Venom rose,
> And thou didst him, who gave thee Bread, expose.
> 'Gainst him a scandalous Preface didst thou write,
> Which thou didst soon expunge, rather than fight.
> § *Sir R. H. who kept him generously at his own House.*
> [Original note].

As I have already pointed out, recently discovered evidence confirms
Shadwell's statement about Dryden's residence under Howard's roof
and tells us that Dryden slept in a "serge bed." Dryden's own statements leave no doubt of his indebtedness to Howard during the early
1660's.[21] The literary quarrel with Howard has yet to be examined
carefully, but it is clear that the "scandalous Preface," that is, the *Defence of the Essay of Dramatic Poesy,* was indeed "expunged." If the
quarrel was terminated by the threat of a duel, as Shadwell implies, no
corroboration can be found in contemporary writings.

[19] For a discussion of the evidence that Dryden was an employee of the Commonwealth
government see pp. 184–86 below.

[20] For a detailed examination of this subject see pp. 186–93.

[21] See especially the Letter to Howard before *Annus mirabilis:* "You have not only been
careful of my fortune, which was the effect of your nobleness, but you have been solicitous
of my reputation, which is that of your kindness."

The last incidents that Shadwell relates from Dryden's early career concern his patroness Anne, Duchess of Monmouth:

> (When turn'd away by him in some small time)
> You in the Peoples ears began to chime,
> And please the Town with your successful Rime.
> When the best Patroness of Wit and Stage,
> The Joy, the Pride, the wonder of the Age,
> Sweet *Annabel* the good, great, witty, fair;
> (Of all this Northern Court, the brightest Star)
> Did on thee, *Bayes,* her sacred beams dispence,
> Who could do ill under such influence?
> She the whole *Court* brought over to thy side,
> And favour flow'd upon thee like a Tide.
> To her thou soon prov'dst an * *ungrateful Knave;*
> So good was she, not only she forgave,
> But did oblige anew, the faithless Slave.
>
> * *When he had thrice broken his Word, Oath, and Bargain with Sir* William Davenant, *he wrote a Letter to this great Lady to pass her word for him to Sir* William, *who would not take his own; which she did. In his Letter he wisht God might never prosper him, his Wife or Children, if he did not keep his Oath and Bargain; which yet in two Months he broke, as several of the Dukes Play-house can testifie.* [Original note].

Since Dryden frequently acknowledged his gratitude and indebtedness to "charming Annabel," Shadwell's lines tell nothing that is very new. They do, however, illustrate well Shadwell's mastery in the art of distortion: on the ground that Dryden was helped by his patroness, we are told that the poet's success was primarily due to her influence.

But the footnote is a different matter: this oath taking is an entirely unknown incident and has never been examined by any of Dryden's or Davenant's biographers. We know little of Dryden's relations with Davenant, except the two passages, one in the Preface to the *Tempest* (1670) and the other in the essay *Of Heroique Plays* (1672), in which Dryden paid tender tribute to his late collaborator and predecessor in the office of laureate. The episode is related with such an air of verisimilitude and show of detail, especially the effective phrase "as several of the Dukes Play-house can testifie," that it cannot be lightly disregarded. Can we believe there is any truth in it? The answer to this question is important, for it is the crux of our reëxamination of the poem.

Once Shadwell is acknowledged to be the author of this poem, the logical consequences must be faced. The careers of the two poets paralleled each other so closely that each had an opportunity for intimate knowledge of the incidents in the other's life: both were at Cambridge, both were in the government service,[22] both had connections with Herringman the publisher, both circulated in the same company of wits and literary noblemen, and both were important figures in the theater. Thus when *Mac Flecknoe* and *The Medal of John Bayes* were written, the authors had ample knowledge of their subject matter.

The detailed examination of Shadwell's poem which we have just made substantiates this fact. In every instance where outside evidence can be produced, Shadwell's anecdotes are consistent with the established details. He distorted and exaggerated, but like every good satirist he based his abuse on a kernel of truth. Because the outside evidence always supports and never contradicts what Shadwell says, even those incidents where corroborative evidence is lacking must be accepted until they can be disproven. The course for future biographers is therefore plain. The anecdotes concerning Dryden's drinking coffee for chocolate, his lodging with Herringman, his expedition to Windsor with Etherege, his tangle with Davenant, and the others, must take their place in Dryden's biography until they are contradicted by new discoveries.

And while logic is being so rigorously applied, one other point should not be forgotten: Shadwell conspicuously omits any reference to the circumstances of Dryden's marriage with Lady Elizabeth Howard. Other passages in the abuses are personal enough and obscene enough to show that he was not holding back any slanderous charge from a sense of delicacy. This negative evidence strongly suggests the conclusion that the story of certain unpleasant circumstances attendant on the marriage was not true. Shadwell had found enough authentically scandalous anecdotes about Dryden without resorting to rumor or fabrication to lengthen his list.

[22] Charles E. Ward, TLS, April 3, 1937, p. 256.

WAS DRYDEN IN HERRINGMAN'S EMPLOY?

Every investigator of Dryden's early life has been baffled by two problems concerning the eight-year period between his departure from Cambridge and his initial financial success in the theater. Was Dryden in the service of Cromwell's government during his first years in London? And, after the collapse of the Protectorate, did he work for the publisher Herringman? The first question has frequently been answered in the affirmative on very unsubstantial grounds. By now enough evidence has been accumulated to prove that Dryden was definitely a government employee between 1656 and 1658. This evidence is of two sorts—the testimony of Dryden's contemporaries, and certain documents in the Public Record Office.

The earliest testimony belongs to the year 1668 and comes from the author of *A Letter from a Gentleman to the Honorable Ed. Howard Esq; Occasioned by a Civiliz'd Epistle of Mr. Dryden's before His Second Edition of His Indian Emperour*. This pamphlet is signed simply "R.F.," and the initials may stand for Richard Flecknoe.[1] Whoever the author may have been, he was well acquainted with the various events in Dryden's early career. He refers to Dryden as "the Squire," and among other things says of him, ". . . the Squire having been employed under his father, a zealous committeeman and Sir Gilbert Pickering, a crafty councellor, in the late times." Since this statement was made within ten years of the supposed event, and made by a person obviously well informed, it carries great weight.

Allusions to this alleged employment were repeated by many of Dryden's opponents in the 1680's and 1690's. The best known of these later

---

[1] This pamphlet was not seen by Malone until after the publication of his Life of Dryden. He made several manuscript notes about it in his own copy of the Life, which will be found transcribed on pp. 124 above. The ascription to Flecknoe was first made by Peter Cunningham, *Gentleman's Magazine*, XXXIV (new series, 1850), 597–99, who suggested that this *Letter* was behind Dryden's annoyance with Flecknoe.

lampoons is *The Medal of John Bayes* (1682). The lines in question are familiar to all Dryden students:

> The next step of Advancement you began,
> Was being Clerk to *Nolls* Lord *Chamberlain*,
> A Sequestrator and Committee-man.[2]

Since this satire was the earliest and best known of the new crop that began in 1682, doubtless the others derived their knowledge of the incident from it.[3] The author, as I have suggested in the preceding chapter, was probably Thomas Shadwell. Though he selected the subject matter of this lampoon for its value as abuse, nearly all of the biographical incidents in the poem have a basis in fact. The "committee-man" allegation may possibly be derived from "R. F.," but considering the obscurity of the *Letter to Howard* and the circumstance that Shadwell knew a good deal about Dryden, I believe that Shadwell's statement is entitled to rank as independent evidence.

The testimony of these contemporaries is corroborated by several documents in the Public Record Office. The earliest one was discovered only a few years ago by Professor Ward. It records payment for moneys "expended for the publique service" between April 3, 1656, and April 9, 1657.[4] Among the persons listed as having received compensation on the latter date was someone bearing the surname "Dryden," who received £3. No Christian name is given for him. Though signed receipts can be found for most of the individuals named on the list, none, unfortunately, exists for Mr. Dryden.

The next document is dated October 19, 1657, and records a payment by Secretary Thurloe to John Driden for £50. It was brought to light by Masson in the course of his researches on Milton and is described by him in the following words:

"Received then of the Right honble. Mr. Secretary Thurloe the sume of ffifty pounds: £50: *by mee,* JOHN DRIDEN," is a receipt, of date "19 October 1657", among Thurloe's papers in the Record office—the words *"by mee,* JOHN DRIDEN" in a neat slant hand different from the body of the receipt. The poet Dryden, it may be remembered, was the cousin and client of Sir Gilbert Pickering, one of the most important men in the Council and one of the most strongly Oliverian. The poet left Cambridge, his biographers tell

---

[2] Lines 97–99.

[3] Among the lampoons that mention this incident are the *Satire to His Muse* (1682) and *The Protestant Satire* (*ca.* 1684). See pages 138–39, above.

[4] S.P. 18/154, f. 230.

us, without this M.A. degree, "about the middle of 1657", and it was a taunt against him afterwards that he had begun his London life as "clerk" to Sir Gilbert. As he cannot have got the £50 from Thurloe for nothing, the probability is that he had been employed, through Sir Gilbert, to do some clerkly or literary work for the Council.[5]

The third and last of these documents bears the date September 7, 1658, a few days after the death of Cromwell. It is a list of minor government employees who were given an allotment of mourning cloth to be worn at Cromwell's funeral. The passage contains the following names, preceded by the cloth allowances they applied for and the amount they received.

9	6	Mr John Milton	Lattin
9	6	Mr Merville	
9	6	Sir Phillip Meadows	Secryes
		Mr Sterry	
9	0	Mr Drayden [6]	

Attention was first called to this series of illustrious names by Professor Pierre Legouis in his *André Marvell.*

De ce texte il ressort que l'allocation de Milton et Marvell a été réduite pour chacun de 9 à 6 yards (même mesure fut prise pour le *Master of the Rolls;* le lord-maire, proposé pour 9 *yards,* les obtint sans reduction), que le nom de Meadows, pourtant revenu de son ambassade en juillet, a été remplacé par celui de Sterry qui continuait donc à travailler dans le même service que Milton, avec ou sans le titre de secrétaire latin, enfin que "Drayden" devait être une sorte de surnuméraire et se vit comme tel refuser l'allocation.[7]

The conclusion to be built on these documents is plain: a certain John Dryden, Driden, or Drayden was employed, continually or intermittently, by the Commonwealth government between April, 1656 and September, 1658, a man whom two well-informed contemporaries identified with the author of *The Essay of Dramatic Poesy* and *Mac Flecknoe.* Neither the records nor his contemporaries provide detailed knowledge of the duties he performed. Until contradictory evidence is discovered, the fact seems clearly established that Dryden was an employee of the Commonwealth government.

The second problem is whether in the years before he attained success

[5] David Masson, *Life of Milton,* 1859–80, V, 375–76.

[6] Dryden's name is omitted in the reference to the document in the *Calendar of State Papers, Domestic,* 1658–59, p. 131.

[7] Pierre Legouis, *André Marvell,* 1928, p. 214.

in the theater Dryden was in the service of the publisher and bookseller, Henry Herringman. Here again the most important testimony is found in *The Medal of John Bayes:*

> He turn'd a Journey-man t'a § Bookseller;
> Writ Prefaces to Books for Meat and Drink,
> And as he paid, he would both write and think.

§ Mr. *Herringman,* who kept him in his House for that purpose. [Original note].[8]

These lines have been quoted by every biographer of Dryden since 1800, but to my knowledge, no one has ever looked into the facts back of Shadwell's statement. Such an investigation should begin with an examination of the books published by Herringman in this period. This I have attempted to do by going through the Stationers' Registers for the years 1656 to 1664, picking out all the entries made by Herringman, and examining each of the books of which copies can be found.

In this six-year period Herringman's name appears about fifty times on the Stationers' Registers.[9] Dryden is known to have been associated with three books published by Herringman during these years. The first is the *Three Poems upon the Death of His Late Highness Oliver Lord Protector of England, Scotland and Ireland,* 1659. It was entered January 20, 1658/9, and contains Dryden's "Heroique Stanzas Consecrated to the Glorious Memory of His Most Serene and Renowned Highness Oliver Late Lord Protector of This Commonwealth." Although Herringman entered the book at Stationers' Hall, his name does not appear on the title page of any known copy. All copies read "Printed by William Wilson, and are to be sold in Well-yard neer Little St. Bartholomew's Hospitall." Perhaps Herringman disposed of the property soon after registering it. The next book is *Poems . . . by the Honorable Sr Robert Howard,* 1660. Entered April 16, 1660, the volume was advertised for sale early in June. To it is prefixed Dryden's verses "To My Honored Friend Sr Robert Howard on His Excellent Poems." Howard ended his "To the Reader" with the remark "I prevailed with a worthy friend to take so much view of my blotted Copies, as to free me from grosse Errors." This friend was unquestionably Dryden, who may have

---

[8] Lines 109–11.

[9] *A Transcript of the Registers of the Worshipful Company of Stationers from 1640–1708.* 3 vols. Privately printed [for the Roxburghe Club], 1913–14. Transcribed by H. R. Plomer. Doubtless Herringman published other books not entered at Stationers Hall, but aside from single poems, none printed 1656–64 are known to me. See p. 287.

become acquainted with Howard through their mutual connections with Herringman. The third book is *Chorea Gigantum, or, The Most Famous Antiquity of Great Britain, Vulgarly Called Stone-heng . . . by Walter Charleton, D^r in Physic,* 1663 (entered September 18, 1662). This volume contains the commendatory verses to Charleton that are well known to every reader of Dryden's poetry.

It should be noted that in this same period Herringman published three other poems by Dryden, none of which was entered on the Stationers' Registers. They are: *Astraea Redux,* June, 1660; *To His Sacred Majesty,* April, 1661; and *To My Lord Chancellor,* 1662. Several reasons can be suggested why Herringman did not register these poems. The most likely is that he did not consider them valuable enough to require protection. These three poems and the "Heroique Stanzas" on Cromwell have every appearance of being ordinary transactions between author and publisher. So too, the commendatory poems to Howard and Charleton require no explanation, for the custom of prefixing such poems was well established.[10] These six publications show that Dryden was already one of Herringman's most active authors.

Of the forty-seven other books that Herringman entered on the Stationers' Registers in the years 1656 to 1664, thirty-five provide no evidence to suggest that Dryden had any concern with their publication. This group includes eight volumes that I have not seen.[11] Perhaps some

[10] The 1651 edition of William Cartwright's *Poems* contains more than fifty commendatory verses.

[11] The entries are in the order in which they appear on the Stationers' Registers.

19 August 1656. *Heroick Education or the Right Method to Train up the Young Nobility and Gentry to Vertue and Learning &c,* "Translated out of the French." According to Donald Wing's *Short Title Catalogue 1641–1700* the Bodleian and the British Museum have copies.

1 December 1656. *The Romance of Players* [*Scarron*] . . . "Translated into English & the scene altered by a Person of Quality." No copy of this edition of the *Comedy Romance* is known to Mr. Wing.

16 January 1656/7. *The Shirke or Buscons Adventures* "Put into English by a person of Honour." No copy is known to Mr. Wing.

29 November 1657. *A Prospective of the Navall Triumph of ye Venitians on ye Turke.* No copy is known to Mr. Wing.

6 September 1658. *Poems Written on several Occasions,* by Jasper Mayne. Unknown to Mr. Wing.

6 December 1659. *Lues venerea,* by John Wynell, M.D. A copy is in the British Museum.

13 February 1659/60. *Honours Geneology,* by John Tilston. Unknown to Mr. Wing.

8 January 1661/2. *The Truth and Reasonableness of Religion delivered by Jesus Christ.* A copy is in Dr. Williams' Library, London.

A few other books have been examined for me at the Bodleian by my friend Frederick W. Bateson, who has reported that they contain nothing likely to have been written by Dryden.

of them were never published. But of the twelve others, I believe the prefatory matter in five may possibly have been written by Dryden. In the remaining seven his pen may conceivably have been employed, but I regard it as unlikely.

The earliest of the five books that require serious consideration is an English translation of *L'Astrée,* by Honoré Durfé, in three volumes, bearing the dates 1657-58. Herringman's name does not appear on the imprint, but on May 13, 1656, when the publication was entered at Stationers' Hall, Herringman was listed as one of the proprietors.[12] Each volume is introduced by a leaf entitled "To the Reader," covering two pages in the first and second volumes and one page in the third volume. In the first two volumes these remarks are signed "J.D.," and the page in the third volume is apparently written by the same hand. Could these prefaces be among the ones that Dryden "writ for meat and drink?" Certain factors argue in favor of his authorship, of which the most important is the conjunction of the initials "J.D." and Herringman's position among the proprietors. Added to this are certain facts about the translator of the volumes, Francis Gifford, Esq. Gifford, like Dryden, was a native of Northamptonshire and also a member of the University of Cambridge during the years 1650–54, when Dryden was there.[13] These circumstances suggest that if "J.D." was Dryden, Gifford may have been the agent who brought about his connection with Herringman.

The content and style of the prefaces tell little. The subject matter is principally a puff for the reading of romances in general and *Astrea* in particular. The allusions are so conventional that they carry no value as evidence, but they contain nothing inconsistent with Dryden's early interests. About the only positive conclusion that can be deduced from the subject matter is that these pages were written by someone who had the interests of the stationer definitely at heart, for the rhetoric of his remarks was intended primarily to increase sales. The style is florid and involved and at first glance is very unlike the lucid vigor characteristic of Dryden's prose. Yet when Dryden's writings of the 1650's—his verses to Hoddes-

[12] The first volume was entered at this date, but volumes two and three were not entered until June 29, 1660. All three volumes were entered by Humphrey Mosely, Thomas Dring, and Henry Herringman. The translator was Francis Gifford, Esq.

[13] According to Venn, *Alumni Cantabrigienses,* Pt. I, Vol. II (1922), p. 213. Gifford matriculated at Queen's College in Lent, 1647/8, proceeded B.A. in 1650/1, and M.A. in 1654. In 1660 he was incorporated at Oxford; he was ordained priest in March 1660/1, and passed the rest of his life in the Church.

don and his letter to Honor Dryden—are compared with these prefaces, it is apparent that the exaggerations and conceits are similar to the style we might expect from the young Cambridge poet. The diction is also suggestive of Dryden, whose early writings abound in gallicisms and other new words. The reader of these prefaces will immediately notice words like "Quixoticall," "cajolleries," and "divertisements." The first use of "quixotical" recorded in the *Oxford English Dictionary* is in 1850, and of "quixotic" in 1815. Use of "cajolleries" is recorded in 1649, and of "divertisements" in 1651. But Dryden was not the only man of his generation who liked to wrap his tongue around new words, and the internal evidence is inconclusive. In order that students may judge for themselves, the pages in question are printed at the end of this chapter.

The external evidence is no more conclusive than the internal. Though Dryden was apparently occupied in a small government office between 1656 and 1658, his duties would not have prevented him from writing these five pages of prefatory prose. On the contrary, it is evident that during the period of government employment he continued to apply himself to literary exercises. The development of his poetical powers to the level they reached in the next decade can hardly be explained in any other way. Examination of the French editions of *L'Astrée* fails to provide other clues. The 1647 edition, for example, contains two prefaces— an "Advertissement au Lecteur" and a shorter one, "Au Lecteur"—but there is no apparent relation between them and the passages from the pen of J.D.[14] An open verdict is clearly in order: I am not convinced that these initials are the signature of John Dryden, but the possibility should be given full attention by all future biographers and editors.

The next one of Herringman's books, in point of time, in which Dryden may have had a hand, is *The Immortality of the Human Soul*, by Dr. Walter Charleton. It was registered on February 16, 1656/7. After the "Epistle Dedicatory," and before the text of the book is "An Advertisement to the Reader," covering one page and signed by Henry Herringman. The principal subject of this advertisement is the advantages of the familiar dialogue as a literary form. Although signed with Herringman's name, the style and learning of the piece make his authorship extremely unlikely. If the page were not signed by Herringman, I should have sus-

---

[14] *L'Astrée de Messire Honoré d'Urfé*, five parts, 1647. The "Advertissement au lecteur" covers leaves a6ᵛ–a8ᵛ of the fourth part. The page addressed "Au lecteur" is in part five, leaf é5.

pected that it came directly from the hand of Charleton himself. Even the signature does not rule Charleton out—indeed, the biographical incidents at the end must have come from him—but it is more likely that anything printed over Herringman's name was written by one of the bookseller's staff rather than by a physician of Charleton's eminence. It is even possible that the preparation of this "Advertisement" was the first meeting of Dryden and Charleton, who several years later sponsored Dryden's candidacy for membership in the Royal Society.[15]

In the next year, on September 22, 1658, Herringman entered another of Dr. Charleton's books on the Stationers' Register. It bore the title, *The Natural History of Nutrition* and was published with the date 1659. Included in the preliminary matter is a page headed, "The Stationer to the Reader," also signed with Herringman's name. This page and the "Advertisement" in the earlier book are parallel problems—some of the information undoubtedly came from Charleton, and it is unlikely that Herringman contributed more than his name. Two circumstances favor the possibility that Dryden may have held the pen: the first is the subject matter, which is very characteristic of Dryden's scientific interests at this time. The references to Dr. Ent, for example, bring to mind the allusion to him in Dryden's poem prefixed to *Chorea gigantum*. The style is equally suggestive of Dryden, especially the gallicism at the end, "to manifest my devoir toward the advance of Knowledge, and service to the Publique." If Dryden wrote any prefaces for Herringman, this is one of the most likely candidates.

A few weeks after Herringman entered Charleton's *Immortality of the Human Soul,* he registered a volume of *Poems* by Dr. Henry King (March 11, 1656/7). Prefixed to this book are four pages headed "The Publishers to the Author" and signed with the names of the stationers, Richard Marriot and Henry Herringman. The epistle makes excuses for publishing the poems allegedly without the knowledge or the permission of Dr. King. I offer it here as another bit of hack writing that may have been done by one of Herringman's "ghost writers."

The last one of Herringman's volumes I have found containing a preface that may have been written by Dryden was published after

---

[15] Dryden was proposed on November 12, 1662, and admitted as a Fellow on November 26, 1662. In September of this year or earlier Dryden had written the verses to Charleton printed before *Chorea gigantum*. In the Folger Shakespeare Library is a presentation copy, "For my Learned & obliging Friend, Mʳ John Driden," described more fully on p. 247, below.

Charles was back on the throne. It was registered on June 6, 1660, and bears the title *Ratts Rhimed to Death, or the Rump Parliament Hang'd up in the Shambles, Being a Collection of Such Ballads & Songs as Were Made on the Late Rump Parliement.* The volume is a collection of twenty-seven ballads that had been previously printed as broadsides. Anthony Wood's copy is dated "14 July 1660," and the Thomason copy is listed under November, 1659.[16] Preceding the text is a prefatory epistle "To the Reader," which covers two and a half pages. This epistle is in vigorous, direct prose, and was definitely written by someone of intelligence and literary awareness. The tone is more pungent than modern readers may desire, but it is typical of much popular writing of the Restoration period. The only allusion worth noting is that to Hobbes's *Leviathan,* a book well known to Dryden and other educated men of his generation. Whether Dryden was responsible for these pages will probably never be known, but if Shadwell was right in saying that Dryden wrote prefaces for Herringman, this gusty "To the Reader" is conspicuously eligible for attribution to him.

Seven other books published by Herringman in this period contain prefaces, advertisements, or "to-the-readers" that could possibly have come from Dryden's pen, but which for various reasons were more probably written by other hands. Though I do not believe Dryden wrote any of them, other investigators may discover evidence which warrants such a conjecture.[17]

16 See H. F. Brooks, *Rump Songs,* Proceedings of the Oxford Bibliographical Society, V (Part 4, 1940), 283–304.

17 The following volumes are listed according to the date of their entry in the Stationers' Registers. Herringman was concerned in all of them.

15 June 1658. *The History of the Wars of Italy* (published 1663), by Pietro Giovanni Capriata, translated by Henry Carey, Earl of Monmouth. Prefixed is an unsigned ."Epistle to the Reader," two pages long. It is in a florid and clumsy style, praising both Capriata and Monmouth.

5 September 1659. *A Collection of English Letters* made by Sir Tobie Matthew, published with the date 1660 on the title page. This volume contains a "To the Reader" extending over seventeen and a half pages. It is unsigned, but is probably by Sir Tobie himself.

29 October 1660. *The Visions and Prophecies concerning Cromwell* (1661), by Abraham Cowley. This was also issued as *The Visions of Ezekiel Grebner.* The *Cromwell* issue has a five-page "Advertisement," which differs textually from the seven-page "Advertisement concerning the Book and Author" in the *Grebner* issue. Both may be by Cowley.

28 April 1661. *Certain Phisiological Essays,* by the Honourable Robert Boyle. It contains an unsigned "Advertisement to the Reader," a page and a half long. I believe Boyle wrote this himself.

20 August 1663. *Verses Lately Written upon Several Occasions,* by Abraham Cowley. There is a six-line notice, signed by "Herringman," saying that this edition follows one

The question asked in the title of this chapter must, unfortunately, be left without a conclusive answer. We know that Dryden did supply prefatory verses for Howard's *Poems* and for *Chorea gigantum,* but these verses have every mark of being acts of personal commendation rather than commissions for Herringman. Of the five volumes whose prefaces are reprinted at the end of this chapter, all of them could have been by Dryden, but in none, even the pages signed "J.D.," is the evidence more than suggestive. Future editors of Dryden's prose must decide for themselves. But when doing so they should give full weight to the testimony of Thomas Shadwell, whose statements of fact in *The Medal of John Bayes* have stood for two hundred and eighty years without contradiction. If Dryden did indeed "turn Journey-man t'a Bookseller" and "writ Prefaces to Books for Meat and Drink," then the following pages contain the most likely products of his pen.[18]

To the Reader

[From Volume I of the English translation of *Astrea,* 1657]

OF all the *Books* that Mankind hath convers'd with, since it was first refin'd by *Letters,* none hath contributed so much to the *civilization* thereof, or gaind that *esteeme* and *Authority* with it, as those of POETRY; by which

---

printed in Dublin. It might have been written by Cowley, by Herringman, or by one of his workmen.

15 February 1663/4. *Pompey,* an English version of Corneille's play, translated by Katherine Philips. In the front of the book is a short "Printer to the Reader." Her biographer, P. W. Souers, considers that she wrote this herself (*The Matchless Orinda,* 1931, p. 194).

9 April 1664, *Poems on Several Occasions,* by Edmund Waller. The pages headed "Printer to the Reader" were probably written by Waller, as his first editor, Elijah Fenton, suggested. Fenton's successor, George Thorn-Drury, did not refute the ascription and printed the pages as Waller's.

[18] Traces of Dryden's pen may be discovered in other books of this period. A case in point is Alexander Brome's edition of *The Poems of Horace . . . Rendred into English Verse by Several Persons.* Though published in 1666, the volume had been in preparation for more than a year, for it was entered on the Stationers' Register on February 28, 1664/5. The editor made use of translations already in print, including some by Panshaw, Hawkins, Holiday, and Cowley. In cases where no English version was available, Brome followed a procedure described in the Dedication, "such as were not *Translated* by others, my self and several friends of mine at my request have attempted." One of these friends, the translator of the last Epistle of Book II (pages 370–79) signed himself "J.D." Could this have been Dryden? Neither the internal nor the external evidence yield any clues. I can discover no other indication of relations between Brome and Dryden, and no record of Dryden's interest in this Epistle. All that can be said is that Dryden is as likely to have authored the lines as any other "J.D." of the period. If this poem could be shown to be his work, it would be his first published piece of translation.

terme I meane, FICTION, in the largest extent. Under *this*, are comprehended the highest & noblest productions of man's wit, ROMANCES; a kinde of writing so full of *charme* and *insinuation*, that even *Religious* worship, in the dis-illuminated times of *Paganism*, was oblig'd to it for most of its *Ceremonies*, & and the strange *influence* it had over the *multitude*. For, what were the *Oracles*, what all ancient *Mythologies*, what *Numa's* pretended correspondence with his Nymph *Ægeria*, but so many politick *Romances*, cunningly advanc'd, to create in the minds of the people a *feare* and *veneration* of some power above humane Lawes, whereby they were deterr'd from those things which were out of *their* reach and cognizance? Hence was it that some stumbled on that *Paradoxe, "That mankinde, look't on generally, had made greater advantages of* Fiction, *than ever it had done of* Truth; the *one*, it seemes, by reason of her nakednesse, finding so much the colder reception; the *other*, disguized in the dresses of *Witt*, and *Eloquence*, the noblest entertainement that could be expected from *reverence, admiration*, and *Idolatry*.

But, if Endeavours of this nature were so succesfull and advantageous to piety & a civill life, in their infancy, while they were yet shrowded in *Fables* and *Oracular* cheats and ambiguities, and lay *levell* to the capacities of the *multitude*, what may not those contribute, that are calculated to the *meridian* of the most *criticall* and most *ingenious*? What was before censur'd as *extravagance* of *imagination*, is now reconcil'd to *probability*, and restrain'd by *judgement*. What falsly *ravish'd* the eager *apprehension* into amazement at impertinent and *Quixoticall* Attempts, does now but gently enflame the minde into an *aemulation* of the perfections, & a *sympathy* for the weakeness & sufferings it finds represented. Thus an excesse of *Austerity* in some hath reduc'd many to a greater *compliance* with and *submission* to *Nature;* and the elevation of the voice in *Singing Masters* above the *note*, does but direct the *Learner* to reach the *tone*.

This, READER, is the designe of the worke thou now hast in thy hands. Here thou find'st a cleare *representation* of the Noblest and most generous *images of life*, and such an accompt of the *passions* and *actions* of *Men*, as few bookes of this nature afford so plentifull; with such variety of excellent discourses, and an extraordinary sententiousnesse, as deservedly celebrate *this* above any *Author* of the kinde. Here thou hast a jealous and distrustfull ASTREA; adespairing, yet faithfull CELADON; a fickle and unconstant HYLAS; and such intricate scenes of *Courtship, Love, Jealousie*, and the other *passions*, as cannot but raise in thee a consideration of humane Affairs, sutable to the severall emergencies. But to close up the *elogies* may be given this worke, with the greatest that any of this kind ever receiv'd, I shall onely adde the judgement of it, of the late famous Cardinall of RICHELIEU, *That he was not to be admitted into the Academy of Wit, who had not been before well read in* ASTREA.

J. D.

To the Reader

[From Volume II of the English translation of *Astrea*, 1658]

HAving in the *Epistle* to the *precedent* Volume insisted on the generall advantages accrewing to Mankind by *Romances,* and particularly by this of *Astrea* above any other, some would haply imagine there were no more to be done in *this,* than to tell the *Reader* that this is a *second* Volume of the same excellent ASTREA, when he hath the Book already in his hands. This were an imagination flat enough, even though, out of an excess of foresight, they should further suspect it were the *Stationer's* designe to commend both, by telling him, that, As good entertainment begets confidence; so the world's kind reception of the *former,* had contributed much to the publishing of this *Second* Volum. No, these are *Cajolleries,* and *Artifices* may haply be excusable before such Books, as, like pittifull *Shewes,* must needs have a *Trumpet* or a *Jack-pudding* at the Doore, that is, such as would surprise people into a credulity, not a little prejudiciall to their *Eyes,* their *memorie,* their *Understanding,* and their *Purses.*

Know therefore, that this proceeds not from *private* Interest, but *publique* satisfaction; and is not so much the designe of the *Stationer,* in point of advantage, as (so welcome is this Piece abroad) an effect of the *Buyer's* expectation and importunity; and thence he peremptorily affirmes, that the better his Bookes sell, the greater obligation he puts on the world. This some may thinke a *Paradox;* but to shew it is demonstrable, I need onely say, that the more a Booke is bought up, the more are people inform'd, the more instructed, the more edifi'd; which who looks not on as of much greater consequence than the price, is a person certainly of no great correspondence with Letters. If so, how then are we oblig'd to those who spend their endeavours and Estates to satisfie our *Curiosity,* to sharpen our *imaginations,* to rectifie our *judgements,* to purifie our *language,* to perfect our *morality,* to regulate our *deportments,* and to heighten and inflame our more generous *inclinations,* nay to acquaint us with all that is *pleasant,* all that is *excellent,* all that is *extraordinary* in human Actions? And these are the true *designs* and *ends* of Works of this nature; These are Academies for the *Lover,* Schools of War for the *Souldier,* and Cabinets for the *Statesman;* they are the Correctives of *passion,* the restoratives of *conversation;* they are the entertainments of the *sound,* and the divertisements of the *sick;* in a word, the most delightful accommodations of *civill* life.

J. D.

Reader,

[From Volume III of the English translation of *Astrea*, 1658]

YOu have in the Epistles to the first and second Volumes of *Astrea,* the design and tendency, as also the advantages of it, & of works of its nature

I mean *Romances*) 'Twill therefore be unnecessary to use repetition thereof: This ensuing (being the continuation and conclusion of the work) exposeth itself to publick view, as necessary to the compleating of its *Individuum*. I can believe it will meet with such only, who prefer an industrious and strict Scrutiny, before a superficial and easie Censuring; such I am sure are nearest the confines of Reason and Civility. The floridness of its Discourses will Apologize for your pains in reading, and its price in your purchasing. Nor needs it other Complement to indulge and ingratiate, then its own suavity, which being degusted, will delight the pallate of the candid and ingenuous, for whom it is accommodated.

An Advertisement to the Reader

[From Dr. Charlton's *The Immortality of the Human Soul*, 1659]

AMong the Ancient Philosophers (as you may remember) nothing was more frequent, than to deliver their opinions and documents, as wel Physical as Moral, in the plain and familiar way of *Dialogue;* and the Reasons, that induced them thereunto, are not unworthy consideration. For, besides the opportunity both of commemorating their worthy Friends, and of introducing several occasional and digressive speculations, that might be, perhaps, nor lesse grateful, nor lesse useful, than the principal Argument proposed; they thereby gave themselves the advantage of freely alleaging the various and different Conceptions and Perswasions of Men, concerning the subject, which they had designed to discuss: Which in the stricter method of Positive and Apodictical Teaching, they could not with equal conveniency do; And how much better we may judge of the truth of any Theorem, when we have heard as wel the principal Reasons that impugne, as those that assert it, is obvious to common observation. Hereunto may be added, that a Discourse digested into the form of a familiar conference, doth by its variety delight, and by its natural freedom and familiarity more gently insinuate itself into the Mind; as is assured by Experience. Now, when you have reflected upon these Considerations, you clearly understand what were the main Motives, which induced the Author of this Treatise, to dispose his Collections and solitary Meditations, on this excellent subject, the *Immortality of Mens Souls,* into a *Dialogue* consisting of Three Persons, the one Propugning, another Impugning that most comfortable Tenent, and the third impartially Determining their Differences. But yet (as I have heard) He had one inducement more to this manner of writing; and that was, that being not long since in *France,* and invited to discourse of the same Argument, He delivered the substance of all that is here spoken by one of the Interlocutors (viz. *Athanasius*) in a free Colloquy, betwixt Himself and two of his honour'd Friends, as they were recreating and reposing themselves in *Luxenburg* Garden in *Paris.* So that in the Circumstances of this Confabulation, there is nothing of Fiction, besides that of Names proper to each of the Speakers. And, as for those; the Parts they bear in the Discourse, sufficiently discover their Derivations.

HENRY HERRINGMAN.

The Stationer to the Reader

[From Dr. Charlton's *Natural History of Nutrition,* 1659]

THat you might be acquainted with the *Occasion* of the Author's writing this discourse, his *Design* therein, and the *Motives* that induced Him to consent to the Publication of it; I have obtained leave of him, to Print also this following *Epistle* of his to that Excellent Person, *Dr. Ent,* to whose peircing and impartial judgment, he thought fit to submit his own, as well concerning the Verity and weight of what his Papers contained, as concerning the fitnesse of their Constitution to endure the publique air. And this Favour I was the more importunate with him for; both because it might evidence his *Modesty,* in distrusting his own *Exactnesse:* and because it might appear, it was not only his *Inclination,* that brought this Book into my hands and so into yours. Besides, I was not so improvident of my own Advantage, as not to understand, how much of *Reputation* the Booke hath acquired to itself, by passing the Examination of a *Man,* whose Universal Learning, and admirable Perspicacity in things of Nature, have conspired to render him as competent a judge of such Treatises, as the World affords. This I say, not to assure you, that *Dr. Ent* found nothing in these Papers, from which He thought fit not to dissent; because, the subjects of Philosophers speculations and Enquiries, being usually very obscure in themselves, it is no rarity to meet with Diversity of Opinions among Them, as well as among the Vulgar: but, thus much I dare avouch, that He dissented but in very few points, and those only concerning such difficulties, that are not yet cleerly determined by Anatomical Observations; and that nevertheless, He pronounced the whole work to have been undertaken upon mature Consideration, and done with singular Care, Industry, and Circumspection. And I doubt not but you also will be of the same Opinion, when you have attentively read the booke; in which confidence I commend it into your hands, being not a little glad of so good an opportunity to manifest my devoir toward the advance of Knowledge, and service of the Publique.

HEN. HERRINGMAN.

The Publishers to the Author

[From *Poems, Elegies, Paradoxes and Sonnets,* by Dr. Henry King, 1657]

Sir,

IT is the common fashion to make some address to the Readers, but we are bold to direct ours to you, who will look on this publication with Anger which others must welcom into the world with Joy.

The Lord *Verulam* comparing ingenious Authors to those who had Orchards ill neighboured, advised them to publish their own labours, lest others might steal the fruit: Had you followed his example, or liked the advice, we had not thus trespassed against your consent, or been forced to an Apology, which cannot but imply a fault committed. The best we can say for our selves is, that if we have injured you it is meerly in your own defence, preventing the present attempts of others, who to their theft would (by their false copies of these Poems) have added violence, and some way have wounded your reputation.

Having been long engaged on better contemplations, you may perhaps look down on these *Juvenilia* (most of them the issues of your youthful Muse) with some disdain; and yet the Courteous Reader may tell you with thanks, that they are not to be despised, being far from Abortive, nor to be disowned, because they are both Modest and Legitimate. And thus if we have offered you a view of your younger face, our hope is you will behold it with an unwrinkled brow, though we have presented the Mirrour against your will.

We confess our design hath been set forward by friends that honour you, who lest the ill publishing might disfigure these things from whence you never expected addition to your credit (sundry times endeavoured and by them defeated) furnished us with some papers which they thought Authentick; we may not turn their favour into an accusation, and therefore give no intimation of their names, but wholly take the blame of this hasty and immethodical impression upon our selves, being persons at a distance, who are fitter to bear it then those who are neerer related. In hope of your pardon we remain

> *Your most devoted servants,*
> RICH: MARRIOT.
> HEN: HERRINGMAN.

To the *Reader*

[From *Ratts Rhimed to Death*, 1660]

Reader,

THis Collection of excellent Ballads on the late *RUMP*, who called themselves the *Parliament*, when they were formerly Printed in loose sheets, might not unfitly be called the Picture of the Members of the *Rump* dissolved, and stinking singly a-part. Being now bound together, they may as fitly be called the Picture of the said *Rump* assembled, and stinking in Consort. If you think this second Edition might be spared, I must borrow my Apology from their Sermons, who were Preachers to the Rump; which, for the most part, were nothing but Repetition and Tautology, or a Rump of staler Mutton hash'd by ill looks, where all the parts being minced exceeding small, lost their order and distinction. And where that which was the Preface would as well have served for the Conclusion; and both the Preface and Conclusion would equally have past for the Middle of the dry Discourse. If you ask me, Why being dead and rotten, the unsavoury remembrance of them is preserved by these Papers: It is, because whilst they lived, they were a kind of Purrezes [19], whose business was to suck the blood of the Nation, and to break our sleeps by stinging; and who never stink more than when they are crusht, and squeezed; and who, in spight of all perfumes, will offend the Nose even when they are dead. I hope you will pardon the ill Tunes to which they are to be sung, there being none bad enough for them; nor any voice so fit as their Speaker's, who, as long as he was the Rump of this Rump, and sate in the Chair, it was a kind of a new Common-wealth, or Mr. *Hobs's* Artificial Man made a *Leviathan,* still breaking wind, and speaking backwards.

[19] Professor George Sherburn has pointed out to me that this word is a printer's error, for "punezes," a variant of "punaise," meaning bedbug.

DRYDEN AND THE KING'S
PLAYHOUSE IN 1678

THE study of Dryden's place in the theater, like the study of the Restoration drama as a whole, begins with the two rival theatrical companies, the one called the Duke's, headed by Sir William Davenant, and that known as the King's Company managed by Thomas Killigrew. Dryden's connection with the King's Company began at the outset of his career as a dramatist. His first play, *The Wild Gallant,* was produced by them on February 5, 1662/3 in their makeshift theater, formerly Gibbons's Tennis Court. The comedy was, to be sure, a confessed failure; the best that the author could call it was "an indifferent success," and Samuel Pepys described it in his diary as "so poor a thing as I ever saw almost." But despite this inauspicious beginning, within a few years Dryden became the leading dramatist of the day and turned out one box office success after another.[1]

Undoubtedly the chief reason for Dryden's connection with the King's Company was his friendship with the rising young politician Sir Robert Howard. It happened that Howard owned a quarter interest in the King's playhouse and was thus the principal nonactor shareholder.[2] It is likely that at this very time Dryden was living at Howard's house in Lincoln's Inn Fields, for a letter-book in the British Museum shows that only a few months after the performance of *The Wild Gallant* Dryden was occupying a "serge bed" in Howard's residence. Before the year was out Dryden had turned friendship into a family connection by marrying Sir Robert's sister, Lady Elizabeth Howard.

During the time that the two bachelors were living together they

---

[1] In his brilliant paper "Elizabethan-Restoration Palimpsest" (MLR, XXXV, 287–319, July, 1940), Professor Alfred Harbage has given evidence indicating that *The Wild Gallant* was not an original play by Dryden, but an old play by Richard Brome, rewritten by Dryden. This suggestion goes far to explain the differences between this comedy—including its ill success on the stage—and Dryden's later plays.

[2] *Restoration Drama,* by Allardyce Nicoll, Cambridge, 1928, p. 282. I am indebted to this book for many references in the following pages.

had collaborated on a play, *The Indian Queen*. The manner in which it was produced was in striking contrast to Dryden's first play. *The Wild Gallant* had been performed at the old theater without even the benefit of painted scenery; *The Indian Queen,* however, was staged at the new Theatre Royal on Brydges Street, and every effort was made to achieve magnificence. Elaborate scenery was provided, new costumes of rich materials were ordered, and no expense was spared to represent the glittering palace of the Ynca of Peru. The result was one of the greatest successes the theater has ever known. John Evelyn described it in his diary as "a tragedy well written, so beautiful with rich scenes as the like has never been seen here." This was in January, 1664. A few months later Dryden gave the company his second comedy, *The Rival Ladies*. It was another hit, described by Pepys as "a very innocent and pretty witty play." But Dryden was intent on providing a sequel to *The Indian Queen,* and the next spring, in April, 1665, the Theatre Royal offered its patrons *The Indian Emperor*. Its success was immediate and lasting, and the play continued to draw large audiences for many years.

In this very month the great plague broke out, and by midsummer it reached such a height that the playhouses were ordered closed. Dryden and his newly acquired wife followed the rest of the fashionable world and retreated to the country, going to the Wiltshire home of Lady Elizabeth's father, the Earl of Berkshire, where they remained for more than a year. Meanwhile the poet kept his pen busy and added to an already considerable reputation by writing *The Essay of Dramatic Poesy, Annus mirabilis,* and also a new comedy, *Secret Love; or, The Maiden Queen*. The theaters were allowed to open again a year and a half later, in the early winter of 1666. About three months afterward, in February, 1667, *The Maiden Queen* was performed. It proved to be another popular success. The play became such a favorite of Charles II that he "graced it with the Title of His Play." The King's Company had reason to count the young author as one of their most profitable assets.

But he was not theirs exclusively for long. Opportunity now arose to join in another collaboration, if it can be so called, for the Duke of Newcastle turned over to Dryden a translation of Molière's *L'Étourdi*. Dryden revised and polished it and adapted it for the stage under the title *Sir Martin Mar-all*. The play was not given to Killigrew's actors, however, but to their rivals, the Duke's Company, headed by Sir William Davenant. It was such a tremendous success that John Downes, the prompter of the Duke's Company, wrote years later that with only one exception it "got the Company more money than any preceding Comedy." But why had Dryden deserted the King's Playhouse for the Duke's? The probable explanation is that the Duke of Newcastle, whose name was not mentioned when the play was printed, was a patron of Davenant and his men. It is likely that before Dryden was called in, the literary Duke had already given the play to Davenant for production at the Lincoln's Inn Fields theater.

Evidently Davenant was favorably impressed with Dryden's ability to doctor up a script, for he induced Dryden to help him adapt Shakespeare's *Tempest* for a revival of the Duke's Theatre. The first performance took place in November, 1667, and added another to the string of successes that streamed from Dryden's pen. But the connection so well begun between Dryden and Davenant was terminated a few months later by Davenant's death in April, 1668. Six days afterwards, Dryden was appointed to succeed him as poet laureate.[3]

Dryden was now on the crest of his popularity as a playwright. He was therefore in an excellent position to bargain for his services, and probably it was at this time, the spring of 1668, that he entered into a formal agreement with the King's Company. By the terms of this agreement Dryden contracted to provide the company with three plays a year, in return for which he received one and one-quarter shares of the company's profits.[4]

Our knowledge of this agreement and of other relations between Dryden and the King's Company during the next ten years is largely based on the document reproduced opposite. It contains the most

---

[3] Was there any connection between this event and Dryden's theatrical affairs? The ramifications of Dryden's official positions have yet to be properly examined.

[4] The earliest reference to this agreement is in the *Key to the Rehearsal,* 1704: "He contracted with the King's Company of Actors, in the Year 1668, for a whole Share, to write them four Plays a year." There were a total of twelve and three-quarters shares in all. The extent to which Dryden entered into the activities of the company is shown by a Chancery suit of 1669, made known by Professor Hotson (*Commonwealth and Restoration Stage,* p. 251, and Appendix, p. 348). In this suit, a scene painter named Isaac Fuller averred that: "One Mr. Dryden (a Poet as this Defendant hath heard that Sometimes makes Plays for the Company of Comedians or Actors in the Bill mentioned) and one Mr. Wright (a Joiner belonging to the said Company) . . . did come unto this Defendant then lying sick at his own house and did propose unto him the painting of the said Scene of an Elysium . . . and to encourage this Defendant to undertake the painting thereof the said Dryden and Wright or one of them told this Defendant he should be well satisfied for the same."

Whereas, upon M.ʳ Dryden's binding himselfe to write 3 Playes a yeare, Hee the said M.ʳ Dryden was admitted & continued at a Sharre in the Kings Playhouse for divers yeares, and received for his share & a quarter 3. or 4. hundred pounds Communibus annis, butt though he received the monyes we received not the Playes, not one in a yeare. After which the House being burnt, the Company in building another contracted great debts, So that the Shares fell much short of what they were formerly. Whereupon M.ʳ Dryden complaining to the Company of his want of profitt, The Company was So kind to him that they not only did not presse him for the Playes which he so engag'd to write for 'em, and for which he was paid beforehand, But they did also at his earnest request give him a third day for his last new Play called All for Love

~~[struck through]~~
~~[struck through]~~
~~[struck through]~~

and at the receipt of the money of the said third day, he acknowledged it as a guift, & a perticular kindnesse of the Company, Yet notwithstanding this kind proceeding M.ʳ Dryden has now jointly with M.ʳ Lee (who was in Pension with us to the last day of our Playing, & shall continue) Written a Play called Oedipus, and given it to the Dukes Company contrary to his said agreem.ᵗ his promise and all gratitude to the great prejudice, and almost undoing of the Company, They being the onely Poets remaining to us.

PETITION OF THE KING'S COMPANY
Recto

Note — Mr Browne being under the like agreemt with
the Dukes house writt a Play called the Destruction
of Jerusalem, and being forced by their refussall
of it to bring it to us, the said Company compell'd
us after the studying of it, to a vast expence in
Scenes and Cloathes to buy off their claymes, by
paying all the pension he had received from them
Amounting to One hundred & twelve pounds paid
by the Kings Company, Besides neare forty pound
he the said Mr Browne paid out off his owne
Pockett.

These things considered, if notwithstanding Mr Drydens
said agreemt promise, & moneys freely given him
for his said last new Play, & the many titles we
have to his Writeings, this Play be budg'd away from
us, We must submit

Charles Killigrew.

Charles Hart

H: Th: Burt

Cardell Goodman

Mich: Mohun

Charles Hart

PETITION OF THE KING'S COMPANY
Verso

important evidence that has been preserved about Dryden's relations with the King's Company. The document is a complaint by the shareholders of the King's Playhouse that Dryden had not lived up to the terms of the agreement and had finally deserted them entirely and given his latest play, *Oedipus,* to the rival theater. Several references in the document help to date it. *All for Love* is spoken of as recently acted, an event which took place in mid-December, 1677. And *Oedipus,* though not performed until the next winter, is described as having been already delivered to the Duke's Company. It is significant that *Limberham,* the first play which Dryden gave the Duke's actors, which was staged in March, 1678, is not mentioned. These facts suggest that the complaint was drawn up in January or February, 1677/8, before *Limberham* had gone into production.

The agreement thus remained in force for the decade 1668 to 1678 and governed the production of nine plays, so that over the period of "diverse years" the average is truly "not one in a year," as the shareholders stated in their complaint.[5] For the next five years, or until 1682, when he began to devote his energies almost entirely to matters of politics and religion, Dryden continued to turn out an average of a play a year: *Limberham* and *Oedipus* in 1678; *Troilus and Cressida* in 1679; *The Spanish Friar* in 1680; and *The Duke of Guise* in 1682. All of them were given to the Duke's Company.

This document therefore marks an important crossroad in the history of the King's Company as well as in the career of John Dryden. As such it deserves more thorough examination than it has hitherto received. It was published as long ago as 1780 by Edmond Malone in the first volume of his *Supplement* to Shakespeare (I, 395) and the history of its preservation is given by Malone in the following words:

Of this paper (which remained for a considerable time in the hands of the Killigrew family, and is now in the possession of Mr. Reed of Staple Inn, by whom it was obligingly communicated to the editor,) the superscription is lost; but it was probably addressed to the lord Chamberlain or the King, about the year 1678.[6]

---

[5] The existence of this contract probably explains why Dryden turned over *The Mistaken Husband* to the company. It would have been easier for him to polish up this old play than to write a new one. Professor Harbage (*loc. cit.*) suggests that the original author was Richard Brome.

[6] From Isaac Reed these papers passed to John Field and were sold as lot 1042 in the sale of his library, January 22, 1827.

Twenty years later Malone reprinted it in his Life of Dryden (1800, I, 73 ff.), and it has been frequently referred to in subsequent histories of the stage. The document is now owned by an eminent American collector, who has kindly allowed me to subject it to various photographic tests.

These tests were necessitated by the inked-over passage of two and one-half lines, which was entirely unmentioned by Malone, probably because he knew of no way in which the original reading could be recovered. With the help of modern photographic devices, however, the over-scoring soon gave up its secret. It was only human to hope that the passage would contain some sensational bit of information about Dryden, but unfortunately such is not the case. Nevertheless, the canceled words are of considerable interest. If the facsimile is compared with the document, the canceled passage can be read in its proper place. The passage in the square brackets is that which was later inked over.

Whereas, upon Mr. Drydens binding himselfe to write 3 Playes a yeare, Hee the said Mr. Dryden was admitted & continued as a Sharer in the King's Playhouse for divers yeares; and received for his Share & a quarter, 3 or 4 hundred pounds, Comunibus annis; but though he received the monyes, we received not the Playes, not one in a yeare. After which, the House being burnt,[7] the Company in building another, contracted great debts,[8] so that the Shares fell much short of what they were formerly. Thereupon Mr. Dryden complaining to the Company of his want of proffit, The Company was so kind to him, that they not onely did not presse him for the Playes which he so engag'd to write for 'em, (and for which he was paid before hand [)] But they did also at his earnest request, give him a third day for his last new Play, call'd All for Love; [9] [Hee promiseing before most part of the Company That they should have the refuseall of all his Playes thenceforward,] and at the receipt of the money of the said third day, he acknowledg'd it as a guift, & a perticular kindnesse of the Company, Yet notwithstanding this kind proceeding Mr. Dryden has now jointly with Mr. Lee (who was in Pension with us to the last dayof our Playing, & shall continue) Written a Play call'd Ædipus,[10] and given it to the Dukes Company, contrary to his said agreemt, his promise, and all gratitude to the great prejudice, and almost undoing of the Company, They being the onely Poets remaining to us. Mr Crowne being under the like agreemt with the Dukes house writt a Play

----

[7] On the evening of January 25, 1671/2.

[8] According to Hotson, *Commonwealth and Restoration Stage* (1928), p. 255, the cost was £3908 11s 5d.

[9] Acted in mid-December, 1677.

[10] Produced by the Duke's Company in midwinter of 1678.

call'd the Destruction of Jerusalem,[11] and being forced by their refuseall of it to bring it to us, the said Company compell'd us after the studying of it, & a vast expence in Scenes and Cloathes to buy off their clayme, by paying all the pension he had received from them Amounting to one hundred & twelve pounds paid by the Kings Company, Besides neare forty pound he the said Mr Crowne paid out of his owne Pocket.

These things consider'd, if notwithstanding Mr. Drydens said agreemt, promise, & moneys freely given him for his said last new Play, & the many titles we have to his Writeings, this Play be Judg'd away from us, We must submit.

> Charles Killigrew.
> Charles Hart.
> Nich. Burt.
> Cardell Goodman.
> Mic. Mohun.

The interpretation of this incident must begin with an answer to two questions: *who* caused this cancellation to be made, and *why* was it done? Since the document was preserved by the Killigrew family and Charles Killigrew's signature tops those of the other shareholders, we may assume, I believe, that the deletion was made with his knowledge and consent. *Why* it was done cannot be certainly determined. If, as the evidence indicates, the paper was drawn up in January or February, 1678, several months had elapsed since Dryden bargained over the remuneration for his greatest play, *All for Love*. Most of the company's revenues were required to meet payments on the heavy debt with which the theater was burdened, and Dryden, who was a keen judge of the value of his own works, did not wish to see all the receipts from the new play flow into the pockets of the mortgagees. The company took the only fair course open to it and agreed to give Dryden what every author, unless he were unlucky enough to be a shareholder in an insolvent theater, had a right to expect, the money taken in at the third performance of the play.

Someone, perhaps Killigrew, retained the impression that during the negotiations Dryden had promised to give the company the refusal of any plays he might write in the future. The phrase, "promising before most part of the Company," has an air of verisimilitude about it, which suggests that the matter was definitely discussed at the time. As for the actual cancellation, the most likely moment would have been when Hart, Burt, Goodman, and Mohun were assembled to sign the paper.

[11] Produced January 12, 1676/7, at the Drury Lane Theatre.

Perhaps one (or more) of them considered that the word "promise" was too strong and caused the statement to be deleted before he would affix his signature. Or a strictly legal consideration may have decided the matter, for a case based on a mere verbal understanding might have been considered too weak to stand in court. But whatever the explanation may be, the canceled passage gives an added glimpse of the scene that took place when Dryden walked into the Drury Lane playhouse some time during the summer of 1677 with the manuscript of *All for Love* under his arm.

In case anyone should be tempted to blame Dryden for leaving the King's Company, a little reflection on the state of its affairs in 1678 will suggest that he followed the only course open to him. Ever since the fire six years earlier the company had been in a shaky position. The new theater in Drury Lane, in spite of its innovations, was struggling under a crushing burden of debt. Trouble broke out among the actors, and attendance became increasingly thin. Dwindling revenues brought increased dissensions, dissensions which were not diminished by the succession of Charles Killigrew to his father's position as manager. In effect, the direction of the company was left in the hands of the old actors, Hart, Mohun, Burt, Lacy, and others, who by 1678 had practically come to the end of their careers. Indeed a few months after this date a number of the younger members of the company, including Cardell Goodman, whose signature appears on this document, deserted the theater and migrated to Edinburgh. There they formed a company to amuse the courtiers who had accompanied the Duke of York on his exile in Scotland.

This, then, was the sad state of the King's Company when the principal members made their complaint against Dryden. The action was the last attempt to preserve a property that had been one of their most valued assets. That Dryden had stuck it out till the last is indicated by the statement in the document that he and Lee were "the only poets remaining to us." Dryden was too much of a realist to waste his efforts on a quarreling and broken company, and he cannot be blamed for not doing so. Three years before, in 1675, he had voiced in the Prologue to *Aurengzebe* his belief that competition was the cause of the difficulty in which the theaters found themselves:

> There needs no care to put a Play-house down,
> 'Tis the most desart place of all the Town:

We and our Neighbours, to speak proudly, are,
Like Monarchs, ruin'd with expensive War . . .

The best practical solution to the problem was a merger of the two companies. The event finally took place in 1682, when the Duke's Company
absorbed its impoverished competitor, in what for face-saving purposes
was called the "Union" of the companies.

Most writers who have had occasion to mention this document have
assumed that it was once officially lodged with the Lord Chamberlain. I
should like to question this assumption, and there are two grounds for
doing so. In the first place we have the testimony of Isaac Reed that
the paper "remained for a considerable time in the hands of the Killigrew family." And, secondly, there is the physical appearance of the
document itself, for it bears no external markings or superscription of
any sort. And here the inked-over passage comes to the fore once
again; official procedure would not permit the acceptance of a mutilated
document.[12]

To anyone who might urge that a fair copy of the petition was filed
with the Lord Chamberlain, I can only say that still other considerations
make it seem unlikely. First of all, there is the fact that Professor Hotson
and others who have combed through the public records have never
found a single trace of this action. Of course many of the Lord Chamberlain's papers pertaining to the theater of this period have not been
preserved, but the negative evidence is not without value.[13] And, lastly,
we are entitled to draw certain inferences from the conduct of Dryden
himself. He does not appear to have paid the slightest attention to the
complaint; *Limberham* was acted on March 11, 1677/8, and *Oedipus,*
which was the specific cause for the complaint, was performed at the beginning of the next winter and achieved a continuous run of ten days,
a noteworthy accomplishment for those years. But whether or not Dryden was ever required to give an official answer to it, this document is
of value for the facts it gives about the leading dramatist of his age and
the theatrical company with which he was long associated.

[12] I owe this suggestion to Mr. E. S. deBeer.

[13] Professor Allardyce Nicoll, who has kindly looked over this paper, has written, "It is
probable that this matter was never officially filed, but manifestly many of the Lord
Chamberlain's papers relating to the theatre between 1660 and 1680 have not been preserved, so that the failure to discover a particular document does not necessarily indicate
that the document was not once in the official archives."

DRYDEN'S LONDON RESIDENCES

FOR the first half-dozen years after he came to London, there is no direct evidence where Dryden lived. It is quite possible, as his nineteenth-century biographers suggested, that he lodged with his relative Sir Gilbert Pickering. Pickering was lord chamberlain to Cromwell, and probably was responsible in some degree for Dryden's employment under Thurloe,[1] Oliver's secretary of state. If this was the case, Dryden would have needed to seek new quarters when, in the winter of 1659, Pickering found it expedient to leave London.

Soon afterward, according to the scurrilous but usually reliable author of *The Medal of John Bayes*,[2] Dryden took lodgings with Herringman, the bookseller and publisher. The suggestion rests on the statement in the satire:

> He turn'd a Journey-man t'a ‡ Bookseller;
> Writ Prefaces to Books for Meat and Drink . . .
>
> ‡ *Mr.* Herringman, *who kept him in his House for that purpose.* [Original note] [3]

We do know that Dryden and Herringman were acquainted early in 1660, for Herringman published *Astraea redux* in the summer of that year.[4] And this same year Herringman brought out a volume of poems by Sir Robert Howard, which contained complimentary verses by Dryden, the first evidence of his acquaintance with the Howard family. Herringman's shop was at the Blue Anchor in the lower walk on the New Exchange, on the south side of the Strand, opposite what

---

[1] For discussion of this subject, see pp. 184–86.

[2] See pp. 171–83 for the evidence that Shadwell was the author of this attack on Dryden and for examples of his veracity.

[3] For an examination of "prefaces" to Herringman's books, in which Dryden may have had a hand, see pp. 187–93.

[4] Judging from the copy in the Thomason Tracts, this poem appeared on June 19, 1660 (*Catalogue,* II, 319). Professor Charles E. Ward, of Duke University, who called this date to my attention, points out that the poem was one among more than thirty written for the occasion.

is now Bedford Street. Pepys and others tell us that it became one of the chief literary meeting places and centers of gossip. Residence with Herringman would have provided Dryden with easy access to most of the *literati* of London, and perhaps it was at the Blue Anchor that the friendship grew up between him and Howard.

The friendship soon ripened into intimacy, with the result made familiar by another passage in *The Medal of John Bayes:*

> Then by th'assistance of a § Noble *Knight,*
> Th'hadst plenty, ease, and liberty to write.
> First like a *Gentleman* he made thee live;
> And on his Bounty thou didst amply thrive.
>
> § *Sir R. H. who kept him generously at his own House.*
> [Original note].

Some details of Dryden's residence with Howard are supplied by the letter-book of Sir Andrew Henley. The Henleys held property in Lincoln's Inn Fields, and one of their tenants was Sir Robert Howard, who occupied "the sixth Doore from Turnstile Holborne Row." On October 8, 1663, in discussing the purchase of the house by Howard, Henley wrote that he wished certain furniture to be excluded from the sale and sent to him at Bramshill, including "the serge Bed Mr Dreiden useth." [5] Thus Dryden's home during these years was probably on the north side of Lincoln's Inn Fields, near the site of the Soane Museum.

In such a case it would be natural to suppose that Dryden continued to live with Howard until his marriage to Howard's sister, but seven weeks after Henley's letter, on November 30, 1663, Dryden stated in his application for a marriage license that he was a resident of the parish of St. Clement Danes. This church is so near to Lincoln's Inn Fields that I questioned whether in 1663 this newly-laid-out district was not indeed part of that parish. I am informed, however, by Mr. S. Harris, the verger of St. Giles-in-the-Fields, that "the whole of Lincoln's Inn Fields was in the parish of St. Giles-in-the-Fields in 1663, and previous to that, and also up to about 1732." The facts can be reconciled by supposing that when Henley took possession of the "serge bed," Dry-

---

[5] The letter-book is in the British Museum, Sloane 813; this letter is on f. 71. See W. S. Clark in MLN, XLII (1927), 160; C. E. Ward in RES, XIII (1937), 298–300, and Clark's rejoinder, RES, XIV (1938), 330–32. Apparently the "serge bed" indicated one with a coverlet or hangings of durable wool.

den left Sir Robert's house and sought other lodgings, finding them in the neighboring parish of St. Clement Danes.

After their marriage the Drydens probably continued in lodgings, as we infer from the jotting of Major Richard Salwey described at length on another page: "Recd this letter from m^r Dryden by a messenger sent on munday night. 6. June 64 at 10. oclock to wch I returnd answer by lett^r y^t I would attend him at his lodging early on the morrow . . ." Efforts to find Dryden in the rate-books of these years have been fruitless. His name is not present in those of St. Dunstan's for 1655–68/9, St. Clement Danes for 1655–88/9, St. Paul's, Covent Garden, for 1664–68, or St. Margaret's, Westminster, for 1664–68.[6] Those of St. Bride's, Fleet Street, do not commence until 1707. Since the rate-books record the names of householders only, the absence of Dryden's name is an indication that during these years he was probably living in lodgings.

During part of this period, from midsummer, 1665, until the autumn of 1666, the Drydens were in Wiltshire, where they had fled at the height of the great plague. By the end of 1666 payment began to come in from the Exchequer of sums which Dryden's father-in-law had given Lady Elizabeth as a dowry. On October 16, 1667, Dryden was able to lend £500 to no less a person than the King himself,[7] and in the years that followed Dryden began to receive generous payments from the theater. When we remember that the family now included an infant son,[8] we have reason for believing that the Drydens wished a home of their own, as well as proof of their means to maintain it.

The first house which we have definite proof that Dryden occupied as a householder was in the parish of St. Martin's-in-the-fields. The rate-books show that he had a residence toward the west end of the north side of Long Acre, from Easter, 1669, until Easter, 1687.

Much has been written about a house in Fetter Lane, where Dryden is said to have resided. Churton Collins pointed out to Saintsbury a house in that street bearing a plate with the statement that Dryden had lived there.[9] Saintsbury was unable to corroborate this evidence,

---

[6] St. Dunstan's rate-books are in the Guildhall; St. Margaret's, Westminster, at Caxton Hall; St. Bride's at the church. The others mentioned, as well as the important St. Martin's and St. Anne's, Soho, books are preserved at the Westminster Public Library, St. Martin's Street, W.C.2: they were examined for me by Mr. Robert G. Sawyer, with the permission and courteous help of Mr. T. A. M. Bishop, archivist to the City of Westminster.

[7] See Ward, RES, XIII (1937), 297–98, and p. 8, above.

[8] Charles, the eldest son, was born at Charlton in 1666 (Malone, Life of Dryden, p. 399).

[9] *Dryden* ("English Men of Letters" series, 1881), pp. 66–67n.

and so was content to say that "if Dryden ever lived here, it must have been between his residence with Herringman and his marriage." Sir Leslie Stephen in the DNB again mentions the house, with the additional details that it was pulled down in 1887 and that Dryden had lived there from 1673 to 1682. A later article, by P. D. Mundy, refers to the house,[10] and in another note [11] Mundy mentions that a reproduction of it was printed in the *Illustrated Family Journal,* March 29, 1845, as well as in Diprose's *Book of the Stage.* H. B. Wheatley also notes the existence of the building in his pamphlet *Gerrard Street and Its Neighbourhood* (1904).

But the rate-books cited a moment ago prove that Dryden was already living in Long Acre beginning Easter, 1669, and that he continued to dwell there for eighteen years. It so happens, moreover, that the Fetter Lane house was not erected until April, 1670. Percy C. Rushen in the *Home Counties Magazine* (Vol. VII [1905], 68–71) has described the articles for constructing it, made between Thomas Sander, of London, gentleman, and Thomas Ratten, citizen and carpenter, and John Jordan, citizen, bricklayer, and tiler. Thus the tale of Dryden's residence in Fetter Lane is an anecdote even less trustworthy than most traditional stories.[12]

---

[10] *Home Counties Magazine,* VI (1904), 169–77. [11] *Ibid.,* p. 326.

[12] An anecdote concerning Dryden and Otway is placed in Fetter Lane by Walter Thornbury in his *Old and New London* (1872), I, pp. 102–3: "Dryden and Otway were contemporaries, and lived, it is said, for some time opposite to each other in Fetter Lane. One morning the latter happened to call upon his brother bard about breakfast-time, but was told by the servant that his master was gone to breakfast with the Earl of Pembroke. 'Very well,' said Otway, 'tell your master that I will call tomorrow morning.' Accordingly he called about the same hour. 'Well, is your master at home now?' 'No, sir; he is just gone to breakfast with the Duke of Buckingham.' 'The d—— he is,' said Otway, and, actuated either by envy, pride, or disappointment, in a kind of involuntary manner, he took up a piece of chalk which lay upon a table which stood upon the landing-place, near Dryden's chamber, and wrote over the door,—
'Here lives Dryden, a poet and a wit.'
The next morning at breakfast, Dryden recognised the handwriting, and told the servant to go to Otway and desire his company to breakfast with him. In the meantime, to Otway's line of
'Here lives Dryden, *a poet and a wit,'*
he added,—
'This was written by Otway, *opposite.'*
When Otway arrived he saw that his line was linked with a rhyme, and being a man of rather petulant disposition, he took it in dudgeon, and turning upon his heel, told Dryden 'that he was welcome to keep his wit and his breakfast to himself.'" The source of this tale is unknown to me. In addition to the usual weakness of such traditional stories this one encounters the obstacle of chronology, for during the period before 1669 when Dryden might have lived in Fetter Lane, Otway was still a schoolboy, going from Winchester to Christ Church in 1669.

Dryden, then, was a householder in Long Acre, paying poor-rate in Easter, 1669, and continuing to do so until Easter, 1687. These dates represent the end of the financial years 1668–69 and 1686–87 (the financial years of English local government authorities still end at Lady Day). And as we should expect, his name is found spelled in various ways—Drayton, Dreydon, Draydon, and Dreaton, in addition to Dryden.[13] Yet in every case the name is followed by "Esq.," indicating that he was acknowledged to be a person of some importance and eliminating the possibility that some other Dryden was referred to.[14] The amount of the poor-rate paid varied from fifteen shillings to eighteen shillings, but was usually the higher figure. These rate-books prove that Dryden was living in Long Acre at the time of the Rose Alley ambuscade, not in Fleet Street or Salisbury Court as has frequently been stated.[15]

To the best of my knowledge the Drydens moved directly from Long Acre to the well-known house in Gerrard Street. Since the poet was still domiciled in Long Acre in the spring of 1687 it is not improbable that he moved to the newly-laid-out Gerrard Street about the time when his fortunes came tumbling down with the Revolution of 1688. Unfortunately there is a gap in the rate-books of St. Anne's, Soho, which includes Gerrard Street, from 1687 to 1690, but in the book dated January 16, 1691/2 John Dryden, Esq., is listed as the fifth householder on the east end of the south side. This is confirmed by a statement in a letter from Dryden to Elmes Steward: "If either your lady or you shall at any time honour me with a letter, my house is in Gerard-street, the fifth door on the left hand, comeing from Newport-street." [16]

That Dryden was already living in Gerrard Street late in 1689 we

[13] In 1680 he is called "Edward," but this is obviously a clerical error.

[14] The John Dryden who was a collector of customs lived in the parish of St. Bride (see Ward in MLN, XLVII, 246–49). This explains the contradictions noted by Robert Bell in *Once a Week* (1st series, I [1859], 307–12): "the rate books of St. Bride's are quoted to show that in 1679 he was living in Fleet Street,—the rate books of St. Martin's are relied upon, with equal confidence, to prove that he was living at the same time in Long Acre." As I have already pointed out, the rate-books for St. Bride's do not begin until 1707.

[15] See Robert Bell, *loc. cit.*, and Wheatley's *Gerrard Street* (p. 4). "Dryden was certainly living in the parish of St. Bride's during this period [1673–82], and Peter Cunningham supposed his residence to be in or near Salisbury Court." W. Marston Acres twice tries to put Dryden in Salisbury Court, in his *Notes on the Historical and Literary Associations of the City of London* (1922, p. 58), and his *London and Westminster in History and Literature* (1923, p. 95).

[16] Scott-Saintsbury, letter XXVIII.

know from the dedication of *Don Sebastian* to the Earl of Leicester, in which Dryden speaks of himself as "a poor inhabitant of his [lord Leicester's] suburbs, whose best prospect is on the garden of Leicester-House." It was there that Dryden did a large part of his translation of Virgil and his *Fables,* "in the ground room next the street," as Pope told Spence.[17] In this house he died on May 1, 1700, and hence was carried to nearby St. Anne's, Soho, to be later disinterred and reburied in Westminster Abbey.

In the first entry of these books the value of the poet's house is given as £44 yearly, and he paid eleven shillings poor-rate. The assessment and payment remained the same through December 22, 1692, but on June 15, 1693, the assessment was dropped to £40, where it remained.[18] The payment of the poor-rate on the latter date was decreased to ten shillings, but in the following years it was increased to thirteen shillings and fourpence. From 1697 there is a gap in the books until June 8, 1700, when "Madam Dryden" paid thirteen shillings and fourpence. To this entry there is a side note, "Emty one quarter," which indicates that Lady Elizabeth moved out soon after her husband's death. She was not there on December 24, 1700, and her name does not reappear, the house being occupied thenceforward by one Lyceant. It should be noted that while living in Gerrard Street Dryden is called "Esq." in all the entries, just as had been done during his residence in Long Acre. This appellation is found after very few names in the rate-books, and is a recognition of Dryden's standing in the community.[19]

[17] *Anecdotes,* ed. Singer, pp. 260–61.

[18] A number of the books are missing, but the figures to December 31, 1697, are consistent.

[19] In the 1930's Dryden's house was distinguished by a huge sign "43" overhanging the sidewalk. As "Richardson's Rehearsal Rooms," it was a well-known address in certain circles, and from morning till night an *olla podrida* of "swing" music poured from its upstairs windows.

DRYDEN'S ABSENCES FROM LONDON

ALMOST without exception the names of the major English poets are still associated with their favorite haunts in the English countryside. Shakespeare and Stratford, Milton and Chalfont St. Giles, Pope and Twickenham, Cowper and Olney, Wordsworth and Grasmere—their names are linked forever. But this does not apply to Dryden. The average reader thinks of "Glorious John" at Will's Coffee-house, or perhaps in Covent Garden. Only the rare individual who has examined the poet's few remaining letters knows how he loved his native Northamptonshire and that he made an excursion thither nearly every summer.

The reasons for his reputation as a London poet are readily apparent. In the strict sense Dryden was not a descriptive poet, for as far as he was concerned, Cooper's Hill, Windsor Forest, and other local beauty spots did not exist. Rather than nature poems, he wrote of people, ideas, and events. Yet although the countryside is absent from his writings, Dryden was far from being, as Prior would have him, a mere "city mouse." The extent and frequency of his absences from town can best be appreciated when they are examined systematically, and so I have gathered the scattered evidence into a chronological review of the subject.

Born in the rural parish of Aldwincle All Saints, in Northamptonshire, Dryden attended the local school at Tichmarsh. About 1644 he was admitted a King's Scholar at Westminster School, and it is probable that this gave the boy his first glimpse of London. In 1650 the young "Alumnus Scholae Westmonasterae" went up to Cambridge to spend the next few years at Trinity College. The journey home to Northamptonshire was a relatively short one, and there are indications that portions of the vacations were spent with his attractive cousin, Honor Dryden, at Canons Ashby, nearby.[1]

[1] Scott-Saintsbury, Vol. XVIII, Letter I. See also Robert Bell's edition of Dryden. 1854, I, 15, 19–20.

In 1654, soon after receiving his degree, Dryden became semi-independent financially as a result of the death of his father. Although part of the following year was passed in Cambridge, he took the road south not long afterward, and by 1657 was established in a small government post under Secretary Thurloe. Except for occasional expeditions he remained in London for the forty-three years left to him. Of these early years, before his reputation had grown, there are no records to indicate Dryden's movements. It is possible, however, that the task of collecting rents from his small estate near Canons Ashby prompted him to return frequently to Northamptonshire.

During the early 1660's Dryden began to achieve literary success, and in December, 1663, he married the daughter of the impecunious Earl of Berkshire. When, a few years later, a series of disasters, including the Plague and the Great Fire, fell on London, the fashionable world fled to the country. From May, 1665, to October, 1666, the theaters were closed, and the young playwright had no reason to remain in town. He retired with his wife to the home of her father at Charlton, in Wiltshire, and while they were there his eldest son, Charles, was born. Here, too, Dryden spent much time in writing, and in November, 1666, he sent up *Annus mirabilis* for his friend and brother-in-law, Sir Robert Howard, to launch in London. In addition to theatrical writing, Dryden did a great deal of critical thinking, and during this period he wrote his great *Essay of Dramatic Poesy*. Since the stay at Charlton had led to money squabbles with Lady Elizabeth's father,[2] we may imagine the Drydens were not sorry to return to London. The immediate occasion for their return was the opening of the theaters and the preparations for the production of Dryden's new and, as it was to prove, very popular play, the *Maiden Queen*.

The years that followed were crowded with success, and Dryden not only became the leading playwright of the day, poet laureate and historiographer royal, but he also developed an intimate acquaintance with the court wits and became well known to the King himself. Unfortunately the personal records for this period are again scanty. In June, 1671, Dryden may have been with the court at Windsor, for we

[2] See Dryden's letter of August 14, 1666, addressed to Sir Robert Long, Auditor of the Exchequer, printed in the *Catalogue of the Collection of Autograph Letters and Historical Documents Formed by Alfred Morrison*, II (1885), 46. This letter was sold to Henry Sotheran Ltd. for £50 at Sotheby's on December 11, 1917.

know that while there the King and the Earl of Rochester looked over the manuscript of *Marriage a la mode*.[3]

During this decade Dryden probably made rent-collecting expeditions to Northamptonshire, especially after the death of his mother in June, 1676. Although we do not know whether he journeyed there in time for her funeral, it was undoubtedly necessary for him to attend to the settlement of the estate, from which he now received an additional £20 a year in rents.

The first indisputable evidence of Dryden's spending the summer in his native district occurs in 1677. On August 20 William Wycherley wrote to the Earl of Mulgrave: "I have no scandalous news to send you for Mʳ Russel is out of Town, nor any Poetical News, for Dryden is in Northampton-shire. When I write to him, I will not fail to make him proud with your Lordship's Compliment." [4] One of Dryden's letters written during this summer has been preserved, and from it we learn that he was staying with his cousin Sir Thomas Elmes at Lilford, near Oundle, where he intended to "drudge for the winter," perhaps revising *All for Love*.[5]

The summer of 1679 again saw Dryden in the country, for he states in the Dedication of *Limberham* that the play was "printed in my absence from town this summer, much against my expectation . . ."

In the spring of the next year, 1680, Dryden may have made an excursion to Oxford. We know that the King visited the University in March. As part of his entertainment a play was performed which ended with an epilogue especially written for the occasion by Dryden. Mr. R. G. Ham, who discovered the epilogue, "pictures" Dryden as taking part in the festivities, but the conjecture has not been substantiated.[6] In August of this year, however, we know he was far from London, for in a news letter dated August 31 and addressed to Narcissus Luttrell, Jacob Tonson added the postscript, "Mr. Dryden is in Staffordshire at

---

[3] See C. E. Ward, PMLA, LI (1936), 786–88. Perhaps this was the visit to Windsor with Sir George Etherege alluded to in *The Medal of John Bayes*. See p. 179.

[4] London *Times Literary Supplement*, April 18, 1935; from a copy of the letter in the Orrery papers at Harvard.

[5] This letter is reproduced in the *Catalogue of the R. B. Adam Library*. For a further account of it see p. 280. During this 1677 visit Dryden filled the end papers of Rymer's *Tragedies of the Last Age Considered* with the notes that he later wove into the Preface of *Troilus and Cressida*, a preface now generally known as *The Grounds of Criticism in Tragedy*. See also pp. 283–85.

[6] Cf. *London Mercury*, March, 1930, p. 421, and also MLN, April, 1931, and May, 1934.

S^r Ch Woolslys & Mr Dugdale at Stafford." [7] Sir Charles Wolseley was an old Cromwellian. In 1660 he had been helped by Sir Robert Howard to obtain a free pardon, but I doubt if this slight connection can explain Dryden's visits. More likely the poet was there with Sir Charles's son Robert, for the latter was a man about court who nursed literary interests and who five years later contributed a preface to Rochester's *Valentinian*.

A question arises about Dryden's whereabouts in December of this same year (1680). On the fourteenth of that month he executed a letter of attorney to one George Ward, appointing him to receive certain sums of money due from the Exchequer. Mr. C. O. Parsons, who first called attention to this document, has suggested, "It is likely that Dryden gave Ward power of attorney because of an intention to absent himself from town." [8] But there are other possible explanations, for example, that the easiest way to extract payment from the Exchequer was to appoint an agent familiar with the procedure; or Dryden may have borrowed money from Ward and assigned his pension in payment. If Dryden did in fact leave London at this unseasonable time, we have no evidence of the journey, although, indeed, there is no record of his whereabouts from this time until the publication of *Absalom and Achitophel* in the following November. Sometime before 1685 Dryden had visited the mouth of the river Trent, for in his note to line 134 of *Threnodia Augustalis* he says that he there saw the eagre, or double tide. The exact time or nature of this expedition cannot now be determined.[9]

During the factious years following his emergence as a party writer, Dryden's health made visits to the country doubly desirable. There are two references to the subject in a letter to Laurence Hyde, earl of Rochester, written probably in the summer of 1683.[10] Beginning with some remarks about his "ill health, which cannot be repaired without immediate retireing into the country," Dryden went on to announce a

---

[7] All Souls MS CLXXI, No. 63. This reference I owe to my friend Mr. E. S. de Beer.

[8] MLN, L, 364–65.

[9] Malone (p. 521) thought that Dryden had visited Richard Jones of Ramsbury, Wilts., for fishing pleasures in the company of Thomas Durfey. Malone was misled by Warton's note on the subject, for it was Durfey who was invited; Dryden is merely quoted, and was not one of the party with Durfey and Jones.

[10] Scott-Saintsbury, Letter VI; so dated by Malone. During June of this year Dryden was at Windsor, for Evelyn records the poet's presence at a dinner given by the earl of Sunderland on the seventeenth. The company was composed almost entirely of the older generation of courtiers.

political service he had undertaken at the King's request: "I am going to write somewhat by his Majesty's command, and cannot stir into the country for my health and studies, till I secure my family from want." These references provide grounds for speculation on Dryden's writing habits and raise the question whether he did not customarily plan to do the heavy work of composition during his absences from London. Indeed, when brought together, the evidence strongly suggests that however much writing Dryden accomplished in town, the long summer visits in the country were occupied with composition.

The summer of the following year, 1684, supplies a good example of the way Dryden spent his time while in the country. From a letter to Jacob Tonson we can visualize the busy poet, deep in multifarious tasks of translation, dramatic writing, and political pamphleteering. Speaking of the forthcoming second volume of the *Miscellany*, he says,

You will have of mine, four Odes of Horace, which I have already translated; another small translation of forty lines from Lucretius; the whole story of Nisus and Eurialus, both in the fifth and the ninth of Virgil's Æneids . . . There will be forty lines more of Virgil in another place, to answer those of Lucretius: I meane those very lines which Montagne has compared in those two poets . . . And for the Act which remains of the Opera, I believe I shall have no leysure to mind it, after I have done what I proposed . . .[11]

As if this full schedule was nothing unusual, he adds, "my business here is to unweary my selfe after my studyes, not to drudge."

To this period belongs an interesting manuscript record which provides a new Dryden anecdote and also throws some light on another of Dryden's absences from London. In a copy of a long poem called *Canidia, or The Witches. A Rhapsody*, by "R. D.," published in 1683, is found the following manuscript note:

Mem^d When m^r Dryden, the great Poet,—was for some moneths at Lodge, in the time of my old Lord Teynham, and some very few years before that Rebellion which was called the Revolution of 1688. my Father Doctor Robt Dixon, Author of Canidia, did comit to m^r Drydens reading one of those Books called Canidia, or the Witches. which Book, after m^r Dryden had well read and considered, he did approve of. And did publickly tell my Father at my Lords Table these words, vizt Dr Dixon, If I had had your Learning, I should have been the best Poet in the World. m^r John Gyles was also one then at Table, who heard the Words spoken, and, as others, did Attest it, to the Honor of the Author.

                                                            Ja: Dixon.

---
[11] Scott-Saintsbury, Letter VII.

"Lodge" is short for Linstead Lodge, the seat of the Lords Teynham; it is about two miles southeast of Sittingbourne, Kent. The "old Lord Teynham" mentioned by Dixon is probably Christopher Roper, fifth baron, who died shortly before July 24, 1689, at Brussels.[12] The Ropers were avowed Roman Catholics,[13] a circumstance which may be a possible explanation of Dryden's visit. As for "Mr. John Gyles," I have been unable to identify him.[14]

This chance record of Dryden's visit to Linstead Lodge illustrates the perplexing nature of any attempt to trace Dryden's visits to the great houses of his noble friends. When and how often, for instance, was he a guest at Knole, the home of his patron for more than thirty years, Charles Sackville, Lord Buckhurst and earl of Dorset? In *Knole and the Sackvilles* (1922), Miss Victoria Sackville-West makes the positive statement, "we know that Dryden was a constant visitor at Knole," and she appends the account of an incident which supposedly occurred on one such occasion. Unfortunately nothing besides the anecdote has remained to substantiate the tradition of these "constant" visits—no dates or other details of any kind.

Similarly there is a strong tradition in the Clifford family that Dryden made at least one visit to Ugbrooke in Devonshire, the seat of his patrons, the Lord Treasurer Clifford and his son Baron Chudleigh. The question has been investigated by Professor Ward, who suggests that *The Hind and the Panther* may have been written there.[15] According to family tradition this was the case. In the seventeenth century, a good proportion of the deer in the park were white, and because of the Dry-

[12] Luttrell, *Brief Relation,* I, 563.

[13] See CSP Dom., 1689, p. 257, where Lord Teynham is mentioned in a list of "known papists."

[14] A note on another flyleaf of this volume, which is now in my possession, adds the following information about the composition of the work: "It is worthy of the Readers Notice That this Canidia was written by my Father, Dr Dixon, in the time of his Visits to my Bro^r Dixon and my self at our Houses. But mostly at my House in Newnham. And consequently from his own House and Library. Nor do I remember he made use of above two or three books at my House, of which the Chief was Cooks Comentary upon Littleton. In short, he seldom had any Books by him, when he wrote, yet see in this Book what vast Reading he shews, and Memory, I think to Admiration. Ja: Dixon" Hitherto the ascription of *Canidia* to Robert Dixon has been tentative (e. g., DNB: "Bibliographers ascribe this crazy work to a Robert Dixon, and it has been suggested that the divine was its author."): but these MS notes by Dixon's son make the equation of R. D. and Robert Dixon, D.D., certain. The royalist divine was rector of Tunstall, about three miles from Linstead, until 1676, when he resigned his living in favor of his son Robert (probably the "brother Dixon" of the note). He lived until 1688.

[15] See RES, XIII (1937), 300–301.

den tradition the white strain has been perpetuated, so that there are now more white deer in this herd than in any other private one in England.[16] One attraction for Dryden would have been the private chapel at Ugbrooke, the oldest post-Reformation chapel in the south of England, where Roman Catholic services were permitted. In Dryden's time it was protected by a pardon from Charles II. The new convert may have retreated there to participate in religious ceremonies without interruption while writing his great *profession de foi*. If any part of the poem was written at Ugbrooke, it would indicate a visit by Dryden in the winter or spring of 1686–87. He himself tells us that *The Hind and the Panther* was composed in spite of "long interruptions of ill health and other hindrances," which suggests that his health may once again have caused him to seek the country air.

During these years Dryden made other visits to the country seats of his patrons, but the excursions cannot be dated exactly. Among his friends was Sir William Leveson Gower, to whom Dryden dedicated *Amphitryon*. A passage in the dedication speaks of a visit sometime before 1690: "the warm Remembrance of your noble Hospitality to me at *Trentham,* when some years ago I visited my Friends and Relations in your Country." Trentham Hall is in Staffordshire, and the only time we can trace Dryden in that county is in August, 1680, when he was "at Sir Charles Woolsley's." Perhaps Dryden was harking back ten years to this occasion.[17]

During the brief reign of James II, when the "new army" was annually concentrated on Hounslow Heath, members of the court party

[16] Unfortunately for the unassailability of this tradition there is a walk known as "Dryden's Walk" at Rushton Hall, Northamptonshire, in which is an urn with a pedestal inscribed:

In Memory of
DRYDEN
Who frequented these Shades
And is here said
To have compos'd his Poem
Of the
HIND & PANTHER

This inscription was said in 1894 to be "now almost illegible." The owner of Rushton Hall in the late seventeenth century was Brien Cokayne, second Viscount Cullen, who died in July, 1687.

[17] In 1691 or early 1692 Dryden read *Cleomenes* at the house of unspecified relatives of Laurence Hyde, earl of Rochester. Similarly at some time before 1693 portions of his translations from Ovid were read at the home of Francis, Lord Radcliffe. Because of lack of evidence to the contrary I have assumed that these readings took place at their town houses rather than their country estates.

often attended the King there. According to a contemporary squib, *Hounslow Camp*,[18] Dryden was frequently one of them. The author reported that thence "daily swarm Prodigious Wights," among whom he will only mention

> The hungry Bard that writes for Pension;
> Old *Squab*, (who's sometimes here I'm told)
> That oft has with his Prince made bold . . .

The problem of dating these visits, if they occurred, is complicated by Dryden's statement in his letter of February 16, 1687, to Sir George Etherege: "I have made my court to the King once in seven months [and] have seen my Lord Chamberlain full as often." [19]

In 1692 Dryden spent the summer in Essex, but I have not been able to determine whom he was visiting. The expedition is mentioned in three letters from Tonson to Dryden, from which we learn that Dryden stayed in Essex until October 10.[20] Whether Dryden also managed to visit Northamptonshire that year is open to question, though the same letter reveals that Tonson had been there. The following summer (1693) Dryden and his bookseller went down there together,[21] so perhaps they were repeating a successful trip made in 1692.

The expedition of 1693 was made in late July or early August, for in a letter to Walsh written in mid-July, Dryden reported, "I spoke for places in the coach too late; there will be none voyd till next weeke." [22] Tonson accompanied Dryden all the way to Northamptonshire, an act of friendship of which Dryden was properly appreciative:

I am much asham'd of my self, that I am so much behind-hand with you in kindness. Above all things I am sensible of your good nature, in bearing me company to this place, wherein, besides the cost, you must needs neglect your own business; but I will endeavour to make you some amends; and therefore I desire you to command me something for your service.[23]

The host who entertained Dryden that summer had never been identified until Professor Ward discovered that it was Sir Matthew Dudley,

[18] *A Third Collection of the Newest and Most Ingenious Poems, Satires, Songs . . . against Popery and Tyranny*, 1689, p. 5; reprinted in *State Poems Continued*, 1697, p. 52 where it is given the date 1686; quoted by Scott in his *Life of Dryden*, 1808, p. 348.
[19] *Letterbook of Sir George Etherege*, pp. 355–57. The editor, Miss Sybil Rosenfeld, does not indicate whether the date is old or new style.
[20] Scott-Saintsbury, Letter VIII.   [21] Scott-Saintsbury, Letter IX.
[22] Scott-Saintsbury, Letter LII. Since no destination is named it would appear that an earlier letter from Dryden to Walsh had referred to plans for this journey.
[23] Scott-Saintsbury, Letter IX.

Bart., of Clapton Manor (Clapton is about two miles from Tichmarsh, and only four from Oundle). Sir Matthew was very busy that summer making arrangements for his wedding to Lady Mary O'Brien, daughter of the Earl of Thomond, who lived at Great Billing, about twenty miles away.[24] Accordingly Dryden complained,

> Sir Matthew is gone abroad, I suspect a wooeing, and his caleche is gone with him; so that I have been but thrice at Tichmarsh, of which you were with me once. This disappointment makes the place wearysome to me, which otherwise wou'd be pleasant.

He passed his time with William Dudley, Sir Matthew's younger brother, and in fishing. Another letter to Tonson, dated September 13, reveals an incident that occurred during another of Sir Matthew's absences:

> Haveing been obliged to sit up all last night almost out of civility to strangers, who were benighted, and to resign my bed to them, I am sleepy all this day; and if I had not taken a very lusty pike that day, they must have gone supperless to bed, foure ladyes and two gentlemen; for Mr. Dudley and I were alone, with but one man and no mayd in the house.[25]

Dryden remained only a week after this event, and returned to London on September nineteenth.

For the summer of 1694 there are no letters or other direct evidence. There is only one hint to go by: in the postscript to his translation of Virgil, Dryden stated that the first *Georgic* and the last *Aeneid* were englished at Denham Court, the seat of his friend Sir William Bowyer. Since the agreement with Tonson, dated June 15, 1694, specified that Dryden was not to receive the first payment until the *Georgics* and the *Eclogues* had been delivered to Tonson, it is reasonable to believe that the first *Georgic* was translated at the earliest opportunity, which event would place Dryden at Denham Court in 1694. If the translation had been made before, it would no doubt have been included, like the third *Georgic,* in Tonson's *Fourth Part of Miscellany Poems,* which was published a year before the signing of the *Virgil* contract.

A portion of 1695 was again spent in the country, for in the Preface Dryden wrote to his son's play *The Husband His Own Cuckold,* he

---

[24] The wedding took place on October the eighth.

[25] Scott-Saintsbury, Letter XIV, misdated 1695. According to Ogilby's *Roads of England,* 1699 edition, pp. 85–86, the main road from London to Oakham, Rutlandshire, passed through Clapton,

speaks of being "absent from town" when the play was produced. Since the theaters were closed during the summer, this indicates that the heavy work of translation had taken Dryden to the country earlier than usual. Thanks to a letter to Tonson belonging to this year, specific information is available. On October 29, the date of the letter, Dryden had completed the seventh *Aeneid* and was about to begin the eighth.[26] Concerning Dryden's whereabouts, Malone made the positive statement that he was then "at Burleigh, the noble mansion of the Earl of Exeter." Malone neglected to give any authority for this statement, but he was probably thinking of a note of Oldys in his copy of Langbaine.[27]

The autumn of 1696 saw Dryden back at Denham Court again with Sir William Bowyer. This fact is established by Dryden's statement that "the greater part of the last AEneid" was translated there. For the date we depend on a letter written on September 3, 1696, by Daniel Bret to Theophilus, seventh Earl of Huntingdon:

One volume of my Lord Rochester's letters is come out, another is speedily designed with a mixture of some of the Duke of Buckingham's and Sir George Etherege's, Mr. Dryden is upon the 12th Book of his Virgil, the 11th is said by good judges to outdo the original; Sir Roger Le Strange hath just finished his Josephus.[28]

Bret's letter is interesting as further evidence of the extent to which the translation was passed round in manuscript and of the anticipation aroused by these previews.

In a letter from Dryden to Tonson, dated November 25 and ascribed to 1696, is another point of some importance. In it Dryden asked Tonson to receive for him the remainder of his Northamptonshire rents, as he himself was too busy to meet the Towcester carrier at Smithfield.[29] This annual business of collecting rents should not be overlooked as motivation for Dryden's movements, since responsibility for his Blakesley farm was one of the reasons why jaunts to Northamptonshire were frequent events in Dryden's summer schedule.

As we have seen, Dryden's friendship with Sir William Bowyer had

[26] Scott-Saintsbury, Letter XV.

[27] "The Story of Mr Dryden's Dream at Lord Exeters at Burghley while he was translating Virgil, as Senior Vario then painting there, related it to the Yorkshire Painter of whom I had it . . ." P. 135 of Oldys's Langbaine.

[28] Historical MSS Commission, Report on the Hastings MSS of the Manor House, Ashby de la Zouche, II (1930), 280–81.

[29] Scott-Saintsbury, Letter XX.

ripened gradually while the *Virgil* was in preparation, and after the great folio had been launched in July, 1697, Dryden returned once again to Denham Court. He must have set out on the eighteenth or nineteenth of August, since on the eighteenth he wrote Sir William Trumbull that he was "just ready to take coach for the country." [30] Whether he went there directly we do not know, but he was at Denham Court early in September, for on the third of this month he wrote a letter from there to his sons at Rome—a long newsy letter which tells among other things, "I am writing a song for St. Cecilia's Feast." [31] During that summer it is also likely that he translated Book I of Ovid's *Art of Love* and two passages from the *Amours*. Had these poems been completed before 1694, they would probably have been included in the *Fourth Part of Miscellany Poems;* and 1697 was Dryden's first free time for translating authors other than Virgil. That these parts of Ovid were finished by 1698 is shown by a reference to them in a letter from Dryden to Tonson ascribed to December, 1697.[32]

The last two summers of Dryden's life were busy ones, and they included the usual amount of traveling. In July, 1698, he received an invitation to visit Sussex as the guest of John Caryll,[33] who is now chiefly remembered as the friend of Alexander Pope. Could it have been here that Pope saw "that great man"? He told Spence many years later, "I saw Mr. Dryden when I was about twelve years of age," [34] and his memory of early events was often inaccurate. Pope was ten years old in 1698.

By October of this year (1698) Dryden had again reached Northamptonshire, accompanied by his favorite son Charles, who had lately returned from Rome. Dryden's letters to Mrs. Steward are full of details about his movements and reveal that his itinerary was from Tichmarsh to Cotterstock, then to Chesterton, and then back to Tichmarsh again.[35] By the beginning of November he had returned to Gerrard Street, where he fell ill for a period of three weeks. Gradually he recovered his

[30] Marquess of Downshire's MSS, Historical MSS Commission, I, Part 2, 761.

[31] Scott-Saintsbury, Letter XXIII.

[32] Scott-Saintsbury, Letter XXVI.

[33] Caryll's copy of Dryden's letter is preserved in the British Museum (Add. MS 28618, f. 84).

[34] *Anecdotes*, ed. Singer, p. 332. Warburton claimed that Pope saw Dryden at Will's Coffee-house. See Malone's manuscript note on the subject among those I have printed, p. 156.

[35] Scott-Saintsbury, Letter XXVII.

health, assisted by a present of marrow puddings from the faithful Mrs. Steward.[36]

The intimacy that existed between the old poet and his Cotterstock relatives throws a mellow glow over Dryden's last years. During the winter months friendly letters conveyed exchanges of presents and literary gossip. On July 11, 1699, Dryden wrote of his expectation of another summer in Northamptonshire.[37] On August 10 he finally set out, again accompanied by his son Charles.[38] They remained until late in September, but were back in London on the twenty-eighth. When safely home Dryden wrote Mrs. Steward an account of the little incidents of the return journey, a letter that will always remain a classic description of coaching days.[39]

From this journey Dryden returned to London for the last time. In December he experienced a bad attack of erysipelas, but recovered strength enough to see the *Fables* published and well received. But the infection was merely banished, not defeated, so that when a new infection started in late April, only a few days passed before Dryden was dead. Since then he has rested in Westminster Abbey at Chaucer's feet. When we pass his grave today we must not forget that Dryden, like Chaucer, was a London poet who also knew and loved the shires of England.

[36] Scott-Saintsbury, Letters XXIX and XXX.   [37] Scott-Saintsbury, Letter XXXIV.
[38] Scott-Saintsbury, Letter XXXVII.
[39] Scott-Saintsbury, Letter XXXVIII. Some readers may prefer letter XXIX, describing the journey a year earlier.

DRYDEN AND WILLIAM WALSH

DRYDEN's generosity to other poets is well known, especially in the later years of his life, when he became the affectionate literary counsellor to many of the younger wits. The traces of his friendship with Congreve, Southerne, Walsh, and Addison are found in the prefaces and post-scripts of various books, as well as in Dryden's correspondence. The best portrait of Dryden in the role of Aristarchus, however, is preserved in the letters between the gray-haired poet and his elegant young friend, William Walsh. Dryden's part of the correspondence has been in print since Robert Bell discovered the letters in the Phillipps collection, and now five of Walsh's letters can be added from one of his early letter books which has lain, long undisturbed, in the British Museum.[1]

Born in 1663, the son of a Worcestershire squire, Walsh had been a gentleman commoner at Wadham College, Oxford, before setting out to travel on the continent, especially in Italy.[2] When he returned to England once more, Walsh began seriously to pursue the life of a wit and a dandy, and soon sprouted modest literary pretensions. Some time after 1686 he made bold to send some of his compositions to Dry-den, but to be sure that his poems were strictly judged, he sent the letter without signing his name. The letter itself has disappeared, but a rough draft is preserved in one of Walsh's notebooks, now MS Malone 9 in the Bodleian.[3] It ends with the request:

---

[1] Add. MS 10434. This volume was known to Malone after his edition of Dryden had been published, and to some later scholars, but the letters to Dryden were never exhumed from it. Professor Ward and I both came upon it independently a few years ago. He will give the full text of the letters, with necessary annotations, in his forthcoming edition of Dryden's correspondence.

[2] In the Preface to *A Dialogue concerning Women* (1691) Dryden relates that Walsh "had improved himself by Travelling." The *Dialogue* itself strongly suggests that Walsh visited Naples (p. 34) and Venice (p. 95), and even that he conversed with Queen Christina of Sweden.

[3] Attention was first called to this letter by Miss Phyllis Freeman, who printed it in the *Bodleian Quarterly Record,* VII (1934), 503–7. From references on other pages in the notebook, Miss Freeman has dated the letter about 1686, when Walsh was twenty-three. On the ground that the first of twenty letters was probably written in 1686 or early 1687,

... deal frankly with mee Sir & let mee know without any complement your real thoughts of 'em, in which I can assure you, you will very much oblidge

S^r

your ff

Dryden's reply, the brief epistle called "Letter L" by Saintsbury, shows that Dryden saw through the ruse at once; it breathes affectionate congratulation:

My Deare Padron,
Nothing cou'd please me better, than to know you as well by the endowments of your mind, as by those of your person. I knew before this discovery, that you were ingenious but not that you were a Poet, & one of the best that these times produce, or the succeeding times can expect. Give me leave not onely to honour, but to love you; and I shall endeavour on my part, to make more advances to you, than you have made to me, who am both by gratitude & by inclination

Your most faithfull humble Servant,

John Dryden.[4]

This encouragement opened the way for a correspondence, heavily literary in tone, which began when Walsh sent more examples of his work to Dryden:

You will see how easy 'tis to encourage an ill Writer into ye troubling you. The favourable opinion you shewd of ye Songs, have made mee send you an Epigram & an Elegy; which I fancy to bee better in their kind than ye Songs, because they are kinds y^t I think I under[stand] better.[5]

The young man followed this up with extended comments on the art of epigram writing. The following sentence has more interest than the rest, for it records one of Dryden's critical dicta dropped among the young men at Will's: "I remember you said [when] wee talkt about

---

she concludes that the rest of the entries were made then. But it is quite possible that the letter to Dryden could have been written in 1689 or 1690.

[4] Because the three letters fit together so neatly as I have arranged them, I am convinced that the "Dear Padron" note is Dryden's reply to Walsh's first application. Against this is the circumstance that Walsh's reply to the "Dear Padron" note is in the British Museum letter-book and dates from about 1689-90. Yet Walsh's epigram which accompanied this letter is in the first letter-book, f. 60^v, which suggests that Walsh used both notebooks in 1689 or 1690. Mr. E. S. deBeer has suggested that Dryden's use of the term "Padron" for Walsh may indicate that Walsh gave money to Dryden. There is no other evidence to support this suggestion.

[5] The opening sentences of a letter covering ff. 8 and 9^r. Although Dryden's name is not given to it, the evidence that it was sent to him is readily apparent.

these things at ye Coffee house y^t [there] were not above 20 good Epigrams in Martial . . ." [6] Dryden's writings show that he was extremely well acquainted with Martial, whom in one place he records as being disdained by "warm young men" [7] and in another "the bottom of all poetry." [8]

The letter concludes with a passage which suggests that Dryden and Walsh were still at the beginning of their friendship:

Tis not Ill assure you Sir out of any want of respect, if I have not made you all the advances imaginable, as you pleasd to tell mee in y^r Letter. But methinks I am ashamed to profess y^t in words y^t I am not able to perform in actions, But I'll assure you, if there were any thing in which I were capable of serving you, you should finde y^t no man in ye World will with more zeal than my self

Dear Sir [etc.] [9]

The best indication of date in this letter is a reference to Walsh's *chef d'œuvre,* the *Dialogue concerning Women:*

I shoud not trouble [you] with these little things, but y^t I have sent you a Discourse I have writt about Women; which I woud beg you at y^r leisure to look over & tell mee your Opinion of it; as also of ye Verses. I see my self 'tis incorrect, but 'twas writt in haste, in obedience to the command of a fair Lady.[10]

The *Dialogue* was finally published in April, 1691,[11] so this letter was probably written some time in the previous year.

Dryden's answer is that printed as Letter XLIX by Saintsbury. In it he made a number of "animadversions" on both the epigram and the dialogue, but passed over the elegy in silence. The letter is one of the best witnesses to Dryden's conscious study of the devices of literary craftsmanship and makes us wish that other letters of such concrete criticism had survived.

Walsh's reply is the next letter in the new manuscript book, and it begins with an acknowledgment of the assistance Dryden had given him:

I give you infinite thanks, Dear Sir, for ye trouble you have given y^r self in y^r Criticism. To tell any body y^r fault wth a design y^t they shoud mend

---

[6] Folio 8. [7] *Dedication of the Aeneis,* Ker ii. 224.
[8] *Discourse on Satire, ibid.* 27. There are at least sixteen references or allusions to Martial in Dryden's works.
[9] Folio 9. [10] Folios 8^v–9^r.
[11] It was advertised in the *London Gazette* for April 20, 1691, No. 2654.

em, is certainly ye highest act of friendship. To tell 'em y^t they may avoid 'em, is an just end of criticising, But to do 'em only, to lessen one mans reputation w^{th}out any design of bettering another, is w^t is properly calld Malice. I shall take care to correct those little faults you finde & w^n you have more leisure shall beg you to look it over again.[12]

The rest of the letter is given over to a discussion of several of the corrections Dryden had suggested. An examination of the finished epigram and *Dialogue* shows that Walsh was not merely polite in expressing his gratitude, for he adopted nearly all Dryden's recommendations.[13] If Dryden sent a reply to this letter, it has not been preserved.

The next twenty pages in the letter-book have nothing to do with Dryden, but folios 29 and 30 contain a letter addressed to him. It begins with an explanation of Walsh's reasons for writing the *Dialogue* and develops into a request to Dryden to write a preface for the volume. There can be no better indication of the easy access which young poets had to Dryden's assistance than Walsh's attitude in the following passage:

The Business therefore is thus, I have hardly confidence enough in it, to print in my own name; on ye other side shoud it bee printed w^{th}out any name at all, it may perhaps never come to bee read; Now if you woud give y^r self ye trouble to write some little preface to it, it might [be] a very great means to recommend it to ye World. Tis true I am no great friend to Letters of Recommendation before Books, nor I believe doe any of solid Judgem^t ever like 'em ye better for it, But this beeing intended only for ye Ladies they are often imposd upon by such things. It is a very usual thing amongst ye French, for one friend to write prefaces for another; however I do not much fancy, y^t manner of doing it wch is a fulsome panegyrick upon ye Work. All y^t I would have done in the case, is to acquaint em, y^t ye Author of it having not confidence enough in ye piece to venture it to ye press, you thought y^t it might pass as well as others y^t they have been troubled with. If you finde any thing in ye manner, of ye Dialogue, in ye Gallantry of ye Apostrophes, or if you think there is somew^t of reading thereon in it, y^t is considerable for a man who professes himself so perfect a Servt to ye Sex, you may please to let 'em know as much. I wou'd by no means impose so far upon y^r friendship, as to desire you to say any thing more y^n w^t you think, but if you think there is any thing tolerable in it, you may let 'em know y^t. . . . If you have leisure to do this & dont think ye piece unworthy it, I will send you th Copy,

---

[12] Folio 9^v.

[13] As will be recognized, the epigram is that on "Gripe and Shifter," found in Walsh's *Letters and Poems*, 1692, p. 104. Professor Ward will print the original version of the epigram from MS Malone 9, f. 60, so that by comparing the two, Dryden's corrections will be easily seen.

wch you may dispose of wth ye same freedom as if it were y^r own, reserving mee a sifficient number of Printed ones, to dispose among my friends. I do not mean y^t you shoud speake of it as a piece of wch ye Author is not known, for tho' I will not venture to put my Name, yet except it is known to bee mine, it will not answer ye Ends for wch I design'd it.

A comparison of this request with the Preface to the *Dialogue concerning Women* shows that Dryden did little more than turn Walsh's suggestions into form and garnish them with a few personal remarks such as the tribute to Waller. If Walsh did indeed send the manuscript to Dryden, as he proposed to do, it is probable that Dryden arranged the details of having it printed. Such a procedure had obvious advantages for the young man in Worcestershire, and perhaps Dryden in turn was able to sell the property to Tonson and to gather a few guineas for his pains.

That Walsh was filled with pride at his intimacy with the great poet can be seen in a somewhat muddled page in a letter addressed to a lady, found on folio 53^r of the letter-book. A postscript to the letter bears the date July 25, 1691. Walsh was writing his fair friend about a rival wit who had, apparently, come out against him with some satirical verses:

Now to tell you ye truth Madam I cannot imagine but this [lampoon of Walsh] was written by some Rival mind: Methinks it savours much of Mr T. Shee corrected by my Lord R: Certanly they had some hand in it, or else Shee woud rather have been put in y^n my L^d D: [between the lines the following was written at a later date than the text: "You cannot imagine how often such Wit of She has gott the better of mine"] However ye business is: I think my self extreamly obliged to him [the following deleted: "y^t can trace Mr Drydens style in my Book & gives mee my L^d D for a M—] for favouring wth Mr Drydens style & my L^d D conversation. If hee takes y^t for an affront I dare answer for him, y^t his Verses were never corrected by Mr Dryden, nor his Company agreeable to my L^d. D. [between the lines was written at a later date: "Hee may see how much more just I am to him y^n hee is to mee, tho hee says maliciously y^t M^r D— writes for mee & y^t my L: D. keeps mee company, yet must do him ye Justice to own y^t I dont believe Mr Dryden ever corrected his verses or y^t my L^d D: ever kept him company."]

It would be tempting to guess at the persons meant by the initials, for example, that "L^{d}D" represents the earl of Dorset, and that "Mr T. Shee" refers to Shadwell, but in view of the slight evidence, conjecture would be idle. There is no likely candidate by the name of "Shee" or "Shea."

The next letter from Walsh to Dryden, Folios 55–57, is dated August 13, 1691. Walsh had spent part of the interval in London, basking in the feeble rays of his literary success, and had recently returned to Worcestershire: "I sent you a letter y^t day I came out of Town by my Chairman, wth a Copy of ye Song to Fulvia enclosed in it, wch I suppose hee deliverd you." Walsh then went into a long synopsis of a treatise "Of the Nature of Love," ending with the request, "Pray let mee know whether you approve of ye design or no, & whether you think it bee w^{t}hin my strength." What Dryden replied is unknown, for no letter from him on the subject has come to light. Yet the fact that nothing came of Walsh's elaborate plans permits the conjecture that Dryden, after a letter or two on the subject, did not press Walsh to carry through his ambitious design.

The end of the letter contains some personal news:

But I trouble you too long at a Trifle, & take you of from Employm^t ye World will bee much more concernd in. Is Cleomenes finisht pray? or have you begun ye other design you told mee of ab^t ye priesthood.

Let mee know w^n you go out of Town & whither. Have you heard out of Staff, I had a letter from London wch told mee ye young Lady was just going to bee marryd to a young L^d whose Name they coud not tell. that is not fair play methinks to take so considerable place wthout proclaiming War.

The reference to *Cleomenes* is useful in helping to date Dryden's illness of this year. It will be remembered that Thomas Southerne recorded in the Epistle Dedicatory of *The Wives Excuse* (1692) that Dryden "falling sick last summer, he bequeathed to my care the last act of his tragedy of *Cleomenes* . . . " [14] Walsh does not mention Dryden's illness, so it probably began after Walsh left London, not many weeks earlier. The design about the "priesthood" may refer to some anticlerical squib that Dryden had in mind, but no other record of it is known.

Once again Dryden's reply is missing, but from Walsh's next letter (ff. 59^v–61) we can judge some of the topics that it contained:

[14] This epistle, it should be noted, has not been found prefixed to any copy of the 1692 edition, but is present before the play in the collected edition of 1721. Professor Noyes has explained the anomaly thus: "My guess is that Southerne wrote his *Epistle Dedicatory* for the 1692 edition, that it got lost in the printer's office and was sent back to him unprinted. Such things happen even today" (personal letter, November 11, 1936).

I am very sorry to hear you have but been well, but hope the Thunder has cleard ye Air, & made it fitter for you tho not perhaps for Poetry I see will still bee reserved to ye same Destiny & meethinks Homer who went ab^t alone wth a Dog & Bell, had somew^t ye advantage of a Man y^t goes about in some sort of Mens Company. But who is ye Lord pray y^t was talkt of for ye fair Lady for this is ye first y^t you told mee of it.

The bulk of the letter is taken up with discussion of Italian and French writers on "the nature of Love," and Walsh's comments indicate that Dryden had recommended that he look into Castiglione and Boileau, among others. Here, again, Dryden's reply has not been preserved. No more news of a personal nature is found in the letter-book, although it is possible that the fair copies may have received some additions before Walsh signed them.

After this letter of the autumn of 1691, the manuscript yields no more Dryden material. Indeed, from this time until May, 1693, other records of the friendship between the two are lacking. Yet, if we may judge from this one year, 1693, the correspondence between the two poets continued and grew more active, more intimate, and more newsy with the passage of time. Three fine specimens have come down to us, dated May 9, sometime in June, and December 12, and they are among the most valuable documents extant for information about Dryden's affairs.[15] No less important is the light they throw on Dryden's personality; such zest for life was remarkable in a sexagenarian whose fortunes had so recently come tumbling down about his head. The letters exude interest in people, a currency of gossip about the latest books and plays, and a keen attention to the latest foreign news. Taken together they show the old poet to have been a remarkable person. The demonstration of such vitality and joy of living on the eve of his "grand climacteric" explains why Dryden, at an age when most men retire to chairs near the window, could take in his stride a translation of the whole of Virgil.

After 1693 records of the friendship between Walsh and Dryden are meager. In the postscript to the *Aeneis* Dryden referred to information received in "a letter from William Walsh, of Abberley, Esq. (who has so long honoured me with his friendship, and who, without flattery, is the best critic of our nation)."[16] So, too, a letter written in

---

[15] Letters LI, LII, and LIII in Scott-Saintsbury.

[16] Walsh was also a five-guinea subscriber to the *Virgil*, and the plate opposite page 94 is dedicated to him.

WILLIAM WALSH TO JOHN DRYDEN

December, 1697, records that Dryden told Tonson how he had seen "the best critic of our nation" at "the coffee house," and had asked his opinion of some verses by Lady Chudleigh.[17] But after this year Walsh's name appears only once more, in a letter of February 23, 1699/1700, in which Dryden reported to his cousin Mrs. Steward that "The poem of the Confederates some think to be Mr. Walsh."

There is no reason to doubt that the friendship between the two poets continued until Dryden's death, and we can only regret that more of the correspondence has not been preserved. But fortunately the eleven letters just quoted show clearly the fine relationship that existed between them. Those from Dryden reveal his personality and interests far more than his prefaces do, informal though they are. The newly recovered letters of Walsh disclose the growth of their friendship and the way that the grand old man of literature held out his hand to a young poet who attempted to follow his steps up Parnassus.

[17] Scott-Saintsbury, Letter XXVI.

DRYDEN AND LANGBAINE

In the history of Oxford as a center of learning, few periods have been more remarkable than the last decade of the seventeenth century. To these years belong Anthony Wood's great *Athenae oxonienses,* Tanner's *Notitia monastica,* Bernard's *Catalogue,* and the work of the "Oxford Saxons" which culminated in Hickes's *Thesaurus,* all of them gigantic monuments of learning and still consulted by scholars and historians. To this decade also belongs the first important book on the history of the English drama, *An Account of the English Dramatick Poets; or, Some Observations and Remarks on the Lives and Writings, of All Those That Have Publish'd Either Comedies [or Other Kinds of Plays] in the English Tongue.* It was written by one of Wood's Headington neighbors, horsy young Gerard Langbaine, the son and heir of the distinguished provost of Queen's College. Langbaine was aware of the frivolity of his octavo compared with the folios of his contemporaries, and he ended his Preface with the remark:

. . . if I can but be so happy as to obtain a Pardon from the more solid part of Mankind, for having mis-spent my Time in these Lighter Studies, I promise for the future, to imploy my self on Subjects of more Weight and Importance.

In this volume Dryden, no longer laureate, but still the chief ornament of the stage, figured more largely than any other dramatist. Of the more than five hundred pages in the book, about a tenth were devoted to him. This prominence was not awarded to the dean of playwrights out of admiration, however, but rather the reverse. Langbaine thought Dryden had harmed and humiliated him, and the young man was out for revenge.

For the origin of his grievance it is necessary to go back several years. Langbaine had early been stage-struck, as is indicated by his first publication, entitled *An Exact Catalogue of All the Comedies [etc.] That Were Ever Yet Printed and Published, till This Present Year 1680.* No trace of animosity toward Dryden is found in it. Probably his attitude was little different from that of his predecessor Kirkman, who in his 1671 catalogue,[1] which Langbaine was here revising, had said,

And although I dare not be absolute in my Opinion, who is the best of this Age, yet I should be very disingenuous if I should not conclude that the *English* Stage is much improved and adorned with the several Writings of several persons of Honour; but, in my Opinion chiefly with those of the most accomplished Mr. *John Dreyden*.

At any rate Langbaine made no attempt to do more than add the titles of Dryden's later plays, including the erroneous ascription to him of *Love in a Wood*. He retained most of Kirkman's errors; for example, he still attributed *Sir Martin Mar-All* and *The Maiden Queen* to Sir Robert Howard.

As far as I can determine, Langbaine's quarrel with Dryden dated from the publication of his second catalogue in November, 1687. To Langbaine's surprise this literary offspring appeared with the spurious title, *Momus triumphans: or, The Plagiaries of the English Stage; Expos'd in a Catalogue of All the [Plays, etc.] With an Account of the Various Originals . . . from Whence Most of Them Have Stole Their Plots.* Although details of the hoax will probably never be known, the outline is clear. Langbaine, snug in Oxford with his horses and his collection of plays, had left the printing to Nicholas Cox in London. As he explained to the reader on the errata leaf: "By reason of my great distance from the Press, several considerable *Errata's* are to be met with . . ." But how "considerable" Langbaine could not have imagined in his wildest nightmares. Someone, probably a person connected with the theater, had become irritated by Langbaine's pedantry and had prevailed upon Cox to issue the catalogue with the *Momus* title page.

Anthony Wood tells in a manuscript note in his copy [2] that five hundred of the *Momus* issue had been sold before Langbaine was able to substitute the correct title leaf, *A New Catalogue of English Plays*. The indignant author inserted an advertisement in the new issue which acknowledged his complete humiliation: "This Brat, of which I am now ashamed to own myself the author, is Published to the World under the Heathenish Name of *Momus Triumphans* . . . My friends may think me Lunatick." And he immediately burned for revenge: "I wish I knew

---

[1] Kirkman's catalogue first appeared in 1661; in 1671 it was revised, brought up to date, and appended to John Dancer's translation of Corneille's *Nicomede*.

[2] Wood's copy of the volume in the Bodleian Library, Wood E.28 (4).

my obliging Gossips who named it that I might thank them as they deserved for their signal Kindness."

Langbaine soon laid the "brat" at Dryden's door. We know little of the reasons that prompted this action, except that Dryden had more cause to perpetrate the prank than any other contemporary writer. The possible motive was that Langbaine's Preface had made some rather stiff charges against Dryden: indeed he was the only playwright singled out for special obloquy. The offending passage is worth quoting at length, since it contains seeds of the hate that flowered in 1691. This is what Langbaine had written about Dryden long before the hoax was perpetrated:

> Thus our *Laureat* himself runs down the *French* Wit in his *Marriage a la Mode,* and steals from *Molliere* in his *Mock Astrologer;* and which makes it more observable, at the same time he does so, pretends in his *Epistle* to justifie himself from the imputation of Theft: *Not unlike the Cunning of a Jugler* (to apply his own Simile to him) [Epistle to the *Spanish* Fryer] *who is always staring us in the Face, and overwhelming us with Gibberish, only that he may gain the opportunity of making the cleanlier conveyance of his Trick.* I will wave the Epistle to this Play, which seems to be the Picture of Bays in little, yet I cannot omit one Observation more, which is, that our *Laureat* should borrow from *Old Flecknoe,* whom he so much despises: and yet whoever pleases to read *Flecknoe's Damoyselles a la Mode,* will find that they have furnisht Mr. *Dryden* with those *refin'd* Expressions which his *Retrenching* Lady *Donna Aurelea* makes use of, as *the Counsellor of the Graces,* and that *furious indigence of Ribbons.* But possibly he will own that he borrow'd them as *Father Flecknoe* did, from *Mollieres Les Precieuses Ridicules* . . . I hope Mr. *Dryden* will pardon me this Discovery, it being absolutely necessary to my design of Restoring what I could to the true Authors: . . . I own that Mr. *Dryden* has many Excellencies which far out-weigh his Faults; he is an excellent *Critick,* and a good Poet, his Stile is smooth and fluent, and he has written well, both in Verse and Prose. I own that I admire him, as much as any man . . . But at the same time I cannot but blame him for taxing others with stealing Characters from him, (as he does *Settle* in his *Notes on Morocco*) when he himself does *the same,* almost in all the Plays he writes; and for arraigning his Predecessours for stealing from the *Ancients,* as he does *Johnson;* which 'tis evident that he himself is guilty of the same.[3]

Whether Dryden actually was involved in the *Momus* title page is a question that cannot be answered definitely. That he never denied it is without significance, for doubtless he would have kept silent if the joke had been perpetrated by other members of the group at Will's. But

[3] Preface.

though Langbaine never directly charged Dryden with the deed, it is plain that he suspected Dryden's complicity. Until evidence is discovered to the contrary, his belief deserves to be accepted.

It is important to observe that behind Langbaine's original criticism there was a personal animus based on the fact that Langbaine pointedly declared his allegiance to Shadwell. At the same time that he singled Dryden out for censure, he saluted Shadwell with praise:

For this reason I must distinguish one of our best Comick-Writers, from the *common Herd* of *Translators;* since though proportionate to his Writings, none of our *modern* Poets have borrow'd less; yet has he dealt ingenuously with the World, and if I mistake not, has *publickly* own'd, either in his Prefaces, or Prologues, all that he has borrow'd; which I the rather take notice of, because it is so *little* practised in *this* Age.[4]

Langbaine's attachment to Shadwell was so notorious that the abridger of the *Account,* Charles Gildon, referred to it parenthetically, "Mr. *Langbain,* (whose το παν Mr. *Shadwell* is) . . ." [5]

Between 1688 and 1691, while Langbaine was preparing his third catalogue, animosity ripened into detestation. He became settled in the belief that Dryden had fathered *Momus triumphans.* Wrath smoldered in the Preface to the new volume, which opened with an allusion to the 1688 catalogue: ". . . the Malice and poor Designes of some of the *Poets* and their Agents, to destroy its Reputation, (by printing a Spurious Title-page, and an uncorrected Preface) . . ." [6] Next followed a retort to the "Objection of a certain *Poet,* who professes he has not stollen half what *I then* accused him of." [7] And in its turn the main Dryden entry is one long abuse of the poet for literary plagiarism and all its variations, robbery, piracy, larceny, embezzlement, burglary, and simple theft. These charges lack any pretense of being reasoned criticism, and they were recognized by others as the product of personal hatred. Furthermore, during the intervening three years the political wheel had inverted Dryden's fortunes: the Tories were out, William III was on the throne, Shadwell had become poet laureate. Langbaine was now able to taunt: "Mr. *Dryden,* I dare presume, little imagined, when he writ that Satyr of Mack-Flecknoe, that the Subject he *there* so much exposes and ridicules, should have ever

---

[4] *Ibid.* The passage has an inset note, "Mr. *Shadwell.*"

[5] *The Lives and Characters of the English Dramatick Poets . . . First Begun by Mr. Langbain, Improv'd and Continued down to This Time, by a Careful Hand* [1698], p. 124.

[6] Preface to *Account,* 1691, p. [1].   [7] *Ibid.,* p. [6].

lived to have succeeded him in wearing the Bays." [8] The naïveté of Langbaine's abuse is balanced by the artlessness of his boasted alliance with the new laureate, Shadwell:

But I am willing to say the less of Mr. *Shadwell*, because I have publickly profess'd a Friendship for him . . . the Reader is not to measure his Merit by Mr. *Dryden's* Standard; since *Socrates*, never was more persecuted by the Inhumane *Aristophanes*, than Mr. *Shadwell* by Mr. *Dryden's* Pen: and with the same injustice . . .[9]

As might be expected, behind the personalities in this quarrel loomed the literary issues of the day, prominent among them the controversy of "the ancients *versus* the moderns." Langbaine's pedantic outlook and his alliance with Shadwell combined to make him a defender of the ancients. He wrote, "[to] proceed to the Vindication of the Ancients . . . I present my self a Champion in the Dead Poets Cause, to vindicate their Fame." [10] On the other hand, since the foundation of the Royal Society Dryden had been a champion of the moderns, though the familiar caricature in Swift's *Battle of the Books* distorts the part he played in the fray.[11]

Directly connected with the quarrel over the ancients and moderns was the disagreement about the sovereignty of Ben Jonson, and here the same individuals were ranged against each other. Since 1668 Shadwell had been one of the most devoted "sons of Ben," [12] whereas Dryden had not only tried to rank Jonson in his rightful place below Shakespeare, but in *Mac Flecknoe* (line 172) had specifically rebuked Shadwell for "arrogating Jonson's hostile name." Accordingly Langbaine took frequent opportunities to attack Dryden for his heretical attitude toward Jonson.[13]

Turning next to Langbaine's favorite cry, "plagiary, plagiary," there are two important points to keep in mind. The first is that even his contemporaries recognized that Langbaine suffered from a fixation.[14]

---

[8] *Account*, p. 443. [9] *Ibid.*, pp. 443–44. [10] *Ibid.*, pp. 134 and 133.

[11] The cross-currents of the controversy make over-simplification dangerous, but Dryden clearly considered himself on the side of the moderns. In a letter to his young friend Walsh in May, 1693 (Scott-Saintsbury, Letter LI) Dryden wrote thus of an essay on which Walsh was engaged: "For I shall be very proud, of your entring into the lists, though not against Rymer; yet as a champion for our cause, who defy the Chorus of the Ancients." See also a passage in the Dedication of *Examen poeticum* (1693), Ker's edition of Dryden's *Essays*, II, 5–6, and his note in the Introduction, I, lxvi–lxvii.

[12] See the Preface to his first play, *The Sullen Lovers*.

[13] *Account*, pp. 136, 145, 281 ff., 444.

[14] For example, the writer in *The Moderator* for June 23, 1692, and Gildon in the Preface to his abridgment of Langbaine: ". . . Mr. *Langbain* seems every where to gratify

His monomania was the point of the *Momus* hoax, and not improbably the printer, Nicholas Cox, was glad to help in the joke, for it could scarcely have been perpetrated without his connivance.

The second consideration is that the charge of plagiarism was an extremely old story to Dryden. More than twenty years earlier, in the prolegomena to both *Tyrannick Love* and the *Mock Astrologer,* he had openly discussed his sources, thus meeting any charge in advance. And at the same time that Langbaine's book was in the press, Dryden had written, "The *Materia Poetica* is as common to all writers, as the *Materia Medica* to all physicians." [15] Moreover, Dryden himself had thrown the word "plagiary" at Shadwell in *Mac Flecknoe,*[16] and it had been flung back at him in *The Medal of John Bayes.*[17] When Langbaine's turn came, ten years later, he could add nothing to these charges except details. And we may doubt if his buzzing recital bothered Dryden to any degree, for there is no record that he took any notice of the affair. Dryden was accustomed to being attacked by veterans.

---

some private Pique, and seldom to regard the Merit of the Person he reflects upon . . . He often commends, *Shirley, Heywood, &c.* and will scarce allow Mr. *Dryden* a Poet; whereas the former have left us no Piece that bears any Proportion to the latter; the *All for Love* of Mr. *Dryden,* were it not for the false *Moral,* wou'd be a Masterpiece that few of the Ancients or Moderns ever equal'd, . ."

[15] Preface to *Don Sebastian,* Malone's edition of the *Prose Works,* II, 190.

[16] Lines 183–84:

> "When did his [Jonson's] Muse from Fletcher scenes purloin,
> As thou whole Eth'rege dost transfuse to thine?"

[17]
> "No Piece did ever from thy self begin;
> Thou can'st no web, from thine own bowels, spin.
> Were from thy Works cull'd out what thou'st purloin'd,
> Even *D—fey* would excel what's left behind.
> Should all thy borrow'd plumes we from thee tear,
> How truly *Poet Squab* would'st thou appear!
> Thou call'st thy self, and Fools call thee, in Rime,
> The goodly *Prince of Poets,* of thy time;
> And Sov'raign power thou dost usurp, *John Bayes,*
> And from all *Poets* thou a Tax dost raise.
> Thou plunder'st all, t'advance thy mighty Name,
> Look'st big, and triumph'st with thy borrow'd fame.
> But art (while swelling thus thou think'st th'art Chief)
> *A servile Imitator and a Thief.*
> All written Wit thou seizest on as prize;
> But that will not thy ravenous mind suffice;
> Though men from thee their inward thoughts conceal,
> *Yet thou the words out of their mouths wilt steal.*
> How little owe we to your Native store,
> Who all you write have heard or read before?"

> > Summer's edition of Shadwell's *Works,* V, 254. For the ascription of this satire to Shadwell see pp. 171–75.

Aside from the abuse, what real information about Dryden does this book contain? Very little indeed. Langbaine had, in fact, specifically disclaimed any attempt to record the poet's biography, by saying, ". . . I shall wave all Particularities of his Life." [18] The reason for this lack of personal detail is that Langbaine does not appear to have ever seen Dryden or to have been much in contact with those that did. His comments and criticisms are no different from those found on some earlier printed page, especially in *The Medal of John Bayes* and *The Reasons of Mr. Bayes's Changing His Religion*. The "Fastidious Brisk" of Headington showed a more limited knowledge of the personalities and theaters of Covent Garden than of his own library of "Nine Hundred and Fourscore English Plays and Masques, besides Drolls and Interludes."

The relations between Dryden and Langbaine still contain many problems for his biographer. Why did Langbaine, who had little or no personal knowledge of Dryden, believe that he had perpetrated the hoax of the spurious title page? Could Shadwell have encouraged the belief, and egged Langbaine on to abusive retaliation in 1691? Several passages in the book suggest such a possibility, but it is no more than a suggestion. Whatever the explanation of Langbaine's conduct, probably no book had a greater effect on Dryden's reputation in the century that followed his death. The *Account of the Dramatic Poets,* for all its limitations remained the chief tool of compilers for more than two generations, and when Birch, Broughton, Baker, Dr. Johnson, and a host of other biographers copied the list of Dryden's dramas from Langbaine, they took not only the facts but many of his abusive remarks about Dryden. The wits at Will's Coffee House may have laughed loud and long over the *Momus* joke, but Langbaine's ghost laughed last.

[18] *Account*, p. 130.

BOOKS FROM DRYDEN'S LIBRARY

In the library of Trinity, Dryden's old college at Cambridge, is a copy of the 1679 edition of Spenser (Adv.a.l.4) which contains numerous manuscript notes and corrections. On the flyleaf is scribbled

> The corrections made in this Book are of Mr
> Dryden's own hand writing
> J Tonson

An examination of the writing confirms Tonson's statement. That the book passed through Tonson's hands is not surprising, since we know that he also had Dryden's copy of Rymer's *Tragedies of the Last Age Considered* from which he extracted Dryden's manuscript notes and published them in the 1711 edition of Beaumont and Fletcher. The wanderings of the Spenser folio, after leaving Tonson's hands, are unknown, except that it contains the bookplate of Thomas Barrett of Lee, Esq.[1] Attention was first called to the volume by W. D. Christie in the "Globe" edition of Dryden's poetical works (1870), page 366.

Traces of Dryden's pen are found on about sixty-five pages. In order to summarize what these annotations tell us about Dryden, we can best group them under three headings. The first group consists of textual corrections and emendations that might have been made by almost any reader. Since the text of the 1679 edition is extremely corrupt, these corrections constitute the largest portion of Dryden's emendations, numbering about thirty-five in all. The misprints of rhyme words were, of course, the most obvious errors, and Dryden made eight such corrections.

The second group contains certain changes that resulted from rather more deliberate thought by Dryden. An example is found in the *Faerie Queene,* Book I, canto viii, stanza 30, line 2, "An old man, with beard as white as snow." This line is a syllable short, and Dryden remedied

---

[1] Note has been deleted.

the deficiency by substituting "aged" for "old": the genuine text reads "old old." One of Dryden's most interesting conjectures is his attempt to fill out the incomplete line which concludes Book II, canto viii, stanza 55:

> Which when he heard, and saw the tokens true,
>   His hart with great affection was embay'd,
>   And to the Prince with bowing reverence due,
>   As to the Patron of his life, thus said;
>   My Lord, my liege, by whose most gracious ayd
>   I live this day, and see my foes subdew'd,
>   What may suffice, to be for meed repay'd
>   Of so great graces, as ye have me shew'd,
> But to be ever bound

Dryden naturally assumed that the text was at fault, and supplied the words "and still those bonds renewd," a very satisfactory ending. Other passages where Dryden tried to regularize Spenser's meter include the following: *Faerie Queene*, III.iii.39, line 9; III.xii.41, line 7; IV.xi.22, line 4; IV.xii.13, line 1; IV.xii.18, line 1. Some of these irregularities were the fault of Spenser, but others are contaminated readings of the 1679 text.

Several times Dryden also attempted to improve on Spenser's choice of word. In each instance he apparently thought he was remedying a corruption, as in II.v.9, line 9, "And falsed oft his blows, t'allude him with such bait." Dryden emended "allude" into "allure" and thus strengthened the line, for "allure" and "bait" form a natural metaphor: yet here again the early editions have a different word, "illude." When I first looked over these alterations, I wondered whether Dryden might have been correcting the 1679 text from an earlier edition, but these examples clearly show that Dryden's changes were his own conjectures, though they are the conjectures of a master poet.

The third group of these jottings is nontextual, and several of them preserve traces of Dryden's personality. Four passages of the *Faerie Queene* contain such comments. Opposite II.ix.6, line 5, he wrote "But were your will, her sold to entertain," he wrote "*sold* heer signifyeth hire." The use of the word as a substantive in this sense had almost died out in Dryden's time. After II.xi.15, line 6, "And those two brethren Gyants did defend," Dryden wrote the partly blotted sentence, "I suppose He means the will and the understanding."

That Dryden followed the narrative carefully is shown by his frequent correction of pronouns and also by his question after V.vii.24, lines 4–5,

> And royal gifts of gold and silver wrought,
> She for a present to their goddess brought,

In the margin Dryden wrote, "Whence had she all this wealth?"

Of Dryden the literary critic there are only two traces. The first is after the last line of III.ix.15, "Confounds both Land and Seas, and Skyes doth over-cast." There he scrawled "an Anticlimax." The other is in the *Shepheardes Calender:* next to line 115 of "October," Dryden wrote, "Orrerism." A glance at the line in question, "But ah, my courage cools ere it be warm," suggests the quality of Orrery's writing of which Dryden was reminded. I can find no other record of this word in Dryden or elsewhere.

Another passage reveals Dryden's practice when he wished to indicate whether a final "ed" should be stressed or unstressed. In line 4 of III.xii.36, "He read and measured many a sad verse," he has crossed out the last "e" in "measured," which was not to be pronounced. This conforms to the usual practice of Dryden's contemporaries.

Among these notes there are allusions to his favorites, Virgil and Chaucer. Before the first stanza of *Faerie Queene* IV.iii, beginning

> O why do wretched men so much desire
> To draw their days unto the utmost date . . .

Dryden wrote "Degeneres Animos timor arguit, et. Virg." [*Aeneid* iv.13.] In the second case Dryden's memory, which Congreve described as "tenacious," played a trick on him. In the gloss after the "Februarie" section of the *Shepheardes Calender,* "E. K." gave the following definition: "*Gride,* perced: An olde word much used of *Lidgate,* but not found (that I know of) in *Chaucer.*" Next to this Dryden wrote "I remember it in Chaucer." The word was not, however, used by Chaucer, and probably Dryden was led astray by its presence in the works of Drayton and Henry More, who had picked up the archaism from Spenser. Yet it is pleasant to see this trace of Dryden's acquaintance with the old English poet with whose dust his own has since mingled in Westminster Abbey.

Only one of these notes is well known to Dryden scholars, that written between stanzas 12 and 13 of *Faerie Queene* VII.vii, where Dryden jotted the words, "Groundwork for a Song on St Cecilias Day." As Christie pointed out, these stanzas contain a celebration of Phoebus, the god of music, which differs greatly from the two St. Cecilia odes that Dryden carried to completion.

A description of this volume would not be complete without mention of another record that it has preserved. Page 274 bears the impression of a thumb print in ink, rather slight, but in the outside margin, where the left thumb would hold the book open. The ink appears to be identical with that used by Dryden throughout the book. Can it with any degree of probability be assigned to Dryden? If it is the poet's, this mark is another vestige of the many hours that the volume rested in his hands.

The affectionate interest in Spenser to which these marginalia testify prompts us to ask, how well acquainted was Dryden with Spenser before the new edition came into his hands? That Dryden had read Spenser as a boy and thought him "a mean poet" in comparison with Du Bartas, he confessed in the dedication of *The Spanish Friar*.[2] A copy of the 1611 folio of Spenser's works has been preserved, which no less a disciple than Alexander Pope treasured as having once belonged to Dryden. It is now in the library of the Bishop of Worcester, at Hartlebury Castle, as, thanks to Bishop Hurd, are many other books from Pope's library. Professor Maynard Mack, to whom I am indebted for an account of the volume, says that on the upper left-hand corner of the title page is written "E Musaeo Jo Drydeni," in Pope's hand. Throughout the book are indications of the thoroughness with which Pope read it, especially the many commas in the margins, which was Pope's characteristic method of indicating passages of special interest. But aside from Pope's inscription there is no other evidence of Dryden's ownership. We are entitled, however, to believe this testimony, for Pope had special opportunities to know the truth of his statement. That Pope was impressed by the association-value is indicated by the fact that this is the only volume among his books with a record of provenance, except those that came to Pope directly from the hands of their authors.

The contrast between the copious annotations in the 1679 volume and the absence of them in the 1611 is reflected in the distribution of the references to Spenser which are sprinkled in Dryden's poems and pref-

[2] Ker's edition of the *Essays*, I, 247.

aces. Of seventeen that are known to me, all except two are later than 1679. This proportion, taken with the evidence from the volumes themselves, suggests that Dryden was comparatively indifferent to Spenser until the appearance of the 1679 edition stimulated a new interest in the "poets' poet." [3]

OTHER BOOKS THAT BELONGED TO DRYDEN

In addition to these two copies of Spenser's poems, I know of only ten other volumes, presumably extant, which, according to evidence of varying authority, once had a place in Dryden's library. (The annotated Rymer, discussed elsewhere at length, is ruled out of this catalogue, because it perished in Sir John Hawkins's fire.) I have examined only five of these volumes, one of the others has been seen by that good friend to Dryden students, Mr. Percy J. Dobell, and one is described by Mr. Hugh Macdonald in his Dryden *Bibliography*.

To begin with those I have examined: the least interesting is a copy of *Expositio epistolarum D. Pauli,* a medieval manuscript now in the British Museum. It carries the press mark Harleian 3253, and inside the front cover are the words "Liber aliquando Johannis Dryden," which is the only evidence connecting the volume with the poet. Nowhere on its vellum pages is there anything to substantiate the alleged ownership. Neither is there among the hundreds of Biblical allusions in Dryden's writings any instance of marked fondness for St. Paul, and there is no reference at all to a commentary on his epistles. Possibly the owner was some other John Dryden.

The next volume is a schoolbook, an interleaved copy of the *Anthologia Graeca,* now in the Harvard University Library (Sumner 134). The flyleaf is covered in schoolboy fashion with the name "Dryden" written about a dozen times, only twice preceded by "John." The handwriting is sufficiently like the poet's to suggest that the book belonged to him, although an equally good case could be made out for his second

---

[3] Dryden's interest in Spenser has led to some rather extravagant suggestions. It is not clear where Hales or Sidney Lee picked up the belief, preserved in the DNB (article "Edmund Spenser"), that the 1679 Spenser was "partly edited" by Dryden. In a recent study (*Two Centuries of Spenserian Scholarship,* 1936), Miss Jewel Wurtsbaugh has echoed this suggestion in her statement that "It is not wholly impossible that [Dryden] may have contributed the biography to the 1679 edition." This wild conjecture is invalidated by the existence of the original manuscript of the biography, in the hand of Brook Bridges (1630–1702). (Item 281 in Catalogue number one of Herbert Ford, of Mevagissey, Cornwall, 1939.)

son, also named John, or for other members of the family, such as
John Driden, of Chesterton. But since the printing is early-seventeenth-
century work, the poet may well have been the youthful owner.

The volume is a 16mo of forty-six pages, without date and place,
but probably printed on the continent.[4] The first few pages are occupied by grammar and rules; the rest of the book is interleaved, these
blank pages having been used for notes bearing on the text and kindred
subjects, some of them apparently in another hand. The Greek text is
interlined with a Latin translation, except on some of the later pages.[5]
On the end paper are scribbled a few mathematical sums, most of them
practice in division. Here the name "Charles Negus" appears twice,
with another "Charles" and two separate "Negus"es. Of this person,
who may have used the volume after Dryden, no record is known to me.

The history of the volume before April 28, 1874, when it was received at Harvard, is recorded in a note on the back flyleaf:

I purchased this book in an Auction of Books Sold by M[r] R. N. Evans in
the month of Jan[y] 1838 for the sum of £1.11—which sum I paid for it in
consideration of its bearing on the first leaf the autograph of the celebrated
Poet, John Dryden; it being the book used by him at Westminster School
where he was educated.

Tho[s] Rodd

March 2. 1838.

There is, of course, no proof that the volume was used in Westminster
School, for the *Anthology* may just as likely have been studied during
university years. Here Thomas Rodd jumped to a conclusion, not only
in the matter of Westminster School, but in the more important belief
that the schoolboy John Dryden was none other than the poet. Probably
the details repeated by Rodd had their origin in some bookseller's catalogue.

Now for the three volumes in Mr. Dobell's Dryden collection, housed
in the Folger Shakespeare Library. The first is a vellum-bound folio,
Sir Francis Bacon's *Of the Advancement and Proficience of Learning,*

---

[4] Mr. W. A. Jackson of the Harvard Library writes to me: "It is unlikely to have been
printed after 1640 and is much more likely to be c. 1600. It contains an ornament of
which at least six copies were used in England 1600–1630 and as such ornaments were obtained at that time mainly from the Low Countries, the use of it there is likely to be as
early or earlier than in England. The type also fits such a date."

[5] Pages 41–45 are interlined, but pp. 34–40 and 46 are not.

1674. The title page bears the signature "John Dryden 1677." I know of no references to this work in any of Dryden's writings.

The second is Dr. Walter Charleton's *Chorea gigantum,* quarto, 1663. It is a presentation copy with the inscription, "For my learned and obliging Friend Mr John Dryden" in Dr. Charleton's handwriting. The volume contains Dryden's complimentary verses to Charleton and is the earlier of two issues bearing the *imprimatur* leaf. A manuscript correction in the text of the poem is undoubtedly in Dryden's hand. It will be remembered that Dr. Charleton sponsored Dryden for membership in the Royal Society, and thus the inscribed volume possesses a great deal of association interest.

The third book is a copy of Monsieur de Scudéry's *Alaric, poème héroique,* octavo, Paris, 1655, bound in the original vellum. On the flyleaf is the signature "John Driden," and "Jean Driden" is inscribed on the engraved title. Mr. Dobell has written to me: "The explanation of the signatures in my *Alaric* is that Dryden wrote his name twice, in English and in French. There can be no doubt both are in his own hand, and Thorn-Drury agreed with me that this was the explanation." The book was acquired from the library of Hornby Castle, Bedale, Yorkshire, the property of the Duke of Leeds (Sotheby's, June 4, 1930). Since the Duke of Leeds inherited Congreve's library, Mr. Dobell suggests that the volume passed from Dryden to Congreve and from Congreve to the library of the Duke of Leeds. This poem made a lasting impression on Dryden, for he referred to it in three of his critical writings: first in the Preface to *Annus mirabilis,* written in 1666 (Ker's edition of the *Essays,* I, 12); then twenty-five years later in the *Discourse concerning the Original and Progress of Satire* (Ker, II, 28), and lastly in the *Dedication of the Aeneis* (Ker, II, 165).

Mr. Macdonald has mentioned two other books that may have belonged to Dryden, of which the first is the British Museum copy of Joshua Poole's *The English Parnassus,* 1657. Says Mr. Macdonald, "The B.M. copy has a MS signature on the title-page which may conceivably be Dryden's. The catalogue tentatively ascribes the Preface—'a short Institution of English Poesie'—to him. It is very unlikely to be by him." [6] I have not seen the signature, so shall not attempt to speculate whether it is Dryden's. It is difficult to think of any motive which would

[6] Item 143 in his Dryden *Bibliography.*

prompt some contemporary to write the name, unless it belonged to one of the five or six other John Drydens who lived in the seventeenth century. Of course it may have been written by a deliberate forger.

Concerning the other matter, whether Dryden may have been the author of the "Institution of English Poesie," Mr. Macdonald has somewhat overstated the case, I think, by labeling it "very unlikely." The Preface is a highly commendable piece of writing, revealing a knowledge of French poetry and Greek and Latin verse forms, and showing that the author had done much careful thinking about the problems of poetry. The fourteen pages are written in a swift clear style that ranks with any other prose of the period. Though it is signed "J.D.," the initials might stand for John Denham, John Donne the younger, John Dauncey, John Dancer, John Drope, or a score of other contemporaries rather than for John Dryden. But there were not many men in England in 1657 with the initials J.D. who combined a knowledge of "the Heroick," "the Lyrick," "Dramatick Poesie," and other types of poetry with the gift of easy exposition possessed by the author of this Preface.

The second volume mentioned by Mr. Macdonald has not been seen by him. It is a copy of Richard Blackmore's *Prince Arthur* (1695). W. C. Hazlitt had it before him when he described it as having "MS. notes of early date, said to be in Dryden's hand." [7] Mr. Macdonald could not find the volume, and until it is rediscovered the verdict must remain open.

The final volume of this brief catalogue now reposes I know not where. It was offered for sale in 1927 by W. H. Robinson of Newcastle-upon-Tyne in his catalogue, Number 18:

264. Dryden. The Reign of Gustavus King of Sweden. Collected out of Histories of those times. Small 4°, unbound, and imperfect. 1658. £5/5/– Presentation inscription on the titlepage, 'Johne Dryden ex dono Edw. Howard.'

This copy of a little-known book raises several pretty problems. The spelling "Johne" cannot be verified until the volume is located in the hands of its present owner. Heretofore this excursion into history has not been credited to Ned Howard: this inscription does not imply that he was the author, but does raise the possibility. But most perplexing of all is the question of the date when Howard made the presentation. If

[7] *Ibid.*, pp. 282n.

it was within the first two years after the publication of the volume, then this inscription is the earliest remaining evidence of Dryden's acquaintance with the Howards and it was Ned, rather than Sir Robert, who introduced Dryden into the family of his future wife.

A glance at these few volumes prompts the question, What has become of Dryden's other books? He must have had a large library, for his writings prove him to have been an extensive reader, and a man of letters in the seventeenth century had to depend primarily on his own bookshelves. Anyone who has rambled in the pages of eighteenth-century book catalogues comes away with the conviction that few volumes with definite association value have been allowed to go begging for shelter. The survival of so few of Dryden's books suggests the conclusion that he rarely wrote his name in them, for otherwise such valuable relics would have been preserved, as these volumes have been.[8]

A NOTE ON DRYDEN PRESENTATION COPIES

Mr. Dobell has also made a record of two volumes purporting to be gift copies from Dryden to others. The first is a copy of the 1700 folio of the *Fables,* with the inscription on the flyleaf, "For My Cousine Mrs Elizabeth Stuart, From the Author." This inscription is repeated three times, the third with the words "John Dryden." It was offered for sale by James G. Commin of 230 High Street, Exeter, in his Catalogue 400 issued in April, 1924. Mr. Dobell, who did not have an opportunity to examine the volume, considers the irregular inscription difficult to explain, and its authenticity has never been certified by a specialist. Mrs. Steward preserved her Dryden letters carefully, with the result that Malone was able to borrow them from her granddaughter in 1799. Thus it is unlikely that a family relic so obviously marked would easily pass out of the family. Moreover, such an inscription would be an obvious mark for any fabricator who had taken the trouble to look through the printed correspondence, for in the letter dated March 12, 1699 (1700), the poet informed his cousin that a presentation copy of the *Fables* was being sent to her. These doubts may be dissipated if the volume can be found and the inscription inspected.

[8] The Duke University Library possesses a copy of *Reliquae sacrae Carolinae,* The Hague, 1651, whose flyleaf bears a signature of two words, the second of which is "Dryden." Professor Ward has informed me that the first word is certainly not John, and the "Dryden" is not in the poet's hand.

The other presentation volume was sold with the library of the Marquess of Lansdowne at Hodgson's on March 27, 1930. It is a large paper copy of the 1693 *Juvenal,* with the autograph inscription on the flyleaf, "For his True Friend Mr [Name obliterated] from the Authour." The text contains a few slight manuscript corrections, and there are also added in the margins of Juvenal's sixth satire a few obscene lines not in the printed text. It sold for £60, and apparently is authentic.

DRYDEN FAMILY TRADITIONS
IN 1799

In the discussion of Malone's contributions to the biography of Dryden I gave a brief account of his applications to representatives of the Dryden family, and quoted from some of the replies he received.[1] The most important result of these inquiries was the recovery of the intimate letters written by Dryden to his young cousin Mrs. Elmes Stewart, of Cotterstock, Northamptonshire. These letters, by virtue of their simple charm, occupy a special place in Dryden's correspondence.

In addition to lending these documents to Malone the Dryden heirs wrote down for him a number of traditional anecdotes that had been kept alive in the Dryden family for a hundred years. Malone inserted most of these anecdotes in his Life of Dryden, where they were available to Scott, Christie, Saintsbury, and other nineteenth-century biographers of the poet. Because no future biographer will be content with such a secondhand source, the letters containing these family traditions are now printed, together with some comments, in order that they can be reinterpreted in the light of new facts unearthed since 1800.

Unsuspected by Malone, another inquirer had written to the Drydens of Canons Ashby early in 1798, or more than a year before Malone decided to write. This was Alexander Stephens, who is remembered today chiefly as the biographer of Horne Tooke. Lady Dryden, in her reply to Stephens's inquiry, sent a generous letter full of family lore. Fortunately a copy of the letter has been preserved by one of the writer's descendants, Percy Dryden Mundy, Esq., who has given me permission to quote from it:[2]

---

[1] Pages 46–49.

[2] The letter was called to my attention by Professor Charles E. Ward, who possesses a transcript. When I wrote to Mr. Mundy, he corrected the text of the letter from his copy, and contributed the notes signed with his name. The copy was made by Mr. Mundy's grandfather, Charles Beville Dryden, the son of the writer of the letter. Since the last part of the letter deals with events not concerning the poet, I have not quoted all of it.

Sir,

I received the favor of your letter and am happy your sentiments meet mine so entirely upon the subject of our correspondence and have no doubt of much approving the productions of your Pen. I am glad you are so far engaged in literary pursuits, they are entertaining rational and beneficial to the Public. It will give me much pleasure to be able to give any hints which may clear up the imperfect knowledge the learned have of the parentage of Mr. J. Dryden my Great Great Uncle that I can easily do he being the Elder Brother of my Great Grandfather but we have not unfortunately any letter or writings of his of his [sic] here he not being (as is too often the case) upon good terms with the then head of the family Sir Robert Dryden but had attached himself to the Second Brother Mr. Dryden of Chesterton in Huntingdonshire with whom Sir Robert was at variance. This I imagine prevented Mr. John Dryden from coming much here tho' he inherited from his father a small Estate at Blakesley a Village three miles from hence which we now possess *by heirship,* it brings in at present a nett rent of £182 12 per annum the Grandfather of the present Tenant was Tenant to the Poet who he says was an excellent Landlord and never raised him a shilling in his life and made heavy complaints against my late Uncle (of whom he also rented several years) for increasing his rent.[3] I believe most of the Circumstances related of him are nearly true—whether his extraordinary judgment in Phisiognomy has been mentioned I do not recollect. his sister married a Mr. Shaw who had a place under Government and was Guardian to my late Uncle his Picture is now here.[4] She and her Brother John were on terms of friendship and often met,[5] his wonderful Knowledge of the effect of the Passions of the Mind on the Mussells of the face used sometime to give him great uneasiness. She was a very nervous woman and he being of a lively turn used jestingly to take pleasure in alarming her. One day sitting next to her at dinner at a friend's house he begged her in a whisper to look at the Butler who was waiting, she accordingly did and asked him his reason as she saw nothing in the Servant particular, he told her that she might depend upon it that the man would soon come to a violent death, she was angry with him for shocking her but did not think any more upon the subject till going two days after to visit the family again she found them in great confusion and was told that the Butler had that morning killed himself—but to proceed to his Genealogy in which my own

---

[3] Malone reported this information in his Life of Dryden, p. 471.

[4] Mr. Mundy does not know the present whereabouts of this portrait. John Shaw was a "Groom in the Accompting House" under the Board of Green Cloth from 1692 to 1704. At Canons Ashby there is a large Royal Arms framed tapestry which is said to have once decorated the room where the Board of Green Cloth sat and to have come to the family through Shaw.

[5] In subsequent letters Lady Dryden corrected the relationship between Dryden and Mrs. Shaw—she was his niece, the daughter of his brother Erasmus. Aside from family tradition there is no record of the•friendship.

is included. The Dryden family is supposed (by themselves) to come originally from Scotland, it was settled here before the Dissolution of the Mon-
asteries by Henry VIII, and inhabited this old Mansion, which was not the
Monastic House, that being purchased many years afterwards by the family
and pulled down in my late Uncles memory.[6] The first of the family we
know anything of was a Mr. Erasmus Dryden so named from the learned
Erasmus with whom he had some connection.[7] He was made a baronet by
James the First,[8] he had several sons, his eldest and successor was Sir John
Dryden [9] who took an active part in the Civil Wars in the time of Charles I
and sat in the long Parliament, the second son of Erasmus went into trade in
the City,[10] the third son settled at Tichmarsh in this County and had two
sons Mr. J. Dryden the person in question and Mr. Erasmus Dryden afterwards Sir Erasmus my Grandfather.[11]

Sir John Dryden the Member in the long Parliament left two sons Sir
Robert and Mr. Dryden of Chesterton to which latter as I said before the Poet
attached himself.

Mr Dryden of Chesterton and the Poet both died before Sir Robert. Sir
Robert and his Brother both died unmarried.

Sir Robert having the Estate in his own Power left it away from the Title
to his second cousin Mr. Edward Dryden (my grandfather) son of Mr.
Erasmus Dryden the Poet's younger Brother, so passed by all the elder
branches. The title went of course to the son of old Sir Erasmus's second
son a person in trade in the city.[12]

He had it only three months and died in this Neighbourhood leaving no
children.

The title then went to the Poet's third son Erasmus Henry (the two elder
being dead, Charles drowned near Windsor and John a Cupbearer to the
Pope dying at Rome).[13]

Sir Erasmus Henry the Poet's third son held the Title only two months and
died and was interred here as appears by the Register. The elder branches

---

[6] Mr. Mundy suggests that Sir John Cope made himself a house out of the monastic
buildings about 1550, a few years before his daughter Elizabeth married John Dryden
of Staff Hill. The house was torn down about 1664.

[7] For Malone's suggestion that the name Erasmus came, not from the famous scholar,
but from an uncle, see page 136.

[8] For details of the Baronetcy see G. E. Cokayne's *Complete Baronetage* (1900), I,
128.

[9] For an account of Sir John Dryden (*ca.* 1580–1658) see *ibid.* He was sheriff for
Northamptonshire in 1634–35, and member of Parliament for the county 1640–53 and
again 1654–55.

[10] William Dryden, of Farndon, Woodford, Northamptonshire, spent part of his life
as a woolen draper in St. Paul's Churchyard. He died December 24, 1660, aged 68.

[11] Sir Erasmus, the poet's younger brother, was born in 1636 and died in 1718.

[12] Sir John Dryden (*ca.* 1635–May 22, 1710) the son of William Dryden of Farndon.

[13] Charles Dryden was drowned in the Thames in mid-August, 1704. The usual date
for the death of the poet's son John is wrong. For evidence that he died in Rome on
April 15, 1703, see p. 282.

being all extinct, the Title came to the Poet's *younger Brother* the last Sir Erasmus my Great Grandfather.

His eldest and only son holding the Estate under Sir Robert's Will, the Estate and Title were again united in my late Uncle who was Mr. Edward Dryden my Grandfather's eldest son.[14] It was the custom in those days when specie was scarce to portion off the younger branches of a family with small portions of land which was the reason of the Poets having the farm we now possess of his, old Erasmus leaving farms to each of his younger sons which are all now added to the family Estate.

The Poet was supposed to be a Catholic, his second son was Cupbearer to the Pope, it is a rule that those who have that honour must have had their families Gentlemen for a certain number of years, the Poet therefore drew up his Genealogy with his own hands and it is now at Rome and the only authentic one to be met with of the Dryden family.[15]

He might probably trace it into Scotland where they would assist him in carrying it up for many centuries.

I fear you will find my account confused, if you do and you will inform me, I will explain it with pleasure.

This letter raises a number of interesting points, which may best be considered after reading the same lady's reply, dated April 20, 1799, to Malone's request, made on April 12, for similar information:

Sir,

The favour of your letter dated the 12th was delivered to me upon my arrival here from town on the 15th, and should with pleasure have been answered immediately, had not a very bad feverish cold confined me to my room and disabled me from writing till the present day. It gives me the highest satisfaction to find that such an able pen as yours is employed upon a subject very worthy of it, that of the life of a great master of poetry and an exalted genius, and extremely happy should I be if I could find among our old books any memorandums of the kind you mention; but there is no such, nor, indeed, any one which bears the least trace of having been in Mr. J. Dryden's family. I have not the smallest doubt that the age put upon the monument is exact, as it was erected (accordingly to my recollection) during the lifetime of his widow, Lady Elsabeth Dryden, and therefore very improbable for the dates to be erroneous.[16] You are quite right as to his descent. Mr. John Dryden and my great-grand-father (the late Sir Erasmus Dryden) were sons of Mr. Dryden of Tichmarsh in this county, who was brother of old Sir John Dryden, a person much engaged in politicks in the reign of

---

[14] Edward Dryden died in November, 1717, age 49.

[15] Several years ago I arranged to have a professional searcher at the Vatican look for this genealogy, but no trace of it could be found.

[16] The monument gave wrong dates for both the birth and the death of Dryden. See Malone, Life of Dryden, pp. 5–6.

Charles I., whose letters we now have.[17] Mr. J. Dryden, the author, died
before Sir Robert Dryden his first cousin (the possessor of this estate and
eldest son of old Sir John), who left the estate by will to Mr. Edward Dryden
my grandfather. Upon his (Sir Robert's) death, the title went to the son
of an elder brother of Mr. Dryden of Tichmarsh, who, surviving only two
months, it descended to the author's youngest son, Sir Erasmus Henry, who
also lived only a few months, and died here of a decline under the tender
care of his worthy uncle, my great-grandfather, and was interred here according to the register, but in what part of the church we know not.[18] This
uncle then succeeded to the title, he was the 4th baronet within the year.[19]
Our farm at Blakesley in this county was Mr. John Dryden the poet's; after
his death it appears (by old accompt books) to have been the jointure of
Lady Elsabeth, for there are many entries of monies paid to Lady Dryden
(as she is termed) by my grandfather's steward, who seems to have been
the receiver of her rents, and as there had been no other Lady Dryden for
nearly fifty years before, it must mean her.[20] This I verily believe to have been
the case, & at her death, it went to my uncle, Sir John Dryden, as heir-at-
law. My late uncle by his will left me all his estates, remainder to my eldest
son, now Sir Edward Dryden.[21] The Blakesley farm has never been either
diminished or added to that I ever heard, the grandson of Mr. Dryden's own
tenant now occupying it. It contains 186 acres, and the net rent is 182 *l.* 12 *s.*
per annum. The grandfather of the present tenant now occupying it (Har-
riotts) used to talk much of the poet, his landlord, said he was the most easy
best landlord in the world, and never once raised his rent during the time
he possessed the estate. From family differences, Mr. John Dryden and
Sir Robert were not on good terms. I have heard that my great-grandfather
and grandfather had many valuable books, but whatever they were, they,
together with most of their plate, were left to my grandmother, from whom
(after passing through the hands of some elderly ladies) they came altogether in the year '87 into the possession of a worthless marine officer, who
I heard sold them for what he could get at the first stall.[22] I am almost
ashamed to add to this prolix detail the circumstance of our not having a
compleat sett of Mr Dryden's works of any edition, I have only two large
folio vols. of plays, date 1701, & to prove to you that I have not been un-
mindful of the subject, I have agreed, thro' a friend with a bookseller in
Bond St., to compleat the sett, w^h he undertakes to do, but it is to be all

---

[17] In Mr. Mundy's opinion these letters are probably still preserved, but at the time of
my inquiry circumstances did not permit him to investigate.

[18] Malone (p. 429) gives December 4, 1710, as the date of interment.

[19] In her next letter Lady Dryden corrected this statement to three baronets within
one year.

[20] These account books are mentioned by Malone on pp. 397, 427–28. They may still
be preserved at Canons Ashby.

[21] Lady Elizabeth married John Turner, Esq., who in 1791 assumed the name Dryden,
and was created baronet in 1795. The present title stems from this creation.

[22] There is no other record of this "worthless marine officer" or of the sale of the books.

mysteriously conducted; mine will be sent up in a week or two. Since my unhappy loss, which has, as I may say, driven me to reside in this very old mansion, I have not been without intentions of leaving some memorial here of so great a character, and have indeed, very lately, been speaking to a statuary about a bust or statue of my great-great-uncle, & about a year and a quarter ago endeavoured to recollect & note down all I had heard my grandmother (who was well acquainted with Mr. & Lady Elsabeth Dryden) had related concerning them. If those little circumstances had not been in print (which I confess my ignorance about), I thought they might be of use to a literary friend who wished for the information, & having occasion to write to him upon another account, I sent him all I could then remember, & which I own I have now nearly forgotten owing to having been immediately after engaged in legal business of very great consequence to me, which obliged me to confine my studies wholly to the practice of law & equity for the last twelve months, and having at last brought it to a successful conclusion, am but just released. The friend I allude to is a Mr. Stephens, who lives at No. 12 South Parade, Queen's Elm, Little Chelsea: a gentleman of literature, good sense, and agreeable conversation. As I do not think he means himself to make any use of my information, I have no doubt he will with pleasure send you any part of my letter to him relating to Mr. John Dryden if you should wish to hear it.

Mr. Pettiward, a gentleman of literature, who, I believe, is still living, & who gave the poet's picture to the University of Cambridge, is also a relation of Mr. Dryden, I should think great-nephew, and must have heard much about him, or by the circumstance of the picture respect his memory properly.[23] I was much puzzled last winter by reading in my leisure evenings the great edition of Ld Orford's works, the prose part of which I never had read before. He says there, speaking of the picture of his mother at Houghton, Catharine Lady Walpole, that she was daughter of sir John Shorter (of, I think, the county of Kent) and great-niece of Dryden the poet.[24] I mentioned this to Mr. Stephens, as I had never heard it before. It is astonishing to me that

---

[23] I am unable to trace this Pettiward. In Venn's *Alumni Cantabrigienses* three persons of the name are listed as belonging to Trinity College: John, who was granted the degree of B.A. in 1773 and M.A. in 1776; Daniel, who was granted the degree of B.A. in 1789 and M.A. in 1792; and Richard, who received the degree of Sacrae Theologiae Professor in 1750. It is difficult to determine which of these three Pettiwards may have been the "gentleman of literature" who presented the portrait of Dryden now in the hall at Trinity College. According to the *Gentleman's Magazine*, L, 155, one John Pettiward, Esq., died at Putney in March, 1780. Since this was twenty years before the date of Lady Dryden's letter, it is unlikely she would say of this gentleman "who, I believe, is still living." Nor would she be likely to have referred to Daniel Pettiward in those words, for he was probably only twenty-six or twenty-seven in 1799. The phrase would apply to Richard Pettiward, who would have been more than seventy years of age, except that a professor of theology would likely be known by his cloth rather than as a "gentleman of literature." Perhaps in due time the records of Trinity College may provide the answer. See p. 288.

[24] For the relationship between Lady Walpole and Dryden see Malone, p. 436*n*.

my grandmother, who was much in the world during Sir Robert Walpole's celebrity, should not dwell much upon the celebrity of such a relation as Lady Walpole, & also of her mother, Lady Shorter, who should have been first cousin to my grandfather. I cannot doubt Lord Orford's assertion, and therefore must conclude a stupor had seized my family respecting all connections & pedigree, and also respecting the merits of the great man in question. I have not yet seen Mr. Harding; he lives twelve miles off, he is my curate, as we are not under episcopal jurisdiction, and I am prioress. My steward keeps the registers, but as Mr. H. has access to them, I doubt not he has given you an accurate statement of the interment of the persons you mention. I will converse upon the subject tomorrow. As soon as I am able I will inspect the steward's books from the beginning of this century, which I am fearful of doing at present, as they are locked up with other writings in a cold place. If I find anything likely to throw any light upon the subject in question, I will send them up to my sister, who resides in town, & who will have the honour of informing you; [25] &, if any variation from the foregoing accounts appears, it may be mentioned in the second edition of the work. I must again say how extremely pleased I am, that such a work is in such proper hands, and after apologising for this uncommonly prolonged letter I beg to subscribe myself, sir, your very obliged and obedient hum^le servant. P.S.—I am glad to hear that Lady Sunderlen is coming to England, & will trouble you with my compliments to her when you see her.[26]

Although the letter to Malone repeats most of the ground covered by the epistle to Stephens, there are three points which Lady Dryden did not send the second time. The first provides an explanation of Dryden's relations with the Canons Ashby branch of the family, headed by Sir John Dryden, the second Baronet and uncle of the poet. Of Sir John's six children, three find a place in biographies of Dryden; Robert, who in 1658 inherited the title and manor, John, of Chesterton, and their sister Honor. The poet's earliest known letter is addressed to Honor, and Robert Bell found other evidence suggesting that Dryden visited Canons Ashby at various times during the early 1650's. There is no record, however, of his being there afterwards, a circumstance which indicates that family tradition is correct in reporting incompatibility between Sir Robert Dryden, the new head of the family, and the future laureate. No indication of relations between Dryden and his cousin John of Chesterton exists before the letter dated October 1, 1698.

[25] From another letter of this series (p. 263) we learn that this sister lived at 11 Hertford Street, Fitzroy Square.

[26] Lady Sunderlin was the wife of Malone's brother, Richard Malone, Baron Sunderlin (1738–1816). The Text of this letter is from *The Collection of Autograph Letters and Historical Documents* formed by Alfred Morrison, III (1896), 156–58.

In the following year Dryden addressed to his "Honour'd Kinsman" the well known poem published with the *Fables* in 1700.

The second concerns the poet's patrimony, the farm at Blakesley. Many details about this property were incorporated in Malone's biography of Dryden, especially the rent account, and the gentle repute in which Dryden was held by his tenants, the Harriott family. But Lady Dryden's letter to Stephens provides a probable explanation of how the farm came to Dryden's father: as a clergyman and younger brother, this small property was "portioned" to him as the only share he could expect from the family estate.

The third incident is of greater interest, the anecdote of Dryden's ability to read faces. Certainly it sounds reasonable enough. Dryden had passed many decades in reading the faces of men of the world, so that the troubled features of a maladjusted country menial would have presented no deep problem to him. Moreover his belief in astrology may well have been accompanied by an interest in other pseudo-sciences, physiognomy among them. Coming directly from the family, this anecdote is entitled to a place with other traditional lore which is included in Dryden's biography.

Lady Dryden's next letter was despatched on April 30, and in it she replied to a number of Malone's specific questions:

I received the favor of your last letter, & have been for some days looking over carefully some of my g^t grandfather's accompt books, which I have gone through to the year 1712.[27] I find in them very frequent mention of his nephew, first by the name of Captain Dryden, which proves him to have been in the army;[28] it appears that on or about the 22nd May, 1710, be succeeded to the baronetage, & that he died, and was enterred here on December 4th, 1710, as appears by the bills of funeral expenses, which are wonderfully small, & I must own a great reflection upon his uncle & my grandfather who were both in opulence. It appears by the book that there was much more money paid to Sir Eras^s Henry's use than could be drawn from Blakesley, probably arising from his commission in the army; he seems

---

[27] These are the account books referred to in the previous letter.

[28] The problem of Sir Erasmus Henry's right to the title "Captain" is not easily solved. It is unlikely that he was an officer of the British army, for his name is not found in the army lists. Moreover, as a Roman Catholic he could not legally have held a commission after the revolution of 1688, at which time he was only nineteen years old. According to Cokayne (*Complete Baronetage*, 1900, I, 129), he "studied at Douay; entered the Noviciate of the Dominicans, 1692; was ordained priest, 1694; sub-prior to the convent of the Holy Cross, Bornheim, 1697–1700." Why he returned to England is unknown, but it is possible that the mental illness from which he suffered at the time of his death had already begun to affect him.

to have been entirely under his uncle's care. You are quite right as to Lady E. Dryden having her thirds of the Blakesley farm, as plainly appears by the book, and the rent was sixty pounds p^r ann., & as it was then unenclosed, it could indeed, be hardly worth more.[29] One passage in the book runs thus;—"September ye 29th, 1712, allowed to my son, Mr. Edward Dryden, upon my Ladey Dryden's accompt, being for thirds tenn pounds for half a year from Lady day, 1712, to September, 1712." Then follows: "This accompt of Lady Dryden's is fairly made up to Michaelmas, September 29, 1712, all receipts in Mr. Shaw's name."[30] Mr. Shaw married the poet's sister, & was in the Board of Green Cloth under Queen Anne, a very respectable man, and probably trustee for Lady E. Dryden. I enclose three bits of paper of memorandums left in the account book of Sir Erasmus, my g^t grandfather's own writing, and which are copied twice on the book. They prove what I have mentioned, & what indeed you partly know, the person he mentions as his daugh^r Dryden was my grandmother, his son's wife. When you have run them over they may be burnt as of no value.[31] I see there were only three successors to the baronetage in 1710, as Sir Robert died in 1708. My father, Bevil Dryden, was the fifth son of Mr. Edward Dryden; he died in London in the year 1761, at the age of 84. My late uncle, who survived all his younger brothers several years, died at this place on the 20 March in the year 1770, in his 65th year. I am sorry I cannot find any account of Lady Elsabeth Dryden (as she always desired and used to be called, tho' I conclude her true name was Elizabeth)[32] later than 1712, but the moment I have leisure, I will search further into the trunk of writings. My grandmother used always to say that the printed accounts of the Dryden family were mostly erroneous, in many instances false, & stories of other families attributed to them. My late aunt has often pointed out to me some of those relations; she used to say that the only authentic pedigree of the Dryden family was at Rome in the Vatican, in the poet's own handwriting in Latin, sent with his son John, who was cup-bearer to the Pope, & died at Rome of a consumption. I suppose it has been mentioned that it was the poet who changed the writing of the name from Driden to Dryden, Sir Robert was much displeased at it; but after his death all the family followed.[33]

---

[29] For an account of this rental see Malone, pp. 440–41.

[30] Malone printed several entries from these account books concerning payments to Lady Elizabeth Dryden; see p. 397, of his Life of Dryden.

[31] It was not in Malone's character to burn any documents, no matter how useless; but no trace of them can be found among the Malone papers in the Bodleian or elsewhere.

[32] No other allusion to this trait of Lady Elizabeth is known to me.

[33] More attention has been focused on the difference in spelling than the subject will warrant. Like other names in the seventeenth century the spelling of Dryden was phonetic: Dreiden, Dreyden and Dreyton are common variations. Though the poet preferred the form to which posterity has become accustomed, instances where he signed himself Driden are familiar enough. The spelling "Dryden" had long been used by the family, for in the church at Canons Ashby the brasses for Sir Erasmus, first Bart. (d. 1632) and for John (d. 1631) son of Sir John, second Bart., are spelled "Dryden." (Notes and Queries, 2d Series, VII, 465. June, 1859).

I am very sorry I cannot inform you of the residence of Mr. Pettiward or his descendant if he is dead; nor do I know any one now living that can. About ten years ago he lived in St. James's Street, was a great antiquarian, had been much in Italy; his mother was niece to the poet, & in case myself or sisters left no issue was heir-at-law to the Dryden estates by my uncle's will, and must have succeeded. I recollect this being mentioned when my late uncle's will was opened & read by his executors. I have heard that several pictures, letters, and manuscripts of the poet's were at Chesterton in Huntingdonshire, the seat of Sir Robert Douglas' [sic] brother, with whom the poet was on very friendly terms.[34] That houses & estate with some estates in this county and Warwickshire belonging to the Drydens went eventually to a nephew of Sir Robert and Mr. Dryden's, Mr. Pigott, and at last, some years ago (since my late uncle's death), came under the hammer, when we bought a small estate in this neighbourhood and Mr. Robert Pigott [35] (known upon the turf by the name of the black prince) died only about a year ago in very bad circumstances.

I fear we shall not find any papers in the possession of Harriott's at Blakesley, they have been such rude unlettered people. My steward has been from home, but shall certainly make a search in a few days.

I am going into Gloucestershire for ten days, and shall not be back till the 13th May, which I am sorry for, as it retards my search; however, I fear I shall not find anything of material consequence. I always heard that Erasmus Dryden, the poet's father, lived at Tichmarsh in this county, but whether Aldwinkle is in that parish I am ignorant.[36] I see by their epistolary correspondence that old Sir John Dryden and his kinsman, Sir Rich[d] Knightley, were of republican principle, but tho' no one can more condemn the sacrifice of so many lives, and particularly the King's, than myself (in which I do not believe they had any share), yet as advocate for truth, I must confess that I think we should have been in a very enslaved state, had that government continued in full power, so that I shall not have my feelings in the least hurt at reading the relation of those facts.[37]

Malone made use of most of the details in this letter, so there is nothing that calls for comment beyond that given in the notes.

One more letter from Lady Dryden completes this series. It is preserved among the Malone papers in the Bodleian, and is dated May 18, 1799. From it we can reconstruct the direct questions which Malone addressed to her, and learn that she sent him certain of the family account books for his own inspection.

[34] I can find no record of Dryden's friendship with anyone named Douglas.

[35] According to the *Gentleman's Magazine*, LXIV, 958, he was "commonly called 'black Pigot' and died at Toulouse on July 7, 1794."

[36] The parishes are, of course, separate.

[37] *The Collection of Autograph Letters and Historical Documents* formed by Alfred Morrison, III (1896), 158–59.

Sir,

I duly received the favor of your letter dated the 13th immediately after my return to this place and began my researches directly, w^h I am glad to say have been in one instance successful.—I am vexed I omitted to inform you that Towcester was our Post Town, w^h would have saved you the trouble of your second favor received yesterday—as Banbury is some miles further from us than Towcester we prefer the latter & more regularly send there. however letters directed to either of those Towns are sure to be brought safe.

Altho I have not as yet examined all the old papers, I have looked over some to the purpose which I will not delay sending to you, from Sir Erasmus's (my G^t Grandfathers) account or rather memorandum books, written strangely, & scarcely to be read. One or two begun in 1661 by Sir Robert Dryden, & used afterwards (for economy as it should seem) by my G^t Grandfather, who I am surprised (from his having been all his life in trade in London) did not write better & keep a more regular account. The memorandums in question appear to be only of what money was expended *here,* chiefly in Masons and Carpenters work etc etc.—from Sir Robert's death or soon after, as my Grandfather laid out a large sum in repairs & his father seems to have taken the employment of paying the men & receiving rents and other money for that purpose. In two of the leaves of the first book you will observe Sir E. Henry named as "Capt. Dryden"; in the two others of the first books, as "Sir Erasmus Dryden", & there follows the account (of which I sent the loose memorandums) of his funeral expences, etc.—I cannot think he was a Catholic, as he would have required at his death some ceremonials of the Church of Rome, w^h would have been mentioned; at least I think something would have appeared that would have countenanced the supposition. Neither do I think his Uncle would have termed him Capt had he not been in *our* Army; but this is all conjecture. I think we may rest assured that he *was not* a priest & that he *was* in the military line; but further than that I fear my papers will not throw any light.—I am quite of your opinion that he was not able intirely to conduct himself: he appears to have had about £70 or £80 per ann.—The second account or rather memorandum is clearer in its meaning tho written equally ill; it there appears plain that Lady E. Dryden's thirds from Blakesley were paid half yearly by her Brother in law Sir Erasmus, to a Mrs Stocks for her use, which I conclude was after her derangement of mind; as you will plainly perceive, her decease is mentioned to have happened before midsummer 1714 & after Lady Day the same year, by two words at the end of the sentence very illegibly scrawled, & which I did not at first reading find out, till led to the examination by the payment being only a q^r of a year, & no other mention made in the subsequent part of the account—I am glad we have found this circumstance which may be relied upon; but where she died or was interred is unlikely to be discovered here: she resided in Lodgings in London when my grandmother visited her; but having, to bad conduct before marriage, united bad conduct afterwards, & having used Mr Dryden very indifferently, the family confined their attentions to formal tea visits, as I have heard.—the name of Sylvius I cannot find mentioned in any book or papers.[38]

In all the account books & and in the common way of speaking the Village is written and pronounced Blakesley, but I think I have seen it written as you mention. I have heard my late Uncle say that Brown Willis (a great visitor here in his day) said it was so named from the river Ooze taking its rise there, & at first was called Black-Oozely; it is a cold soil, Hedges and Timber Trees thrive there but very ill; tho' the land is mostly valuable for agriculture, it is three miles and a half from this place & is four miles & a half from Towcester, the Chester Road.—I perceive by looking more accurately over the accounts that I have made a mistake as to M[rs] Shaw, she was the poets niece not his sister, she was Sir Erasmus (his brothers) daughter, as he terms her in one page of the book "Daughter Shaw," "M[r] S. Son Shaw." She had been much with the poet & a great friendship subsisted between them.—Of his sisters I know very little except M[rs] Sandwell, I fancy one was a M[rs] England who turned Methodist, & died in such low circumstances my late uncle was written to by one of the teachers, & he sent money for the funeral, for w[h] he had a very grateful letter from the Teacher with a kind of sermon added to it—[39]

In regard to the erroneous accounts of the Family I can at present recollect but two, tho' my Grandmother said that most of the published pedigree was very much so. The first is a Story that I believe Bridges has taken from another Author, of several Brothers resolving not to marry, or casting lots which should marry first, (I forgot which for I have not the books).[40] My late Aunt used to say that story belonged to a family about eight miles from hence.—The second, that the first Sir Erasmus was a Schoolmaster, this was absolutely denied, indeed it appears highly improbable, as he possessed this House & part of the Estate, which never belonged to the Monastery or the Cope family into which he married: he was rich enough to fit up a room to receive the Queen of James the 1st on her progress; the cieling of which is now intire & is ornamented with the Thistle in every state of bloom, as a compliment to his Majesty; besides I think the aristocratic disposition of those times would hardly have conferred a Baronetage upon a Schoolmaster.[41] I believe the family is (not without reason) supposed to

---

[38] Malone inserted most of these details in his account of Lady Elizabeth Dryden, pp. 394–98. An account of Lady Anne Sylvius is on p. 396, and further details can be found in *The Ashstead Estate and Its Howard Possessors,* by the Reverend Francis Puget, 1873, pp. 115–17.

[39] Malone inserted a reference to this sister in the copy corrected for the second edition. See page 136, above.

[40] Malone did not repeat this story.

[41] Mr. Mundy writes that this tradition probably grew out of the fact that David Dryden (1563–96) was a schoolmaster at Daventry, Northamptonshire. This David was a nephew to John Dryden, of Canons Ashby, the father of Sir Erasmus Dryden, first Bart. See page 136, above, for Malone's manuscript note on the subject.

have come originally from Scotland: and I have been told that the name is not so uncommon there as it is in England, which corroborates the opinion.—

Should I make any other discoveries amongst the old receipts I will with pleasure inform you directly, feeling myself must interested in the subject.— The Accounts are in long parchment bound Ledger Books, the leaves cut out are of little value as they will probably never be looked into again; but if you will take the trouble any time before August next to order them to be sent directed to me, to my sister Miss Drydens at No 11 Hertford St. Fitzroy Sq^r it will be quite time enough. I am very glad to hear Lady Sunderlen is arrived safe in England, & beg you will permit me to trouble you with my compliments to her—and believe me to remain Sir with great respect your obliged & very obed^t

Humble Ser^t.

Elizth Dryden

Canons Ashby. 18th May 99

P.S. I am very glad you can disprove the absurd story of the funeral of Dryden which I never believed, being a most strange account.—Surely Charles Dryden had some small place about the Court.—the story of the prediction of his misfortunes & death (which he found in his fathers pocket book) was intirely credited by my grandmother, Mr & Mrs Shaw & in consequence all the family; but that seems strange he was certainly drowned. I had read so little about the poet that I never knew the foolish account of his funeral till after I married & left this place—.

Although this letter is full of detailed information, it raises almost as many questions as it settles. And this is its value to us; Malone made use of all the points that could be easily incorporated in his biography, but left many of the problems unsolved and some of them unmentioned. Did Dryden's son Erasmus die a Roman Catholic, or was he denied Catholic burial? Where is Lady Elizabeth buried? Did Dryden have any relations with his sisters, Mrs. Sandwell and Mrs. England (the Methodist)? What was Charles Dryden's "small place about the court"? Probably the answers to these questions will never be known. Yet by calling attention to them, the way is opened for later investigators who may stumble upon a chance clue, and pursue the search to its ultimate conclusion.

The final document in this reconstruction of family anecdotes is a letter from Miss Honor Pigott, a distant cousin of the Dryden family.[42] In general her lore merely paralleled stories and facts already known to

---

[42] For the exact relationship between Miss Pigott and the Dryden family, see page 47, above.

Malone. Nevertheless, her letter of June 15, 1799, is worth giving in full, because of the additional information which it contains.

Lansdowne House   Bath
June ye 15th 1799

Sir.

I am Highly gratified at present in my Correspondence with you & at any Mite of Information I can give concerning Our Great Relation, tho still *Mortified* that I can Only give fragments from my Memory of what I have heard in my Earlyer days of Our Dryden Conection, & this Knowledge I Cheifly gain'd from a very Worthy Old Aunt who Lived with her Grandmother & Mrs Honor Dryden in Shrewsbury (& Early Years are seldom forgot) She was their particular Favorite Mrs Pigott left her the Interest of 600 £ to be paid her Independent of Richard Lyster Esqr her Husband for she was Married at sixteen & was the Anne Pigott Mr John Dryden Left 2000 to [in] his Will, she allways mention'd them & M^r J Dryden as the best people in the world, so did all the Town of Shrewsbury who in my Time remember'd them, & they Left considerable Benefactions to the Churches there, Mrs Honor Dryden I have heard was a very superior Character Both in Goodness & Understanding. I have heard my Aunt Lyster say *she had never been Handsome* But very Attractive to the Men & had several Great Offers but Having been Ill Used by her Cousin Sr Gibert Pickering she determined never to Marry, Prehaps she might Like a Life of Celibacy as well as her five Brothers (tho I dare Answer she took No *Vow*— The family allways seem'd to Look Up to her with the greatest Atention for I have been lately reading several of Mr John Drydens & the family Letters to her wrote with a deal of Good Sense & Sentiment, but it was not the Age of Sentiment (as the present especially in Letter writing. I am sure it will strike you as singular that these Letters should be Preserv'd & None of the Poets, but when we Consider what is No Loss Can't be Worth taking your surprise will Cease & Who wou'd not turn Theif (Conscience Laid Aside) for *such a Prize* as the Poets Letters,—In the very neighbourod of Chesterton & almost in the next field at Alwanton Lived Doctor Timothy Neve [43] who you must well know was the greatest Antiquarian & Colecter of Paper's in the last Age. Mr Robert Smyth an Equal searcher of Knowledge was Another Near Neighbour of whom you will read a very particular of [sic] in the Gentleman's Magazine for 1796,[44] I have often dined with them at Chesterton & there seem'd a great degree of family Intimacy, & Can we think it Possible that these two Greedy Men, for such a Prey would be Inatentive to get Drydens Letters in their Possession, for they have certainly been Glean'd from the family But pray

---

[43] An account of Timothy Neve (1724–98) is in the DNB.

[44] This short biographical sketch of Smyth, undoubtedly by John Nichols, appeared in the *Gentleman's Magazine* for August, 1796, LXVI, 637–38.

Observe I mention this as *Probable* tho not as *Fact,* & have been more Particular as it may Lead you thro a Rugged road (prehaps) to discover these Most Valuable Letters I dont doubt but you have read the Dryden Pedigree in Collins's Baronetage 1791 & I have Little doubt but it was Given by the said Mr Robert Smyth for it seems very Particular & most Parts very Authentick, But I am rather perplex'd [by] what he says in regard to Sr John Drydens three daughters as I allways thought my Great Grandmother was the Eldest Sister & Mrs Sneyd the yongest, but if it will be any source of satifaction I will get more Certainty of it, Our Lamented Picture of the Poet's at Chesterton I have often Look'd at with the greatest pleasure it was a Half Length & [obliteration] a Large Wig, with a Wreath of Bays In His Hand much in the Stile of the Print in the Octavo Edition of Virgil, By Riley, But Older & the Hands were most Beautifully painted.—

I Hear all the Ormond Papers are still Lock'd Up in the Old Castle of Kilkenny. I woud advise you to write to Lady Eleanor Butler at Llangollen in Denbighshire she is Aunt to the present Earl of Ormond & I think she will be most Willing & Able to give you Some Assistance, for she has all the Knowledge of her Ancestors & a Noble Nature with it to Enlighten others, besides I have heard her express the greatest Esteem for Dryden & she will be Delighted that you are going to Introduce Him in a New Dress.[45] —I would Likewise advise you to make an Application to Colonel Sneyd who is now with the Staffordshire Militia near Windsor.—for I have only mention'd it to the Ladies of that family.—I saw Once at Keel in Staffordshire a Picture of the Poets which the Sneyds fancy'd Sr Godfrey Knellers But it might be Rileys or Clostermans who were great Copyers of Sr Godfrey Kneller's.[46] I supose you have some reason to think Charles Dryden mention'd in Mr John Drydens Will was Son to the Poet as I hear you are perplex'd concerning the Date but is it not possible? He might have some other Cousin of that Name: for such a Man & such a *fortune* must have Cousins Out of all Numbering, when the Pasture was so Rich to feed Upon, But I can procure you a sight of the Will soon which will determine all Doubt. I have just been reading again the family Letters & I have Heard my Mother say (who had a very good Understanding) that Mr John Drydens Letters were thought Equaly Good to the Poets there certainly seems a Rich Vein of Good Sense & Character in all his Letters to His Sister Mrs Honor Dryden & all the Balm of Human Kindness, By what I have heard from Many He had a Character that cou'd not be Complimented even by his Cousins Charming Poem, for He was a Man Above all Praise There is One Lady in the family that I have quite Lost which is Mrs Elizabeth Dryden I have Read she was Grandmother to Dean Swift & if so, Dryden & Swift

---

[45] Apparently Malone was unsuccessful in his attempt to gain access to the Ormond papers, for the representatives of the Duke of Ormond are listed among the "Persons in whose cabinets letters written by Dryden may probably be found."

[46] Malone's remarks on this portrait are on page 435 of his Life of Dryden. It is now owned by Mr. Mundy.

were second Cousins, & I have often heard our family mention Dryden, Swift, & Addison being nearly related to Us [47] & I shoud be sorry to Lose so Rich a Source for want of proper Information, & cou'd Immagine Swift had gathered some Embers of Drydens Poetic fire which Drydens Superior Genious coud not Want, for Drydens Muse seem'd Inspiration I have often heard my Aunt Lyster *say* her Cousin John Dryden & his Wife were very Unhappy, for she was of a most sad temper & He was often Obliged (I supose for Peace) to seperate from her, & my Aunt said spent often those days at Chesterton, for the family never Liked his Conection—

I have Likewise often heard mention'd from the *Best* Authoritys the Gift of the 500 £ long before the year 1760, & by Dates I shoud supose the Picture was presented to Chesterton very soon after the Gift.—

M^r J Dryden of Chesterton Purchased the very Valuable Living of Edgmond near Newport in Shropshire & his three Nephew Pigotts Have successively Enjoy'd it, being his Nephew, Great Nephew, & now Great Great Nephew who is my Brother & tho' the Purchase was small, the Living now produces Above a thousand a year & is Held with Chetwynd. My G Grandmother gave a very Handsome Pulpit Cloth to Edgmond Church & the Communion Plate, She & Mrs Honor Dryden Left a considerable Benefaction to the Poor of Both Parishes—I mention these trifles, as to an Editor a Trifle may Lead to an Event, & it shews the Opulence of the Dryden family, Mrs Honor Dryden I beleive was Burry'd at Chetwin of which I expect Information every day & where she died—[Two lines obliterated].

My Father Died in the year 1770 at which time my Sister & self Look'd over all the papers at Chesterton, & shoud have been delighted to have found any fragment of Drydens Pen. But I am too certain none was there, but it is strongly in my Memory that Mr Robert Smyth Gain'd Drydens Letters, & that I heard my Mother Once say—"That," Mr Smyth who has dined with Us has Gain'd a Number of *family* Letters from your Grandfathers Indolence," I am surprised they were never *advertised* for I beleive many of them might Go into very Low Hands as I have traiced *One* of them —lately Monopolized by a Servant who Lived with my G Grandmother in Shrewsbury & to whom she Left an Annuity—(viz Blakeway— [48]

I was much surprised this morning at a Libary in seeing the Print to Drydens Works by Derrick taken from a Picture of S^r G Kneller 1798 [sic] which was the Date I suposed that our Picture at Chesterton was taken, but this Print of Derricks was quite in a different stile, & a most frightful Hand, But Both are represented greatly in the Vale of Years, Ours was in a Wig—Derrics in his Own Hair, I must supose Derrick was Led into some Error in this Point as He was in several Points of Drydens Life—

---

[47] For the relationship between Dryden and Swift see Malone, Life of Dryden, p. 238, and an article by Mr. Mundy in *Notes and Queries*, CXLVII (July–December, 1924), 243, 279, 334.

[48] For other details about this letter see pp. 46–47, above.

We have a very fine folio of Drydens Fables which seems one of the Best Impressions of the first Edition & I have allways heard the Poet presented his Cousin at Chesterton with it—

You Sir have given me a new Chain of Memory By your Enquirys of family Annecdotes, which I had been willing to forget *in the Pains of Memory* which all familys must feel but none more than Mine, If ever I see you at Bath I shall with pleasure shew you the Dryden family Letters & If I have given you any Information my Reward will be sufficient. In the Numerous Biographers of Drydens I am surprised Our Family has never been apply'd to before, But Dear Doctor Johnson (who was certainly his Best Biographer) was allways Toiling with Indolence & often found the End but never *the Easy* Road to Knowledge—I think I have answer'd all your Questions & a deal More so I will release you from a tedious Letter with assuring you that I am Dear Sir

Your Sincere Humble Serv
Honor Pigott

I am surprised Mr L Powys coud not give more Information as I have seen him lately at Bath & he was conected with the Poets family.[49]

Several of these anecdotes are familiar enough, because Malone examined them thoroughly in his biography. In this group are the traditions that Dryden and Swift were second cousins and the tale that the epistle to John Driden, of Chesterton, had been rewarded by a gift of £500. The letter also provides one bit of relief for the searcher after Dryden documents. It is Miss Pigott's statement that in 1770 she made a thorough search of all the papers at Chesterton and found none of the poet's.

Less reassuring is her firm conviction that the two greedy antiquaries, Dr. Timothy Neve and the Reverend Robert Smyth, who had been frequent visitors at Chesterton, took all the Dryden papers they could find. There is no indication, however, that Malone was impressed by the charge, and in the century and a half that has elapsed since 1799 no Dryden papers have come to the surface that could be traced to either Neve or Smyth. Neve's descendants were intelligent enough to have made such documents public, and a large portion of Smyth's collections ultimately reached John Nichols. Nichols sets us speculating again, however, by reporting that many of Smyth's papers were supposed to have been destroyed by an illiterate brother.[50]

For the future biographers of John Dryden these letters pose many

[49] This letter is Bodley MS Malone 27, 16, ff. 147–50.
[50] Nichols's *Literary Anecdotes*, V, 48.

problems. Probably most of the family traditions can never be completely substantiated or demolished, but they deserve to be collected and preserved. Where there is smoke, it is never safe to preclude the possibility of fire.

SHORTER STUDIES

DRYDEN'S VERSES ON KONINGSMARK

On Sunday, February 12, 1681/2, an incident occurred which threw the whole of London into an uproar. Thomas Thynne, the wealthy young friend of the Duke of Monmouth, was riding down Pall Mall in his coach, when three men on horseback seized the reins, stopped the coach, and fired at Thynne with a blunderbuss, wounding him mortally. A hue and cry was raised, and within twenty-four hours the assassins were captured, but not before the Whigs had converted the murder into a political crisis. They claimed that the attack was intended to be on the Duke of Monmouth, who had been riding in the coach with Thynne and had alighted just a few moments before the coach was halted. The excitement was so great that the King himself examined the murderers, one of whom, in his confession, implicated the well-known Swedish nobleman, Count Charles John Koningsmark.

The evidence of Koningsmark's complicity was circumstantial, but very strong. Known to be the unsuccessful rival of Thynne for the hand of an heiress, the Count had twice tried to lure Thynne into a duel. His connections with Captain Vratz, the chief assassin, were very close, and when Koningsmark was arrested, he was trying to flee the country in disguise. But though the three murderers were condemned and executed, Count Koningsmark was acquitted and allowed to leave the country unmolested. Popular indignation ran high, for the crowd was with the Whigs. The Tories, on the other hand, felt the incident had been exploited at their expense, so they tended to absolve Koningsmark of complicity and to laud his unquestioned courage and military prowess.

These events provide a background for some verses that are found on the back flyleaf of a volume in the Dobell Dryden collection, now installed in the Folger Shakespeare Library. They are quoted with the permission of the director, Dr. Joseph Quincy Adams:

"Under C^t Koningsmarks picture by Mr Dryden—

To blast thy name or to condemn thy Cause
This argues malice, that arraigns the Laws.
True Justice on Suspicion is not built,
And bare surmises prove no actual Guilt.
Thy well known Courage could no Aid demand,
Nor didst thou need a mercinary hand,
Let this thy Injur'd Reputation right,
He dares not murther, who can dare to fight."

The book is a copy of *Poetical Miscellanies: the Sixth Part,* 1709 [Case 172 (6) (a)]. In the front is written "Francasci Gregor de Med. Templo" and also "E Libri 1709." These inscriptions indicate that Gregor probably bought the book when it first appeared. Since the verses are in the same hand and ink as the signature, it seems likely that they were copied at the same time or shortly afterward.

Whether these lines are actually by Dryden is a decision that can be left to the next editor of his poetical works. Certainly the couplets are not an example of Dryden at his best. Perhaps they were dashed off on the spur of the moment when Dryden was looking at the portrait for the first time.[1] The sentiments are consistent with those that Dryden, as a strong Tory, probably felt. He had already given his opinion of Thynne in *Absalom and Achitophel,* where Monmouth's "wealthy western friend" was dubbed Issachar, after the "strong ass" of Genesis. But though these circumstances are suggestive, the only real evidence is the fact that Francis Gregor, when he copied the verses a few years after Dryden's death, acted in full belief that they were written by Dryden. In the absence of contradictory evidence Gregor's testimony is enough, in my opinion, to allow the verses to be accepted as Dryden's.

DRYDEN AND THOMAS SPRAT

Relations between Dryden and Sprat began, as far as we know, in 1659, when Dryden's *Heroick Stanzas* on Cromwell were published in the same volume with elegies by Waller and Sprat, the latter then fresh from Wadham College. Except for commendatory verses, this was the literary debut for both Sprat and Dryden.

The next record we have of their acquaintance is December 16, 1661,

---

[1] The only portrait of Koningsmark to which I have found reference is one by Michael Dahl. Since Dahl was a native of Sweden, he probably had easy access to Koningsmark. The present whereabouts of the portrait is unknown to me.

when they went together to the first performance of Cowley's *Cutter of Coleman Street*. Cowley, the "darling" of Dryden's youth, was well known to Sprat, and after the play the latter took Dryden with him to console Cowley on its failure.[1]

While at Oxford, Sprat had been a protégé of Dr. Wilkins and had taken a leading part in the Royal Society during its early years, when Dryden was also a member. Whether Dryden was ever active in the society is a debatable question, but if he was, its meetings would have provided occasions for further contact with Sprat.

After these early years, however, the relations between Sprat and the new poet laureate were far from congenial. Sprat is reported by a contemporary writer to have had a finger in the *Rehearsal*,[2] and scholars concur in the belief.[3]

The explanation for such a change in Sprat's attitude may possibly be found in a report that appeared in a Dutch paper. The *Hollantsche Mercurius*, published at Haarlem, in 1670, announced on page 85 (Vol. XX) that in June, 1669, Sprat had been provisionally appointed to succeed Howell as historiographer-royal:

Dese dagen Monsr. Howel, History-Schrijver van sijn Majesteyts van Engelants Huys, overlijdende, is hem im provisie gesuccedeert in dat Ampt Monsr. Spratt, den Autheur van de Historie van de Konincklijche Compagnie, ende van de leste Oorlogen van Engelant met Vranckrijck, Hollant en Denemarcken, met een betragelijcke Stijl, groote kennisse en exactitude.[4]

Given the situation that a rivalry existed for the post of historiographer-royal, and that Sprat resented Dryden's success in gaining the appointment, Sprat's participation in the *Rehearsal* is provided with an additional motive.

DRYDEN AND HIS "COSEN SALWEY"

On an island with a total population of six million, where large families were the rule, it was inevitable that many of the gentry should be related, either closely or distantly. The Dryden family was no exception,

[1] See Dennis's *The Comical Gallant*, 1702 (*The Critical Works of John Dennis*, I, 289, edited by E. N. Hooker, Baltimore, 1939), and Johnson's *Lives of the Poets*, ed. G. Birkbeck Hill, I (1905), 14, 66.

[2] See "The Session of the Poets," in *Poems on Affairs of State*, 1697, p. 206.

[3] Among them Professor Arthur Mizener, who has made a special study of George Villiers, second Duke of Buckingham.

[4] My attention was directed to this quotation by Mr. E. S. deBeer, who informed me that as far as is known, Sprat was not responsible for the second work attributed to him.

and the young poet who came down from Cambridge to London in the troubled days of the Protectorate was not without benefit of family connections.

Of these relations we are here concerned with the descendants of Humphrey Salwey, of Stanford Court, Worcestershire. After attending Brasenose College and the Inner Temple, Humphrey retired to his lands in Worcestershire, and there produced eleven sons and three daughters.[1] Of the sons, the eldest, Edward, followed his father's footsteps to Brasenose and the Inner Temple, before marrying Dorothy, daughter of Sir Erasmus Dryden, and a sister of the poet's father, in March, 1629. As a wedding present Humphrey settled Stanford Manor on his son.[2] In due course the couple had four children, only one of whom was a boy—named Edward after his father.

For some reason this Edward did not follow his father and grandfather to Oxford, but went directly to the Inner Temple, where he was admitted in November, 1649. In 1658 he was called to the Bar. During his early years in London, we may imagine that Edward and his cousin John spent an occasional hour in each other's company. The only souvenir we have of their friendship, however, is a letter in Dryden's hand written in 1664, to Edward's uncle, the old Cromwellian soldier, Major Richard Salwey.

With the help of this letter we can reconstruct a very tense moment in family affairs, a situation that supplied the plots of innumerable dramas during the next hundred years and more—scheming for the family estate. Edward was unmarried, and as long as he remained so, the rest of the family could not keep the future of his estate out of their minds. Uncle Richard had a son to provide for, and as a man of action he naturally functioned as chief counsellor on family matters involving property. This, then, was the setting in June, 1664, when Edward, the young inheritor of the estate, fell gravely ill of a fever.

When Dryden discovered him in this condition, he knew that there

[1] According to Foster's *Alumni Oxonienses* he matriculated at Brasenose on November 8, 1590, aged 15, and proceeded B.A. February 16, 1592/3. Cooke's *Students Admitted to the Inner Temple* shows that Humphrey was admitted there also in November, 1590. See also the DNB under Richard Salwey.

[2] Baker, *History of Northamptonshire*, II (1841), 6, and *Victoria History of Worcestershire*, IV, 343. Salwey was appointed assessment commissioner for Worcestershire in 1656 and sat in the House of Commons for Droitwich from January to April, 1659: see W. R. Williams, *Parliamentary History of the County of Worcester*, 1897, p. 126.

Honoured S[r]

I was this evening with my Deare cosen
Salwey, whose feavor thanks be to god
I find much abated, yet calling to mind
those many sad differences suden deaths
occasion in familyes, I deemed it my duty
out of that sincere affection I owe him
and his relations, to be his remembra-
cers as to ye settlement of his estate
to which I found him very inclinable
, to which purpose hee ingaged mee heare
tily and humbly to beg your pardon for
those unbeseeming expressions, the violence
of his distemper forced him to utter, allso
he earnestly requests that you will favour
him wth your company to morrow betwixt
seaven and eight of the clock in ye morning
and that .... wth you in Leek-
more and in .... ye latter I have some
acquaintance w[th], but as to ye former if
you'l be pleased to write a word or two
to him by this messenger, my man shall
carry it to him, be pleased to write where
he lodges. I shall send very erly to morrow
to enquire after my cosens health, for

[left margin, written vertically:]
... it be not pretty will continued [?] esteeme it very
strainge to see ... him in relation of this nature I hope
S[r] you will not faast any of his consideration one my behalfe I
beg in theire for Sir ... Salwey to ... him very faithful
and y[e] worthy relations, who shall ... in a very frend
and hardest ... Dryden

JOHN DRYDEN
The Salwey Portrait

was no time to lose and dispatched the following letter to Major Salwey: [3]

These / For y^e much honour^d, / Rich: Salwey Esqr / at Mr Warings house [4] / in Gratias Street/

Honour^d S^r

I was this evening with my Deare cosen Salwey, whose feaver thanks be to god I find much abated, yet calling to mind those many sad differences sudden deaths occasion in families, I deemed it my duty out of that sincere affection I owe him and his relations, to be his remembracer as to ye settlement of his estate, to which I found him very inclinable to wch purpose he engaged mee heartily and humbly to beg your pardon for those unbeseeming expressions, the violence of his distempers forced him to vtter, allso he ernestly requests that you will favour him wth your company to morrow betwixt seven and eight of the clock in ye morning and that there may be wth you Mr Leckmore and Mr West,[5] ye latter I have some acquaintance w^th, but as to ye fomer if youl' be pleased to write a word or two to him by this messenger, my man shall carry it to him, be pleased to write where he lodges. I shall send very early to morrow to enquire after my Cosens health, for if he be not pretty well composed, I deeme it very incovenient to disturbe him wth occasions of this nature. I hope S^r you will not putt any other construction on my intentions her[e]in then my sincere desires to serve him your selfe and y^r worthy relations, who shall ever be y^r reddy friend and servant

J Driden.

The news set the old soldier on the alert, and he acted at once. Being a methodical man he recorded the details of the incident on the outside leaf of the letter:

Recd this letter from m^r Dryden by a messenger sent on munday night. 6. June 64 at 10 oclock to wch I returnd answer by lett^r y^t I would attend him at his lodging [6] early on the morrow & did accordingly before 8. of ye clock. but then understood my nephew was not in condition to be spoken wth about the contents therof. More over y^t my nephew being in very good temp[er] & composure from 12. oclock ye p[r]eceding day till 10. at night. did that euening declare he would settle his estate. also that he nev[er]

[3] Now in the possession of Captain Roger Salwey, of Overton, Ludlow, Salop., who has kindly allowed me to make use of it.

[4] Major Salwey had been prisoner in the Tower the previous winter on a charge of "treasonable designs." On November 2 he gave his address as "lodging with Mr. Waring, his father in law in Grace church street." (Cal. S. P. Domestic, 1663, p. 325). Salwey was released on February 3, 1663/4.

[5] Probably attorneys or attorneys' clerks, about whom I can offer no information.

[6] See p. 210.

intended his sisters should haue his lands, but y^t (as oftimes before he had told him in his health.) he resolud to settle it upon his uncle R. S. & his heires—yet charged wth such sumes of money as might make up his sisters portons to be 2000^l a peice or better. & sd his uncle was most dear to him & one y^t had neuer offended him & to w^m hee always comitted the guidance of all his concerns.

Mr Dryden adding y^t he thought it was reasonable ye effect of this resolutio[n] shuld stil be p[ro]secuted & would endeaur to dispose his neece [7] therto & dobted not of accompt. Thurs   This in p[r]esence of mr Checkley [8]

A week after Dryden's letter the matter was not yet settled, and Major Salwey added another memorandum:

M^e

munday ye 13. June m^r checkley rec. 2. letters fro[m] Neece Rogers one of wch signd wth her name & Neece Eliz. on ye tuesday he shewd mee wth m^r Courten and then told vs, y^t surely m^r Ed. Salwey had settled his estate & made his will. for y^t about a year & half since he came one day to his house & told him, he had now don his great worke for y^t he had that day settled his estate and made his will. to wch m^r checkley replyed. Hee hoped his mynd would now be at rest. Also y^t he had frequently heard my nephew say he would settle his estate upo[n] mee & my sonn. greatly advancyng my care of him at all times specially in his minority w^n he sd, (but for mee) he might haue starued for y^t he was maynteyned by mee. also during his minority coming once to see his mother at worcester at w^h instant m^r Checkley was present. his mother upbrayded his being so fyne in apparel & s^d [s]he knew not how he came by it, except he rob^d for it by ye high way.

Moreov[er] y^t he often s^d to mr Checkley he would nev[er] leaue his lands to his sisters but would charge it so, as y^t their portion might be worth to each about 2000^l—

But alas for the hopes of the heirs collateral; the young man did not leave the estate to them after all, and at his death it passed to his three sisters [9] and eventually to the "Elizabeth" mentioned in the letter, wife of Sir Francis Winnington, and so out of the Salwey family.[10] But in spite of the undramatic ending to the story, the letter is valuable for the glimpse it gives of Dryden at this early and obscure period in his life.

---

[7] A term loosely applied to any female relative.

[8] Evidently Major Salwey's agent.

[9] Edward Salwey's will cannot be found at Somerset House; it is presumably at Worcester.

[10] *Victoria History of Worcestershire*, IV, 343.

WILLIAM OLDYS ON DRYDEN

Anyone who seeks biographical information about Dryden and his contemporaries will sooner or later come face to face with William Oldys. Though the published writings of this insatiable antiquary are many, it is his manuscript notes that are most frequently quoted. They are referred to so often by his successors—Steevens, Nichols, Malone, Thoms, as well as by A . H. Bullen and other writers for the *Dictionary of National Biography*—that by the end of the nineteenth century Oldys's fame far surpassed the modest repute in which he was held at the time of his death in 1762. His almost legendary reputation is reflected in the words written in 1894 by Henry T. Scott in his treatise on *Autograph Collecting* (page 16): "It is certain that Oldys possessed some valuable information concerning Shakespeare, and intended to publish a life of that poet. He also made collections for a life of Dryden which must have been invaluable." Like many of Oldys's other projects, his life of Dryden never got written, but his manuscript notes on Dryden have been quoted so frequently that it is worth while to single them out for examination.

It is not known how early Oldys began to collect material on Dryden, but without doubt the process was one of gradual accumulation. However, one reference to "Broughtons Pref to the late Edit of his Poems" [1] indicates he was well into the task shortly after 1743, in the period when he and Samuel Johnson were making their post-mortem of the books in the library of Oldys's late patron the second Earl of Oxford. In another place we hear that about seven years later Oldys planned definitely to complete the biography in book form:

Rememb^r my large Bundle of Pamphlets all written by, for or ag^t Mr Dryden in Fol, Q^o, & 8° and my Chronological Draught or Skeleton of his personal story, to be enlargd into a Life of him when that shall be publishd, wch is to be written by Mr Broughton for the Biogr. Britannica [*ibid.,* p. 131].

As all who have tracked Oldys along the margins of his books would expect, a special "parchment book in 4to" was employed for notes. Another reference gives more detail:

---

[1] Oldys's annotated copy of Langbaine's *Account of the English Dramatic Poets*, in the British Museum, p. 130.

I have it [Hunt's *Municipal Rights,* etc.] now transcribd in 3 Sides 4⁰ It lies in my Yellow Parchm^t Volume 4⁰ in wch is entred ab^t 150 Transcripts in Prose and Verse relating to the Life Character & Writings of Mr Dryden [*ibid.,* p. 163].

That these were not separate volumes is revealed by a third entry, "copied . . . at length into the Yellow Book for Dryden's Life" (p. 152). These collections, the pamphlets and the book of notes and references, have disappeared, and their location, if they are still extant, is unknown.

But even without these materials we can form an estimate of Oldys's approach to this biographical undertaking. This is possible by observing the Drydeniana he jotted down in the documents still preserved, especially his copy of Langbaine. Crowded along the margins of the Dryden pages, are a variety of notes designed for biographical use, including (p. 130) a long list of books containing allusions to Dryden. Most of them are by quondam opponents of Dryden. A few pages later (p. 176) Oldys set out a full list of Dryden's "Enemies who wrote ag^t him."

Among these marginalia Oldys records the existence of the letter to Rochester (p. 131).[2] Probably he scribbled this note after he had first encountered it in the Harleian Library. But when he conjectured that it was dated about 1680 Oldys made one of his occasional slips, for the letter belongs to an earlier period, perhaps July, 1673. A few pages earlier our curiosity is provoked by the entry:

The Story of Mr Dryden's Dream at Lord Exeters at Burghley while he was translating Virgil, as Senior Vario then painting there, related it to the Yorkshire Painter of whom I had it lies in the Parchment Book in Q⁰ designed for his Life: [*written later:*] Now entered therein [p. 135].[3]

But the answer will be known only when the "Parchm^t Book in Q⁰" comes to light again.

More of these jottings are worth repeating: ". . . I have heard, by a Relation of his, that he had also some personal Estate to the last ab^t 100^ll p An." (p. 135). This report, as Malone observed, "appears to have been not far from the truth."[4] Another note may have come from the same member of the Dryden family: "Dryden had a Sister Married to

---

[2] Scott-Sainsbury, Letter II.

[3] Quite possibly Oldys had heard this anecdote during his sojourn in Yorkshire about 1728–30. For the indication that Dryden's visit took place in 1695, see p. 223.

[4] Malone, Life of Dryden, p. 444*n.*

Shelmardine the Bookseller in Little Brittain another to Sandwell a Tobacconist in Newgate Str." (p. 176).[5]

Whether the loss of Oldys's life of Dryden is a matter of regret, depends on what it would have been like had he completed it. Any attempt at answering this question should take into account Oldys's other biographical writings, especially his *Life of Raleigh*. The latter is the first great scholarly biography ever written by an Englishman and is a remarkable achievement of documentation. But even if it had been on this scale, the chief value of Oldys's life of Dryden would have been as a collection of data, mostly drawn from out-of-the-way sources. Oldys led his generation in the utilization of manuscript collections for biography, and there is every reason to suppose that the life of Dryden would have possessed this characteristic merit.

On the other hand Oldys's deficiencies should not be forgotten, particularly that he was far from a master of prose style. For this reason we can conjecture that Oldys's life of Dryden, like his other lives, would have been notable more as a repository of useful information than as a readable biography. It should be remembered that Oldys and his contemporaries were not properly critical of anecdote and tradition. Like Thomas Birch in the *General Dictionary,* Oldys had mastered the art of collecting materials, but he had never learned to sift them. Doubtless another drawback to this Dryden biography would have been Oldys's great dependence upon the large collections like that in the Harleian Library, the Lambeth Library, and the College of Arms for his information. Here he would have been handicapped, for they yield little about Dryden. Since a large portion of his materials ultimately came into Malone's hands, it may be doubted whether the absence of Oldys's biography leaves a serious gap in Dryden studies.

THE DRYDEN LETTERS AT KNOLE

When Malone began his search for Dryden letters by applying to the descendants of Dryden's friends and patrons, he had special hopes of success among the Dorset papers at Knole. There, he believed, would be found letters written to the Restoration wit and Lord Chamberlain

---

[5] Probably the father of the Thomas Shelmerdine who was located in Little Britain from 1698: perhaps the Ralph Shelmerdine who was a bookseller in Manchester from 1661. See Plomer's *Dictionary of Booksellers and Printers 1668–1725,* p. 269.

to William III, Charles Sackville, sixth earl of Dorset and earl of Middlesex.

The story of Malone's unsuccessful application may be pieced together from the one letter of the correspondence that remains.[1] Dated June 25, 1799, it is from Nathaniel W. Wraxall (later created baronet, and remembered today for his *Memoirs of My Own Time*), and indicates that at this period Wraxall was engaged at Knole in a literary capacity. From Wraxall's letter we learn that Malone's initial inquiry had been answered by Wraxall to the effect that the Duchess of Dorset would not allow Malone to see or use the Dorset Papers. Malone, whose social position had heretofore opened all doors before him, was not accustomed to such treatment, and suspected Wraxall of playing his own game. Thus he retorted hotly:

From Enquiries which I have made, I can say with Certainty, that you have her Grace's Permission to communicate the Letters in question.

To this charge Wraxall sent a detailed reply:

. . . the Duchess fully means to give to the World the 'Dorset & Middlesex' Papers. Among these, whenever they appear, any letters of Dryden, if such should be found, (for hitherto only three have appeared;) may be published with those of Sir Kenelm Digby, of Sir John Suckling, of Prior, Shadwell, & many other eminent Persons of the last Century. I am sure, therefore, you will feel, that the Duchess of Dorset, by giving away any Letters in the Dorset collection, would frustrate the Object which she has in her own Contemplation.

The remainder of the letter contained what was intended to be a concrete rebuttal of the duplicity Malone had implied, for Wraxall had the Duchess frank the cover as evidence that the matter had been laid before her.

This letter, then, is the authority upon which Malone based his statement in the Life of Dryden (p. 569) that "Among the Dorset Papers are at least three letters, written by our authour to his patron, Charles, Earl of Dorset." And since these words were printed (1800), nearly every serious Dryden student has tried, at one time or another, to obtain a glimpse of the letters.

When Scott began work on his *Life of Dryden,* only five years after Malone's had been published, these Dorset letters were his most coveted quarry. They provided an obvious opportunity to garnish his life with

[1] Bodley MS Malone 27, f. 171.

new documents. He attempted to reach them through the medium of his friend Lady Abercorn, as his letter to her reveals. On September 20, 1806, he wrote:

I am very anxious to procure copies if possible of three original letters that are among the Duke of Dorset's papers written by Dryden to his Grace's ancestor the witty Earl of Dorset. I am quite at a loss for a channel to approach this great man: perhaps your Ladyship may be able either to give me some assistance or at least your kind advice. If he is accessible to any of our Scottish nobles I could contrive, directly or indirectly to procure their mediation. It is of the greatest consequence to me to procure them if possible.[2]

Then on February 11, 1807, he wrote her again on the same subject:

"One of my principal reasons for visiting London this spring is that I may avail myself of your ladyships goodness in procuring me a passport to the Dorset papers."[3] The reply Scott received is not preserved in detail, but his edition of Dryden shows that he did not obtain use of the letters. The only reference to the matter is found on page 370 of his *Life*: ". . . to [Dorset's] bounty Dryden had frequently recourse in cases of emergency." *

* Such, I understand, is the general purport of some letters of Dryden's, in possession of the Dorset family, which contain certain particulars rendering them unfit for publication. [Original note].

Now this statement is important, for it indicates that Scott received an authentic answer to his well-introduced application. From it we can infer three things: that the letters were in existence in 1807, that at least one contained evidence of direct financial assistance to Dryden, and that at least one of them was written to the taste of the Restoration earl. So little, then, do we know about the letters that survived at Knole for a century after the death of Dryden's patron.

Of these three letters, only one still remains among the Dorset papers.[4] It is that which Mr. Charles J. Phillips printed in the first volume of his *History of the Sackville Family* [1930], page 444.[5] Unfortunately

[2] *Letters 1787–1807*, p. 318.
[3] *Ibid.*, p. 350.
[4] Most of the Dorset papers were recently deposited at the Public Record Office. By some chance the name Dryden does not appear in the manuscript handlist that is deposited with them.
[5] It is dated "Octob: 7th Thursday," which could be in 1680, 1686, or 1697. Yet the subject matter indicates it belongs in 1691. In that year October 7th fell on a Wednesday, and possibly Dryden made a mistake of one day in dating it.

this letter fits neither qualification suggested by Scott: it asks a favor, apparently an official one, but contains no evidence of direct financial help; and likewise there is no suggestion of ribald subject matter.

Among the few Dryden letters which have come to light during the last hundred years is the one printed in the catalogue of the R. B. Adam Johnsonian library (1929, III, 87 verso). It was written about August, 1677, while Dryden was spending the summer in Northamptonshire, probably with his cousin Sir Thomas Elmes, of Lilford.[6] Although without a superscription, there are several indications that the letter was sent to Dorset. It is addressed to "your Lordship," and the subject matter consists of topics agreeable to Dorset's appetite, news of a Miss Tresham, known as "the flower of Northamptonshire," and comments on the newest book of literary criticism, Rymer's *Tragedies of the Last Age Considered*. Moreover, penciled on the reverse are the words

> John Dryden
> Without date
> To Charles E. of D—t.[7]

Since this writing is in Wraxall's hand, the case seems fairly evident that the letter is one of the three which were at Knole in 1799. How it was smuggled out and sold is a tale unlikely to be recaptured, for there is no record of its provenance before Mr. Adam acquired it.

If this letter is accepted as the second of the three from Knole, the third one is still missing. Sackville family tradition, knowing nothing of a specific total of three letters, has explained the absence of additional Dryden correspondence on the ground that one of the nineteenth-century descendants destroyed a number of letters because their Restoration flavor was offensive to Victorian taste and deprecatory to the memory of his illustrious ancestor. This tradition is consistent with the known evidence, for the third letter has completely disappeared from view, and it is the only one that could have contained "particulars unfit

---

[6] It can be dated with the help of a letter from Wycherley to Mulgrave written on August 20, 1677 (described at length in the *Times Literary Supplement* for April 18, 1935), which says "Dryden is in Northamptonshire" and speaks of Rymer's book as "lately published." Both these matters are integral parts of Dryden's letter.

[7] I owe this information to the late D. B. Gilchrist, the librarian of the University of Rochester, where the Adam Library is now on deposit. Photographs which Mr. Gilchrist sent me were compared with Wraxall MSS in the Yale Library. Miss Emily Hall confirmed the identification.

for publication." Until facts to the contrary are produced I shall feel content that only three letters from Dryden to the Earl of Dorset were preserved and that they have been accounted for.

JOHN DRYDEN, JUNIOR, AND THE DUKE OF SHREWSBURY

Though all three of Dryden's sons made the pilgrimage to Rome, only one of them stayed there. Charles, the eldest, returned to London about 1697 or 1698, was drowned while swimming in the Thames near Datchet, and was buried at Windsor August 20, 1704. Erasmus-Henry, the youngest, resided at Rome till 1697, when he was sent to the convent of Holy Cross, Bornheim: there he was subprior until 1700, returning to England soon after his father's death. He ultimately became baronet, but died soon after his succession to the title in 1710, apparently afflicted by mental disorders.

Little is known of the last years of the second son, John, who went to Rome with Charles about 1692. In 1700 he made a tour of Italy and Malta with a Mr. Cecil, and an account of his journey was published in 1776. Malone, who first investigated the lives of Dryden's family, could find no definite information on the closing years of John's life, saying only, "Soon after his return to Rome from that excursion [through Italy and Malta], (January 28, 1701, N.S.) he is said to have died there, of a fever." [1]

But a sketchy record of John's life in Rome, as well as a definite date for his death, can be extracted from the manuscript journal of Charles Talbot, Duke of Shrewsbury. Shrewsbury, a convert to Anglicanism from Roman Catholicism, had held various high offices in the governments of James II and William III, but in 1700 he resigned from office, owing to ill health and unwillingness to take further part in public life, and then went abroad until 1707. The early period of this exile was spent at Rome, where he settled among the English colony in 1701, and his journal, which extends from 1700 to 1706,[2] mentions John Dryden, Junior, fairly frequently.

---

[1] Life of Dryden, p. 425. In the DNB this statement is telescoped into the words, "He died at Rome 28 Jan. 1701."

[2] Historical MSS Commission, 1903, *Report of the MSS of the Duke of Buccleuch*, II (Part 2), 746–99. The journal is entirely in his grace's hand and is paged 1–493.

The first entry concerning the poet's son occurs on November 26, 1701: "After dinner young Dreyden came to see me; he is like his father . . ." From this time on there are frequent records of hours spent in Dryden's company:

12 Dec. 1701: . . . Mr. Cecil, Monsr. Walgrave, and Mr. Dreyden dined with me.

6 Jan. 1702   I dined alone. Mr. Dreyden came to see me. I went with him to see some statues bespoke for Lord Exeter, to a man that makes fine tables, set him at home, and went . . .

7 Jan.   This morning I went with Mr. Dreyden to Carlo Marat; . . . Mr. Dreyden dined with me. We went [to] Joseppe Chiary, a scholar of Ca. Marat's, and [who] does now better than his master. . . . We saw some pictures at Sig. Faulconier's; we went to a bookseller's. I set Mr. Dre[yden] at home.

16 Jan.   Mr. Dreyden dined with me. We went to see pictures of a gen[tlema]n at the Vatican; he set me down at the P[rincess] Carpegna['s].

17 Jan.   This morning I went with Mr. Dreyden; saw the Chiesa Nuova . . . Mr. Dreyden and Flamarin dined with me.

20 Jan.   Was visited by Mr. Dreyden, the Bishop El[l]is, Sir Tho. Morgan, Mr. Lewis, and la Roche.

23 Jan.   I went this morning with Mr. Dreyden, and bespoke two tables. He and young Rizzi dined with me. We went to see pictures.

26 Jan.   [again went together to see pictures]

1 Feb.   Went with Mr. Dreyden to Villa Borghese, where I met Mr. Cotton, Webb, and St. Johns.

And so the diary continues with other references, for February 5 and 7, March 12 and 28, April 17, May 3, June 2, July 23, November 30, and February 7, 1703. Usually Dryden and the Duke dined together or went out to see pictures or other objects of virtu, which at this period made Rome the center of the artistic world.

The last entry to interest us is very brief. It occurs on April 16, 1703, and says simply "Mr. Dreyden died this morning, about an hour after midnight." No cause is mentioned, but it is not improbable that John succumbed to the sudden fever of which report had reached Malone. Unfortunately these brief records tell nothing about John's father, but with their help we can establish the fate of the only son who followed his father in the theater, at however great a distance.

DRYDEN'S "HEADS OF AN ANSWER TO RYMER"

The location of the original text of Dryden's notes on Rymer was unknown to Malone when he was preparing his edition of Dryden's prose works, and in Appendix V to Vol. I, Part 1, he said,

Rymer's "Essay on the Tragedies of the last Age," in the blank leaves of which Dryden wrote several observations on that work, was some years ago in the library of the late David Garrick, Esq.; but Mrs. Garrick has informed me, that it is now not to be found there. It would be a publick benefit, if the person into whose hands this book has fallen, would give notice of it; as there is some doubt whether those remarks have been arranged in the order intended by the author.[1]

But some time later its fate became known to him. Among his notes to Langbaine is the following:

. . . I have printed this Essay in my Edition of the Prose works of Dryden. I had however some doubt whether Johnson printed it quite correctly for the reasons there assigned and wished to have examined the book from which he printed, containing Dryden's MS. but after his death Sir John Hawkins finding it in his Library carried it off, as well as every other book in which there was anything written, and it was afterwards consumed in the fire that destroyed his house in Queen's Square in the year 1786 or 1787.[2]

A modified version of this passage was entered in his own copy of the Life of Dryden.

At present we have three texts of these notes. The first is found in Tonson's 1711 edition of *The Works of Beaumont and Fletcher,* I (Preface), xii ff. Since Rymer's *Tragedies of the Last Age Considered* had dealt with three plays by those authors, the inclusion of Dryden's rejoinder was considered appropriate. To print the notes was easy, since the volume was then in Tonson's hands.

The second text is Johnson's. It contains wide differences in the order of the paragraphs. This is shown by representing the order in the 1711 text as 1–52: the order in which Johnson printed them is 34, 51–52, 35–38, 1–6, 29–33, 39–50, 7–28.

The third text is that printed by Saintsbury. He was apparently unaware of the existence of the 1711 printing and took his version from a copy made in 1726 by W. Harte, probably the friend of Pope and later

---

[1] Pages 569–70.   [2] Bodley Malone E 61, pp. 203–4.

of Johnson.[3] The most noticeable variation from the 1711 text is the omission of paragraph 22. Harte also made a number of contractions such as "can't" where Tonson had printed "cannot." But these small differences prove nothing, since they may have been the result of indifferent or rapid copying. It would be difficult to show that Harte's copy is independent of the 1711 text.

Both Tonson's and Johnson's texts appear to have been taken from the original volume, and the only important question is whether we can determine the order in which Dryden's notes should be printed. Having been written "on the blank leaves, before the Beginning, and the End of the Book," these notes were probably not in any fixed arrangement. Dryden may have filled the back fly leaves before using the front ones, or *vice-versa*. Likewise he may have written some notes on the margins of the pages, notes which never were gathered in any proper sequence. This probable state of disarray dooms to failure any attempt to establish the order by linking up the notes with the passages in Rymer to which Dryden may have been replying.

The sequence in which Tonson printed the notes has one point in its favor—Tonson's statement, "just as he left them be pleased to take them then here verbatim inserted." These words may have applied, however, to the fact that Dryden's jottings were printed as notes rather than rewritten into a formal answer to Rymer. If it could be established that Harte's text was more than a copy, it would provide strong support for Tonson's order.

In favor of Johnson's arrangement little can be said, yet there is one circumstance to plead for it. The 1711 text begins with the excellent introductory paragraph: "He who undertakes to answer this excellent critique of Mr. Rymer, in behalf of our English poets against the Greek, ought to do it in this manner . . ." If this passage had come first inside the cover, Johnson, even with all the carelessness of which he was capable, could scarcely have disregarded it as the most effective introduction. The fact that Johnson began *in medias res* constitutes a negative argument of some weight against Tonson's order and in favor of Johnson's less satisfactory beginning. This reasoning would explain Tonson's arrangement as opportunism.

If the key were to be found in internal evidence, we should look for it in the thought transitions between the misplaced paragraphs. These

[3] Professor Ward informs me that this volume is now in the Folger Shakespeare Library.

are between paragraphs 34 and 51, 52 and 35, 38 and 1, 6 and 29, 33 and 39, and 50 and 7. Examination of them fails to throw any light on the problem, for in spite of Tonson's effective beginning, Johnson's links are on the whole superior. The nearest approach to an argument for Johnson's order would be based on the link between paragraphs 33 and 39. Paragraph 39 begins with the line, "And if we should grant that the Greeks performed this better." The pronoun "this" dovetails exactly with the previous paragraph as Johnson printed it. However, a sufficiently good antecedent for the pronoun can also be found in paragraph 38, immediately preceding, in Tonson's text, so that no weight can be attached to this instance.

The truth is that we should probably be equally baffled if we had Dryden's handwriting before us. He doubtless jotted down the notes as they occurred to him, and their arrangement would depend entirely on how he synthesized them afterward. But Sir John Hawkins's action in carrying off this valuable book has given us the pleasure of speculating on a highly interesting problem.[4]

DRYDEN'S BAPTISM

For more than two centuries the circumstances of Dryden's birth were in doubt. Malone gave the birth date correctly, but warned his readers that it rested on "no satisfactory evidence." [1] August 9, 1631, has now been accepted on the authority of a horoscope preserved among the papers of John Aubrey.[2]

The date of Dryden's christening has perplexed his biographers even more. Malone wrote "I have in vain endeavoured to ascertain the precise time of his baptism . . . the ancient register of the parish of All-Saints is unfortunately either lost or mislaid; the earliest extant commencing in the year 1650." [3] Malone was particularly anxious to find the baptismal record, because in 1681 one of the squibs attacking *Absalom and Achitophel* had raised the question whether Dryden had ever been baptized:

> ". . . a certain poet undertook,
> That men and manners deals in without book;

---

[4] For a discussion of the relation between these *Heads of an Answer to Rymer* and the Preface to *Troilus and Cressida* see F. G. Walcott in the *Philological Quarterly*, XV (1936), 194–214. See also George Watson, "Dryden's First Answer to Rymer," RES, XIV (1963), 17–23.

[1] Malone, Life of Dryden, p. 3.   [2] Bodley MS Ashmole 243, f. 209.

[3] M .l. ne, Life of Dryden, pp. 8–9.

And might not more to Gospel-truth belong,
Than he (*if christened*) does by name of John." [4]

This charge has not been taken seriously by any biographer of Dryden except the latest one, Mr. Christopher Hollis, who in 1933 declared it "probable enough" that Dryden was never baptized.[5]

This view has been challenged by Mr. Percy Dryden Mundy, who called attention to the registers of the nearby parish of Tichmarsh, where the Drydens lived beginning in 1632 or perhaps earlier.[6] Only fifteen months after the poet's birth, his sister Agnes was baptized at Tichmarsh, and the registers contain records of the baptism of eight more of Dryden's younger brothers and sisters. From these facts Mr. Mundy drew the conclusion: "There appears no reason why John Dryden's parents should have been averse from baptism in 1631, and in favor of it in 1632 and in subsequent years." [7]

By some freak of fate, however, a record of Dryden's baptism has been preserved. It is in the Bodleian among the papers of John Bridges, the historian of Northamptonshire.[8] The sheet containing it is a partial transcript of a parish register, and seems to be part of a letter to Bridges. There is no definite indication that the register was for the parish of All Saints, but I believe the assumption is a fair one. The entry reads: "1631 Johannes filius Erasm Dryden Generos. bapt. 14. Aug." This date is five days after Dryden was born. Bridges began to collect materials for *The History and Antiquities of Northamptonshire* in 1719 and died in 1724, so the information probably came to him during the intervening five years. It refutes once and for all the accusation that Dryden was "a bristled Baptist bred."

---

[4] Quoted by Malone, Life of Dryden, p. 9, from *Poetical Reflections . . . on "Absalom and Achitophel."*

[5] *Dryden,* by Christopher Hollis, London, 1933, p. 12.

[6] *Notes and Queries,* CLXXIII (1937), 225.   [7] *Ibid.*

[8] Bodley MS Top. Northants. C. 17, f. 167.

ADDENDA AND CORRIGENDA

Page 91. Did Sir Henry Dryden own a letter from Dryden to Edmund Waller? This question arises from the *Report Presented to the Cambridge Antiquarian Society at Its First General Meeting, May 6, 1841,* by its twenty-year-old secretary, James Orchard Halliwell. At the end of the report is a list of books and manuscripts presented to the society, and among them (p. 22) is *"A Letter from John Dryden to Waller: printed for private circulation* and presented by Sir Henry Dryden Bart." Search for the pamphlet proved fruitless, for a reason that became clear when in December, 1963, I purchased at Sotheby's the Dryden-Walsh letter of December 12, 1691 (Ward's number 28). With it came various other items, including the printed facsimile which carries the printed title, LETTER/ of/ JOHN DRYDEN/ to WILLIAM WALER,/ FROM THE ORIGIONAL AT CANON'S ASHBY;/ PRESENTED TO/ THE REV. SIR HENRY DRYDEN,/ BY/ SAMUEL BUTLER,/ BISHOP OF LITCHFIELD AND COVENTRY. In ink "WALER" has been altered to "WALSH."

Page 92. With the Dryden-Walsh letter described above, there came also a letter of Honor Dryden written to Sir Erasmus Dryden, the poet's younger brother. Its chief interest is as a specimen of the remarkable spelling, capitalization, and freedom from punctuation employed by gentlewomen of that time.

Sir,

Rosamas my Seruse to you and to all my Cossens and I Expected to a seeane you a Srusbrurey before now this poore man hase binn Sick a greate while and bad and I understand that you are Angrey for him being Sent to ashbey but he Could not help it he has bine a seruant to our fameley for[merl]y and I desier you to Sett him at worck and in so doing you will a bleig your seruant

Oner Dreden

[Addressed:]

For Sir Rosamas
Dreyden at
Cannons ashbey

Pages 187–88. Information about other books published by Herringman have been called to my attention. Percy J. Dobell sent me *A Judicious View of the Businesses Which are at This Time between France and the House of Austria . . . Translated out of French, by a Person of Honour*, London, Printed by W. Wilson for Henry Herringman, 1657 (*Stationer's Registers*, March 11, 1656/7). He also sent the same book with the title *The Grand Differences between France, Spain and the Empire . . . By an Impartiall Hand*, London, Printed for Henry Herringman, 1657. The volumes (now in the Yale University Library) carry a preliminary note of one and a half pages, headed "A Character of this Worke" which Mr. Dobell considered may have been an early effort of Dryden's. It could have been written by Herringman, himself, or any literate hand.

The volume registered with the title *The Shirke or Buscon's Adventures* "Put into English by a person of Honour" is undoubtedly *The Life and Adventures of Buscon the witty Spaniard* [with] *The Provident Knight* "Translated by J.D." 1657. I have not seen the book, but the "J.D." is interesting, especially in light of the entry as by "a person of Honour." A second edition appeared in 1670.

Copies of *A Prospective of the Navall Triumph*, translated by Sir Thomas Higgons from the Italian of Busenello, are in Yale and Texas, where Miss Mary Tom Osborne used it for her *Advice-to-a Painter Poems*, 1949. This poem served as a model for Waller's adaption of the genre to political satire. There is no indication that Dryden had any connection with the publication.

The published title of *The Truth and Reasonableness of Religion* was *A Short Discourse of the Truth etc;* Professor Brice Harris writes that other copies are in the Library of Congress, the University of Illinois, and the McAlpin Collection, the author being Sir Henry Yelverton.

Page 193. Professor Harris has also written that the *Pompey* (1664) published by Herringman was translated by Waller and four collaborators. Similarly he pointed out that the "J.D." in Brome's edition of *Horace* was undoubtedly Sir John Denham.

Page 216. As Professor Bredvold pointed out to me, Dryden's visit to Oxford occurred in 1680/1, not 1680.

Page 219. Professor Brice Harris, who has made a special study of Charles Sackville, earl of Dorset, reports that his lordship's favorite seat was not Knole, but Copt Hall in Essex, where Dryden would more likely have visited him, if he ever did so.

Page 246. Percy Dryden Mundy reported that a Negus family lived in Aldwincle.

Page 250. Two other association books are recorded in Macdonald's *Bibliography of Dryden:* Wood's copy of *Religio laici* in the Bodleian which has "Exdono Auctoris" on the title page (p. 34), and another copy of the same poem in the National Library of Wales (MS. 5295E) with autograph corrections said to be in Dryden's hand. The Huntington Library has two books that former owners believed had belonged to Dryden. *Godfred of Bulloigne,* 1600 (Huntington 69618), carries the signature "John Dryden 1695" at the top of the title page in a hand unlike the poet's. Huntington 121981, a copy of the 1697 octavo edition of the *Satires of Juvenal* carries on the first flyleaf Dryden's verses to Granville (1698) signed "John Dryden," again not in his hand.

Page 256. The portrait of Dryden was given to Trinity College in 1753 by R. M. Pettiward. According to Mr. P. D. Mundy it is by Thomas Hudson. (*Notes and Queries,* clxv, 194.)

Page 271. Dryden and Sprat were, of course, brought together in the early days of the Royal Society (Ward, *Life,* 31, 339), though Dryden soon lost interest in it. Both Dryden and Sprat were among the twenty-two members appointed in December, 1664, to study ways to improve the English Language.

Dryden also put many of Sprat's arguments from *Observations on Monsieur Sorbier's Voyage into England* (1665) into the mouth of Neander in his celebrated *Essay* (see George Williamson, "The Occasion of *An Essay of Dramatic Poesy,*" *Modern Philology* XLIV [1946], 1–9).

Page 280. Professor Brice Harris has written, "I have heard on good, though not final, authority that one of the nineteenth-century descendants of the Sackvilles was fond of gratifying his friends by giving them desirable items from his family papers when they expressed unusual interest in them. I suggest this as a more plausible leak than theft.

Page 281. A few bits of information can be added about Dryden's sons, Charles and John. In the Bodleian there is a letter dated June 30, 1693, and received July 20 from their uncle, Cardinal Howard, writing from Rome to Lord Medford at St. Germain and thus indirectly to the exiled James II (Carte 209ƒ74). One passage reads,

"and now that wee are in expectation of his Mat^{ies} speedy restoration, so many will petition for favours, that I must also be one of them beforehand, begging of his Mat^{ie} (and y^r Lo^{ps} favour in it) that heare, being two Brothers Catholique gentleman caled Mr Charles and John Draytons (sonnes to the famous Poet Laureat Drayton in London) one wheareof I hav^e in the interim gotta place of Cameriero d'Honore with our ould man, and th'other liveth with me, but they alwaise desiring to serve theyr natural King, and both theyr father and they having beene alwaise faithfull, would have gone to serve him in france had it not beene to putt him to straights amongst so many others for their maintenance; whearefore my humble request is that his Mat^{ie} will please to make them his Gentlemen Ushers daly wayters in Ordinary in his Presence Chamber, or Groomes of his Privey Chamber, at his returne into England, wch honor I am confident they will both as faithfully and decently performe, theyr father being a Convert, and theyr mother a Cath^c Sister to ye Lord Berkshire."

The Cardinal included his two nephews in his will, drawn in Rome June 9, 1694, leaving to "Mr. John & Mr. Charles Dryden fifty Roman Crownes a—piece" (*Catholic Record Society Publications,* XXV [1925], 90). New details have also come to light about Erasmus-Henry. See P. D. Mundy, "Dryden's Dominican Son" in *Notes and Queries,* October 27, 1951, CXCVI, 472–73, and Ward, p. 363.

INDEX